Language, Culture, and History

Essays by Mary R. Haas

Selected and Introduced
by Anwar S. Dil

Stanford University Press, Stanford, California   1978

Language Science and National Development

A Series Sponsored by the
Linguistic Research Group of Pakistan

General Editor: Anwar S. Dil

Stanford University Press
Stanford, California
© 1978 by Mary R. Haas
Printed in the United States of America
ISBN 0-8047-0983-1
LC 78-59373

Contents

Acknowledgments

The Linguistic Research Group of Pakistan and the General Editor of the Language Science and National Development Series are deeply grateful to Professor Mary R. Haas, Associate Member of the Group, for giving us the privilege of presenting her selected writings as the eleventh volume in our series established in 1970 to commemorate the International Education Year.

We are indebted to the editors and publishers of the following publications. The ready permission on the part of the holders of the copyrights, acknowledged in each case, is a proof of the existing international cooperation and goodwill that gives hope for better collaboration among scholars of all nations for international exchange of knowledge.

Men's and Women's Speech in Koasati. Language 20. 142-149 (1944), with permission of the Linguistic Society of America.
Interlingual Word Taboos. American Anthropologist 53. 338-344 (1951), with permission of the American Anthropological Association.
Thai Word Games. Journal of American Folklore 70. 173-175 (1957), reproduced with permission of the American Folklore Society.
Burmese Disguised Speech. The Bulletin of the Institute of History and Philology, Vol. XXXIX, pp. 277-285 (1969), Academia Sinica.
Sibling Terms as Used by Marriage Partners. Southwestern Journal of Anthropology 25. 228-235 (1969), with permission of the Editors.
The Declining Descent Rule for Rank in Thailand: A Correction. American Anthropologist 53. 585-587 (1951), with permission

of the American Anthropological Association. Title revised as "The Declining Descent Rule for Rank in Thailand" in this volume.

Techniques of Intensifying in Thai. Word 2. 127-130 (1946), by permission of the Linguistic Circle of New York.

The Use of Numeral Classifiers in Thai. Language 18. 201-205 (1942), with permission of the Linguistic Society of America.

The Use of Numeral Classifiers in Burmese. Semitic and Oriental Studies, University of California Publications in Semitic Philology, Volume XI (Berkeley: University of California Press, 1951), pp. 191-200, with permission of the publisher.

The Expression of the Diminutive. Studies in Linguistics in Honor of George L. Trager, ed. by M. Estellie Smith (The Hague: Mouton, 1973), pp. 148-152, with permission of the publisher. © 1973 Mouton, The Hague.

Some French Loan-Words in Tunica. Romance Philology, Volume 1, No. 2 (November 1947), pp. 145-148, with permission of the University of California Press. © 1947 by The Regents of the University of California. Title revised as "Some French Loanwords in Tunica" in this volume.

The Menomini Terms for Playing Cards. International Journal of American Linguistics, IJAL/Native American Text Series 34. 217 (1968), with permission of The University of Chicago Press.

The Linguist as a Teacher of Languages. Language 19. 203-208 (1943), with permission of the Linguistic Society of America.

What Belongs in a Bilingual Dictionary? Problems in Lexicography, ed. by Fred W. Householder and Sol Saporta (Bloomington: Indiana University Press, 1962), pp. 45-50, with permission of the publisher.

Anthropological Linguistics: History. Perspectives in Anthropology 1976, ed. by Anthony F.C. Wallace et al. A Special Publication of the American Anthropological Association, No. 10, pp. 33-47 (1977), with permission of the American Anthropological Association. Revised and expanded with title changed as "The Study of American Indian Languages: A Brief Historical Sketch" in this volume.

Grammar or Lexicon? The American Indian Side of the Question from Duponceau to Powell. International Journal of American Linguistics, IJAL/Native American Text Series 35. 239-255 (1969), with permission of The University of Chicago Press. Title revised as "The Problem of Classifying American Indian Languages: From Duponceau to Powell" in this volume.

'Exclusive' and 'Inclusive': A Look at Early Usage. Interna-
tional Journal of American Linguistics, IJAL/Native American Text
Series 35. 1-6 (1969), with permission of The University of Chicago
Press.

Problems of American Indian Philology. Language and Texts:
The Nature of Linguistic Evidence, ed. by Herbert H. Paper (Ann
Arbor: Center for Coordination of Ancient and Modern Studies, The
University of Michigan, 1975), pp. 89-106, with permission of the
publisher.

Boas, Sapir, and Bloomfield. American Indian Languages
and American Linguistics, ed. by Wallace L. Chafe (Lisse: The de
Ridder Press, 1976), pp. 59-69, with permission of the publisher.
Title revised as "Boas, Sapir, and Bloomfield: Their Contribution to
American Indian Linguistics" in this volume.

Linguistics and History. The Scientific Study of Language;
The Role of the Linguistic Society of America, ed. by Anwar S. Dil
(Abbottabad, Pakistan: Linguistic Research Group of Pakistan, forth-
coming), pp. 136-147, with permission of the Linguistic Research
Group of Pakistan. © 1978 LRGP, Abbottabad, Pakistan.

Historical Linguistics and the Genetic Relationship of Languages. Current Trends in Linguistics: 3: Theoretical Foundations,
ed. by Thomas A. Sebeok (The Hague: Mouton and Co., 1966), pp. 113-
154, with permission of the publisher. © 1966 Mouton, The Hague.

The Position of Apalachee in the Muskogean Family. Inter-
national Journal of American Linguistics, IJAL/Native American
Text Series 15. 121-127 (1949), with permission of The University of
Chicago Press.

Noun Incorporation in the Muskogean Languages. Language
17. 311-315 (1941), with permission of the Linguistic Society of
America.

Classificatory Verbs in Muskogee. International Journal of
American Linguistics, IJAL/Native American Text Series 14. 244-
246 (1948), with permission of The University of Chicago Press.

Prehistory and Diffusion. The Prehistory of Languages, by
Mary R. Haas (The Hague-Paris: Mouton, 1969), Chapter 5, pp. 78-
97, with permission of the publisher. © 1969 Mouton, The Hague.

Language and Taxonomy in Northwestern California. American Anthropologist 69. 358-362 (1967), with permission of the American Anthropological Association.

Consonant Symbolism in Northwestern California: A Problem in Diffusion. Languages and Cultures of Western North America,

ed. by Earl H. Swanson, Jr. (Pocatello: The Idaho State University
Press, 1970), pp. 86-96, with permission of the publisher.
        The Northern California Linguistic Area. Hokan Studies,
ed. by Margaret Langdon and Shirley Silver (The Hague-Paris:
Mouton, 1976), pp. 347-359, with permission of the publisher. © 1976
Mouton, The Hague.

        Dr. Afia Dil, Lecturer in Linguistics, United States Inter-
national University, San Diego, must be thanked for her help in many
ways. Kamran Dil of Mt. Carmel High School, San Diego, assisted
the Editor in library research and several matters of detail. Typing
of the camera-ready manuscript has been done by Jacquelyn Bailey of
the United States International University and she certainly deserves a
word of appreciation.

EDITOR'S NOTE

        These essays have been reprinted from the originals with
only minor changes made in the interest of uniformity of style and
appearance. In cases where substantive revisions have been made
proper notation has been added. Misprints and mistakes appearing
in the originals have been corrected in consultation with the author.
In some cases references, notes and bibliographical entries have
been updated. Footnotes marked by asterisks have been added by
the Editor.

Introduction

Mary Rosamond Haas was born in Richmond, Indiana, on January 23, 1910. After receiving her A.B. degree from Earlham College, in her hometown, in 1930, she studied linguistics under Edward Sapir, initially at the University of Chicago and later, with her husband Morris Swadesh (whom she had met in Chicago), at Yale. She completed her Ph.D. degree in 1935 with a dissertation on Tunica, a language with only one speaker living at that time, a man in Louisiana who remembered the language though he had not spoken it since 1915. Her next project, undertaken with the encouragement of Sapir, Franz Boas, and Leonard Bloomfield, was an extensive field study of the Natchez, Creek, and Koasati languages, which occupied her for nearly six years.

From 1941 to 1943, Dr. Haas was a research fellow of the American Council of Learned Societies working on the Thai language. In 1942, after a year teaching Thai at the University of Michigan, she moved to the University of California, Berkeley, as an instructor in the Army Specialized Training Program. Later she was appointed Lecturer in Thai and Linguistics, and in 1947 she was made Assistant Professor. From 1957 to her retirement in 1977 she was Professor of Linguistics at Berkeley; she served as chairman of the Linguistics department for a number of years. In 1964 she established the Survey of California Indian Languages along with Murray B. Emeneau, and she served that project as program coordinator until retirement.

Dr. Haas has taught as a visiting professor at Linguistic Society of America institutes and the Canadian Institute of Linguistics, and at a number of universities in the United States, Canada, and

Australia. She has served the Linguistic Society of America as its
Vice-President in 1956 and as its President in 1963, being one of
only two women presidents in the Society's fifty-five-year history.
She was the LSA Professor in 1970. She is a Fellow of the American
Anthropological Association and the American Association for the
Advancement of Science. In recent years she has been widely honored.
In 1974 she was elected to the American Academy of Arts and Sciences.
In 1975 and 1976 she was awarded honorary degrees by Northwestern
University and the University of Chicago, respectively. Later in 1976
she was named Distinguished Lecturer of the American Anthropologi-
cal Association and was presented the Berkeley Citation by her university. In 1977 the Yale Graduate School Association awarded her
its Wilbur Lucius Cross Medal in recognition of her distinguished
career as a scholar and teacher.

Dr. Haas started her fruitful career as a specialist in Amerindian languages with an article on Nitinat published with Morris
Swadesh in 1932. Her monograph on Tunica, a revised version of her
dissertation published as the fourth volume of Boas's Handbook of
American Indian Languages (1941), was hailed by George L. Trager
in Language as not only "an important contribution to American linguistics" but "one of the best and most thorough descriptions of a
language. . .the reviewer has ever encountered." Haas's classificatory work on Muskogean and Algonkian languages has also been well
received; and she is currently working on her extensive collections
on Natchez, a language that has now become extinct.

She did her first work on the Thai language during the Second
World War, and her famous paper "The Linguist as a Teacher of Languages" (1943) well evokes the spirit of that golden age of applied linguistics and second-language teaching in the United States. Her classroom materials, notably Spoken Thai (1946 and 1948), written with her
second husband Heng R. Subhanka, have been used by thousands of beginning students. Her most valuable contribution in this field, however, is her Thai-English Student's Dictionary (1964), which has ad-
ditionally proved a rich source for sociolinguistic purposes, thanks
to her pioneering classification of Thai words as vulgar, common,
colloquial, elegant, or literary. Although her ambitious project of a
larger dictionary had to be abandoned, her essay "What Belongs in a
Bilingual Dictionary?" (1962) offers her mature thoughts on the subject for the benefit of lexicographers in general.

During her work with Thai and Burmese (which she used as a field language in her methods course), Dr. Haas brought forth a harvest of delightful papers on such phenomena as interlingual word taboos, word games, disguised speech, sibling terms as used by marriage partners, and the declining-descent rule for social rank, as well as a series of meticulous explorations of the use of numeral classifiers and techniques of intensification and reduplication. Some of her earliest studies anticipate the central concerns of sociolinguistics. For example, her classic 1944 essay on men's and women's speech in Koasati, which opens this volume, is frequently cited in discussions of women's speech as part of the women's rights movement; and her paper on French loanwords in Tunica offers striking proof that language cannot be studied in isolation from its sociocultural context.

The work for which Mary Haas may perhaps be longest remembered is in the prehistory of languages, or what she calls "a kind of linguistic archaeology." Based on the principle of the regularity of linguistic change, this field of study has contributed greatly to the reconstruction of earlier forms of languages. In particular, Dr. Haas's work on Amerindian languages has helped to dispel some widely held misconceptions about unwritten languages, notably the notion that such languages change too rapidly to permit a reliable reconstruction of their proto-forms. As she demonstrates in her monograph The Prehistory of Languages (1969, reprinted in 1978), this is not so: not only do all languages change in much the same ways in their phonology, morphology, and vocabulary, but their written or unwritten status neither significantly retards nor accelerates such change.

Mary Haas's painstaking studies in the Thai and Amerindian languages and cultures not only form an admirable body of linguistic scholarship, but offer challenging directions for the study of language and culture relationships across the world. We are proud to present her essays in our series.

Anwar S. Dil

United States International University
San Diego, California
March 17, 1978

**Language, Culture,
and History**

Part I. Sociolinguistics and Language Science

1 | Men's and Women's Speech in Koasati

I

Kosasati is a Muskogean language now spoken in southwestern Louisiana.[1] One of the most interesting features of the language is the fact that the speech of women differs in certain well-defined respects from that of men. The differences may be described by means of a fairly simple set of rules, and the most concise way to formulate them is to set up the forms used by women as basic and to derive the forms used by men from these. While this procedure is preferred because of the greater expediency it offers in the formulation of the rules, it is in most instances arbitrary. In a few instances, however, the speech of women is seen to be somewhat more archaic than that of men and to this extent it is possible to justify the procedure on historical grounds.

The differences between the two types of speech are confined to certain indicative and imperative forms of verbal paradigms. In order to simplify the statement of the rules governing the forms which differ in these paradigms, the rules governing the identical forms are presented first. These are as follows:

(1) If the women's form ends in a vowel, the men's form is the same. Examples:

W or M

lakawwilí	'I lifted it'[2]
oktawhiská	'you stirred it'
iskó	'he drank'

(2) If the women's form ends in č̣, the men's form is the same. Examples:

W or M

lakáwč̌	'you are lifting it'
hí·č̌	'he is looking at it'
č̌a ·kháč̌	'you (pl.) are chopping it'

The remaining rules take care of the instances in which the forms used by men differ from those used by women. The first three of these provide for the cases in which the men's forms substitute an s for the nasalization of a final vowel or for certain final consonants of the women's forms.

(3) If the women's form ends in a nasalized vowel, the men's form substitutes an s for the nasalization. Examples:

W	M	
lakawtakkǫ́	lakawtakkós	'I am not lifting it'
lakawwą́·	lakawwá·s	'he will lift it'
ką·	ká·s	'he is saying'

(4) If the women's form has the falling pitch-stress on its final syllable and ends in a short vowel followed by l, the men's form substitutes the high pitch stress for the falling pitch-stress and an s for the l. Examples:

W	M	
lakawwîl	lakawwís	'I am lifting it'
molhîl	molhís	'we are peeling it'
lakawhôl	lakawhós	'lift it!' (addressed to second person plural)

(5) If the women's form has the falling pitch-stress on its final syllable and ends in a short vowel followed by n, the men's form retains the falling pitch-stress but substitutes an s for the n and lengthens the preceding vowel. Examples:

W	M	
lakawčîn	lakawčî·s	'don't lift it!'
tačilwân	tačilwâ·s	'don't sing!'
iltočihnôn	iltočihnô·s	'don't work!'

The last rule takes care of the instances in which the men's forms differ from the women's by the simple addition of an s.

(6) If the women's form ends in a short or long vowel plus one or two consonants, the men's form adds an s except under the following circumstances: when the women's form ends in č, rule 2; when the women's form has the falling pitch-stress on its final syllable and ends in a short vowel followed by l, rule 4; when the women's form has the falling pitch-stress on its final syllable and ends in a short vowel followed by n, rule 5. (It should also be noted that t + s regularly contracts to č.) Examples:

W	M	
lakáw	lakáws	'he is lifting it'
lakáwwitak	lakáwwitaks	'let me lift it'
mól	móls	'he is peeling it'[3]
lakáwwilit	lakáwwilič	'I lifted it'
í·p	í·ps	'he is eating it'
ta·ɬ	ta·ɬs	'he is weaving it'
tačílw	tačílws	'you are singing'
iltolí·hn	iltolí·hns	'we are working'
mí·sl	mí·sls	'he is blinking'

This completes the rules governing the differences between the speech of men and of women. The table below summarizes these rules by showing in condensed form the final part of the word. Note that a stands for any vowel, k for any consonant, while other letters and diacritics have their proper phonetic value.

W	M	W	M
a	a	ân	â·s
č	č	ak	aks
a	as	a·k	a·ks
a·	a·s	akk	akks
âl	ás	a·kk	a·kks

It sometimes happens that several of these rules operate within the same paradigm and in such a case the differences between the speech of the two sexes is particularly striking. This is illustrated in the three singular paradigms given below:

W	M	
o·tîl	o·tís	'I am building a fire'
ó·st	ó·sč	'you are building a fire'
ó·t	ó·č	'he is building a fire'
lakawwîl	lakawwís	'I am lifting it'
lakáwč	lakáwč	'you are lifting it'
lakáw	lakáws	'he is lifting it'
ka·hâl	ka·hás	'I am saying'
í·sk	í·sks	'you are saying'
kạ·	ká·s	'he is saying'

As has been mentioned, in some instances the speech of women appears to be more archaic than that of men. In rule 4 it is pointed out that when the women's form has a falling pitch-stress on the final syllable and ends in a short vowel followed by l, the men's form substitutes a high pitch-stress for the falling pitch-stress and an s for the l. In the cases that fall under this rule the women's forms are more archaic than those of men. In a first person singular present progressive form like lakawwîl (w. sp.) the -l is the first person singular sign and is related to the suffix -li which is used in the aorist and certain other paradigms; compare lakawwîl (w. sp.) 'I am lifting it' with lakawwilí (w. or m. sp.) 'I lifted it'. The men's form corresponding to lakawwîl, however, is lakawwís and in it the personal sign is missing. The archaism of women's speech is further illustrated in a first person plural present progressive form like lakawhîl (w. sp.). Here the personal sign is -hil, related to the first person plural sign -hilí which is used in the aorist and certain other paradigms; compare lakawhîl (w. sp.) 'we are lifting it' with lakawhilí (w. or m. sp.) 'we lifted it'. The men's form corresponding to lakawhîl is lakawhís; the l of the ending -hil has been lost.

This concludes the technical discussion of the differences between men's and women's speech in Koasati. It is of interest to note that at the present time only middle-aged and elderly women use the women's forms, while younger women are now using the forms characteristic of men's speech. The attitude of older Indians toward the two forms of speech is also interesting. One of my men informants thinks that the speech of women is better than that of men. He said that women talk 'easy, slow, and soft. It sounds pretty. Men's speech has too much ssss.'

Members of each sex are quite familiar with both types of speech and can use either as occasion demands. Thus if a man is telling a tale he will use women's forms when quoting a female character; similarly, if a woman is telling a tale she will use men's forms when quoting a male character. Moreover, parents were formerly accustomed to correct the speech of children of either sex, since each child was trained to use the forms appropriate to his or her sex.

II

Other Muskogean languages appear to have had at one time differences between the speech of men and of women similar to those preserved in Koasati down to the present day. Creek men and women of the present day speak in exactly the same way, both using the forms which were once used only by men. But occasionally the archaic women's forms are preserved in tales where a female character is talking. At first these strange forms were puzzling to me — they were like nothing in ordinary speech; but after I discovered the phenomenon of sex differences in speech in the related Koasati language and learned the nature of these differences, it became clear that these puzzling forms were those formerly used by women. The matter was then carefully checked with some of the older people and these were also able to identify the forms as archaic women's speech.

The examples that I found in Muskogee in this way are not very numerous, but here again the women's forms appear to be basic. The only rule discovered is as follows: Women's forms end in a long vowel with a falling pitch-stress while the corresponding men's forms shift the stress to the penultimate syllable, altering it to a high pitch-stress, and in addition shorten the long vowel and add s. If the shortened vowel is i it is often dropped altogether. Examples:

W	M	
okikâ·	okíkas	'he was'[4]
ó·kickî·	ó·kíckis	'you are'
o·kakaŋkî·	o·kakáŋks	'I meant' (short i dropped)
apo·kiphoykâ·	apo·kiphóykas	'let him stay'

These few examples are practically all that have been discovered; but when coupled with the evidence from the Koasati, the
evidence here seems conclusive for the postulation of a former special
women's speech among the Creeks.

Gatschet[5] tells us that Hitchiti also once had special forms of
speech used by women and he gives brief but convincing proof of this
fact when he speaks of 'the ending -i of the verbs, standing instead of
the -is of the male dialect.' Gatschet also thinks that the forms used
by women were merely more archaic and that long ago men used these
forms also; but he offers no proof for this assumption and I think it is
more reasonable to assume that the so-called 'ancient' language was
actually used only by women. That it was considered 'ancient' by the
Hitchiti themselves probably means no more than that women no longer regularly used these forms in ordinary conversation.

Evidence for the presence of a difference between the speech
of men and of women has been brought forth for three of the Muskogean
languages. In a paper on The Classification of the Muskogean Languages,[6] I presented the evidence for classifying these languages into
two primary divisions, the Western and the Eastern. The Western
division consists only of Choctaw and Chickasaw, but the Eastern division may be divided into three subdivisions, namely Alabama plus
Koasati, Hitchiti plus Mikasuki, and Muskogee (Creek) plus Seminole.
It is thus seen that the evidence for sex differences in speech comes
entirely from the Eastern division and that each of the main subdivisions is known to have possessed the trait. Whether or not it was
at one time present in the languages of the Western division also is
not now known.

III

Languages which contain major or minor differences between the speech of men and of women are not so rare as might be

supposed. From the evidence that has been given in the two preceding sections it appears that most of the Muskogean languages, originally spoken throughout a large part of the southeastern United States, may have had such differences. Sapir[7] has published evidence that such differences existed in Yana, an Indian language of California, while Jenness[8] speaks of their occurrence among the aboriginal languages of Canada, saying: 'More strange to Europeans were the slight differences in speech between men and women that appeared in a few languages. There were sometimes mere differences in vocabulary, certain words being used by women only; but in Siouan and in the Eskimo dialect of Baffin Island there were also slight differences in grammatical form.'

That this phenomenon occurred also in South America is evidenced by the fact that Carib has become almost the classical example of sex differences in speech. The phenomenon occurs also in Asia. Borgoras[9] has demonstrated its existence in Chukchee, spoken far to the north in eastern Siberia, and it is also found in less extensive form in Thai, spoken far to the south in the Indo-Chinese peninsula.

An interesting trait apparently related to this is that in which the sex of the hearer is of grammatical importance. Taking both traits together we find that there are three main types in which the sex of speaker and/or hearer is grammatically relevant. These three types are shown in the following table.

	Speaker	Hearer
Type I	M	M or W
	W	M or W
Type II	M or W	M
	M or W	W
Type III	M	M
	M	W
	W	M
	W	W

The ways in which these types of differences may be actualized are varied, but most of them fall into one or the other of the two following categories: (1) differences in vocabulary, possible in all three types shown in the diagram; and (2) differences in the pronunciation of many or most words, common in Type I.

A few examples of these three types of differences and the ways in which they are actualized may be presented here.

In Thai there are two important differences which fall into Type I and which are actualized by a difference in vocabulary items. The first of these differences is seen in the use of the pronoun phŏm 'I'[10] by men and the use of the pronoun dìchăn 'I' by women. There are many other pronouns that can be used, depending on the relative rank of speaker and hearer, the degree of intimacy between speaker and hearer, or the kinship between speaker and hearer. The pronouns phŏm and dìchăn are used in ordinary polite conversation (not intimate) when speaker and hearer are of equal rank.

The second difference in the speech of men and of women in Thai is in the use of certain polite particles. These are placed at the end of the sentence, particularly in questions and answers and in certain formulaic expressions such as those meaning 'Thank you', 'Excuse me', and the like. The polite particle used by men is khráb; those used by women are khá? (in questions) and khâ? (in answers or statements).

Although Type I differences are shown by only four vocabulary items (two for men and two for women), the polite particles are used frequently and, because of this frequency, an ordinary conversation is characterized by considerable difference in men's and women's speech.

In Yana[11] the forms used by women are shortened and altered at the end so that in this case (in contrast to Koasati) the men's forms appear to be basic. Thus where a man says ʔauna a woman says ʔauh 'fire'.

In Chukchee[12] also sex differences in speech are indicated by altering the words; Borgoras mentions two varieties of this, presumably occurring in different dialects. In the first variety the men's form appears to be basic and the rule for determining the women's form, according to Borgoras, is as follows: 'Women generally substitute š for č and r, particularly after weak vowels. They also substitute šš for rk and čh.'[13] Therefore where a man says rámkɪčhɪn 'people', a woman says šámkɪššɪn. And, quoting Borgoras again,

'The sounds č and r are quite frequent; so that the speech of women, with its ever-recurring š, sounds quite peculiar, and is not easily understood by an inexperienced ear.'

In the second variety of differences in Chukchee the women's forms appear to be basic. According to Borgoras, 'The men, particularly in the Kolyma district, drop intervocalic consonants, principally n and t. In this case the two adjoining vowels are assimilated.' Example: nɪtváɣênat (w. sp.) vs. nɪtváɣaat (m. sp.)

Instances of Type II, where the sex of the hearer is of importance, are not so common as instances of Type I. One interesting instance, though, is found in the Tunica[14] language of Louisiana. Here the differences are found only in the pronominal system, and consist in the use of different words, prefixes, or suffixes. Moreover, the differences are maintained in three numbers, singular, dual, and plural, though in certain paradigms the dual and plural forms have fallen together. Altogether these differences occur in eight different paradigms. Examples:

	Hearer	Singular	Dual	Plural
Semelfactive	M	-ʔa	-wi ʼna	-wi ʼti
Suffixes	W	-ʔi	-hi ʼna	-hi ʼti
Independent	M	-má	wi ʼnima	
Pronouns	W	hɛ ʼma	hi ʼnima	

Instances where Type II is combined with Type I to produce Type III are found in some of the Siouan languages, such as the now extinct Biloxi. Here there was an elaborate system of Type III forms in use — for example in the imperative of verbs. The following sample set, worked out by Dorsey,[15] means 'Carry it'!

	Singular	Plural
M to M	ki-kaŋkoʼ	kiʼ-takaŋkoʼ
M or W to W	ki-tki ʼ	kiʼ-tatkiʼ
W to M	ki-tate ʼ	kiʼ-tatuteʼ

The Biloxi picture is complicated not only by a full set of Type III forms in both singular and plural but by an additional set of singular and plural forms which are used by both sexes when speaking to children, thus: ki 'carry it!' (sing.) and kituʼ 'carry it!' (pl.)

NOTES

[1] The collection of materials on the Koasati language comprised a part of the work done on the history of the towns of the Creek Confederacy under a grant from the Penrose Fund of the American Philosophical Society in 1938-39.

Other languages mentioned in this paper for which the materials quoted are taken from my own notes are Muskogee (Creek), Tunica, and Thai. Linguistic materials on Muskogee were collected during field work among the Creek Indians (in Oklahoma) in 1936 and 1937 through two grants made by the Department of Anthropology, Yale University. Linguistic materials on Tunica (in Louisiana) were obtained principally in 1933 under the auspices of the Committee on Research in American Native Languages of the American Council of Learned Societies. My work on Thai was done for the Committee of the National School of Modern Oriental Languages and Civilizations of the American Council of Learned Societies.

[2] Briefly described, the sounds of the Koasati language are as follows: The vowels are i, a, and o; they may occur either with or without the length phoneme. Short i = [ɪ] (but [e] finally), a = [ʌ], o = [ʊ]; long i· = [e·], a· = [a·], o· = [o·]. All vowels occur also nasalized. Consonants are as follows: voiceless stops p, t, k; voiceless affricate č; voiced stop b; voiceless spirants f, ł, h; semivowels y, w; lateral l; nasals m, n. There are two pitch-stresses in Koasati, the high (ˊ) and the falling (ˆ). All syllables preceding the stressed syllables are high in pitch, except that an open syllable containing a short vowel is low.

[3] The l is not lost here because the word does not have the falling pitch-stress; contrast with rule 4.

[4] The sounds of the Muskogee language are similar to those of Koasati (note 2) except that the Muskogee stops are voiceless lenes and there is an additional nasal ŋ. A fuller description is given in my article Ablaut and its Function in Muskogee, Lang. 16.149-50. The rules for the pitch-stresses are also similar to those of Koasati; but in Muskogee, when two high pitch-stresses occur in the same word, the level of the second is lower than that of the first. Unstressed final syllables are very low in pitch.

[5] Albert S. Gatschet, A Migration Legend of the Creek Indians, 1.79 (Philadelphia, 1884).

[6]In Language, Culture, and Personality 41-56, ed. by Spier, Hallowell, and Newman.

[7]Edward Sapir, Male and Female Forms of Speech in Yana, Donum Natalicium Schrijnen 79-85.

[8]Diamond Jenness, The Indians of Canada, Bull. 65, National Museum of Canada (Ontario, 1932). I am indebted to Dr. Erminie W. Voegelin for this reference.

[9]Waldemar Borgoras, Chukchee, in Handbook of American Indian Languages 2. 631-903.

[10]The phonetic symbols used in the Thai examples quoted here have their usual values except that ph stands for [p'], ch for [ȡ'], and kh for [k']. There are five tones, the even or middle (unmarked), the low (`), the falling (^), the high (´), and the rising (ˇ). A fuller description of Thai sounds is found in my article The Use of Numeral Classifiers in Thai, Lang. 18.201-2, footnote 2.

[11]Sapir, op. cit.

[12]Borgoras, op. cit. 665-6.

[13]The phonetic symbols used by Borgoras in the examples quoted have their usual values except that ṣ̌ is [c] (or, as he says 'like z in German Zeit') and that ệ is [E]. Borgoras also indicated that the consonant ṣ̌ [c] is used only by women, op. cit. 645.

[14]Mary R. Haas, Tunica, in Handbook of American Indian Languages 4. 1-143.

[15]James O. Dorsey and John R. Swanton, A Dictionary of the Biloxi and Ofo Languages, Bureau of American Ethnology, Bull. 47 (Washington, 1912); see p. 3. I have made a few changes in the spelling used by Dorsey and Swanton so that the phonetic symbols used would correspond to those in common use today. I have also put the M-to-W and the W-to-W forms together, since they are identical, though Dorsey listed them separately.

2 | Interlingual Word Taboos

Some years ago, a Creek Indian informant in Oklahoma stated that the Indians tended to avoid the use of certain words of their own language when white people were around. It turned out that the avoided words were those which bear some phonetic similarity to the "four-letter" words of English. These words were avoided even though it is doubtful that a white person not knowing Creek would, when overhearing Creek utterances delivered at a normal rate of speed for that language, be likely to catch these words and attach any special significance to them. For one thing, not understanding the language, he would be unlikely to concentrate sufficiently to notice the rather rare sequences of sounds which might cause him to think he was hearing English obscene words.

How then did the taboo develop? It may be suggested that it arose as a direct result of bilingualism among the Creeks. The more English they knew and used, the more conscious they would be of the phonetic similarity between certain Creek syllables (no full words or even morphemes coincide) and the tabooed words of English. Thus the avoidance grew as bilingualism increased among the Creeks (white people normally do not learn Creek) and as they came more and more to think in terms of the white man's taboos.

Among the words pointed out as being avoided are the following: fákki "soil, earth, clay," apíswa "meat, flesh," and apíssi· "fat (adj.)."[1] Creek monosyllabic words are very rare. Hence the words given here all contain more than one syllable, only one of which bears any resemblance to an English tabooed word. The resemblance may appear to be strengthened by the fact that it is the accented syllable which bears the similarity, but composite words containing the words quoted above may also be avoided, and in such cases the accent has generally shifted to another syllable, e. g. fakkitalá·swa "clay, " fakkinú·4a "brick, " and apisnihá· "meat fat. "

A few years later it became apparent that Thai students studying in this country also tend to avoid certain words of their own language which bear a phonetic resemblance to English obscene words. Here again they avoid the words only when English speakers are about, but the reason for the avoidance appears to stem from their own un-certainty about the propriety of using the words because of their know-ledge of English. The tradition of avoidance is a continuous one. Thai students already residing in this country teach each succeeding group of newly arrived students about the taboo, and in this way the avoidance is kept alive from year to year. [2]

The phonetic nature of Thai is such that there are more words on the taboo list than there are in Creek. Furthermore, since Thai is largely, though not exclusively, monosyllabic, the words tend to bear a greater resemblance to the English tabooed words than do the cor-responding avoided words of Creek.

These secondarily tabooed words of Thai include the follow-ing: fàg "sheath, (bean-) pod, " fág (1) "to hatch," (2) "a kind of pump-kin or squash, "phríg "(chili) pepper, " and khán "to crush, squeeze out."[3] In connection with the last word, it is to be noted that there are other words having the same sequence of sounds except for the tone, e. g. khan (1) "to itch," (2) classifier for vehicles and other objects, and khǎn (1) "to be funny," (2) "to crow," (3) "water-bowl," but it is only the word having the high tone that bears, to the Thai ear, a strong resemblance to the English tabooed word. The reason for this is two-fold: (1) English words with final stop consonants are borrowed into Thai with a high tone, e. g. kέb "(gun-) cap," kɔ́g "(water-) tap," and (2) the high tone on a syllable lacking a final stop is accompanied by glottal stricture when spoken in isolation or when occurring in phrase-final position. The Thai ear equates the final stop of the English word with the glottal stricture of the Thai word; hence the English word, as pronounced in English, sounds like the Thai word khán, whereas khan and khǎn do not.

The word phríg "(chili) pepper" (also used as an abbreviation for phrígthaj "ground pepper, esp. black pepper") caused one group of

students to be faced with a dilemma, since, when eating out, it was
necessary to use this word frequently. In order to observe their self-
imposed taboo and at the same time provide themselves with a substitute term, this group adopted the device of translating the obscene
connotation of the word (if interpreted as English) into the elegant Thai
term of the same meaning, namely lyŋ "the lingam" (derived from the
Sanskrit term). Thus in one limited circle of intimates (men), the
word lyŋ acquired a secondary meaning "pepper" by the round-about
method of translating a Thai word as if it were an English word. This
example of transference of meaning is exceptionally revealing for two
reasons: (1) Most types of vulgarity[4] and familiarity of speech are
not avoided by the Thai among intimates (generally persons of the same
sex- and age-group). Therefore, although lyŋ actually has the meaning
they were trying to avoid when using it as a substitute for phríg (if this
is interpreted as English), this particular substitution must, under the
circumstances, have been virtually, if not actually spontaneous. (2)
Vulgarity and familiarity of speech should be avoided in the presence
of those who are not intimates. Therefore since the word phríg might
be overheard by persons who were not intimates (in this case, speakers of English) and since, in this event, it was liable to interpretation
as an obscenity, the word had to be scrupulously avoided.

Other instances of avoidance also occur in Thai. These are
particularly interesting in that they are far less likely to be misin-
terpreted as obscenities by speakers of English than are the words
quoted above. Thai has no phoneme š (English sh), the nearest equivalent sound being the phoneme ch, an aspirated palatal stop. Another
sound bearing a certain resemblance to English š, from the Thai
point of view, is c, an unaspirated palatal stop. In pronouncing English
words the normal substitution for English š is Thai ch, but avoidance
taboos, of the type mentioned above, extend also to Thai words beginning in c. As a consequence of this, the following words also often
come into the tabooed category: chíd "to be close, near" and cĭd
"heart, mind" (< Pali-Sanskrit citta). The latter word occasionally
occurs as a component of given names in Thai, and at least one man
whose name was sŏmcìd, literally "suiting the heart" (a very pleasing name in Thai), was so embarrassed by this fact that he avoided
the use of his Thai name wherever possible while residing in this
country and adopted an English nickname instead.[5] Other examples
of name-changing under somewhat comparable circumstances are
taken up in a later section of this paper.

The examples of avoided words quoted in the immediately preceding paragraphs range all the way from words whose phonetic resemblance to English tabooed words is very close to others whose resemblance is so slight as to escape detection by the average speaker of English. Therefore the careful avoidance of these words in the presence of speakers of English arises from an exceptionally acute anxiety about the proprieties and niceties of speech. This anxiety is very well reflected in the Thai language itself, for one of its most prominent characteristics is the existence of a very large number of synonymous sets of words differentiated only by the varying degrees of vulgarity and politeness associated with their use.[6] The Thai is consequently willing to go to extreme lengths to avoid even the slightest suspicion of vulgarity. Vulgar speech, when used, is deliberate and intentional. To give the impression of vulgarity unwittingly is unthinkable.

The problem of tabooed words also exists in reverse. That is, certain perfectly harmless English words may bear a phonetic resemblance to tabooed or obscene words in other languages. A striking example of this is found in the Nootka Indian language of Vancouver Island.[7] The English word such bears so close a resemblance to Nootka sač "vagina omens" that teachers entrusted with the training of young Indians find it virtually impossible to persuade their girl students to utter the English word under any circumstances.

Other examples occur in Thai. The English word yet closely resembles the Thai word jéd "to have intercourse" (vulgar and impolite). The resemblance is heightened by the fact that the Thai word has a high tone. Thai taboos against the use of words which correspond in meaning to the English "four-letter" words are not puritanical in origin, as they are in English. Most of the words are at least considered printable in certain situations, for example, in dictionaries, or in textbooks designed to instruct students concerning words which must be avoided in the presence of royalty. The word under consideration here, however, is an exception — it has not been found listed in any Thai dictionary, nor in a textbook. Even so, the word is not one which would be avoided among intimates (i.e., persons of the same sex- and age-group). Nevertheless, the English word yet is very often a source of embarrassment to the Thai, particularly girls studying English in school, since the Thai word is definitely

one of several which would be avoided in the classroom. The English
word key also causes embarrassment to some, because of its resemblance to the Thai word khîi "excrement" or "to void excrement" (vulgar), and since English monosyllables not having final stop consonants
are often borrowed into Thai with a falling tone; hence a Thai, when
first learning English, would pronounce key exactly as khîi. However,
the Thai word khîi, though vulgar, falls somewhat short of being obscene and its use is permissible in some circumstances. For example,
words like khîiphŷŋ "beeswax" (lit. "bee-excrement") or phrǐgkhîinǔu
"bird chili or guinea pepper" (lit., "mouse-excrement pepper"), and
numerous other similar words, are generally quite freely used without
fear of the stigma of vulgarity. Such words would, however, be strictly avoided in the presence of royalty.

        Two other examples of accidental phonetic resemblances be-
tween perfectly harmless words of one language and impolite or obscene words of another language may be cited here.

        The first example involves the Chinese and Burmese lan-
guages and the locale is Rangoon. At least two common Chinese family names, Li and Chi, sound like Burmese lî "phallus" and chî "excrement."[8] It has not been possible to ascertain the attitude of the
Rangoon Chinese toward the matter beyond the statement of a Burmese
informant to the effect that it is not serious enough to cause the
Chinese to change their names; contrast this with the example taken
up in the immediately succeeding paragraphs. Burmese Rangoonians,
on the other hand, are quite aware of the interlingual similarity and
cannot help but find it amusing; at the same time they feel that the
resulting ambiguity is somewhat alleviated by the use of a title meaning "Mr." in front of the name.

        The second example involves interlingual similarities be-
tween impolite or unflattering words and personal, that is, given
names. This situation arises between Northeastern Thai and Central
Thai and the locale is Bangkok. There are a number of given names
of not infrequent occurrence among the Northeastern Thai which sound
vulgar or impolite in the Bangkok dialect (Central Thai). Other given
names sometimes used in Northeastern Thailand are of a type which
is considered highly unflattering or derogatory in the Bangkok area.

As a consequence, a Northeastern Thai bearing one of these given names, will, on going to Bangkok, be obliged to change his name.[9]

One not uncommon northeastern Thai name is tâw,[10] a personal name of a man, sometimes of a woman.[11] This is equivalent to Bangkok tâw, which in one of its meanings is an obscene term meaning "vagina."[12] In northeastern Thailand animal names are sometimes used as personal names; in the Bangkok area, names of this type are strictly avoided. Thus NE măa, personal name (m. or w.), also means "dog"; Bangkok măa means only "dog" and would never be used as a name. NE thúj, personal name (m.), is equivalent to Bangkok thuj "water buffalo having abnormal or stunted horns." NE sĕen, personal name (m.), is equivalent to Bangkok sĕen "rufous stump-tailed monkey" (not found in Northeastern Thailand). NE thŏon, personal name (m.), also refers to a kind of monkey found in the northeast; there is no Bangkok equivalent, but the name would be changed in Bangkok because it refers to a kind of animal. NE tūn, personal name (m. or w.), also means "bamboo-rat," and is equivalent to Bangkok tùn which means not only "bamboo-rat" but also occurs in a common phrase ŋ̂ooŋâw tàwtùn "extremely stupid."

The last example quoted above is changed not only because it refers to an animal but also because it is unflattering in its reference to stupidity. Other names are changed solely because they are un-flattering, e.g. NE kỹm, personal name (m.), which also means "not clever." Though it has no Bangkok equivalent, it is changed because it fails to meet Bangkok concepts of suitability in a name. If the parents dislike or hate their daughter they may name her thŏom, which also means "not pretty and not good, rather stupid." The word has no Bangkok equivalent, but its connotation in the northeast is so unflattering that it will be changed.

A few northeastern Thai personal names are changed because they are considered unpleasing in sound. Some of these have no other meaning but are changed solely because of their sound, e.g. NE pỹy, a common personal name (m.). Others have other meanings besides their use as names, but they are changed because of their sound rather than because of their meaning, e.g. NE mỹy, personal name (m.), also meaning "black gunpowder," and NE mỹm, personal name (w.), also meaning "black."[13]

A common stimulus for name-changing among the Northeastern Thai arises when the person bearing the name goes to Bangkok. Some persons, however, may change their names even though
they remain at home, particularly upon attaining an official position.
But even in this latter event, the change appears to be due to the influence of the culture of the capital, since standards for what befits
a person attaining an official position are set largely in Bangkok. Note
that not all instances of name-changing quoted above are the result of
interlingual word taboos, i.e., word taboos arising from interlingual
ambiguity. All, however, are the result of taboos imposed by another
culture.

The problem of interlingual word taboos has, as far as is
known, received little if any attention among linguists. Many other
examples could no doubt be adduced if some attention were given to
the matter.[14] It is a type of problem that can easily escape notice,
particularly if the period of field contact is short. The Creek-English
and Thai-English examples cited came to attention accidentally after
periods of long contact and in informal conversations, not during for-
malized questioning periods. The Chinese-Burmese and Northeastern
Thai-Central Thai examples, on the other hand, were uncovered by
direct questioning after interest was aroused in discovering more examples of such taboos.

In general it is the speakers of the minority language who
feel obliged to observe the taboo, which, though the result of contact,
is not actually imposed by the speakers of the majority language; for
the latter, in their ignorance of the minority language (except when
proper names are involved), are normally quite unaware of the problem.

The examples brought forth in this paper illustrate two quite
different types of situations. The Creek-English example is the result of acculturation. The same is true of the Northeast Thai-Central
Thai example. In both of these instances it is conceivable that in time
the supposedly objectionable words of the minority language may become obsolete or obsolescent.[15] The Thai-English example, on the
other hand, is a matter of temporary avoidance and will never have
any permanent influence on the Thai language. Thai students may try
to avoid certain English-sounding Thai words while residing in this
country, but they do not continue to observe the taboo after they return

to their own country, even though some speakers of English also reside there. The Chinese-Burmese example is interesting for still
another reason. Here, even though the interlingual ambiguity causes
amusement to the majority group (Burmese), the minority group
(Chinese) has no inclination to be affected by this attitude and makes
no attempt to effect an adaptation or change.

NOTES

[1]The Creek (or Muskogee) language has the following consonants: voiceless unaspirated or weakly aspirated stops p, t, k and
affricate c; voiceless spirants f, s, ł, h; voiced semivowels y, w;
voiced nasals m, n, and defective -ŋ- (of rare occurrence); voiced
lateral l. Vowels are i [ɪ], a [ʌ], u [ʊ], i· [i·], a· [a·], u· [o·], and
the rare -e- (occurring only before y).

[2]Since the Thai do not immigrate to this country, the taboo
exists only among students. Occasionally a student is found who is
uninterested in observing the taboo. Such a student will usually be
found to have come from a section of Thailand other than Bangkok or
its environs. Elaborate gradations of politeness and vulgarity of
speech are particularly characteristic of the Bangkok area.

[3]The Thai consonants are: voiced stops b, d, -g; voiceless unaspirated stops p, t, c (palatal stop), k, ʔ; voiceless aspirated stops ph, th, ch, kh; voiceless spirants f, s, h; voiced semivowels j [y], w; voiced nasals m, n, ŋ; voiced liquids l, r. The
vowels are: front unrounded i, e, ɛ [æ]; central unrounded y, ə, a;
back rounded u, o, ɔ. All nine of these vowels may occur doubled
(phonetically lengthened, e.g., ii, ee, ɛɛ, etc., and the heterophonous vowel clusters ia, ya, and ua also occur. There are five tones:
middle (unmarked), low (ˋ), falling (ˆ), high (ˊ), and rising (ˇ). The
final stops b, d, and g are briefly voiced but unreleased; they therefore resemble the English final stops p, t, and k.

[4]The word "vulgarity" is not used here as a loose synonym
for "obscenity." The Thai word jàab, which I translate "to be vulgar," for lack of a more adequate term, has a much wider application
than "obscene." Thus, to touch the head of another person, to call
attention to one's feet by kicking or any unnecessary movement, to use
certain pronouns of derogatory connotation, to use any of various kinds
of uncouth language, whether obscene or not, to speak loudly or laugh
hilariously, all these things are jàab. It is in this sense, then, that

the words "vulgar" and "vulgarity" are to be understood when they are used with reference to the Thai.

[5] Many others also adopt English nicknames for various other reasons.

[6] Thus there are at least eleven words meaning "to eat" connoting varying degrees of politeness or vulgarity. Such elaboration of speech is largely restricted to the Bangkok area. In other parts of the country other dialects are spoken, and these are marked by greater simplicity in this respect than is the Bangkok dialect.

[7] Edward Sapir and Morris Swadesh, Nootka Texts (William Dwight Whitney Linguistic Series, Yale University, 1939).

[8] In the Burmese words quoted here l and ch are more or less equivalent to English l and ch; i is [i]; the tone mark (ˆ) indicates a high tone in nonfinal position or a falling tone in final position.

[9] If he does not, he will lay himself open to constant teasing and ridicule.

[10] Northeastern Thai is not phonemically identical with Central Thai (see note 3). Northeastern Thai has a consonant phoneme ñ (the palatal nasal), not found in Central Thai, and lacks ch and r, which are common in Central Thai. The vowels, on the other hand, have the same values in the two dialects, though they often differ in their distribution. Northeastern Thai has seven tones, as follows: high-falling (ˊ), lower high level (ˉ), lower high-falling (ˆ), mid level (unmarked), low level (ˋ), very low low level (˜), and rising (ˇ). The tonal equivalences between Northeastern Thai and Central Thai normally follow certain regular rules.

[11] Some northeastern personal names may be given either to men or to women, some only to men, and some only to women. Each name is marked accordingly.

[12] There are at least seven Bangkok words having this meaning; the one cited here is very nearly at the bottom of the scale in degree of vulgarity. The Bangkok word is either tâw or tàw. However, the tonal equivalences between Northeastern Thai and Central Thai are such that NE tâw is equivalent (in sound correspondence, not in meaning) to Bangkok tâw but not to tàw.

[13] "Black," as a name, is not usually considered unflattering.

[14] Certain conditions, however, have to be present before the problem arises. First of all, the phonetic conditions must be present. In other words, the languages which come in contact must have certain sounds and sequences of sounds in common. For example, Japanese speakers residing in this country do not encounter this problem

because Japanese is utterly lacking in the sequences of sounds which are found to occur in English "four-letter" words. Similarly, Burmese students studying in this country are likewise untroubled by the problem because Burmese lacks the necessary sounds and sound sequences.

[15]Of course it is also possible that Creek as a language may die out before the taboo imposed from English has had time to exercise its full effect.

3 | Thai Word Games

Thai schoolchildren between the ages of ten and eighteen often amuse themselves by playing games based upon a knowledge of words or vocabulary.[1] There are two principal types of games. The first type may be called the Identical Initial Syllable Game and is based upon a knowledge of Thai words only. The second type may be called the Rhyming Translation Game since it is a game in which each successive Thai word must rhyme with the English translation of the preceding word. Or it may be played by starting with an English word and then each successive English word must rhyme with the Thai translation of the preceding English word.

The first type of game is particularly popular with younger children whose vocabulary in Thai is still somewhat limited. It is a good game to be played when it is raining outdoors or when the children prefer to sit and talk instead of exercising. The second type of game, since it is more complicated and involves a knowledge of two languages, is more likely to be preferred by the older children.

The principal purpose of both games is to enlarge the children's vocabulary, the first in Thai, the second in English. But more immediate incentives are also often provided in the form of a reward for the winner and penalties for the losers. The first loser is the first one who fails to supply an additional word when his turn comes around. One after another of the players drops out and the last child left is the winner. A penalty for the loser or losers is usually decided upon in advance. A loser may have to wash the dishes or clean up the room for the winner. Or perhaps he has to drink a bottle of water or sing a song. Another type of penalty permits the winner to knock on the knees of the loser for five or ten times, depending on what has been stipulated in advance.

The Identical Initial Syllable Game is considered easier than the Rhyming Translation Game and it is most often played by younger children as an aid to enlarging their vocabulary in their own language. The game always involves Thai disyllabic, or less commonly, polysyllabic words. Thai has many disyllabic words beginning in syllables like ka-, kra-, kha-, pra-, ta-, tha-, ma-, ra-, la-, wi-, sa-, and ʔa-.[2] Therefore the game can be played many times without any repetition of vocabulary items involved. The child who starts the game has the advantage of being able to select a word beginning in a syllable which he favors. If he starts out with a word like sabaaj 'to be well, comfortable,' the other players must quickly start thinking of other words beginning in sa-, e.g., sabùu 'soap,' sadùag 'to be convenient,' sadɛɛŋ 'to show,' saʔàad 'to be clean,' sadùd 'to stumble,' etc.

Sometimes further refinements are introduced to make the game more interesting and also more difficult. Of the literally dozens of Thai words which begin in the syllable kra-, only a limited number refer to birds and animals. To make the game more exciting, then, the children may limit the permitted words to those which have this type of reference, e.g., kracɔ̂ɔg 'sparrow,'[3] kratàaj 'rabbit,' krarɔ̂ɔg 'squirrel,' krasǎa 'heron,' krabyy 'water buffalo,' etc. Other types of words beginning in kra-, such as krapǎw 'pocket,' kradàad 'paper,' kradùug 'bone,' krasǔn 'bullet,' etc., would not be permissible.

Another popular game consists in trying to think of words which begin in the syllable ma- and refer to plants or trees bearing edible fruit. One reason for the popularity of this game is that there are a large number of words which come in this category[4] and so the game can be kept going longer. Examples are mamûaŋ 'mango' makhɣ̌a 'eggplant,' makhǎam 'tamarind,' maphráaw 'coconut,' maráʔ 'bitter melon,' manaaw 'lemon, lime,' madɣ̀a 'fig,' etc. This variety of the game is sometimes brought to an end in a way peculiar to it alone. The child who can think of no more names of fruits beginning in ma- says maŋèeg. This is not the name of a fruit but a threat to knock someone on the head. As the losing player utters this word he holds up his clenched fist in a threatening gesture. The winner, however, still exacts whatever penalty was agreed upon, e.g., knocking upon the knees of the loser.

A more difficult variety of the Identical Initial Syllable Game involves words beginning in the syllable cam-. Words beginning in

this syllable are mostly elegant and learned and literary, [5] and many
of them would not be known to Thai children until they have entered
a more advanced stage in their study of their own language. There is
no semantic limitation set when playing the game with this syllable.
Since the semantic categories of the words beginning in cam- are quite
varied, such a limitation would not be feasible. Examples are:
camnuan 'amount, quantity,' camnáb 'to overtake, arrest,' camphûag
'species, kind,' camdəəm 'origin, originally,' camləəi 'defendant,'
camrəən 'to improve,' camrú? 'to be beautiful' (rare and literary), etc.

  Older children who have begun the study of English are more
likely to amuse themselves by playing the Rhyming Translation Game.
The one who starts the game again has a certain advantage since he
may begin either in Thai or in English, though both languages are involved no matter which language is used in starting. If he chooses
Thai, he gives a Thai word and its English translation. The next player must produce another Thai word which rhymes with the English
translation of the first word. The game then proceeds in this fashion
until only one player is left. An example of the way the game may be
played when starting with Thai is as follows:

1st player:	'kɔ̀b'	plɛɛwâa (means)	'frog'
2nd player:	'hɔ̀ɔg'	"	"	'spear'
3rd player:	'mia'	"	"	'wife'
4th player:	'hâj'	"	"	'give'

For variety the game may also be played by starting out in English.
An example of this method of playing is as follows:

1st player:	'eat'	plɛɛwâa (means)	'kin'
2nd player:	'sin'	"	"	'bàab'
3rd player:	'harp'	"	"	'phin'
4th player:	'fin'	"	"	'khrîib'

  Perfect rhymes between two different languages are often
difficult if not impossible to achieve. And the reader unfamiliar with
Thai phonetics may be puzzled by one or two points involved in the
rhymes occurring in the examples cited. English "spear" can be
rhymed with Thai mia because the Thai vowel cluster ia is very close
in sound to the British pronunciation of -ear, -ere, etc. English

"wife" can be rhymed with Thai hâj because in Thai only one consonant can stand in syllable-final position and it would therefore be impossible to find any closer rhyme in Thai.[6]

Both types of games, besides providing amusement for the
children who play them, are also of considerable educational value.
It is easy to see why the Rhyming Translation Game is preferred by
older children. It obviously requires considerably more skill and
quicker thinking than the Identical Initial Syllable Game. In the latter
game the child with a good memory can plan ahead and think up a
large number of words beginning in the chosen syllable while the other
players are giving their words. In the Rhyming Translation Game, on
the other hand, it is impossible to plan ahead. Therefore the best
player will be the one who has a large enough vocabulary in English to
be able to come up with a rhyming word on a moment's notice.

NOTES

[1]My first information about Thai word-games was obtained
more than ten years ago from Ubol Huvanandana, who has also supplied examples of words used in the Identical Initial Syllable Game.
Additional information, particularly about the Rhyming Translation
Game, was given to me recently by Waiwit Buddhari, who is working
as Thai Linguistic Informant on the Thai Dictionary Project, Institute
of East Asian Studies, University of California, Berkeley. He also
provided examples of words used in the Rhyming Translation Game.
[2]If these syllables are pronounced in isolation, that is, other
than as the first syllables of longer words, they are pronounced as
kà ʔ, krà ʔ, khà ʔ, prà ʔ, tà ʔ thâ ʔ, máʔ, ráʔ, láʔ, wíʔ, sàʔ, and ʔàʔ.
The Thai consonants are: voiced stops b, d, -g; voiceless
unaspirated stops p, t, c (palatal stop), k ʔ; voiceless aspirated stops
ph, th, ch, kh; voiceless spirants f, s, h; voiced semivowels j [y],
w; voiced nasals m, n, ŋ; voiced liquids l, r. The vowels are front
unrounded i, e, ɛ [æ]; central unrounded y [ɨ], ə, a; back rounded u,
o, ɔ. All nine of these vowels may occur doubled (phonetically lengthened), e.g., ii, ee, ɛɛ, etc., and the heterophonous vowel clusters
ia, ya, and ua also occur. There are five tones: middle (unmarked),
low (`), falling (^), high ('), and rising (ˇ). See also Mary R. Haas,
The Thai System of Writing, American Council of Learned Societies
(Washington, D. C., 1955).

³Terms referring to birds are normally preceded by the word nóg 'bird.' Hence one would normally say nógkracɔ̀og 'sparrow,' and nógkrasǎa 'heron.' For the purposes of this variety of the Identical Initial Syllable Game, however, the term nóg is dropped. The names of the animals are not preceded by any generalizing term.

⁴The syllable ma- (máʔ) as the first syllable of the name of a tree or plant bearing edible fruit is actually, etymologically speaking, a generalizing term referring to edible fruits, and that is why there are so many words beginning in this syllable which come in this category. Compare the use of nóg described in note 3.

⁵Most, if not all of them, are probably of Cambodian origin.

⁶When English words are borrowed into Thai they also conform to this same pattern. Thus the English word "mile" has been borrowed into Thai as maj.

4 | Burmese Disguised Speech

1. Although disguised speech[1] of one sort or another is
fairly common among the languages of the world, good descriptions
of the manner in which the disguise is accomplished are still rather
difficult to find.[2] Languages of Southeast Asia and the Pacific seem
to have several varieties. Materials obtained from Burmese speakers
between 1948-52 illustrate a number of these varieties and therefore
seem to deserve a systematic presentation.[3]

Languages like Thai and Burmese have a type of syllable
structure which can usefully be described in terms of an <u>initial</u> (i. e.
the initial consonant or consonant cluster)[4] and a <u>final</u> (i. e. the
vowel plus tone plus consonant, if any). Both languages have developed a kind of speech disguise in which the initials of affected
syllables remain fixed while the finals are reversed. The Thai call
this <u>khamphŭan</u> ("word-reverse") or "reversed speech"[5] and the
Burmese call it <u>zəgəleynv</u>[6] ("speech-disguise") or "disguised speech. "
Some Burmese also refer to it as <u>zəgəhwɛ?</u> ("speech-hide") or "secret speech. "[7]

This is reminiscent of the type of speech distortion known in
English as a "Spoonerism. " The chief difference is that in English
it is usually the syllable-initial which is reversed and — at least in
the most amusing instances — both renditions have meaning (e. g.
half-[f]ormed [w]ish → half-warmed fish).[8] In Thai and Burmese,
on the other hand, it is the syllable-final which is reversed and,
since the reversed rendition is for the purpose of befuddlement and
concealment, it may or may not have meaning. For example

Thai k[ôn] j[àj] "bottom big" → kàjjôn "chicken wrinkled"[9]

(1) Burmese b[eynx] z[ax] "opium-eater" → baxzeynx

However, it sometimes happens that one phrase is the mirror image, so to speak, of another and so it is not surprising to learn that "people like to joke with this," e.g.

(2) k[aw?] y[owx] "straw' ↔ k[owx] y[aw?] 'nine (people)"[10]

There are also other types of speech distortion found in Burmese and some of these more nearly resemble what is called "Pig Latin" in English. These are described briefly in 5.

The principal users of disguised speech in Burma, as elsewhere, are school children and teenagers. They may employ it as a secret language for use among age-mates or for secrecy or joking among brothers and sisters. The favorite kind among the Burmese is z əgəleynv and children generally pick it up from listening to clowns who may use it during dancing festivals (with dancers, clowns, and orchestra) staged for the entertainment of villagers. It is also used for euphemism or concealment and a few phrases have come to have rather wide currency even among adults. References to the eating or smoking of opium are among these, as can be seen in example (1). Another example is:

(3) buv hyeynxdev ← b[eynx] hy[uv]dev "to smoke opium"

In addition, the use of z əgəleynv to disguise derogatory connotation has given rise to a number of expressions including the following very common one:

(4) khwav θeyxδeyx ← khw[eyx] θ[av]δav "little better than dogs" i.e. "very foolish" (khweyx "dog(s)," θav "to surpass").

2. Phonological rules for Burmese can be conveniently stated in terms of the basic form of a morpheme which is modified (or not modified) by preposed morphemes. These basic forms show the maximum differentiation of the initial consonant, e.g. kowv "to" (for kowv ~ gowv in definable circumstances), khəleyx "young" (for khəleyx ~ gəleyx in definable circumstances). Previous statements concerning the changes governed by these morphophonemic rules are to be found in "The Use of Numeral Classifiers in Burmese"[11] and

and in Cornyn's <u>Outline of Burmese Grammar</u>.[12] In the present paper the rules are summarized as the background for the special rules
needed to explain the construction of disguised words.

3. Burmese preposed morphemes end in ʔ(the glottal stop),
H (a special morphophonemic symbol), ə (a reduced vowel), or a full
vowel or diphthong (nasalized or nonnasalized) with distinctive tone
(v, x, or q).[13]

Burmese basic forms begin in one of three kinds of consonants: nonchangeable, limited changeable, and changeable. The nonchangeable consonants are the voiced stops and spirants (b, d, g, z,
δ), the voiced and voiceless sonorants (m, n, ŋ, l, w, y, hm, hn,
hŋ, hl, hw, hy,)[14] and the glottal stop and spirant (ʔ, h). The limited changeable consonants are the aspirated voiceless stops and
spirants (ph, th, kh, sh, and also θ which behaves like an aspirated
spirant) and the changeable consonants are the unaspirated voiceless
stops and spirants (p, t, k, and s).

It is not necessary to make any further statement about nonchangeable consonants since they remain the same in all environments.
The following rules apply to limited changeable and changeable
consonants.

(i)   Limited changeable and changeable consonants remain
       unchanged after ʔ and H and H is then deleted.

(ii)   Limited changeable consonants remain unchanged
       after ə.

(iii) Changeable consonants change to their voiced counter-
       parts after ə.

(iv)   Elsewhere both limited changeable and changeable con-
       sonants change to their voiced counterparts and h (as-
       piration) is deleted.

A couple of sets of forms are sufficient to illustrate these rules. In
the first column below the preposed morphemes tə "one," hnəH "two,"
θownx "three," and thyawʔ "six" are combined with the morpheme

thawnv "thousand" and in the second column they are combined with
kawnv, clf. for animals. The number of the rule involved follows the
gloss.

Limited changeable	Changeable

təthawnv "one thousand" (ii)   təgawnv "one (animal)" (iii)
hnəthawnv "two thousand" (i)   hnəkawnv "two (animals)" (i)
ɵownxdawnv "three thousand" (iv)   ɵownxgawnv "three (animals)" (iv)
thyawʔthawnv "six thousand" (i)   thyawʔkawnv "six (animals)" (i)

4. Before stating the rules which apply to the formation of
disguised speech, it will be helpful to present the Burmese syllabic
canon. This is of two types, full and reduced, as shown below: [15]

$$\text{Full:} \quad C\ (y)\ (w)\ V \begin{Bmatrix} nas \\ ʔ \end{Bmatrix}^{T}$$
$$\text{Reduced:} \quad C \qquad\qquad ə$$

The syllable is further conveniently divided into two parts, the Initial,
composed of the C (and following glides, if any), and the Final, composed of the V plus T (with nasalization or glottal stop, if either).
Full syllables may occur in any position in the word but a reduced
syllable may not be the ultima. Normal words contain either full
syllables or a combination of reduced and full syllables. Hence every
word will contain at least one full syllable and, if there is only one
full syllable, it will be the ultima. Examples:

mix "fire"   theminx "cooked rice"
lavmev "will come"   lavmelax "will (you) come?"
duxyinxbinv "durian tree"   məsaxbux "won't eat"
leʔhmaʔ "ticket"   keləthaynv "chair"

Normal nondisguised words are the terminal strings which
result from the application of the morphophonemic rules (3). Many
such words can be subjected to an additional rule to produce the kind
of disguised speech briefly described above (1). There is, however,
a class of words to which this additional rule cannot be applied. Since
a reduced syllable may not be the ultima, two-syllable words with ə
in the first syllable and three-syllable words with ə in the first two

syllables cannot be reversed. Examples of words of this class are
thəminx and kələthaynv listed above. All other types of words can be
converted into disguised speech by the application of the following
rule:

(v)   Reverse the Finals of the first and last full syllables
        of a word.

	Nondisguised	Disguised
(5)	(l[eʔ]hm[aʔ] "ticket	laʔhmeʔ
(6)	m[ix]b[owv] "fireplace"	mowvbix
(7)	s[av]ʔ[owʔ] "book"	sowʔʔav
(8)	l[av]ʔ[ownx] "come here!"	lownxʔav
(9)	b[uv]davy[ownv] "railroad station	bownvdavyuv
(10)	ʔəy[eʔ]ph[owv] "liquor distillery"	ʔəyowvpheʔ
(11)	θəy[eʔ]θ[ix] "mango"	θəyixθeʔ
(12)	m[ix]yəth[ax] "train"	maxyəthix
(13)	məl[av]b[ux] "won't come"	məluxbav
(14)	ʔəy[eʔ]θəm[ax] "drunkard"	ʔəyaxθəmeʔ

(v. a) Across word boundaries reverse the Finals of the first
        full syllable of each word.

	Nondisguised	Disguised
(15)	b[ev]gowv θw[ax] "go where?"	baxgowv θwex
(16)	b[eynx] hy[uv]dev "to smoke opium"	buv hyeynxdev

(v. b) If reduplication is involved both occurrences are sub-
        jected to the same change.

	Nondisguised	Disguised
(17)	khw[eyx] θ[av]δav See (4).	khwav θeyxδeyx

Since any glides which follow the initial C are treated as part
of the Initial their placement is normally unaffected by the reversal
rule, e. g.

	Nondisguised	Disguised
(18)	mapy[ox]b[ux] "won't talk"	mǝpyuxbox
(19)	ŋǝhmy[ax]d[anv] "fishing-rod"	ŋǝhmyanvdax
(20)	ŋǝpy[ox]δ[ix] "banana"	ŋǝpyixδox
(21)	θw[ax]m[ev] "will go"	θwevmax

See also (15) and (17) above. However, even in reversal the combination *CwuT is avoided.[16] Hence a restriction must be introduced before the reversal rule is applied to the effect that:

$$Cw + V.. \text{ in the env. } Cu \rightarrow C + wV ..$$

We therefore have:

	Nondisguised	Disguised
(22)	mǝhl[wex]b[ux] "won't swing"	mǝhluxbwex
	not *mǝhlw[ex]b[ux] to avoid:	*mǝhlwuxbex
(23)	mǝθ[wax]b[ux] "won't go"	mǝθuxbwax
	Contrast (21) above.	

There is some evidence that there may still be other restriction rules, at least for some speakers, e.g.

$$Cw \ V.. \text{ in the env. } Ci \text{ nonnas} \rightarrow C \ wV$$

This would explain the following example:

	Nondisguised	Disguised
(24)	m[ix]δ[weyx] "charcoal"	mweyxδix

However, this example is not firm because the informant first gave meyxδwix as the disguised form and then corrected himself saying that mweyxδix is better. In normal speech *CwiT seems not to occur and the speaker with a sensitive ear would want to avoid it in disguised speech as well. But it is possible that not all speakers are equally fastidious. There are no restrictions in normal speech on the occurrence of Cwi nas T, e.g. kwiṇxdev "to make a ring (as for the finger)," but nasalized i is lowered to [ɪ].

5. Most Burmese speakers prefer to use the term zəgəleynv only of disguised speech formed through the use of the reversal rule (v) shown in 4. However, they are also usually acquainted with one or more other kinds of ciphered speech. These remind one of our more familiar Pig Latin and all are characterized by the addition of **extrane-ous** phonological material. Each type can be generated from normal speech by the operation of a special rule with the proviso that, as in zəgəleynv, reduced syllables are not subject to **alteration**. The sim-plest type is covered by the following rule:

(vi) In each normal full syllable use -inx as Final in place of the normal Final, then add the unaltered full syl-lable and a word boundary.

(25) Unaltered: θw[ax]m[ev] "will go"
      Altered: θwinxθwax minxmev

(vi. a) A reduced syllable preceding the full syllable will be added along with the unaltered full syllable.

(26) Unaltered: məθw[ax]b[ux]l[ax] "won't (he) go?"
      Altered: məθwinx məθwax bwinxbux linxlax

The remaining types[17] are slightly more sophisticated and involve the insertion of an extraneous Final plus Initial between the normal Initial and Final so that each single full syllable is replaced by two full syllables. There is, moreover, a certain phonological similarity among all of them, viz. , that the extraneous Final always contains the vowel a (though variation is achieved by changing the tone or by using it in a diphthong followed by ?) while the extraneous Initial is always t-.

(vii) Insert Final -ay? and Initial t- between the Initial and Final of each full syllable and add a word boundary.

(27) Unaltered: b[ev]g[owv] θw[ax]məl[ex] "Where are (you) going?"
      Altered: bay?tev gay?towv θway?tax məlay?tex.

(viii) Insert Final -aq and Initial t- between the Initial and Final of each full syllable and add a word boundary.

(28)   Unaltered: sh[ax] y[uv] "bring the salt!"
       Altered: shaqtax yaqtuv.

(ix)   Insert Final -av and Initial t- between the Initial and
       Final of each full syllable and add a word boundary.

(29)   Unaltered: sh[ax] "salt"
       Altered: shavtax.

The last type involves the insertion of two different patterns of Final
plus Initial in alternation:

(x)   Insert Final -av and Initial t- between the Initial and
       Final of the first full syllable and Final -eʔ and Initial
       t- between the Initial and Final of the next full syllable
       and add a word boundary after each operation.

(30)   Unaltered: sh[ax] y[uv] "bring the salt"
       Altered: shavtax yeʔtuv.

In another example which is similar to this the first inserted Final is
-aq in place of -av and the rule for the alternate Final is not entirely
clear.

(31)   Unaltered: m[aq] tw[eyv] sh[ax] y[uv] "Ma Twey
                       (name), bring the salt!"
       Altered: maqtaq tyeʔtweyv shaqtax yaqtuv.

This is only one example of this type at hand and it is not clear
whether the proper name tweyv→ tyeʔtweyv is to be interpreted as
tw[eyv] with the insertion of -eʔ-t- and the substitution of y for w or
whether a new type of insertion is involved, namely -yeʔ-t-, and that
t[weyv] → tyeʔtweyv. The point cannot be settled without more examples
of the treatment of Initial Cw.

        6. In addition to their intrinsic interest as examples of lin-
guistic play, studies of disguised or altered speech can also be used
as illustrations of phonological theory. An earlier draft of the present paper was written more than a decade ago and at that time I was
disturbed by the fact that examples of zǝgǝleynv frequently appeared
to constitute exceptions to morphophonemic rule (iv). [18] Thus:

(32)   θiʔpinv "tree" → θinvpiʔ, not *θinvbiʔ.

(33)   məθawʔphux "won't drink" → məθuxphawʔ, not
*məθuxbawʔ.

(34)   məθawʔthyinv "don't want to drink" → məθinvthyawʔ,
not *məθinvdyawʔ.

(35)   siʔθax "soldier" → saxθiʔ, not *saxδiʔ.

See also examples (10), (11), and (14).

The difficulty, however, vanishes when it is recognized that morphophonemic rule (v), specifying the reversal of Finals, must be applied
after the other rules. Hence Burmese z_ə_g_ə_leynv differs from standard
Burmese by the addition of a single rule and no other statements need
to be made. This is comparable to the statement made by Morris Halle
in regard to the most economical method of describing the difference
between Pig Latin and General American. [19]

The study of Burmese disguised speech also highlights some
problems regarding the phonological nature of the Burmese syllable.
Thus the restriction rules preceding example (22) and (23) show that
even though initial Cw is usually treated as an inseparable unit in the
application of the reversal rule (e.g. example [21]), the avoidance of
combinations like *CwuT and *CwiT takes precedence over the intact-
ness of the initial consonant cluster. Therefore in the structure of the
Burmese syllable the position of noninitial w is somewhat ambivalent.
It normally belongs with the Initial but in some instances it can be
taken as part of the Final. This may turn out to be significant in the
predication of future sound changes and/or the elucidation of earlier
ones.

NOTES

[1] Harold C. Conklin has used the similar term "speech disguise" in his paper on "Tagalog Speech Disguise," Language 32.136-
139 (1956). I am indebted to him for several interesting discussions of
types of linguistic play some years ago. Various points in the present
paper have also benefited from discussions with my colleagues, Pro-
fessors Haruo Aoki, William S.-Y. Wang, and Karl E. Zimmer.

[2]What material there is exists in widely scattered sources and in various languages. An important paper, recently called to my attention by Professor Wang, is Y.R. Chao's study in Chinese which may be translated as "Eight Varieties of Secret Speech," BHIP 23.312-354 (1931).

[3]This work was done under the auspices of the Department of Oriental Languages, University of California, Berkeley. My chief informant at that time was Maung (now U) Tha Hto, but other speakers also contributed information; this is indicated in the notes where pertinent.

[4]The second consonant in standard Thai of Bangkok is l, r, or w. In the Burmese of Rangoon it is normally y or w and w may also occur as a third consonant after y. In these languages these second- or third-position liquids or glides are not treated as part of the vocalic nucleus but as part of the consonantal "initial."

[5]Information about Thai reversed speech was obtained some years ago from Mr. Heng Subhanka and Dr. Kaw Swasdi Panish. The terminology employed by some of the languages of the Philippines is similar to the Thai term. The Tagalog, for instance, have a variety of phonological types of disguised speech all of which are called baliktád "which in other contexts means 'inside-out, upside-down, inverted, or backward'" (Conklin, op. cit., p. 136). The Hanunóo also indulge in various kinds of phonological distortion which they call "sinulih 'turned wrong-side-up'" (Conklin, "Linguistic Play in its Cultural Context," Language 35.631-636 (1959)).

[6]Burmese tones are indicated in this paper by means of arbitrary letters: v, for the long low level tone; x, for the long high tone; q, for a rapidly falling tone with weak glottal stricture. Syllables which end in ʔ have an extra high pitch on the preceding vowel (which is always very short), but no other pitch precedes ʔ and so no tonal indication needs to be made in this position. In this interpretation final ʔ is considered a consonant and not, as previously, a kind of "tone." See Mary R. Haas, "The Use of Numeral Classifiers in Burmese," pp. 191-200 in Semitic and Oriental Studies (= University of California Publications in Semitic Philology Vol. XI (1951)).

[7]The morpheme hweʔ is rare in occurrence but is also found in the expression hyowx hweʔtev "hides secretly" and is related to phweʔ, as in phweʔtev "(he) hides"; information obtained from Maung Soe Win and friends who were attending Colorado School of Mines, Colorado, in 1952.

[8]The reversable or movable segments are placed in square brackets in this and other examples throughout the paper. Although the most usual type of reversal in English affects the syllable-initial, occasional instances of the reversal of finals are also encountered, e.g. it is c[us]tomary to k[iss] the bride → it is kisstomary to cuss the bride.

[9]In Thai, as in Burmese, many instances of reversed speech are either accidentally or intentionally meaningful.

[10]Parentheses are placed around "people" since the Burmese term being translated is the classifier for people and not the noun meaning "people."

[11]Mary R. Haas, op.cit.

[12]William S. Cornyn, Outline of Burmese Grammar, Language Dissertation No. 38 (1944).

[13]The values of the tonal symbols are described in note 6.

[14]Many writers on Burmese linguistics treat hy as the spirant [š], an interpretation which overlooks two important facts about Burmese phonology. (1) Although Burmese y in noninitial position can be described as a glide, in initial position it is always strongly spirantized and resembles [ž] except that contact is made in the y-position; therefore to treat a ž-like sound in y-position as y but a š-like sound in y-position as š completely obscures the relationship between these two sounds. (2) If hy was a true spirant it would be one of the changeable consonants like s which regularly changes to z in circumstances described in rules (iii) and (iv). Although hy is indeed the voiceless counterpart of y, it does not belong to the class of changeable consonants any more than do hw, hm, hn, and hn which are the voiceless counterparts of w, m, n, and n, respectively. It is also worthy of note that hy is written as such in the Burmese orthography (but in devanagari symbols).

[15]C = consonant, V = vowel, T = tone v, x, or q (as described in note 6), nas = nasalization of the vowel (written as n, e.g. lanx "road"), ʔ = glottal stop, here considered a consonant which automatically induces a high-pitched tone.

[16]The combination CyiT however, is not avoided; see example (20). It also occurs in normal words, e.g. nyivduv "equally."

[17]The type described in rule (vii) was first brought to my attention by Dr. R. B. Jones who learned of it from his Karen informant, Saw Judson Aung. According to Burmese informants there is considerable individual variation in the types of ciphered speech.

Moreover, this kind of speech is not considered pleasing to the ear though zəgəleynv is.

[18] My earlier statement was as follows:

> Regular morphophonemic rules are suspended; thus voiceless unaspirated and aspirated stops are not changed to their homorganic voiced stops after v, x, and q. In other words, the twisted [disguised] form is an automatic reversal based on the straight [non-disguised] forms without any other change.

It is somewhat difficult now to see why this should have appeared so troublesome in the early fifties. However, this very fact points up some of the changes that have taken place in phonological theory since that time. See Morris Halle, "Phonology in Generative Grammar," Word 18.54-72 (1962).

[19] Halle, op. cit., pp. 62-63.

5 | Sibling Terms as Used by Marriage Partners

I

In a recent issue of the <u>American Anthropologist</u> Wolf discusses a Chinese case of incest taboo, with special reference to the village of Hsiachichou, "located near the town of Hsulin on the southwestern edge of the Tapei basin in northern Taiwan" (1966: 883), where two types of patrilocal and one type of uxorilocal marriage are practiced. The significant difference between the two types of patrilocal marriage lies in the age of the bride when she enters the home of the groom. In one case she is an adult, and in the "alternative" case

> she enters her future husband's home as a child. . .
> seldom more than three years of age and often less
> than a year. . .[She] becomes a member of the house-
> hold and a daughter-in-law, but. . .she is not imme-
> diately presented to the family's ancestors. This. . .
> does not take place until she is old enough to fulfill
> the role of wife. In the meantime she and her parents
> are affinally related <u>to the groom's parents</u>, but she
> is not in fact married to the groom (Wolf 1966: 884;
> underlining added).

It is not the purpose of the present paper to discuss Wolf's conclusions (1966: 891) regarding the reactions of the villagers to this type of marriage as indicating that "the intimate childhood association of the parties to such a marriage creates a strong emotional resistance to sexual relations." What I do wish to show, however, is that the kinship terminology used by the couple is probably ambiguous and therefore of dubious value as an argument in favor of his interpretation.

In Hsiachichou the couple even address one
another with the same terms used by true siblings.
As the older of the two, the boy receives from his
future wife the term ā-hîa "older brother"; he ad-
dresses the girl by her personal name, in the same
way that he would address any younger sister. Under these conditions it would not be very surprising
if the couple <u>came to think of each other as brother
and sister, or at least as a kind of brother and sis-
ter</u>. . .[One] girl who had herself refused to marry
a boy whose family she had joined as a child. . .
[commented], "I just couldn't do it. It was too em-
barrassing. Imagine marrying your brother!"
(Wolf 1966: 893; underlining added).

It is not possible properly to assess the implications of this
passage without considerably more information about the kinship usage among the people of Hsiachichou. In order to show why this is so,
I should like to digress a moment and present corresponding kinship
terminological information for some of the cultures (or societies) of
Southeast Asia.

II

Among the Thai it is necessary to distinguish three ways in
which kinship terms may be used: 1) as nouns (N), 2) as pronouns (P), and 3) as titles (T) preceding a given name. Thus phɔ̂ɔ N
(Haas 1964: 366)[1] is strictly a referential term meaning "father";
phɔ̂ɔ P is a 1st person pronoun "I, Father" if a father is speaking to
his child, while the derived polite khunphɔ̂ɔ P is used as a 2nd or 3rd
person pronoun "you, he, Father" if a child is speaking to or of his
father; but phɔ̂ɔ T is placed before the first name of boys as a title,[2]
e. g. , phɔ̂ɔdɛɛŋ "Master Daeng," and the whole expression may then
also be used as a 2nd or 3rd person pronoun, especially by family
servants of long standing and sometimes even by acquaintances (non-
intimate friends) of the family. Since this situation may seem strange
at first, it should be observed that English usage affords a close parallel, viz. 1) <u>father</u> N, the referential term, 2) <u>Father</u> P, 1st person
when used by the father and 2nd or 3rd person when used by the child,
though certain substitutes such as <u>Daddy</u> are now generally preferred

in this usage, and 3) <u>Father T</u>, as in <u>Father Brown</u>, a title used with
the surname of certain priests.[3] In order to highlight the likenesses
and differences among these three types of use in the two languages a
simple componential analysis is shown in Table 1, with Thai on the
left and English on the right. While Thai and English are similar in
the triple use of a few terms, Thai differs from English in that there
are similar, though not parallel, <u>triple uses for all consanguineal
terms</u>.

Table 1

Uses of Thai phôɔ and English <u>Father</u>

	phôɔ			father		
	N	P	T	N	P	T
+1 Generation	+	+	−	+	+	−
Male	+	+	+	+	+	+
Adult	+	+	−	+	+	+
Having child	+	+	−	+	+	−

For the purposes of the present discussion, however, we are
interested only in the terminology employed by marriage partners.
As far as Thai terminology is concerned, husbands and wives are af-
fines. The words phǔa N "husband" (p. 340) and mia N "wife" (p. 409),
like all other Thai affinal terms, are used only as nouns with their
proper denotative meanings and are never employed as pronouns or
titles with extended meanings. Instead, pronominal usage for all affinal relatives is based on the most nearly appropriate consanguineal
term. For husbands and wives, obviously, the only appropriate terms
are the sibling terms, because husband and wife, like brother and
sister (or, in Thai, older sibling and younger sibling), belong to the
same genealogical level. The Thai sibling terms are phîi N "older
sibling" (p. 372) and nɔ́ɔŋ N "younger sibling" (p. 257). As pronouns,
these terms have extensions comparable to those previously illustrated for phôɔ "father." Thus phîi P is used as a first person pronoun "I" in the following situations:[4] 1) oSb to ySb, 2) H to W, 3) man
or woman to yBW or ySH (unless, optionally, one of these latter is
older than ego), and 4), nonobligatorily, an older person to a slightly
younger person. Correlatively, the derived polite term khunphîi P
is used as a 2nd or 3rd person pronoun in the following situations:
1) ySb to oSb, 2) W to H, 3) man or woman to oBW or oSH (unless

one of these latter is younger than ego), and 4), nonobligatorily, a younger person to a slightly older person. Table 2 shows a simple componential analysis of the noun and pronoun uses of phîi.

Table 2

Some Uses of Thai phîi

	N phîi	P(1) phîi	P(2) phîi	N phǔa	P(3) phîi	T phîi
Same generation	+	+	+	+	+	+
Older	+	+	±	±	+	+
Same Parent(s)	+	+	−	−	−	±
Male	±	±	+	+	±	±
Female	±	±	−	−	±	±

It also shows clearly that pronominal use (1) has the same analysis as phîi N "older sibling," while pronominal use (2) has a significantly different analysis which in turn is the same as phǔa N "husband," thus corroborating the equation

$$\text{phîi N} \quad : \quad \text{phîi P(1)} \quad : : \quad \text{phǔa N} \quad : \quad \text{phîi P(2)}$$

For the sake of completeness the analysis of phîi T is also shown. It may be placed before the given name of oSb, oBW, oSH, or a slightly older unrelated person of either sex.

III

A somewhat similar state of affairs exists in Burmese. Again, it is the blood kin terms that assume additional uses as pronouns and, though to a much lesser extent, as titles. Cooke (1968: 91) tells us that "affinal kin are pronominally designated by the same terms as blood kin" and that these pronominally used kin terms are extended to include "close friends of kin, kin of close friends, and also individuals accepted into the family." In Burmese the sibling terms used by a woman are ʔakowv N "older brother of man or woman" and mawnv N "younger brother of woman."[5] Either of these can be reduplicated and used as a term of endearment by wife speaking to husband, thus: kowvkowv P "you" (W to H) or mawnvmawnv P "you (W to H, a common affectionate usage). A man, however, does not use a kin term in these circumstances. He may use khinv P in speaking to wife or sweetheart, or, if he prefers, he may use her second name (the second of two given names) reduplicated, e. g. , hlaqhlaq (based on mav-hlaq).

Burmese usage differs from Thai usage in at least one other important respect. Unlike Thai, "brother and sister terms are a-voided. . .between brother-in-law and sister-in-law, since <u>such terms are reserved for husband and wife</u>" (Cooke 1968: 91; underlining added).

IV

To complete the picture in Southeast Asia, we find that Viet-namese usage is also similar to that of Thai and Burmese (Cooke 1968: 127-129; also Emeneau 1951, Thompson 1965). Thus, anh "older brother of man or woman" is used as 1st person pronoun (H to W) and as 2nd person pronoun (W to H). Similarly, em "younger sibling of man or woman" is used as 1st person pronoun (W to H) and as 2nd person pronoun (H to W). Cooke (1968: 129) adds that it is chiefly "youthful couples" who follow this usage. In addition to being used pronominally to or by a wife, em is also used in a similar fashion to or by a close female intimate. But Cooke makes a special point of the fact that "ordinarily em will not be used by or to a woman who is close enough to ego's wife's age to give rise to misunderstanding." The term chi N "older sister of man or woman" also needs to be mentioned briefly. It is paired with anh N in "anh chi 'elder brother-elder sis-ter' (a pair used pronominally chiefly in displaced reference to a hus-band and wife)" (Cooke 1968: 126).

V

These three examples are sufficient to make it clear that the use of sibling terms between husband and wife in the three societies is normal and uncomplicated. It can be referred to as one kind of dis-placement usage.[6] Such use does not imply that a woman confuses her husband with her brother, or a man his wife with his sister. Clearly the basic implication of the usage is simply "person of ego's gener-ation," not "person sharing one or both parents with ego." In Viet-namese, indeed, the use of em is so likely to imply wife or sweetheart that it will be avoided in use by or to a woman close to ego's wife's

age (other than actual sister), and in Burmese there is an avoidance
of sibling terms between brother-in-law and sister-in-law because
these are "reserved for husband and wife."

This brings us back to the situation described by Wolf for the
village of Hsiachichou in Taiwan. We learn that the majority of the
population is descended from "18th-century immigrants from the
Chuanchou district of southern Fukien" (Wolf 1966: 897, fn. 2). In
view of what we have been discussing in regard to sibling terms as
used by marriage partners in Southeast Asia, we see that Wolf's description of the address terminology used by betrothed children raised
in the same household might at some point be open to more than one
interpretation. In other words, we need to know if this displacement
usage of sibling terms is found between ordinary husbands and wives
in Hsiachichou. A recently interviewed speaker[7] of a Min (Fukienese)
dialect from Changhua, Taiwan provides the following information for
his area.[8] The terms for "older brother" and "younger sister" are
used by a wife and a husband, respectively, particularly by the newly
married in a romantic mood, and they therefore correspond closely
in use to such English terms as sweetheart, honey, baby, etc. At the
same time actual siblings also use the appropriate sibling terms in
address, but "older brother" and "older sister" are particularly characteristic of polite (educated, cultivated) usage. On the other hand,
younger siblings may be addressed as "younger brother" and "younger
sister" or by personal name without differentiation on the polite usage
scale. Correspondingly, the uneducated use personal names for all
siblings, older as well as younger.

If the situation regarding the use of sibling terms is the same
in Hsiachichou as it is in Changhua, there exists a strong possibility
of a serious conflict in the implications of the usage as the children
grow older. At first the implication would be attestation of an as-if
sibling status. But sooner or later the intended marriage partners
would learn that in certain circumstances the usage implies sweetheart or marital status. This discovery might very well take place
in early adolescence and the psychological burden imposed by the ambiguity in the address terminology could become the cause of extreme
embarrassment. In the societies of Southeast Asia the use of sibling
terms by marriage partners does not give rise to any serious ambiguity, but in Taiwan where one form of marriage prescribes that the

intended bride be raised as a younger sister in the same household, we cannot argue away the ambiguity. Here older brother = sweetheart-husband and younger sister = sweetheart-wife, and one wonders how the transition is made. Perhaps the high percentage of unhappiness in such marriages, as reported by Wolf, is to be ascribed to the difficulty of making the transition with respect to a single individual. In other words, the same man cannot be both "older brother" and "sweetheart-husband" and the same woman cannot be both "younger sister" and "sweetheart-wife" in spite of the identity of the term used in each case. The tragic irony of the situation can best be brought into focus by the following illustration. While a man obligated to marry a young woman whom he was raised to think of as a younger sister (or at least a kind of younger sister) might well be unable to call his wife "younger sister" in a romantic sense (or even to think of her in a romantic sense), he would probably experience no difficulty whatever in using the very same term to address his mistress.

Almost the entire theoretical fabric of kinship terminology is based on the denotative meanings of the several terms, and extended meanings reflected in address terminology have been largely neglected. Conflicts of the type revealed in the Taiwan situation need further study; the theoretical fabric will never be as strong as it should be until it can adequately account for all varieties of meaning.

NOTES

[1] The Thai-English Student's Dictionary (Haas 1964) is arranged according to the Thai (a non-Roman) alphabet. As an aid to those who do not read Thai, the page number for each kin term is shown following its gloss.
[2] The word may also be used as a title, in certain circumstances, before the first names of men as well as boys.
[3] We should actually distinguish four uses: noun (term of reference), addressive (term of address), pronoun, and title. These various uses of many English kin terms seem nowhere to have been carefully described. Our dictionaries are also much less helpful than they should be. For example, Webster's Third International Dictionary mentions the use of father in direct address only in reference to ecclesiastics, and the pronominal use of the word is not mentioned at all.

⁴The following abbreviations are used here for kin terms: H,
husband; W, wife; oSb, older sibling; ySb, younger sibling; BW,
brother's wife; SH, sister's husband.

⁵This information is taken from my own field notes on Burmese usage (c. 1951-53). Important information is to be found in
Cooke (1968: 88, 90, 91, 96, 97), and some support is also found in
Cornyn and Musgrave (1958). Burling's (1965) paper is almost wholly
concerned with the referential use of Burmese kin terms. Although
he lists kóukóu (kowvkowv) under qakou (ʔakowv), he does not adequately define its use (1965: 108).

The phonetic system used here is the same as that found in
Cooke (1968: 69), which in turn is based on Haas (1951). The letters
v and q are used as tonal markers, v for the low tone and q for the
rapid falling tone with glottal stricture.

⁶Cooke also uses the terms "displaced" and "displacement"
(1968: 50, 126, and passim) but usually with reference to the use of
kin terms for nonkin: e.g., "Kin terms are used pronominally with
blood kin and affinal kin, and most forms also have a displaced usage
denoting nonkin" (1968: 126; underlining added). In my own use of the
terms I include the use of blood kin terms for affinal kin as one type
of displacement.

⁷I am indebted to Mr. Hsin-I Hsieh for providing the information presented here. The form of marriage which places the little
girl in her intended husband's family at a tender age is also known in
Mr. Hsieh's part of Taiwan, though it is considered a degrading arrangement for the girl.

⁸Information about possible similar use on mainland China
is meager. The most detailed study of Chinese terms of address is
that by Chao (1956), but he confines himself to standard Peiping, i.e.,
Peking usage. He makes no mention of the use of sibling terms by
husband and wife, and this would seem to imply their nonuse in that
locality. On the other hand, my colleague William S.-Y. Wang tells
me that the special sibling usage is found in contemporary movies.
Specifically, the wife can use the term for "older brother," and the
husband can use either the term for "younger sister" or for "older
sister." The relative age factor is not vis-à-vis her husband, but
reflects her ranking among her own sisters.

BIBLIOGRAPHY

Burling, Robbins
   1965 "Burmese Kinship Terminology," in Formal Semantic Analy-
         sis (ed. by E. A. Hammel), pp. 106-117. American Anthro-
         pologist, Special Publication, vol. 67, no. 5, part 2.
Chao, Yuen Ren
   1956 Chinese Terms of Address. Language 32:217-241.
Cooke, Joseph R.
   1968 Pronominal Reference in Thai, Burmese, and Vietnamese.
         University of California Publications in Linguistics, vol. 52.
Cornyn, William S., and John K. Musgrave
   1958 Burmese Glossary. Washington: American Council of
         Learned Societies.
Emeneau, Murray B.
   1951 Studies in Vietnamese (Annamese) Grammar. University of
         California Publications in Linguistics, vol. 8.
Haas, Mary R.
   1951 The Use of Burmese Numeral Classifiers. University of
         California Publications in Semitic Philology 40:191-200.
   1964 Thai-English Student's Dictionary. Stanford: Stanford Uni-
         versity Press.
Spencer, Robert F.
   1945 The Annamese Kinship System. Southwestern Journal of
         Anthropology 1:284-309.
Thompson, Lawrence C.
   1965 A Vietnamese Grammar. Seattle: University of Washington
         Press.
Wolf, Arthur P.
   1966 Childhood Association, Sexual Attraction, and the Incest
         Taboo: a Chinese Case. American Anthropologist 68:883-898.

6 | The Declining Descent Rule for Rank in Thailand

In his recent article "Thailand — a Loosely Structured Social System" (American Anthropologist 52, 181-193 [1950]), the late John F. Embree briefly describes the "declining descent rule" as applied to rank in Thailand. This rule, as applied to royal rank and based on a quotation from Graham,[1] is correctly described. But in the sentences immediately following, Embree applies this same declining descent rule to ranks conferred by the king, and he also implies that conferred ranks were awarded, in part at least, to counteract the effects of the declining descent rule. This seems to have arisen from a failure to distinguish between two separate but coexistent types of rank.

The Thai language makes a neat distinction between the two major types of rank[2] by the use of the two terms, câwnaaj[3] "royal personage, royalty" and khǔnnaaŋ, "noble or honored person, the nobility."[4] The term câwnaaj includes the king and his consorts, his children, grandchildren, great-grandchildren, and great-great-grandchildren. The declining descent rule applies only to this type of rank, since each succeeding generation is of a lower rank. Thus the children of the king and queen are Somdet Chao Fa (sǒmdèd câwfáa),[5] those of the king and his wives not of royal birth are Phra Ong Chao (phrá ʔoŋcâw); the grandchildren are Mom Chao (mɔ̌mcâw); the great-grandchildren are Mom Rajawongs (mɔ̌mráadcháwoŋ): and the great-great-grandchildren are Mom Luang (mɔ̌mlǔaŋ).[6] As a general rule, each person in this system stays in the same rank throughout life. However, when a new king is crowned, an additional royal line of descent is set up with the new king at the top; his descendants from then on receive their proper rank in the system through him and not through their relationship to the previous king. Moreover, in rare cases a

person having the rank of Mom Chao is raised to the rank of Phra Ong
Chao.[7] A recent instance of this type is exemplified in the person of
Prince Wan Waithayakon Worawan (phrá?oŋcâw wanwajthájaakɔɔn
wɔɔráwan),[8] the present Thai Ambassador to the United States. By
birth he was a Mom Chao, but in recognition of services during the
bloodless revolution of 1932 (B. E. 2475), he was raised to the rank
of Phra Ong Chao by an act of parliament. His children, according
to the declining descent rule, are now Mom Chao. His brothers, on
the other hand, have not been elevated in rank and they are therefore
also Mom Chao. Even more recently, King Bhumibol Aduladej
(phrábàadsŏmdèd phrácâwjùuhŭa phuumíphon ?àduulàdèed, while in
Thailand in the spring of 1950 for his coronation, honored two other
royal persons by elevating them from the rank of Mom Chao to the
rank of Phra Ong Chao.[9]

     Proceeding now to the system of ranks denoted by the term
khŭnnaaŋ, we find that this includes all persons who have been honored by the king with a special conferred rank. The six most important
degrees of conferred rank, in descending order, are as follows:
Somdet Chao Phya (sŏmdèd câwphrájaa), Chao Phya (câwphrájaa),
Phya (phrájaa), Phra (phrá?) Luang (lŭaŋ), and Khun (khŭn).[10] A rank
within this system belongs to the individual alone — in other words,
it is in no way dependent on any rank conferred on his father, nor will
his son be able to acquire a rank by virtue of his father's rank.[11]
Conferred ranks are bestowed in recognition for service to the government, and a given rank and a given office often go hand in hand. A
document issued by King Chulalongkorn in 1886, and translated by
Frankfurter, also emphasizes these same points in the following
words:

> The nobles (khŭnnaaŋ) in our State are not an hered-
> itary class as in Western countries. The custom regarding
> them is near to that prevailing in China, where dignity and
> office are combined. If a person has a dignity, he occupies
> at the same time an office. If he leaves such office, his dig-
> nity ceases, unless the King allow him to keep his dignity on
> account of services rendered. For that reason most of the
> nobles remain in the Government service during [their] life
> time . . .[12]

     Moreover, a given conferred rank is not necessarily fixed
for life, since a man may hope to be raised to a higher rank (or even

a succession of higher ranks) as a reward for greater and more important services to the government. [13]

From the foregoing it will be clear that the two types of rank are not dependent upon or influenced by each other at any point. Royal rank is determined solely by blood and even if a man is raised from the rank of Mom Chao to the rank of Phra Ong Chao, this elevation is possible because he is already of royal blood. This is in contrast to conferred rank, which belongs to the individual alone and is not hereditary. Confusion between the two types of rank may have arisen in the minds of some because of the fact that a person of royal blood could also be awarded a conferred rank. Such a person would then have two separate kinds of titles, one dependent on his royal blood, the other dependent on his status within the system of conferred ranks. Commoners, however, could attain only one kind of rank, namely a conferred rank.

One important point remains to be made about these two systems of rank in Thailand. After the revolution of 1932, it was decided that the system of conferred ranks should be abandoned. No change has been made in the system or royal ranks. [14] The present situation with regard to conferred ranks, then, is as follows: No new conferred ranks have been bestowed since 1932. Persons who had been given a conferred rank prior to 1932 have been permitted to keep this rank and its title if they so desire. As a result, some individuals have retained their rank and title (which includes a new name along with the title), while others have elected to abandon their rank and title and have resumed their former names. Phya Anuman Rajadhon (phrájaa ʔanúmaan ráadcháthon), Chief of the Department of Fine Arts in Bangkok, is one who has retained his rank and title. On the other hand, Luang Kovit Abhaiwongse (lǔaŋ khoowít ʔàphajwoŋ), [15] a prominent political figure, has abandoned his title and has resumed his former name; he is therefore now known as Nai Khuang Abhaiwongse (naaj khuaŋ ʔàphajwoŋ). [16]

NOTES

[1]Graham, 1912, p. 216; also Graham, 1923, vol. 1, p. 231.

[2]The author is indebted to Mr. Kaw Swasdi Panish (kɔɔ sàwàddiphaanít) for many helpful suggestions in connection with the writing of this communication.

[3]The Thai consonants are: voiced stops, b̲, d̲, -g; voiceless unaspirated stops p̲, t̲, c̲ (palatal stop), k̲, ?; voiceless aspirated
stops ph̲, th̲, ch̲, kh̲; voiceless spirants f̲, s̲, h̲; voiced semivowels
j̲ [y], w̲; voiced nasals m̲, n̲, ŋ̲; voiced liquids l̲, r̲. The vowels are:
front unrounded i̲, e̲, ɛ̲ [æ]; central unrounded y̲, ə̲, a̲; back rounded
u̲, o̲, ɔ̲. All nine of these vowels may occur doubled (phonetically
lengthened), e.g. ii̲, ee̲, ɛɛ̲, etc., and the heterophonous vowel clusters ia̲, ya̲, and ua̲ also occur. There are five tones: middle (unmarked), low (ˋ), falling (ˆ), high (ˊ), and rising (ˇ).

[4]The use of the term "nobility" must not be taken to imply
any connection whatsoever with royalty.

[5]Several different systems of transliteration and transcription of Thai words are in use. Occasionally a writer will use more
than one of these in the same book or article. For this reason words
are quoted in phonemic writing to avoid ambiguity. Titles and proper
names are quoted in one of their more usual Romanized spellings followed by a phonemic transcription in parentheses.

[6]The children of Mom Luang are commoners.

[7]Graham, 1923, vol. 1, p. 231.

[8]In some books Prince Wan's name is transliterated as
Varnvaidyakarn Varavarn.

[9]Standard, May 13, 1950.

[10]Cartwright, in speaking of these titles, says: "These titles are somewhat like the European orders of knighthood, and therefore must on no account be translated by such words as Baron, Mar-
quis, etc. as they are not hereditary; and also for the reason that
many of them are titles appertaining to particular offices or official
positions in the Government Service" (1930, p. 274).

[11]This is not to say that the children of a man high in the system of conferred ranks do not acquire prestige by this fact; it simply
means that these ranks are not hereditary.

[12]Frankfurter, 1900, pp. 124-125. Frankfurter gives the full
document in Thai (pp. 120-124) followed by an English translation
(pp. 124-130). The full translation is commended to those who wish to
know something of the system of conferred ranks as of 1886; a brief
history of the system is also given. In the portion quoted here, the
present writer has inserted the Thai word khŭnnaaŋ in parenthesis
after the word "nobles" to indicate that this is the word used in the
Thai text.

[13]In former times, at least, a conferred rank could also be
"revoked at the Royal will" (Cartwright, p. 273).

[14]However, persons of royal blood (at least those of the rank of Mom Chao and upwards) were thenceforth considered "above" politics.

[15]The names following a man's conferred title are conferred with the title and, as a general rule, are entirely different from the names he used previous to the assumption of his rank (see also Graham, 1923, vol. 1, p. 307). Nai Khuang's family name, Abhaiwongse, however, carries great prestige; it was therefore retained when he was given his full title of Luang Kovit Abhaiwongse.

[16]Nai (naaj) can best be translated "Mr."; in other words, it is a general title for any man without rank.

BIBLIOGRAPHY

Cartwright, B. O.
  1930 The Students' Manual of the Siamese Language (revised ed.),
        Bangkok.
Frankfurter, O.
  1900 Elements of Siamese Grammar. Bangkok.
Graham, W. A.
  1912 Siam, a Handbook of Practical, Commercial, and Political
        Information. London.
  1923 Siam. London, 2 vols. (A revised and enlarged edition of
        the above.)
Standard, May 13, 1950. Bangkok. (An English language weekly
        newspaper.)

There are two special ways of intensifying degree in Thai which are of particular interest. The first involves the use of special lexical elements which may be used in conjunction with only one, or rarely two or three words in the language, while the second involves the use of a special type of reduplication.

As an example of the use of a special lexical element we have the word ʔam which is used only in conjunction with màj 'to be new' in the phrase màj ʔam 'to be brand new.'[1] There are not a great many words of this type, but a number of common descriptive verbs, such as those meaning 'to be hot, cold, wet, dry,' the principal colors, and a few others, have special words which can be used with them to intensify their meaning. These special words may be referred to as restricted modifiers because their range of usage is definitely limited. A few other examples are:

> cúag in khǎaw cúag 'to be pure white'
> bʏ̌y in dam bʏ̌y 'to be jet black'
> chɔ́og in pìag chɔ́og 'to be sopping wet'
> phàag in hɛ̂ɛŋ phàag 'to be bone dry'
> tʏ̂y in mʏ̂yd tʏ̂y 'to be pitch dark'

Occasionally there are two restricted modifiers which may be used with the same word, but as a rule they have a slight difference in meaning. Thus chíab is used with jen 'to be cold' to give jen chíab meaning 'to be ice-cold,' while chŷyd is used with the same word to give jen chŷyd meaning 'to be stone cold' (as food). Similarly, cɛ́ɛd is used with dɛɛŋ 'to be red' to give dɛɛŋ cɛ́ɛd 'to be bright red,' while cɛ̌ɛ is used with dɛɛŋ to give dɛɛŋ cɛ̌ɛ meaning 'to be intensely red.'

Now and then two restricted modifiers used with the same word are differentiated only by vocalic ablaut and, as a rule, some people use one form, other people the other. Thus we have wĕeŋ or its ablaut mate wŏoŋ used with baw 'to be light of weight' giving baw wĕeŋ or baw wŏoŋ meaning 'to be extremely light, light as a feather.' Pairs like wĕeŋ and wŏoŋ have probably arisen from the splitting of reduplicated words; compare rŏoŋrĕeŋ 'to be sparse, widely scattered.' This type of reduplication, wherein a back rounded vowel is paired with a front unrounded vowel of the same height, is very common in Thai.[2]

In some instances we find that the same restricted modifier can be used in two different ways, but the two ways are often related. Thus chɔ̌og is used with plag in plag chɔ̌og 'to be sopping wet' and it is also used with fŏn tòg 'it is raining' in fŏn tòg chɔ̌og 'it is raining hard (that is, drenchingly)'. Similarly, we find that câa is used with sàwàaŋ 'to be bright' in sàwàaŋ câa 'to be dazzling bright' and with dɛ̀ɛd 'sunlight' in dɛ̀ɛd câa 'dazzling sunlight.' In addition to the type of examples just given there are a few instances of restricted modifiers being used with words of unrelated meaning. Thus câa just given is also used with rɔ́ɔŋ 'to cry' giving rɔ́ɔŋ câa 'to cry hard' (speaking of an infant). Similarly, tŷy is used with mŷyd 'to be dark' to give mŷyd tŷy 'to be pitch dark' and also with ʔim 'to be full, satiated' to give ʔim tŷy 'to be very full, stuffed.'

Words like chɔ̌og, câa, and tŷy give us the clue to the origin of these restricted modifiers. All of them at one time probably had a separate meaning and could be used in more than one way; but later on through constant association with one or two words they eventually came to be used only with such words.

At this point it is of interest to note that English has words which are similar in function to the restricted modifiers of Thai. Examples (some of which were used in the translations of Thai expressions above) are found in pitch dark, pitch black, bone dry, jet black, crystal clear, stone cold, stone deaf, stone blind, sopping wet, brand new, chock-full or chuck-full. The English examples given are different from the Thai examples in one important respect, namely, most of the words modifying the adjectives clearly have an independent existence. However, in their function as modifiers of adjectives

they are restricted in use to one or two words. Thus jet is used in
jet black, but isn't used to modify any other adjective. Stone, on the
other hand, is used with three words, cold and deaf and blind, but beyond this it is not likely to be used to modify any other adjective.
Most of the English examples appear to have arisen as analogies.
Thus pitch-dark is equivalent to dark as pitch. However, in this connection it is important to observe that not all analogies have been converted into special phrases like pitch dark. For example, we very often
say hot as fire but hardly ever fire-hot; we say clear as a bell but not
bell-clear. For this reason phrases like pitch dark, bone dry and
crystal clear occupy a unique place in English lexicography just as
Thai restricted modifiers occupy a unique place in Thai lexicography.

       Turning now to the second special technique of intensifying,
that involving a special type of reduplication, we find there are numerous examples like the following:

               ˈdǐidii 'to be exceedingly good'
               ˈsǔajsǔaj 'to be extremely pretty'

       The reduplication used in this function has two special fea-
tures: (1) The changed form of the element is placed first, in contrast to other types of reduplication found in the language. (2) The
first element is always spoken on an emphatic high tone which is higher in pitch than the normal high tone.

       These two special features require some illustration. First
let us compare the position of the changed element in nonemphatic reduplication with that in emphatic reduplication, as shown in the examples below:

                          Nonemphatic

        Nonreduplicated   Reduplicated
jûŋ 'to be tangled, confused'   jûŋjîŋ 'to be complicated'
kràsíb 'to whisper'   kràsíbkràsâab 'to whisper'
tum imitative of drumbeat   tumtum imitative of beating
                                  a drum
                          Emphatic
dii 'to be good'   ˈdǐidii 'to be extremely good'
wǎan 'to be sweet'   ˈwǎanwǎan 'to be extremely
                                  sweet'

The examples above illustrate the fact that whereas in nonemphatic reduplication the modified element comes last, in emphatic reduplication it comes first.

The nature of the emphatic high tone is also important in this type of reduplication. The basic word may have any one of the five tones, the middle, the low, the falling, the high, or the rising. But the first element in emphatic reduplication will always have the same tone, namely the emphatic high, as shown below:

	Simple	Reduplicated
Middle	dii 'to be good'	'díidii
Low	ʔm̀ 'to be full'	'ʔḿ ʔm̀
Falling	jâag 'to be difficult'	'jáagjâag
High	rɔ́ɔn 'to be hot'	'rɔ́ɔnrɔ́ɔn
Rising	wǎan 'to be sweet'	'wáanwǎan

The emphatic high tone is not parallel to the basic five tones of Thai because it does not serve to differentiate lexical elements; it is never found in contrasting series like naa 'field,' nàa in nɔ́ɔjnàa 'custard apple,' nâa 'face,' náa 'younger maternal uncle or aunt,' nǎa 'to be thick.' Phonemically, the emphatic high tone can be treated as a modification of the high tone, since its pitch contour is high level.[3] It is, however, not identical with the high tone as is easily heard in cases where a high-toned word enters into emphatic reduplication, as 'rɔ́ɔnrɔ́ɔn 'to be extremely hot,' for the emphatic high is always higher in pitch and usually more protracted in length than the normal high. The special features of the emphatic tone may be grouped together phonemically as features induced by emphasis. It should also be mentioned that the emphatic high tone is not confined in usage to intensive reduplication. It also occurs in other circumstances, such as exclamations and the like, e.g. 'ʔújtaaj (exclamation of surprise used by women).

A striking parallel to Thai intensive reduplication is found in some local varieties of English. In Louisiana, for example, expressions like it's ho-ot hot, he's goo-ood good, it's re-ed red are heard frequently. In this kind of reduplication the first element is drawn out in length and quite high in pitch; the second element has normal length and pitch. Although intensive reduplication as such does not seem to be geographically widespread in English, the treatment of the

first element in such reduplication differs very little from the unre-
duplicated intensification of General American English heard in such
expressions as he's a goo-ood boy.

In conclusion a few comparisons between the two Thai techniques may be given. Restricted modifiers are used to intensify degree with a comparatively limited number of words. Emphatic reduplication, on the other hand, may be freely used to intensify the meaning of practically all descriptive verbs (so-called adjectives being
actually verbs in Thai). For this reason emphatic reduplication is
numerically by far the more important device for intensifying degree.
However, there are certain differences in usage between the two types
of intensification: (1) Women seem to use emphatic reduplication
with greater frequency than men, whereas both sexes employ restricted modifiers with about equal frequency. (2) Emphatic reduplication
is more important in the spoken language than in the written language
(except, of course, in actual conversational material, such as is
found in novels), while restricted modifiers are characteristic of both
the spoken and the written language.

NOTES

This paper was read at the Summer Meeting of the Linguistic
Society of America held in Ann Arbor in August, 1946.

I am indebted to Miss Poonsapaya Graiyong, Miss Krongthong
Chutima, and Mr. Heng Subhanka for their help in supplying examples
of the phenomena.

[1]Phonetic symbols used for Thai require a few explanations:
ph th kh ch are aspirates, like English p t k ch; but p t k c are unaspirated, like Spanish p t k ch. The high front semivowel (English y)
is shown by i̯, while y represents a high central unrounded vowel.
The tones are shown as: unmarked for middle, ´ for high, ` for low,
^ for falling, ˇ for rising.

[2]See M. R. Haas, Types of Reduplication in Thai, Studies in
Linguistics 1.4.1-6.

[3]In the Thai alphabet (of Indic origin) all tones are clearly
marked, but the emphatic is written as a simple high tone. The reader knows that emphatic reduplication is involved if he finds a high tone
paired with some other tone in a reduplicated form. A high tone paired
with another high tone is ambiguous, it being then impossible to tell
whether simple reduplication or emphatic reduplication is involved.

8 | The Use of Numeral Classifiers in Thai

1. The numeral classifiers[1] of Thai constitute an important syntactic word-class of the language and are employed with all nouns denoting objects which may be counted (e.g. 'man', 'house', 'word'). In most cases it is impossible to devise rules which will serve as an infallible guide in choosing the proper classifier to be employed with any given noun. For this reason it is desirable to memorize the classifier to be used with a noun at the same time that one learns the noun, just as in French or German one must memorize the gender of each noun.

There are some eighty or ninety special classifiers to be found in the language[2] and some of these words have no other meaning or function. In addition there are many nouns which are repeated to serve as their own classifiers, and this increases considerably the total number of words which are employed in this manner.

2. There are five classifiers commonly used with nouns referring to human beings; the choice of classifier to be used depends largely upon the rank or station in life of the individual or individuals referred to. The highest of these is ʔoɲ,[3] used for the king and queen, for princes and princesses, and for dukes and duchesses. The term rû·b is generally used in referring to talapoins, but some people employ ʔoɲ in place of rû·b. The term thân is employed for nobles below the rank of duke and sometimes also for high-ranking officials in the army and navy. The term next in order is na·j, which may be used in referring to individuals slightly above the common people in rank or position in life. The term most generally used in referring to human beings is khon, which is also the ordinary word for 'person'. Thus one says khon sɔ̌·ŋ-khon 'two people',[4] phû·jiŋ sǎ·m-khon 'three women', khru· lǎ·j-khon 'many teachers'.

Sacred or awesome beings are also arranged in a series of ranks which is reflected in the choice of classifier. For gods or angels ʔoŋ is commonly used, while giants and certain large-bodied ghosts of folklore are classified by means of the word ton, which is not used elsewhere in the language. Various kinds of smaller ghosts are classed with animals and therefore take the classifier tua. Interestingly enough, the word sòb 'corpse' (which usually serves as its own classifier, e.g. sòb sì·-sòb 'four corpses') is also occasionally classified by means of tua.

Contrary to what is true of other words referring to animals, the word for elephant has its own special classifier, namely chýag, a word which otherwise has the meaning 'rope'. This is explained by the fact that the elephant is a sacred animal. All other animals and all birds, fish, reptiles, and insects take the classifier tua, which is also one of the words meaning 'body'. Thus one says, chá·ŋ sɔ̌·ŋ-chýag 'two elephants', but mǎ· sìb-tua 'ten dogs', kàj sǎ·m-tua 'three chickens', ŋu· sì·-tua 'four snakes'. In a similar manner a herd of elephants is classified by means of the special word khlò·ŋ, while herds or flocks of other animals and of birds are classified with the word fǔ·ŋ, e.g. chá·ŋ nɣ̀ŋ-khlò·ŋ 'one herd of elephants', nɔ́g nɣ̀ŋ-fǔ·ŋ 'one flock of birds'.

So far we have been dealing with the classifiers used with nouns referring to animates. When we turn to nouns referring to inanimates we find a host of different classifiers. In some instances the size, shape, or function of the object referred to serves as a partial guide in determining which classifier should be used. Thus the word lêm is employed with the word for book and with words referring to edged or pointed objects, such as knives, sickles, needles. Boats and certain other objects which float on the water take the classifier lam, while houses and buildings take the classifier lǎŋ. The word baj, which means 'leaf' when used as a noun, is employed as the classifier not only for all kinds of leaves but also for various types of containers, such as cups, bottles, boxes, buckets, baskets, and the like. In a number of other instances, however, the choice of classifier is entirely arbitrary. Thus the word tua, ordinarily used with animals, is also employed with the words for table, chair, penpoint. Among the words which are repeated as their own classifiers may be mentioned kham 'word' (e.g. kham sì·-kham 'four words'), myaŋ 'city', hɔ̂ŋ 'room'.

Sometimes certain special notions are included in the context by means of the classifier employed. When this happens, the classifiers have a function similar to that of the so-called 'counters' of English, such as the words 'grain', 'pile', 'heap', 'strand', or 'coil' when these are employed with numerals. And, as in English, it often happens that different classifiers may be used with the same noun with a corresponding difference in meaning, e.g. sa·j nŷn-méd 'one grain of sand' vs. sa·j nŷŋ-kɔ·ŋ 'one pile of sand'; kràdà·d nŷŋ-phɛ̀n 'one sheet of paper' vs. kràdà·d nŷŋ-táŋ 'one pile of paper' or kràdà·d nŷŋ-kɔ·ŋ 'one (disorderly) heap of paper'; lûad nŷŋ-sên 'one strand of wire' vs. lûad nŷŋ-khòd 'one coil of wire'; phǒm nŷŋ-sên 'one strand of hair' vs. phǒm nŷŋ-pɔ·j 'one lock of hair' or phǒm nŷŋ-lɔ·n 'one wave of hair'.

The few examples given in the preceding paragraphs will serve to show that we cannot make rules covering the choice of classifier to be used in every given instance. The use of classifiers is a matter that must be treated not only as a part of the grammar of the language but also as a part of its lexicography. For this reason the most useful type of dictionary for the language would be one which provided each noun entry with a parenthetical indication of the classifier required to be used with it.

3. The classifiers of Thai are used in a great many types of noun-phrases, and under certain circumstances are also employed as noun substitutes. When one has acquired a mastery of their various uses one has conquered the most difficult phase of the syntax of the noun. The most important of these uses are described in the following paragraphs.

Classifiers are employed when nouns are accompanied by quantifiers, indicators, or adjectives. The term Quantifier is used for all numerals (except sǔ·n 'zero', used only in arithmetical or mathematical calculations) and for such words as lǎ·j 'many', kì· 'how many', and ba·ŋ 'some' (used only with countables, never with continuals such as water). The term Indicator is used for demonstrative and interrogative adjectives and a special function of the word nŷŋ 'one', while all other types of adjectives are referred to simply as Adjectives.

The use of a classifier is obligatory when a noun is accompanied by a quantifier and the word-order employed is <u>Noun</u> + <u>Quantifier</u> + <u>Classifier</u>, e. g. mǎ· sɔ̌· ŋ-tua 'two dogs' (lit. 'dog two-body'), mǎ· lǎ· j-tua 'many dogs', mǎ· kì· -tua 'how many dogs'.

In precise speech a classifier is also used when a noun is accompanied by an indicator or an adjective; in this case the word-order is <u>Noun</u> + <u>Classifier</u> + <u>Indicator</u> or <u>Adjective</u>, e. g. mǎ· tua-nî· 'this dog' (lit. 'dog body-this'), mǎ· tua-nǎj 'which dog', mǎ· tua-lég 'the little dog'. In less precise speech, on the other hand, it is sometimes ·possible to omit the classifier, e. g. mǎ· -nî· 'this dog', mǎ· -lég 'the little dog'. It also seems to be true that the use of a classifier in these circumstances, e. g. mǎ· tua-nî· , denotes a higher degree of particularization, such as might be rendered in English by the expression 'this very dog'. When numeral adjectives are employed, the classifier may never be omitted, e. g. mǎ· tua-thî· sɔ̌· ŋ 'the second dog'.

It will be noted that the position of a classifier in relation to a quantifier differs from its position in relation to an indicator or an adjective. An interesting fact to be observed in this connection is that the numeral nỳ ŋ 'one' may occur in either position with a resultant difference in meaning. In the one case it tells us how many objects there are and is therefore employed as a quantifier, e. g. mǎ· nỳ ŋ-tua 'one dog'. In the other case it gives us a construction comparable to the English use of an indefinite article and is therefore employed as an indicator, e. g. mǎ· tua-nỳ ŋ 'a dog'.

A number of more complex constructions may be made in which quantifiers, indicators, and adjectives are combined in various ways. The rules of word-order which obtain in such constructions are as follows:

Noun + classifier + adjective + classifier + indicator, e. g.
mǎ· tua-lég tua-nǎn 'that little dog' (lit. 'dog body-little body-that'); mǎ· tua-lég tua-nỳ ŋ 'a little dog'.
Noun + classifier + adjective + quantifier + classifier, e. g.
mǎ· tua-lég sɔ̌· ŋ-tua 'two little dogs' (lit. 'dog body-little two-body'); mǎ· tua-lég kì· -tua 'how many little dogs'.
Noun + classifier + adjective + quantifier + classifier + indicator, e. g. mǎ· tua-lég sɔ̌· ŋ-tua-nǎn 'those two little dogs' (lit. 'dog body-little two-body-that').

In each of these constructions the first classifier may sometimes be omitted with the reservations made above.

4. The classifiers of Thai are also freely used as noun substitutes and in this event they may often be translated by means of
the English pronoun 'one'. This is best illustrated by the following
series of sentences:

> chǎn mi· mǎ· sɔ̌· ŋ-tua. 'I have two dogs.'
> tua-níˑ jàj. 'This one is big.' tua-nán lég. 'That one is
>   little.'
> Q. khun tɔ̀ŋka·n tua-nǎj. 'Which one do you want?'
> A. tua-lég. 'The little one.'
> khǎw mi· mǎ· lǎ·j-tua. 'He has many dogs.'
> Q. khun tɔ̌ŋka·n kì·tua. 'How many do you want?'
> A. sì·-tua. 'Four.'

Note that in the last sentence a classifier must accompany the quantifier whereas in English we may use a numeral alone.

5. There are a number of words in Thai which may be called
'independent' classifiers, since they are used with quantifiers, indicators, and adjectives, but never accompany nouns. Their English
equivalents are classed as nouns, but the Thai words are identified as
classifiers by the rules of word-order.

One set of independent classifiers consists of words denoting
periods of time, such as wan 'day', khy·n 'night', dyaŋ 'month', pi·
'year'. When these words are quantified the quantifier precedes them,
e.g. sǎ·m-wan 'three days, for three days'; nỳŋ-pi· 'one year, for
one year'. (If these words were nouns the quantifier would have to follow them and be followed in its turn by a classifier.) In a manner
comparable to its behavior with nouns accompanied by classifiers, the
word nỳŋ 'one' may follow as well as precede the independent classifier, but in this event the meaning conveyed is one of temporal location rather than of temporal duration. Hence wan-nỳŋ khǎw klàb ma·
means 'one day he came back' while khǎw jù· thî·ní·nỳŋ-wan means
'he stayed here for one day'. When the independent classifiers are
accompanied by indicators or adjectives, such words always follow
the classifier, e.g. pi·-thî·sɔ̌·ŋ 'the second year'.

Another set of independent classifiers consists of words indicating how many times an event takes place. The most common of

such words are khráŋ and hŏn, which may be used more or less in-
terchangeably, e.g. khăw wîŋ sɔ̌· ŋ-khráŋ or khăw wîŋ sɔ̌· ŋ-hŏn 'he
ran twice'. Note that here again the quantifier precedes the independent classifier. Moreover, there is once more a difference between
such an expression as nỳŋ-khráŋ 'one time, once' (in which the word
nỳŋ precedes the classifier) and khráŋ-nỳŋ 'once upon a time' (in
which it follows the classifier). Other independent classifiers of this
type impart an aspectival meaning to the context. Thus thi· includes
the notion of instantaneousness or momentaneousness, as in khăw tè?
nỳŋ-thi·, which may be best rendered into English as 'he gave a kick'.
It is also possible to say khăw tè? nỳŋ-khráŋ or khăw tè? nỳŋ-hŏn 'he
kicked once', but when either of these words is employed there is no
indication that the action is momentaneous. Another word with an
overtone of aspect is khra·w, which conveys the notion of prolonged
or durativized action, as in lom phád nỳŋ-khra·w 'the wind blew
once'.

NOTES

My work on the Thai language is being carried on at the University of
Michigan for the Committee on the National School of Modern Oriental
Languages and Civilizations of the American Council of Learned So-
cieties.
        I also wish to express my indebtedness to my Thai friends at
the University of Michigan, particularly to Dr. Malai Huvanandana,
Mr. Heng Subhanka, Miss Ubol Guvanasen, and Miss Poonsapaya
Graiyong.

[1]Numeral classifiers or numeratives are often referred to
by a number of other names, such as 'Numeralwörter' (F. J. Wer-
shoven, Lehr- und Lesebuch der Siamesischen Sprache 65-8 [Wien,
Pest, Leipzig, 1892]), 'Zählwörter' (Walther Trittel, Einführung in
das Siamesische 72 [Berlin and Leipzig, 1930]), 'numeral designa-
tions' (D. J. B. Pallegoix, Dictionnaire Siamois Francais Anglais,
revu par J. L. Vey 32 [Bangkok, 1896]), and 'descriptive words' (O.
Frankfurter, Elements of Siamese Grammar 49-55 [Bangkok, 1900]).
        In this paper they are introduced as numeral classifiers and
thereafter referred to simply as classifiers. This latter term is to
be preferred to most of the others, since it is better to avoid emphasis on the use of these words with numerals. While it is true that

they are required when numerals are used, they also have many
other uses, as shown in this paper.

[2]One of the most complete lists of classifiers to be found in
published works is that given by Frankfurter, loc. cit. It is of little
use to the general reader, however, since the terms and illustrations
are written in the Thai alphabet.

[3]A brief explanation of the Thai phonemic symbols used in
this paper may be given here. The consonants are as follows: three
voiced stops, b, d, and -g (-g occurring only in syllabic final position); glottal stop, ʔ; four voiceless unaspirated stops, p, t, c [č],
and k; four corresponding voiceless aspirated stops, ph, th, ch, and
kh; three voiceless spirants f, s, and h; seven voiced sonorants, w,
j, m, n, ŋ, l, and r. There are nine vowels: i, e, ɛ [æ], y [ɨ], ǝ
[ö], a, u, o, and ɔ. These may occur both short and long, thus: i
and i·, e and e·, etc. The long vowels, however, are probably to be
considered double vowels on the phonemic level, since they configu-
rate in all respects with the heterophonous vowel clusters, ia, ya
[ɨa], and ua. The vowel a is always nasalized when it follows ʔ or h,
and all vowels are nasalized when preceded or followed by nasal consonants. There are five tones: even or middle (left unmarked), low
(ˋ), falling (ˆ), high (ˊ), and rising (ˇ). In the case of vowel clusters
the tonal marks are placed, for orthographic convenience, over the
first vowel, e.g. hǔa 'head'. The falling and the high tones are characterized by strong glottal stricture if the syllable ends in a vowel or
a sonorant (e.g. nâ· 'face', chá· 'slowly', wîŋ 'to run', nán 'that'),
but not if it ends in a stop consonant (e.g. mî·d 'knife').

[4]The hyphen in this example and others to follow indicates
internal open juncture.

9 | The Use of Numeral Classifiers in Burmese

The use of numeral classifiers is a feature shared in common by many of the languages of East Asia and the Pacific. They occur, for example, in Chinese,[1] Japanese, Korean, Annamese [Vietnamese],[2] Siamese (Thai), Burmese, Karen,[3] Malay, and Tagalog.[4] Details and frequency of usage vary from language to language. A comparative, or better, contrastive, exposition of the variations in usage among the several languages would make an interesting and valuable study. But before this can be adequately undertaken, separate descriptions of the use of classifiers in the various languages are needed. It is the purpose of this paper to describe the use of classifiers in colloquial Burmese.[5]

I

Classifier phrases[6] in Burmese consist of a numeral plus classifier. They are frequently used with a preceding noun which names the entity being counted,[7] e.g., sawnv hnathev 'two blankets' (sawnv 'blanket'; hnathev < hna-, combining form of 'two,' + -thev, clf. for clothlike objects). Some classifier phrases, however, are of a type which need not be used with a preceding noun, e.g., thyaw?-laq 'six months' (< thyaw? 'six' + laq 'month').

The combining of a numeral and a classifier to form a classifier phrase is accomplished in accordance with regular morphophonemic rules. The ordinary numerals from one to ten are: ti? 'one'; hni? 'two'; 9ownx 'three'; leyx 'four'; nax 'five'; thyaw? 'six'; khunv-hni? 'seven'; hyi? 'eight'; kowx 'nine'; tashev 'ten.' Most of these numerals combine with classifiers without change of form. Others, however, have special combining forms which are used with classifiers and with other numerals (multiples of ten). These special combining forms are as follows: ta- 'one' (< ti ?); hna- 'two' (< hni ?); khunvhna- or khunvna- 'seven' (< khunvhni ?); shev- or -shev 'ten' (cf. tashev 'ten' < ta- 'one' + -shev). There is also another number word which appears only in classifier phrases (i.e., is never used independently) and its only form is the combining form bevhna- 'how many ?' e.g., sawnv bevhnathev 'how many blankets ?'

The morphophonemic rules[8] which operate when numerals are combined with classifiers are as follows:

1) If the basic form of a bound morpheme (here, classifier) begins in a voiceless unaspirated or aspirated stop or spirant (p, ph; t, th; k, kh; s, sh; θ), such stop or spirant changes to its homorganic voiced counterpart (b, d, g, z, ð) when combined with a preceding morpheme (here, numeral) having tones 1 (v), 2 (x), or 3 (q), e.g.,

> θi ʔpinv ŋaxbinv 'five trees' (ŋaxbinv < ŋax 'five' + -pinv, clf.
>   for trees, strands of hair, threads); contrast with θi ʔpinv
>   thyaw ʔpinv 'six trees' (thyaw ʔpinv < thyaw ʔ 'six' + -pinv)
> phawnv leyxbawnv 'four rafts' (leyxbawnv < leyx 'four' +
>   -phawnv, clf. for rafts)
> le ʔhma ʔ shevzawnv 'ten tickets' (shevzawnv < shev- 'ten' +
>   -sawnv, clf. for things written)
> ʔeynv shevzawnv 'ten houses' (shevzawnv < shev- 'ten' +
>   -shawnv, clf. for annexes)
> si ʔθax ŋaxðow ʔ 'five groups of soldiers' (used in counting
>   successive groups) (ŋaxðow ʔ < ŋax 'five' + -θow ʔ, clf.
>   meaning 'group' or 'batch')

2) When combined with the numeral ta-'one,' the voiceless unaspirated stops and the voiceless unaspirated spirant s change to their voiced counterparts, while the voiceless aspirated stops, the voiceless aspirated spirant sh, and the voiceless unaspirated spirant θ remain unchanged, e.g.,

> θi ʔpinv tabinv 'one tree' (tabinv < ta- + -pinv)
> le ʔhma ʔ tazawnv 'one ticket' (tazawnv < ta- + -sawnv)
> ʔeynv tashawnv 'one house' (tashawnv < ta- + -shawnv)
> si ʔθax taθow ʔ 'one group of soldiers' (taθow ʔ < ta- + -θow ʔ)

3) When combined with a morpheme (here, numeral) having tone 4 (ʔ) or with one whose combining form ends in atonic -a- (excepting only ta- 'one' and the combining forms of certain nouns), both voiceless unaspirated and voiceless aspirated stops or spirants remain unchanged.

> θiʔpinv hnapinv 'two trees' (hnapinv < hna- 'two' + -pinv)
> leʔhmaʔ thyawʔsawnv 'six tickets' (thyawʔsawnv < thyawʔ
>   'six' + -sawnv)
> ʔeynv khunvhnashawnv 'seven houses' (khunvhnashawnv <
>   khunvhna- 'seven' + -shawnv)
> sawnv bevhnathev 'how many blankets?' (bevhnathev < bevhna-
>   'how many?' + -thev, clf. for clothlike objects)

4) If the basic form of a bound morpheme (here, classifier) begins in a voiced stop or spirant (b, d, g, z), in a voiced sonorant (m, n, ŋ, l, y, w), in a voiceless sonorant (hm, hn, hŋ, hl, hy), in the aspirate h or in ʔ, no change takes place, no matter what the nature of the preceding morpheme may be, e.g.,

> zeyx tazeyx 'one market'; zeyx thyawʔzeyx 'eight markets'
>   (-zeyx, clf. for markets)
> luv tayawʔ 'one person'; luv hyiʔyawʔ 'eight people' (-yawʔ,
>   clf. for ordinary people)
> ʔahmuq tahmuq 'one legal case'; ʔahmuq shevhmuq 'ten le-
>   gal cases' (-hmuq, clf. for legal cases)

II

Cornyn divides Burmese classifiers into three types,[9] which may be summarized here.

Type 1 classifiers are those which may be used with various nouns, the choice of classifier generally depending on some outward characteristic of the entity referred to by the noun. Classifiers for people, for animals, for fruit and round objects, for flat objects, for long slender objects, for clothlike objects, etc., come in this category. Some classifiers of this type are:

-yaw?, clf. for ordinary people, e.g., <u>luv shevyaw?</u> 'ten
  people'; <u>lexðamax ŋaxyaw?</u> 'five farmers'

-kawnv, clf. for animals, e.g., <u>nwax ɵownxgawnv</u> 'three
  oxen'

-lownx, clf. for fruit, for spherical or cubical objects, for
  certain types of buildings, e.g., <u>?ownxðix leyxlownx</u> 'four
  coconuts'; <u>ti?tav talownx</u> 'one box'

-thya?, clf. for flat objects, e.g., <u>kovzox hnathya?</u> 'two
  rugs'; <u>hmanv ɵownxdya?</u> 'three mirrors'

-thyawnx, clf. for long slender objects, e.g., <u>dow? ta-
thyawnx</u> 'one stick'; <u>kalawnvdanv ŋaxdyawnx</u> 'five pens'

-thev, clf. for clothlike objects, e.g., <u>lownvdyiv hnathev</u>
  'two Burmese-type skirts'; <u>sawnv leyxdev</u> 'four blankets'

Type 2 classifiers are identical with the noun they classify
or else are identical with a part of that noun (the second element or
head of compound nouns). A few classifiers of this type are:

-?eynv, clf. for houses when ?eynv is the noun, e.g., ?eynv
  <u>hna?eynv</u> 'two houses'[10]

-tay?, clf. for buildings when <u>tay?</u> is the noun or the head of
  a compound noun, e.g., <u>tay? ɵownxday?</u> 'three brick buildings'; <u>savday? taday?</u> 'one post office'; <u>banvday? hnatay?</u>
  'two banks'

-pwex, clf. for festivals when <u>pwex</u> is the noun or the head
  of a compound noun, e.g., <u>pwex tabwex</u> 'one festival';
  <u>hleyvbwex hnapwex</u> 'two boat races'

Type 3 classifiers are those used in classifier phrases which
do not require a preceding noun. Classifiers referring to units of
money, to units of time, to times (instances), etc., fall into this category. It is convenient further to subdivide these as follows: 3a,
those which are used only in classifier phrases, and 3b, those which
can also be used independently. Some classifiers of type 3a are:

-tya? 'rupee,' e.g., <u>tadya?</u> 'one rupee'; <u>hnatya?</u> 'two
rupees'

-pex 'anna,' e.g., <u>tabex</u> 'one anna'; <u>hyi?pex</u> 'eight annas'

-ye? 'day' (i.e., 'period of twenty-four hours'), e.g., <u>taye?</u>
  'one day'; <u>shevye?</u> 'ten days'

-hni? 'year,' e.g., <u>tahni?</u> 'one year'; <u>kowxhni?</u> 'nine years'
-khav 'time, instance,' e.g., <u>takhav</u> 'one time, once' <u>bev-hnakhav</u> 'how many times?'; <u>ɕownxgav</u> 'three times'

Some classifiers of type 3b are:

<u>laq</u> 'month, moon,' e.g., <u>talaq</u> 'one month,' <u>leyxlaq</u> 'four
    months'
<u>nyaq</u> 'night,' e.g., <u>tanyaq</u> 'one night'; <u>ɕownxnyaq</u> 'three
    nights'

III

The division of classifiers into the three types mentioned in the preceding section is useful not only for the reasons already given, but also for the purpose of stating the rules for their use with numerals above ten which are multiples of ten. The following are the rules which apply:

1) Classifiers of type 1 may not be appended to numerals above ten which are multiples of ten. Instead they are appended to a proclitic <u>?a-</u> to form a numberless classifier phrase[11] which is then followed by the numeral as a separate word. A few examples will make this clear:

<u>luv ?ayaw? hnashev</u> 'twenty people' (<u>luv</u>, noun meaning 'per-
    son'; <u>?ayaw?</u>, numberless classifier phrase < <u>?a-</u> + <u>-yaw?</u>,
    clf. for ordinary people; <u>hnashev</u> 'twenty')
<u>luv ?ayaw? ɕownxzev</u> 'thirty people' (<u>ɕownxzev</u> 'thirty')
<u>luv ?ayaw? tayav</u> 'one hundred people' (<u>tayav</u> 'one hundred')
<u>luv ?ayaw? tayaq hnashev</u> 'one hundred and twenty people'
    (<u>tayaq</u>, special form of <u>tayav</u> used when another number is
    added to it)
<u>luv ?ayaw? hnathawnq leyxyaq ṇaxzev</u> 'two thousand four hun-
    dred and fifty people' (<u>hnathawnq</u>, adding-on form[12] of
    <u>hnathawnv</u> 'two thousand'; <u>leyxyaq</u>, adding-on form of
    <u>leyxyav</u> 'four hundred'; <u>ṇaxzev</u> 'fifty')

But note that as soon as the classifier is used in an expression containing a numeral which is not a multiple of ten (e.g., 21,

136, etc.) the proclitic ʔa- is again replaced by a digital numeral[13] and the word order reverts to that used in ordinary noun-counting expressions containing digital numerals. Contrast the examples below with those immediately above:

> luv hnasheq tayawʔ 'twenty-one people' (hnasheq, adding-on
> form of hnashev 'twenty'; tayawʔ < ta- 'one' + -yawʔ)
> luv hnayaq ɵownxzeq leyxyawʔ 'two hundred and thirty-four
> people' (hnayaq, adding-on form of hnayav 'two hundred';
> ɵownxzeq, adding-on form of ɵownxzev 'thirty'; leyxyawʔ
> < leyx 'four' + -yawʔ)

A few additional examples of type 1 classifiers used in numberless classifier phrases are as follows:

> tyevðix ʔalownx hnashev 'twenty buttons' (tyevðix 'button';
> ʔalownx < ʔa- + -lownx, clf. for fruit, for spherical or
> cubical objects; hnashev 'twenty')
> nwax ʔakawnv leyxzev 'forty oxen' (nwax 'ox'; ʔakawnv < ʔa-
> + -kawnv, clf. for animals; leyxzev 'forty')
> sawnv ʔathev tayav 'one hundred blankets' (sawnv 'blanket';
> ʔathev < ʔa- + -thev, clf. for clothlike objects; tayav 'one
> hundred')

2) Unlike classifier of type 1, classifiers of type 2 are always omitted when their nouns are employed with numerals above ten that are multiples of ten.[14] The numeral then follows directly after the noun. Examples:

> ʔeynv hnashev 'twenty houses' (ʔeynv 'house'; hnashev 'twen-
> ty'); contrast with ʔeynv hnasheq taʔeynv 'twenty-one
> houses' (hnasheq, adding-on form of hnashev; taʔeynv < ta-
> 'one + -ʔeynv, clf. for ʔeynv 'house')[15]
> myowq ɳaxzev 'fifty cities'; contrast with myowq ɳaxzeq
> leyxmyowq 'fifty-four cities' (-myowq, clf. for myowq
> 'city')
> savdayʔ ɵownxzev 'thirty post offices' (-tayʔ, clf. for tayʔ
> 'brick building' and for compound nouns having tayʔ as their
> head)
> ʔalowʔ leyxzev 'forty jobs' (-lowʔ, clf. for ʔalowʔ 'job')

When classifiers of type 2 are used with the numeral 'ten' (and not one of its multiples), two kinds of treatment are possible. The classifier may be appended to the combining form <u>shev-</u> 'ten' (preferred treatment), or the classifier may be omitted entirely, in which case the independent numeral <u>tashev</u> 'ten' follows immediately after the noun, e.g.,

ʔeynv shevʔeynv 'ten houses,' or <u>ʔeynv tashev</u> 'ten houses'

(Of these two forms, the informant much prefers the former.)

3) Classifiers of type 3a are treated like classifiers of type 1, i.e., they are not appended directly to numerals above ten which are multiples of ten. Instead, they take the proclitic <u>ʔa-</u> to form a numberless classifier phrase and are then followed by the numeral as a separate word. Classifiers of type 3a are therefore treated exactly like classifiers of type 1 except that they are not preceded by a noun. Examples:

> ʔakhav hnashev 'twenty times' (-<u>khav</u> 'time, instance'); contrast with <u>hnasheq takhav</u> 'twenty-one times'
> ʔakhawʔ θownxzev 'thirty times, trips' (-<u>khawʔ</u> 'time in the sense of trip'); contrast with <u>θownxzeq θownxgawʔ</u> 'thirty-three trips'
> ʔahniʔ ṇaxzev 'fifty years' (-<u>hniʔ</u> 'year'); contrast with <u>ṇaxzeq hnahniʔ</u> 'fifty-two years'
> ʔapyax hnashev 'twenty pice' (-<u>pyax</u> 'pice'). This expression is equivalent to <u>ṇaxbex</u> 'five annas' (-<u>pex</u> 'anna')

In contrast to classifiers of type 3a, classifiers of type 3b do not take the proclitic <u>ʔa-</u>. Otherwise they are treated like classifiers of type 3a, and numerals above ten which are multiples of ten follow the simple classifier as an independent word. Examples:

> <u>laq hnashev</u> 'twenty months'; contrast with <u>hnasheq talaq</u> 'twenty-one months'
> <u>nyaq hnashev</u> 'twenty nights'; contrast with <u>hnasheq tanyaq</u> 'twenty-one nights'
> <u>navyiv</u> θownxzev 'thirty hours'; contrast with <u>θownxzeq hnanavyiv</u> 'thirty-two hours'

IV

There is one other numeral which should be mentioned here, namely, ʔasey? 'twenty-five, quarter of a hundred.' Although it may be used in the meaning 'twenty-five,' it does not replace the ordinary numeral hnasheq ŋax 'twenty-five' when one is counting consecutively.

The rules for the use of ʔasey? are exactly the same as those already given for numerals above ten which are multiples of ten, and it is therefore the only numeral not divisible by ten which is treated in this fashion. (Note that the rules for the use of ʔasey? do not apply to hnasheq ŋax). Examples of the use of ʔasey? are:

> luv ʔayaw? ʔasey? 'quarter of a hundred people' (ʔayaw?, numberless classifier phrase); contrast with luv hnasheq ŋaxyaw? 'twenty-five people'
> sheyxley? ʔasey? 'quarter of a hundred cigarettes' (clf. of type 2 omitted); contrast with sheyxley? hnasheq ŋaxley? 'twenty-five cigarettes'

V

It sometimes happens that more than one numeral is used in the same noun-counting expression. In general only two numerals will be used in this way, but on rare occasions three are so used. There are three main types of constructions to be distinguished:

1) In a few fixed constructions only the second or last numeral is combined with a classifier, e.g.,

> luv leyx ŋaxyawʔlaw? 'about four (or) five people' (leyx 'four'; ŋaxyaw? < ŋax 'five' + -yaw?; -law? 'about, nearly,' postclitic which may be added to classifier phrases; see section IX below)
> luv leyx ŋax thyaw ʔyaw ʔlaw? 'very few people, a handful of people' (lit., 'about four-five-six people')[16]

Although the particular combination of three numerals illustrated above is a very common combination and one which may be used with various classifiers, other instances of the use of three numerals appear to be rather rare. Two other interesting examples which have come to my attention are:

luv leyx ŋax hyiʔyawʔlawʔ 'about four to eight people' (lit. , 'about four-five-eight people')
luv leyx ŋax shevyawʔlawʔ 'about four to ten people' (lit. , 'about four-five-ten people')

2) In most constructions involving numbers less than one hundred the classifier is used with each numeral. It must be used with each numeral if one of them has a special combining form which cannot be used alone (viz. , ta- 'one,' hna- 'two,' khunvhna- 'seven,' shev- 'ten'), e. g. ,

luv tayawʔ hnayawʔlawʔ 'about one (or) two people'
luv hnayawʔ θownxyawʔlawʔ 'about two (or) three people'
luv shevyawʔ ʔayawʔ hnashevlawʔ 'about ten (or) twenty people.' (For the use of ʔayawʔ, see section III, rule 1.)

3) In constructions which involve numerals referring to hundreds and thousands (and other higher numbers which are multiples of ten) classifiers of types 1 or 2 are generally omitted, e. g. ,

luv tayav hnayavlawʔ 'about one (or) two hundred people' (-yav 'hundred')[17]
luv hnathawnv θownxdawnvlawʔ 'about two (or) three thousand people' (-thawnv 'thousand')

Classifiers of type 3, however, may not be omitted since they are used without preceding noun, e. g. ,

ʔatyeyv tayav hnayav 'one (or) two hundred times' (ʔatyeyv, numberless classifier phrase < ʔa- + -tyeyv 'time, instance')

VI

Classifier phrases in which the classifier is doubled or repeated are occasionally used with special meanings.[18] Common meanings are 'any one (out of a group), ' 'one or another,' 'somebody or other.' The numeral employed in such phrases is always ta- 'one,' e.g.,

> tayaw ʔyaw ʔ lavbav. 'Any one (of you) please come here!'
> (or) 'One or another (of you) please come here!' (tayaw ʔ-
> yaw ʔ < ta- + -yaw ʔ, clf. for people doubled)
> tayaw ʔyaw ʔ lavmev. 'Somebody or other will come'

Note that a preceding noun is not required in these particular expressions. Other examples, some with and some without a preceding noun, are as follows:

> tagawnvgawnvdoq ǫeyvhmavbex. 'One or another (of them,
> e.g., oxen) will surely die' (said if all the oxen are sick).
> (tagawnvgawnv < ta- + -kawnv, clf. for animals doubled)
> sav ʔow ʔ ta ʔow ʔʔow ʔ wevmev. '(I)'ll buy any one (of the)
> books (in this collection).' (ta ʔow ʔʔow ʔ < ta- + - ʔow ʔ, clf.
> for books doubled)
> takhuqguq wevmev. '(I)'ll buy any one (of these things).'
> (-khuq, general clf. for things and one which is sometimes
> substituted for other classifiers)

Occasionally the doubling of the classifier gives a meaning equivalent to the English expression 'one by one,' as in

> yeyvdweyv taze ʔze ʔ tyaq neyvdev. 'The water is falling drop
> by drop.' (-se ʔ, clf. for drops of water)

VII

Sometimes two classifier phrases are used with the same noun (expressed or implied). An interesting combination of this type is one in which the first classifier phrase employs the normal classifier for the noun used or implied while the second classifier phrase employs the classifier -leyv.[19] The numeral employed in both phrases is ta-, e.g.,

> tayaw ʔ taleyv ǫwaxbowq kawnxdev. 'Somebody (unspecified)
> had better go.' (tayaw ʔ < ta- + -yaw ʔ, clf. for people, fol-
> lowed by taleyv < ta- + -leyv)

takhuq taleyvdoq hyiqbowq kawnxdev. 'It's good to have at
   least one.' (takhuq < ta- + -khuq, general clf. for things,
   followed by taleyv)
sav ʔow ʔ ta ʔow ʔ taleyvhmaq mahyiqbuxlax. 'Isn't there a
   single book ?' (ta ʔow ʔ < ta- + - ʔow ʔ, clf. for books, followed by taleyv)

Note also that a positive reply to the last example above calls
for the use of a classifier phrase with doubled classifier (section VI),
viz.,

ta ʔow ʔ ʔow ʔ hyiqdev. 'There are some (books)'

VIII

This section and those which immediately follow are given
over to discussion of postclitic elements which may be attached to
classifier phrases.

When the total quantity involved exceeds one, the notion of
one-half is expressed by adding the postclitic -khwex (or -gwex)[20] to
the classifier phrase, e.g.,

yeyv takhwe ʔkhwex 'one and one-half cups of water' (takhwe ʔ
   < ta- + -khwe ʔ 'cup')
phyinv ŋaxgay ʔkhwex 'five and one-half yards of cloth'
   (ŋaxgay ʔ < ŋax 'five + -gay ʔ 'yard')
shevhni ʔkhwex 'ten and one-half years'
tanavyivgwex 'an hour and a half'

When one-half is itself the total quantity, two types of constructions are found: (1) the word tawe ʔ 'one-half' is placed after the
classifier, or (2) the postclitic -we ʔ is added to the classifier, e.g.,

yeyv khwe ʔ tawe ʔ one-half cup of water'
phyinv gay ʔwe ʔ 'one-half yard of cloth'
laq tawe ʔ (or) laqwe ʔ 'one-half month'
navyivwe ʔ 'half an hour'

Language, Culture, and History

Chart 1

Clf. phrase (num.+elf.)	-khwex	-law?, etc.	-hav, etc.
1) hnanavyiv			
2) hnanavyiv + -khwex			
3) hnanavyiv		+ -law?	
4) hnanavyiv			+ -hmav
5) hnanavyiv + -khwex		+ -law?	
6) hnanavyiv + -khwex			+ -hmav
7) hnanavyiv + -khwex		+ -law?	+ -hmav

Translations: (1) hnanavyiv 'two o'clock; two hours'; (2) hnanavyivgwex 'two-thirty; two and a half hours'; (3) hnanavyivlaw? 'about two o'clock; about two hours'; (4) hnanavyivhmav 'at two o'clock'; (5) hnanavyivgwexlaw? 'about two-thirty; about two hours'; (6) hnanavyivgwexhmav 'at two-thirty'; (7) hnanavyivgwexlaw?hmav 'at about two-thirty.'

Chart 2

Demonst.	Noun mod.	Noun or pronoun	Clf. phrase (+ postclitics)
1)		luv	hnayaw?
2)		ɵuvdowq	hnayaw?salownx
3) div		luv	hnayaw?
4)	puqdeq	luv	hnayaw?
5) div	puqdeq	luv	hnayaw?
6) div	puqdeq	luv	hnayaw?kowv

Translations: (1) luv hnayaw? 'two men'; (2) ɵuvdowq hnayaw?salownx 'both of them'; (3) div luv hnayaw? 'these two men'; (4) puqdeq luv hnayaw? 'two short men'; (5) div puqdeq luv hnayaw? 'these two short men'; (6) div puqdeq luv hnayaw?kowv 'these two short men (as recipients of action).'

IX

Postclitic elements which serve as numeral modifiers may also be added to the classifier phrase. Or, if a numberless classifier phrase is used (section III), the postclitic is added directly to the last numeral. Numeral modifiers include such postclitics as -law? 'about, nearly,' -salownx (or -zalownx) 'all,' and -thex (or -dex) 'alone; only (. . . out of a larger number).'[21] Examples:

> luv shevyaw?law? 'about ten people' (postclitic -law? added to classifier phrase)
> luv ?ayaw? hnashevlaw? 'about twenty people' (postclitic added to numeral which follows numberless classifier phrase)
> luv shevyaw?salownx 'all ten people' (-salownx 'all')
> dax hnathyawnxzalownx 'both knives' (-salownx 'all')
> tayaw?thex lavdev '(I) alone came' (-thex 'only')
> dax hnathyawnxdex the?tev 'only two of the knives are sharp' (-thex 'only')

Classifier phrases are often used with preceding pronoun in place of preceding noun. Such usage is common when numeral modifiers are also used, e.g.,

> ǝuvdowq ǝownxyaw?salownx lavdev,'All three of them came.'
> (ǝuvdowg 'they' < ǝuv 'he, she' + -towq, plural postclitic)
> ǝuvdowq hnayaw?thex lavdev. 'Only two of them came.'

X

Postclitics whose function it is to define the relation between a noun expression and the main verb of the sentence may also be added to classifier phrases or to the last numeral in a nouncounting expression. Elements like -hav, denoting the subject or actor, -kowv, denoting the recipient of the action or place or time to which, -hmav, denoting place or time at which, and -kaq, denoting source or agency, come in this category.[22] Postclitics of this type may be conveniently referred to as relational postclitics. If more than one postclitic is added to the classifier phrase or to the last numeral in a noun-counting expression, the relational postclitic takes final position, e.g.,

hnanavyivgwexlaw ʔhmav lavbav. 'Please come at about half
   past two.' (hnanavyiv 'two o'clock'; first postclitic -khwex
   'and a half'; second postclitic -law ʔ 'about'; third postclitic
   -hmav 'at')
tyunvdov wevgeqdeq khexdanv hnathyawnxzalownxhav nivdev.
   'Both of the pencils which I bought are red.' (hnathyawnx,
   classifier phrase; first postclitic -salownx 'all'; second
   postclitic -hav, denoting subject)

It should be noted that relational postclitics may also be added directly to nouns or pronouns, e.g., luvhav 'the man,' zeyxgowv
'to the market,' myowqgaq 'from the town.' But if a classifier phrase
is used, they are attached, not to the noun or pronoun, but to the
classifier phrase or to the last numeral in a noun-counting expression

XI

Accompanying this discussion are two charts showing the order of elements in noun expressions which contain a classifier phrase.
Chart 1 shows the order of postclitics used with classifier phrases
when a type 3 classifier is used; the same order applies to classifiers
of types 1 and 2. The first column shows the classifier phrase (numeral + classifier), the second column shows -khwex 'and a half'
(section VIII), the third column shows the numeral modifier, e.g.,
-law ʔ 'about,' -thex 'only' (section IX), and the last column shows the
relational postclitic (section X). The full forms with translations are
given below the chart.

Chart 2 shows the relative order of words in noun expressions which contain a classifier phrase. The first column shows the
demonstrative (e.g., div 'this'), the second column shows the noun
modifier, the third column shows the noun[23] or pronoun, and the
fourth column shows the classifier phrase plus its various postclitics
(cf. chart 1). Translations are provided below the chart.

NOTES

[1]Brief descriptions of the use of classifiers (also called
'measures' by some and 'counters' by others) are to be found in some

of the manuals of the Holt Spoken Language Series, viz., Charles F.
Hockett, Spoken Chinese; Bernard Bloch and Eleanor Harz Jorden,
Spoken Japanese; Fred Lukoff, Spoken Korean; Mary R. Haas and
Heng R. Subhanka, Spoken Thai; William S. Cornyn, Spoken Burmese;
Isadore Dyen, Spoken Malay. For separate discussions of the use of
classifiers in individual languages, see also: Edward H. Schafer,Jr.,
"Noun Classifiers in Classical Chinese," Language, 24 (1948), 408-
413; Mary R. Haas, "The Use of Numeral Classifiers in Thai," Lan-
guage, 18 (1942), 201-205.

[2]Information from Professor Murray B. Emeneau.

[3]Information from Mr. R. B. Jones.

[4]Information from Mr. Harold C. Conklin.

[5]My work on Burmese is a corollary of a course entitled
"Linguistics Laboratory" in which we have been using the services of
a Burmese informant for the purpose of demonstrating field methods
in linguistics. Our informant for the course in 1947-1948 was Mr.
Patrick Nyunt or Maung Htin Myint. Our present informant (1948-
1949) is Maung Tha Hto. Both informants are recent arrivals from
Rangoon.

[6]A brief description of Burmese classifiers is to be found in
William S. Cornyn, Outline of Burmese Grammar (Language Dissertation No. 38, 1944). Classifiers are treated on pp. 26-28. Cornyn
defines the three types of classifiers (see section II of the present paper) and lists some of the more important classifiers of each type.
The term "classifier phrase" is based on his usage.

[7]There are two good descriptions of Burmese phonemics.
One is by Cornyn, op. cit., pp. 7-10. The other is by Raven I.
McDavid, Jr., and is entitled "Burmese Phonemics" (Studies in Linguistics, Vol. 3, No. 1, 1945, pp. 6-18). In general I follow the
transcription employed by McDavid, but I follow Cornyn in writing
the initial glottal stop (ʔ). I differ from both in writing /ty/ where
they write /c/, /thy/ where they write /ch/, and /dy/ where they
write /j/. This is a minor point of difference and my justification
for it is that the palatal semivowel /y/ is as prominent in a word
like tyax 'tiger' as it is in a word like pyax 'bee.' One other point of
difference is a matter of convenience of transcription only, viz.,
tone 1 is here symbolized by the letter v placed at the end of the syllable, tone 2 by the letter x, and tone 3 by the letter q. Cornyn and
McDavid, on the other hand use the acute accent (ˊ) for tone 1, the
circumflex (ˆ) for tone 2, and the grave accent (ˋ) for tone 3. Thus,

lavdev 'comes' is equivalent to their lᴀ́dé, pyax 'bee' is equivalent to
their pyᴀ̂, and laq 'moon' is equivalent to their lᴀ̀. I retain their use
of final ? for tone 4 (following McDavid in details where the two differ), e. g. , ti? 'one,' le?hma? 'ticket.'

    [8] These morphophonemic rules are not restricted in their use
to numeral-plus-classifier combinations; they apply throughout the
language whenever two morphemes are combined into one word. See
also Cornyn, op. cit. , p. 10. The usage of my informants differs
from the rules he gives in one instance only. He cites taca? (tatya?)
as varying with taja? (tadya?) 'one rupee' and implies that after atonic syllables replacements of voiceless consonants by voiced ones are
not fixed (p. 10). Both of my informants insist that only tadya? is
correct. In this connection it is to be noted that there are two kinds
of atonic -a- on the morphophonemic level. One kind behaves like
ta- (see rule 2, section I of the present paper); the other kind causes
no change in the basic form of the following morpheme (see rule 3,
section I).

    [9] Cornyn, op. cit. , pp. 26-27.

    [10] The noun ?eynv 'house' can also be used with certain type I
classifiers, e.g. , ?eynv hnalownx 'two houses,' ?eynv hnashawnv
'two houses (as annexes).'

    [11] The term 'numberless classifier phrase' is used to refer
to a classifier phrase which does not contain a numeral.

    [12] The term 'adding-on form' is used to refer to the special
form taken by numerals which are multiples of ten (including ten)
when another numeral which is added to it follows. The adding-on
forms of numerals always have tone 3 (q) if the basic form has tone 1
(v).

    [13] The term 'digital numeral' is used to refer to any number
from one to nine inclusive.

    [14] In Cornyn's description, op. cit. , pp. 26-27, classifiers
of type 1 as well as those of type 2 omit the classifier when used with
numerals which are multiples of ten (including ten). The usage described here was provided independently by both of my informants. It
is probable that there is some variation in usage for different speakers.

    [15] See footnote 10.

    [16] Although ŋax 'five' and thyaw? 'six' are used together when
leyx 'four' precedes, the two are not otherwise used together. They
are avoided because of the ambiguity resulting from the fact that ŋax
also means 'fish' and thyaw? also means 'dried.'

[17]It is also possible to say luv ʔayawʔ tayav hnayav, but the numberless classifier phrase is commonly omitted in constructions of this type.

[18]Cornyn, op. cit., p. 33, gives only the meaning 'one by one.' Compare the last example in this section, where tazeʔzeʔ means 'drop by drop.'

[19]As yet I have not discovered any other use for the classifier -leyv.

[20]This variation is in accordance with the regular morphophonemic rule; see section I.

[21]This list is not intended to be exhaustive.

[22]See also Cornyn, op. cit., pp. 18-19; -hav is often omitted.

[23]Note also that in certain expressions the noun is combined with its modifier, e.g., luvgawnx 'a good man' (< luv + kawnx 'to be good'), luvgawnx hnayawʔ 'two good men.'

10 | The Expression of the Diminutive

In Honor of George L. Trager

1. Introduction

It is safe to say, I think, that the notion of the diminutive is a language universal, or at any rate, a near-universal. On the other hand, the opposite notion, that of the augmentative, is much less commonly found. And when it is found, it is overtly contrasted with the diminutive, but the converse is not true. In other words, the presence of an augmentative implies the presence of a diminutive but not vice versa.

The diminutive also usually carries with it a number of affective connotations which range from endearment to tenderness through mild belittlement or deprecation to outright derogation and insult. Although this fact is fairly generally recognized, there are very few careful studies of the range of connotations in a particular language. The problem is deserving of wider attention.

2. Range of Methods for Expressing Diminution

In the present paper, however, I am not concerned with the semantic range of the diminutive notion, except incidentally, but with the range of methods of expression. These show considerable variation but may be grouped into six main categories: (1) consonant and/or vowel symbolism, (2) reduplication, (3) affixation, (4) syntactic modification, (5) suppletion, and (6) grammatical displacement. Most of these can be illustrated from English. Thus the word tiny may be changed to teeny by substituting high /iy/ for /ay/, an instance of vowel symbolism (1). Teeny may be further diminutivized as teeny-weeny through reduplication (2) with w replacing the initial consonant, here t, in the reduplicated element. The common diminutive suffix -y or -ie, as in daddy, mommy, Johnny, and doggie, illustrates the category of affixation (3). A less common, and usually more intimate, diminutive suffix is -s, as in moms, pops, etc., but it can also be combined with the more common -y, as in momsy, popsy. And the result may be further subjected to reduplication of the ablauting w type, as in popsy-wopsy (Haas 1942: 5).

Syntactic modification (4) is also common in English to express the diminutive. The adjective little is frequently employed in this way. Thus in speaking to a child, one might use 'little hand' rather than 'hand' or, combined with the use of suffixation, 'little footsie' rather than 'foot'. While it is true that the hand or foot of a child is little in comparison to that of an adult, the chief function of the use of little here is to connote affection. Similar use is frequently applied to pets, e.g., 'little paw', even though the animal may be full-grown. Moreover, in many situations, the connotation of affection can slip into that of belittlement or even derogation. Thus when a husband speaks of 'the little woman' the adjective connotes mild, or perhaps jocular, belittlement rather than affection. Other English adjectives function in a somewhat similar fashion. One of these is old, as when a youngster speaks affectionately of his 'old dog', and his 'old sled', or his 'old skates', and somewhat less than affectionately of his 'old teacher'.

Grammatical displacement (6) can be illustrated by the use of third person pronouns in place of the second person, as in 'Does she want mommy to wash her little hands?' A further displacement, connoting even greater diminutivization (as in speaking to a toddler), is seen in the use of the neuter pronoun it rather than the gender-differentiated he or she, as in 'Does it want mommy to wash its little hands?' In languages with gender classes of nouns with or without agreeing adjectives, the displacement commonly consists in gender switching, e.g., feminine for masculine, or masculine for feminine (see also section 3.4. of this article).

As far as I am aware, suppletion (5) is in general very rare, but Natchez uses it as one device (for the other, see section 3.2. of this article) for expressing the diminutive of verbs.[1] Thus the

auxiliary verb -ho·ʔis, as in han-ho·ʔis 'to build normal-sized ones'
is replaced by -helu·ʔis, in han-helu·ʔis 'to build little ones'. Here
its suppletive use marks it as diminutive, but in other uses it is nondiminutive, e.g., halas-helu·ʔis 'to kick a normal-sized one'.

3. Locus of Application of the Diminutive

        1. There is not only a considerable range in the methods of
expressing the diminutive, there is also a difference among these
methods in their locus of application. If the diminutive is expressed
by consonant and/or vowel symbolism only, then all words in a given
stretch of speech may be equally affected. The only constraint is
phonological. But as often as not the usage is limited to nouns or
nouns and verbs. Thus in Yurok t is replaced by č and l by r (Robins
1958:13-14),[2] e.g., nondim. pontet 'ashes' vs. dim. pənčəč 'dust',
nondim. seʔlet 'to scrape off (e.g., mud)' vs.dim. seʔreč 'to whittle'.

        Affixation is also usually restricted to nouns or nouns and
verbs. Thus in Creek any noun may be diminutivized by the use of the
suffix -uci, e.g., nondim. łałí 'fish' and dim. łałíci 'minnow'.[3] But
in Wiyot the diminutive suffix -oc or -ic is used with verbs as well as
nouns, e.g., nondim. tak- 'spruce' and dim. cakic 'young spruce' and
nondim. loliswił 'he sings' vs. rórišwocił 'he hums' (Reichard 1925;
Teeter 1959). Furthermore, if a language uses both sound symbolism
and affixation, the symbolic change is likely to be limited to those
words which undergo affixation. This is illustrated in the Wiyot examples just given where the use of the diminutive suffix also requires
that t, s, and l be replaced by c, š, and r, respectively.

        2. In Natchez the diminutive is expressed by a suffix for
nouns and by an infix for verbs. The diminutive suffix of nouns is
-(y)i·nuh, as in nondim. ʔu· 'road' vs. dim. ʔu·yi·nuh 'trail'. The
diminutivization of verbs is somewhat more complex. The infix -li-
appears in words like heliyahku·s 'to find little ones' vs. heyahku·s
'to find normal-sized ones'. But other verbs take -et- or -eti-, e.g.,
nondim. hapiti·s 'a normal-sized one to walk' vs. dim. hetpiti·s 'a
little one to walk', and haci·s 'a normal-sized one to live' vs. hetici·s
'a little one to live'. A few verbs use suppletion, as has already been
illustrated in section 2 of this article.

3. The use of reduplication appears to be somewhat more diffuse, but it too occurs most often with nouns, somewhat less often with verbs and adjectives. The Salish languages in particular make extensive use of reduplication in expressing the diminutive.[4] Thus in Snohomish we find nondim. čali? 'heart' vs. dim. čačəli? 'little heart' and nondim. ?ibac 'grandchild' vs. dim. ?i?ibac 'pet name for grandchild'. The same device is used with verbs to express "reduced activity or state for bases that translate English verbs and adjectives". (Hess 1966:351-352).[5]

But reduplication also occurs in combination with other devices, especially sound symbolism. Nez Perce, a Sahaptian language (Aoki 1968), makes some use of vowel as well as consonant symbolism and these are also often accompanied by reduplication. Nondiminutives s̱, ṉ, ḵ, and e̱, are replaced by c, l, q, and a, respectively, in diminutive forms. Thus we find nondim. se·x 'onion' vs. ca·xcá·x 'wild onion' and the nondim. elements sikem 'horse' and -qen 'young of animals' vs. ciqá·mqal 'dog'.

4. One of the most highly developed examples of sound-symbolism is found in Wishram, a Chinookan language (Sapir 1911). In diminutive formations nonglottalized consonants are replaced by glottalized, back velar (q, x̱, etc.) by velar (ḵ, x, etc.) and hushing sibilants and affricates by plain sibilants and affricates. Thus we have nondim. i-géč 'nose' vs.dim. i-k̓éč, non-dim. a-q̓oxl 'knee'[6] vs. dim. a-k̓úxl, and nondim. wá-kš̱ən 'finger' vs. dim. wá-ksən. Wishram also has gender displacement as a part of the process of diminutivization. Sapir (1911:641) points out that "several nouns on becoming diminutive in form at the same time change to a more suitable gender, masculines often becoming feminines..., neuters..., or diminutive duals". Thus we find nondim. i-šgán (masc.) 'cedar board' vs. dim. wa-skán (fem.) 'box' and dim. of dim. wá-cḵun (fem.) 'cup'.

4. Other Special Domains of Use for the Diminutive

In many languages the use of the diminutive may have other kinds of special domains of use. In particular, words employed in 'baby talk' (Ferguson 1964) are often heavily subjected to diminutivization. The English use of -y, -ie in 'horsie', or 'little' in 'little coat', or both plus displacement in 'its little shoesies' illustrates the point. In Nootka another set of domains is illustrated in the abnormal types of speech (Sapir 1915a), most of which require the use of the diminutive suffix as well, presumably because of its belittling or de- rogatory connotation. In many languages kinship terms are particu- larly likely to be subjected to diminutivization, sometimes largely in vocative forms, sometimes in other situations. Nez Perce goes a step further and uses the diminutive whenever there is 'possession by first person' in kinship terms, e.g., naʔcíˑc (dim.) 'my paternal aunt' vs. ʔimsíˑs (nondim.) 'your paternal aunt'. Thus in the domain of kin terms the Nez Perce diminutive serves to reinforce the notion of 'one's own' vs. 'that of others'. Similarly, but without being limi- ted to kin terms, a Snohomish speaker "often uses the attenuative [diminutive] in referring to his own possessions in order to indicate humility" (Hess 1966:351-352). Snohomish also has at least one do- main where the use of the diminutive is rejected by some informants, namely its use with "certain male kinship terms".

In Yurok a somewhat different dimension is found with certain nouns, for the diminutive form is sometimes people-oriented in con- trast to a nondiminutive which is animal-oriented. Thus the dim. wenčok^{W}s means 'woman' in contrast to nondim. wentok s 'female (of animal or bird)' and dim. ček^{W}s means '(human) heart' while nondim. tek^{W}sa ʔr is 'heart (of salmon)' (Haas 1970).

Finally, as can be seen in the examples already given (in sections 2. and 3.2.), Natchez is particularly interesting in that verbal diminutivization refers to the subject when the verb is intransitive, but to the object when it is transitive.

NOTES

[1]This information is taken from my own field notes on the Natchez language.
[2]In addition to the consonant symbolism there is sometimes vowel symbolism as well, particularly the replacement of any vowel by ə.
[3]This information is taken from my own field notes on the Creek language.
[4]Sapir (1915b) first described this in detail in reference to Comox.

⁵Hess uses "chameleon morphology" for reduplication, "attenuative" for diminutive, and "augmentative" for several types of pluralization. Reduplication is also used to express the last-named of these, e.g., čáliʔ 'heart', čalčaliʔ 'hearts'. It is also used for the pluralization of diminutives already formed by reduplication, e.g., čačəliʔ 'little heart', čačačəliʔ 'little hearts'.

⁶Sapir's orthography has been changed to modern usage. Most changes require no special explanation. However, Sapir's x̱ = present x and his x = present x.

REFERENCES

Aoki, Haruo
  1968 "Nez Perce Grammar" Ph.D. thesis (Berkeley, University of California).
Ferguson, Charles A.
  1964 "Baby Talk in Six Languages" in The Ethnography of Communication, eds., John J. Gumperz and Dell Hymes (= American Anthropologist 66:6, Part 2:103-114).
Haas, Mary R.
  1942 "Types of Reduplication in Thai (With Some Comparisons and Contrasts Taken from English)", Studies in Linguistics 1:4. 1-6.
  1970 "Consonant Symbolism in Northwestern California: A Problem in Diffusion" in Language and Cultures of Western North America, Earl H. Swanson, Jr., ed. (Pocatello, Idaho State University Press).
Hess, Thomas M.
  1966 "Snohomish Chameleon Morphology", International Journal of American Linguistics 32:350-356.
Reichard, Gladys A.
  1925 "Wiyot Grammar and Texts". University of California Publications in American Archeology and Ethnology 22:1-215 (Berkeley).
Robins, R. H.
  1958 "The Yurok Language", University of California Publications in Linguistics 15 (Berkeley and Los Angeles).

Sapir, Edward
  1911 "Diminutive and Augmentative Consonantism in Wishram" in
       Handbook of American Indian Languages, Franz Boas, ed.
       (= Bureau of American Ethnology, Bulletin 40, Part 1,
       Washington, D.C.), pp. 638-645.
  1915a Abnormal Types of Speech in Nootka (= Canada Department
        of Mines, Geological Survey, Memoir 62, Anthropological
        Series, No. 5) (Ottawa).
  1915b Noun Reduplication in Comox, a Salish Language of Vancouver
        Island (= Canada Department of Mines, Geological Survey,
        Memoir 63, Anthropological Series, No. 6) (Ottawa).
Teeter, Karl V.
  1959 "Consonant Harmony in Wiyot (With a Note on Cree)", Inter-
       national Journal of American Linguistics 25: 41-43.

Tunica is a virtually extinct American Indian language now remembered by only one speaker, an elderly man living near Marksville, in Avoyelles Parish, Louisiana. This is in the French belt of Louisiana, and until quite recently, French was the principal language spoken there. Even today one hears almost as much French as English spoken on the streets of Marksville; and postal clerks, bank tellers, and shopkeepers find it necessary to be able to speak both languages in order to handle their business properly.

It is therefore not surprising that the Tunica language should have quite a few loanwords from French. Rather, it is surprising that it does not have more. However, the Tunica, as their numbers dwindled, found it increasingly difficult to keep up the use of their ancient language, and so, instead of adapting it to the needs of modern times (by borrowing if necessary), they simply adopted French as their native tongue. Strangely enough, before this transition was fully completed, English became increasingly important in that area, and now all the people of Tunica blood living near Marksville speak not only French but some English as well.

Before listing the words which have been borrowed from French, it will be convenient to list the vowels and consonants of Tunica so that it will be possible to show what phonetic adaptations had to be made in taking over words from a foreign source. The Tunica vowels[1] are i, e, ɛ[æ], a, ɔ, o, and u. The symbol ɛ stands for a front vowel similar to Eng. a, as in cat; while ɔ stands for a back-rounded vowel similar to Eng. a, as in call. The remaining vowels have their continental values. The basic consonants are: voiceless stops p, t, k, ʔ; voiceless affricate č; voiceless spirants s, š, h; semivowels y,

w; nasals m, n; lateral l; trilled r. The symbol ʔ stands for the
glottal stop, č is similar to Eng. ch, š to Eng. sh. Some borrowed
words contain the following additional consonants: voiced stops b, d,
g; voiceless spirant f. Borrowed words (not only from French but
from other American Indian languages) have thus influenced Tunica
not only lexically, but phonemically as well.

The following Tunica words, arranged in alphabetical order,
constitute direct borrowings from French: [2]

> dí su, "dime" < dix sous
> kaʼfi, "coffee" < café
> koʼti, "to knit" < tricoter
> miʼnu, "cat" < minon
> saʼmdi, "Saturday" < samedi
> šaʼwana, "Chinese" < chinois (with metathesis)
> suʼhpi, "to eat supper" < souper
> teʼni, "to ring" < tinter
> teʼšuni, "to eat breakfast" < déjeuner
> tiʼni, "to dine" < dîner

The phonetic and other changes that have taken place in the borrowing
process are explained below:

1) All free stems in Tunica have an intrinsic stress on the
first syllable; hence the borrowings listed above all have such a
stress.

2) The French vowels i, or î, a, and ou are borrowed as
Tunica i, a, and u, respectively, as in diʼsu, saʼmdi, and the vowels
of the first syllables of kaʼfi, miʼnu, suʼhpi, and tiʼni. The only exception is šaʼwana < chinois, where French i is irregularly represented
by Tunica a.

3) The French vowel eu is borrowed as Tunica u, as in teʼ-
šuni < déjeuner.

4) The French vowel é or er is borrowed as Tunica e when
occurring in a stressed syllable, e.g., teʼšuni. Unstressed syllables
in Tunica tend to avoid all vowels except i, a, and u; hence é or er

is borrowed as i in Tunica unstressed syllables, as in the final syllables of ka'fi, ko'ti, su'hpi, te'ni, te'šuni, and ti'ni.

5) The French vowel o is borrowed as o in a stressed syllable, e.g., kóti, but as u in an unstressed syllable, e.g., mínu.

6) The French vowel of the first syllable of tinter is higher than the Tunica vowel written ε; hence it is taken over as e, as in te'ni.

7) The French combined sound oi is taken over as Tunica wa, as in ša'wana < chinois.

8) Sometimes French voiced stops are represented by voiceless stops in Tunica, e.g., ti'ni < dîner, te'šuni < déjeuner. At other times they are represented by voiced stops in Tunica, as in di'su < dix sous and sa'mdi < samedi. Since Tunica voiced stops occur only in words of foreign or probably foreign origin (partly French, partly other American Indian languages), those borrowings which contain voiceless stops for French voiced stops must have been taken over earlier than those which have voiced stops for French voiced stops.

9) Both the French voiceless spirant ch and the French voiced spirant j are borrowed as the Tunica voiceless š, as in ša'-wana < chinois and te'šuni < déjeuner.

10) The word ka'fi is the only Tunica word in which the sound f occurs, and thus we have an occurrence of a borrowed phoneme as well as a borrowed word. Some of the near-by American Indian languages have the sound f, notably the Muskogean languages, and therefore it is quite natural that they should use this sound when they take over the word "coffee," e.g., Creek ká·fi. Among those near-by languages which do not have f, however, Tunica is the only one which fails to make a substitution of some other sound or sounds for f. Thus Natchez substitutes W (voiceless w) for f, as in ka·Wih, "coffee,"[3] while Chitimacha substitutes the consonant cluster hp, as in kahpi, "coffee."[4]

11) The French consonants c, m, n, p, s, and t are taken over as Tunica k, m, n, p, s, and t, respectively, as in ka'fi, mínu, su'hpi, and te'ni.

12) It would appear that in taking over the word <u>tricoter</u> as ko̓ti, the Tunica dropped the first syllable, and this could be explained on the basis of the fact that Tunica verb stems rarely have more than two syllables. (The word te̓šuni has a special explanation, given below.) On the other hand, it is also possible that the local French pronunciation of <u>tricoter</u> is 'coter. Since I did not record the local French term, I do not know which explanation is the true one.

13) Certain changes are at present unexplainable, viz., the addition of the h in su̓hpi < <u>souper</u> and the loss of the second <u>t</u> in <u>tinter</u>, which was taken over as te̓ni.

14) The most interesting change that has taken place is the morphological treatment accorded to the word te̓šuni. Since most Tunica verb stems are disyllabic, te̓šuni has been interpreted as a verb stem te̓šu + -ni, a causative suffix. The causative suffix is regularly used in the infinitive and some other morphological forms of causative verbs. But certain other morphological situations regularly call for the use of a paradigmatic form of the causative auxiliary - ʔu̓ta and in these situations the causative suffix -ni must be dropped. Therefore a paradigmatic form like te̓šʔuta, "he ate breakfast" (< té̓šu + - ʔúta) shows that té̓šuni, despite its French origin, has been completely adapted to the morphological structure of Tunica. Note that te̓ni, "to ring," and ti̓ni, "to dine," are not treated as causative verbs, because they have only two syllables, and it is therefore not necessary to interpret -ni as a suffix when fitting these stems into the normal stem patterns of Tunica.

NOTES

[1]Mary R. Haas, <u>Tunica</u>, 1941, pp. 13-14.
[2]Ibid., pp. 86-87.
[3]Taken from my own field notes on Natchez.
[4]Morris Swadesh, <u>Chitimacha</u> (in <u>Linguistic Structures of North America</u>, by Harry Hoijer and others, 1946), p. 312.

Terms for playing cards are all too seldom collected by field workers. While doing some work on a Chipewyan dialect last summer I discovered that many of their terms are borrowed from French.[1] I remembered that Bloomfield had also collected card terms in Menomini,[2] in part at least because he was interested in their gender classification.[3] Looking at the list again I saw that the Menomini terms for the suits are also from French though Menomini has disguised their origin somewhat more radically than Chipewyan has. For example, whereas Chipewyan borrows French nouns complete with article, Menomini omits the article. Menomini phonetic adaptations include n for French r, s for French f, and an intercalated vowel in a consonant cluster. The Menomini names for the suits and their French originals are: pi·k spade (Fr. le pique). The word has also been adapted as the general term for playing card. tanɛ·s club (Fr. le trèfle). ka·no·w diamond (Fr. le carreau). keyo·n heart (Fr. le coeur).

In all probability a great many of the American Indian languages lying within the old canoe-trading area have borrowed card playing terms from French.

NOTES

While teaching at the Canadian Summer Institute of Linguistics at the University of Alberta, Edmonton, I was able to do some work with a Chipewyan speaker at Camsell Hospital.

[1]The Chipewyan terms are included in my Notes on a Chipewyan Dialect, IJAL 34.3. 165-75 (1968)

[2] Leonard Bloomfield, The Menomini Language, New Haven and London (1962).   The card terms are on p. 36.

[3] With the exception of the term for <u>ten-spot</u>, they are all classed as animate nouns.

13 | The Linguist as a Teacher of Languages

I

Today there is a greater need than ever before in the history of the world for learning foreign languages — especially the languages of the Orient — and for learning them as quickly and as efficiently as possible. Yet at every turn we encounter the belief that oriental languages are so mysterious and so intricate that they simply cannot be learned, at least not by English-speaking people. Recently I heard an American woman say to her Chinese companion, 'You know that we could never learn Chinese!' I did not hear the reply; but it might well have been, 'If thousands of Chinese can learn English, why can't Americans learn Chinese? Surely English must be as difficult for the Chinese as their language is for you.' The truth is that we consider the languages of the Orient impossible to learn because we feel no actual need for learning them; whereas Orientals in every part of Asia do feel a need for learning English and therefore learn it. As soon as we take a real interest in the Orient and in other once-remote parts of the world, we shall be as well able to learn their languages as Orientals are to learn ours.

However, even if someone has this interest, he will encounter many obstacles in his attempts to learn an oriental language. The chances are that he will find no trained teachers of the language; and what may discourage him still more, he will probably find very few textbooks, all or nearly all so badly designed as to be quite useless. How then is he to learn the language?

Popular advice on this problem runs something like this: 'The best thing to do is to go to the country where the language is spoken

and pick it up there. If you cannot do that, perhaps you can find someone who has lived there and persuade him to teach you. Or there may
be a native speaker of the language somewhere in this country who
could give you lessons.' Let us see what is likely to happen to someone who adopts advice of this kind.

Suppose first that he can go to the country where the language
is spoken. Here he will try to acquire it by 'absorption' or with the
help of a native teacher. We have all known immigrants who learned
English by this method; we have observed their bewildering pronunciation and their jumbled grammar; and yet, in the face of our experience, most of us still believe that this is the best way to learn a
foreign language. If the student is exceptionally gifted, he will acquire some knowledge of the language simply by hearing it constantly
spoken around him; but unless he can afford to spend many years of
his life in the foreign country and is willing to keep up his efforts to
learn the language, he is likely to have only fair success. Westerners often assume that Orientals are willing to accept almost any mispronunciation of their languages (since these are virtually 'unpro-
nounceable' anyway); but in fact our mistakes are just as ridiculous
to them as theirs are to us. Others like to think that Orientals will
overlook our mistakes because they are too polite to laugh at us; but
if we want to escape at least covert ridicule we must return the
Orientals' politeness and do them the courtesy of trying to speak their
languages correctly. The truth is that many Westerners who have
learned an oriental language by 'picking it up' in Asia so mispronounce
and misconstrue it that they are scarcely understood except by those
natives who know enough English to anticipate and make allowances
for their mistakes.

If the student finds it impossible to go to the country where
the language is spoken, he may decide instead to employ the services
of a returned traveler as teacher. If the latter really knows the language well and speaks it fluently and correctly, then he can be considered the equivalent of a native speaker. But how is the student to
judge of this important matter ? How is he to be sure that the returned traveler is not one of those Westerners whose speech the natives consider comical or even incomprehensible ? Any assurance

which the traveler himself may offer on this point is obviously worth-
less.

Finally, the student may be lucky enough to find a native
speaker of the language who is willing to teach him. Now surely, we
might suppose, he will be able to learn the language well; but again
there is a snag. To learn a language from a native speaker one must
have a technique for eliciting the proper information from him, and
a method for analyzing and organizing the information when the speaker has supplied it. Few people have this technical equipment; yet
without it, a student cannot hope to make much headway. Even in the
matter of pronunciation — in some ways the most superficial of the
difficulties facing him — he can make little progress unless he has
been trained in general phonetics; for the native speaker, to whom of
course all the sounds of his own language are 'natural', [1] cannot explain to the student why and in what respects he mispronounces, or
tell him how to produce the sounds which happen not to occur in the
student's language. The guidebooks that have been written to assist
the student are often more confusing than no help at all. One such
book, written for Europeans learning Thai (Siamese), can come no
closer than this to a description of the voiceless unaspirated stops
k̲, t̲, p̲: the first is '3/4 G and 1/4 K', the second is 'a mean between
the sound of T and D', the last is '2/3 P and 1/3 B.'[2]

At this point we seem to have reached an impasse. Is there
then no method for learning a difficult foreign language without adequate textbooks and trained teachers?

The answer is an inspiring one: any language can be learned,
quickly and correctly, by a trained linguist working with a native
speaker, whom he treats not as a teacher but purely as a source of
information. The linguist is thoroughly trained in phonetics and in
grammatical analysis; in the most favorable case he has already analyzed one or more languages before he approaches the one to be
learned. His method is simple. He persuades his informant (the
native speaker) to talk in the foreign language; he listens carefully,
and writes down what the informant says in a phonetic alphabet, which
he converts as soon as possible into a practical orthography (a phonemic transcription); he compares and analyzes the forms of the new
language; and classifies them in terms of its own grammatical system,

without reference to the grammar of English or of any other language previously known to him. Moreover, the linguist imitates everything the informant says, and keeps on imitating until the informant is completely satisfied with his pronunciation; it is by this means that he learns the language — not by asking the informant how he makes this or that sound, or why he speaks a sentence in this way and not in that.

A more detailed discussion of the method is to be found in two booklets recently issued by the Linguistic Society of America: Outline Guide for the Practical Study of Foreign Languages, by Leonard Bloomfield; and Outline of Linguistic Analysis, by Bernard Bloch and George L. Trager. The first of these tells how the relevant information is most efficiently obtained from a native speaker; the second tells how the information, once obtained, is most efficiently analyzed.

II

Many of the fundamental features of the method described in these booklets were first developed in the study of American Indian languages, which often present unusually difficult phonetic and grammatical systems. Those who have used the method to analyze and describe American Indian languages have known all along that it could be applied with equal success to any language, written or unwritten; but this fact has only recently been proved. Proof came when a group of scholars (several of whom had previously worked on American Indian languages) were engaged by the Intensive Language Program of the American Council of Learned Societies to apply this method to the study of oriental languages.

The successful application of the method to the analysis and description of a number of oriental languages was notable in itself. But equally important was the demonstration that the method is also useful in teaching — more useful, in fact, than almost any other previously tried. For the latter purpose it may be used in two ways:

(1) The students may participate with the linguist, under his direction, in the analysis of the language to be learned. If the linguist himself is new to the language, the students and he learn it together; if he has already studied it, they follow in his footsteps. In

either case his function is that of a guide: he shows the students how
to get the necessary linguistic material from the informant, leads
them to infer the grammatical structure from the examples they collect, helps them to analyze and classify what they have recorded. At
the end of such a course the students not only have a good knowledge
of the language, but are equipped to learn any language in the world
by their own efforts. Those who have once acquired this technique
regard it as a priceless treasure.

(2) The linguist may study the language by himself, analyze
the linguistic material in advance, and organize the grammar for presentation to his students. The informant is still necessary to act as
a model for imitation, but the linguist now actively teaches instead of
only guiding.

The first of these methods is indispensible for teaching those
who wish to master the technique of linguistic analysis and to engage
in linguistic research of their own. (It is to such students that the
booklets by Bloomfield and by Bloch and Trager are most useful.)
The second way is, strictly speaking, a teaching method adapted to
the particular language; it therefore produces faster results for those
interested primarily in the given language, and is much better suited
to the needs of students who are not far enough advanced to do research. It is the second method which promises to be the more widely
used in teaching specific languages.

III

Since many persons have come to regard this method of
teaching a particular language as superior to the traditional methods
of instruction, it may be of interest to describe some of its more important characteristics.

In the first place the teaching is done by a trained linguist,
working with the assistance of a native speaker — except, of course,
in the rare cases where the native speaker is a linguist himself. Two
questions should be answered at this point: (1) If the linguist has
learned the language, why does he need the help of a native speaker ?
— because not even the best grammar-book or dictionary can replace
the native speaker's unique knowledge of what can be said in his

language in any situation; and because students should be allowed to imitate only a native speaker's pronunciation. (2) If a native speaker, for these two reasons, must be always present, why is it necessary to have a linguist also? — because only a linguist has the technical knowledge necessary to help the students in their imitation and in their learning of the language. No one, simply by virtue of speaking a language, can describe its phonetic system or analyze and correct a foreigner's mispronunciation; no one, simply because he is fluent himself, can present the grammatical structure of his language in such a way as to lead others to fluency by the shortest possible route. Only a linguist can do these things.

The actual teaching procedure varies according to the special requirements of the language to be taught and the experience of the linguist in charge of each course. In what follows I shall describe the procedure used for my own classes in Thai.[3] Other linguists, teaching other languages, would modify my practice here and there, perhaps omitting some features of it or introducing innovations of their own; but all would probably agree on the principles that underlie the procedure.

Students in the Thai classes are first of all taught to use a phonemic notation for writing the language, so that they may concentrate on pronunciation from the very beginning. Until they are sufficiently advanced to begin the study of the traditional native system of writing, they carry on all their work with the use of this phonemic notation. This practice reflects one of the basic assumptions of our method: speaking must come before reading.

About half the students' time is devoted to class work of the more traditional kind, with grammatical discussion, word study, translation of Thai into English and of English into Thai, drill on troublesome points of grammar, and the like. The other half of their time is spent on drill intended to develop good pronunciation and, later on, the ability to converse in Thai. (My classes have been small. Where classes are larger, students must be divided into groups of not more than five or six for the drill work.) The drill consists of three kinds of exercises: (1) Exercises of imitation train students to imitate exactly what they hear, so that they may be understood by native speakers; (2) Exercises of dictation train students to write down what they hear, so that they may improve the sharpness of their perception and equip themselves to record new words even before they have learned the traditional native alphabet; and (3) Exercises of recognition and response train them to understand and answer what they hear, so that they may gain experience in the actual use of the language as a means of social intercourse. All of these exercises are conducted by a native speaker (with or without the linguist's supervision), so that the students always hear the language spoken under the most favorable conditions.

Experience has shown the three types of exercises to be so interwoven in their benefits that an improvement in one kind of skill means an improvement in the other two kinds also: as a student's pronunciation improves, so do his ability to record words in the phonemic notation and his ability to recognize and respond to what he hears.

Note that a student does not practice the pronunciation of words by himself until he is well able to do so. In the exercises of imitation he must always listen to the informant and imitate exactly what he hears, practicing each word until the informant is satisfied with his pronunciation. Later on he may attempt to pronounce words and phrases which he has not heard; but if he flounders too much, he must return at once to the imitative process. This method may seem needlessly slow and over-careful; but it is only by such training that a student can acquire the sort of pronunciation which any native speaker — even one who knows no other language — will understand. Imitation can hardly be overdone; whereas bad habits formed in practicing alone may resist all efforts to correct them.

The exercises of dictation are intended to improve the student's ability to hear, not his ability to spell. In the early stages of the work the informant dictates only words which the class have already studied; a little later he dictates short sentences containing familiar words, then sentences containing new words, and finally whole passages with old and new words mingled. In the later stages the student begins to learn how to correct his own mistakes by comparing the troublesome feature of a new word with a similar feature of some word already known. Thus, if he cannot readily identify the tone of a new word, he asks the informant to pronounce the word

beside one whose tone is known to him, and continues this process
until he finds a known word whose tone matches that of the new one.
By a similar procedure he can determine any phonetic feature that
he meets with — the timbre of a vowel, the aspiration or nonaspira-
tion of a consonant, and so on. When he has acquired facility in this
kind of work he is on his way to competence in handling the language.

Exercises of recognition and response may begin quite early.
In the first stages the informant reads Thai sentences which have already been studied in class, and the student tries to give an English
translation as quickly as possible. When the student can understand
through hearing everything that he has learned through reading, he
has made an important forward step. Later the informant asks simple questions in Thai, to be answered by the student in the same language. In the final stage, the informant and the student engage in actual conversation; this will of course be as simple or as difficult as
the student's advancement allows.

All three types of exercise are given concurrently. When
the student has become proficient in all three, he can understand a
native speaker, he can make himself understood, and he can write
down any word in the language, whether or not he has heard it before,
in the phonemic notation which he has learned. These three skills
give him not only a fair practical command of the language, but also
the tools which will enable him to learn more and more of the language as readily as a native speaker does.

After the student has learned several hundred words and has
acquired reasonable facility in conversation through the use of the
phonemic writing alone, then — but not until then — he begins to
learn the traditional system of writing. For this purpose he does not
absolutely need to have achieved the degree of competence here assumed; but if he has achieved it, his progress in learning the native
system of writing will be far more rapid. Indeed, his background
knowledge of the spoken language puts him practically on the same
footing with native speakers when they, as children, begin the study
of their traditional writing system. Peculiarities and irregularities
in the native spelling can nearly always be most easily explained
through the use of the phonemic writing, so that this remains a useful tool even when the student is learning to supplant it by the traditional orthography.

IV

It has been my experience, and the experience of others teaching by similar methods, that students like to learn a foreign language in this way. They acquire a good knowledge of the spoken language, and their progress in the written language is unusually rapid as a result. Their daily contact with a native speaker, their continual efforts to understand him and to make him understand, give them a sense of reality, and the assurance that they are actually on the way, from the very start, toward practical mastery of the language as a means of intercourse with native speakers. The ability to converse in a foreign language — surely the most important single benefit to be derived from language study — is too often neglected or taken for granted. It comes only through long, laborious drill, through constant hard work; but most students are willing, even glad, to do what is required of them, because they see quite clearly — or can easily be made to see — the practical usefulness of these lessons.

NOTES

[1]This applies to native speakers of English as of other languages. A Thai girl studying in this country was once encouragingly told to pronounce th 'naturally'.

[2]B.O. Cartwright, The Student's Manual of the Siamese Language 10-1 (rev. ed., Bangkok, 1930).

[3]My study of Thai was made possible by a fellowship from the National School of Modern Oriental Languages and Civilizations, under the auspices of the American Council of Learned Societies. My intensive courses in this language at the University of Michigan have been sponsored by the Council's Intensive Language Program.

14 | What Belongs in a Bilingual Dictionary?

1. Ideally speaking, the bilingual dictionary would anticipate every conceivable need of the prospective user. (1) It would provide for each word or expression in the source language (SL) just the
right translation in the target language (TL) including, most importantly, the one needed for the passage in hand. (2) It would contain
all the words, locutions, circumlocutions, and idioms that any user
might ever want to look up. (3) It would contain all the inflectional,
derivational, syntactic and semantic information that any user might
ever need. (4) It would contain information on all levels of usage, including special warnings about words not to be used in the presence of
ladies, in the presence of children, or to or in the presence of one's
superiors. (5) It would contain all personal names, names of person-
ages past and present, place names, names of famous books and plays,
names of characters therein, and any other names that any user might
want to look up. (6) It would contain all the specialized vocabulary
items of all the sciences, professions, manufacturing industries, and
trades, each carefully and appropriately labelled as to its field. (7)
It would contain all necessary information about correct spellings, as
well as information on alternate or commonly-encountered incorrect
spellings. (8) It would include all the information needed to instruct
the user in the proper way to pronounce each word so as to be inde-
tectable from the pronunciation of a native speaker.

But this is not all. In order to be truly ideal the bilingual
dictionary would have to meet not less than three other tests. (9) It
ought to be equally oriented to speakers of both languages. (10) It
ought to be as well-adapted to purposes of machine translation as it is
to human translation. (11) Above all, it should be compact — at the
most no bigger than Random House's ACD or Webster's Collegiate.

A final desideratum, (12), not on a par with the others, would be the inclusion of illustrations to picture items unfamiliar to speakers of the target language.

2. The desiderata listed as items (1) to (8) above are important, I think, for all bilingual dictionaries. If all these were properly executed virtual completeness would be assured, but in most cases several volumes would be needed to accommodate the results. It is for this reason that item (11), pointing out the value of compactness, is necessary. In order to achieve this compactness certain limitations have to be introduced. The nature and extent of these limitations should, however, be independently determined for each pair of languages. In general the compactness should be achieved by the omission of entries rather than by the neglect of any of our first eight desiderata.

To the best of my knowledge, no existing bilingual dictionary contains all of these features.[1] Most dictionaries are quite lackadaisical about (4), information on levels of usage. Really troublesome words are omitted altogether.[2] Many otherwise excellent bilingual dictionaries omit item (5), names, or relegate it to a separate section of the dictionary, or, more commonly, to several separate sections, viz., personal names, place names, etc. This is not only wasteful of the time and energy of the user, it sometimes occasions strange-looking gaps in the main part of the dictionary. Thus The Concise Oxford French Dictionary contains in its French-English part the following entries on p. 877:

> voltaire, fauteuil-voltaire (voltɛr, fotoej-voltɛr), s. m. [f. prop. n. Voltaire] Voltaire (armchair).
> voltairianisme (voltɛrjanism), s. m. [f. Voltaire] Voltairianism, voltairism.
> voltairien, -ne (voltɛrjɛ̃), adj. Voltairian.

The proper name Voltaire, however, from which all these are derived, is nowhere to be found; it is not even given separately in the List of Names.

3. So far we have considered only items (1) to (8) and have concluded that they are all useful, provided they are tempered with item (11), the ideal of compactness. What about items (9) and (10)?

Are they also necessary and useful? Or can one or the other or both be dispensed with?

At the present time I am not prepared to discuss item (10), usefulness for machine translation. The demands made by machine translation may differ too much from those required for human translation. I suspect, however, that dictionaries prepared for machine translation will eventually lead to ways of improving dictionaries intended primarily for human use.

This leaves item (9), which states that the ideal bilingual dictionary should serve the needs of the speakers of both languages with equal felicity. This is the only one, I think, which must be dispensed with, at least as long as we must continue to use our present types of book format. (The reason is largely that it cannot be accomplished without introducing cumbersomeness — pronunciation, for example, would have to be shown for both languages in every entry.) Having to give up this ideal is unfortunate, though, because this one, more than any other, is tacitly assumed by the public to be the one above all others which is fulfilled. Worse yet, there is rarely, if ever, any specific warning to the potential user that such, indeed, is not actually the case. If a given French-English dictionary is useful to an American who wishes to translate spoken or written French into English, how can it be that this same book is not equally useful to the Frenchman who has the same goal in mind? The answer is that there are innumerable covert facts about English which are known to the native speaker thereof, but which are not at all clear or obvious to the native speaker of French. Book-publishers can scarcely be expected to take kindly to the thought, but it is nevertheless true that bilingual dictionaries should be titled in such a way that the language of the intended user is made clear, e. g., <u>French-English Dictionary for Americans</u> as against <u>French-English Dictionary for Frenchmen</u>. What is even more deplorable, however, is the fact that often the compilers are not aware of the problems involved. Thinking they are preparing a dictionary for speakers of both languages, they may easily end up producing a dictionary which is not as useful as it should be to speakers of either language.

A couple of examples taken from Thai-English and English-Thai will help show why such a separation of goals is necessary. In

Manich's <u>Thai-English Dictionary</u>, a handy volume which has seen
many editions, the word /rɔ́ɔŋ/ which means 'to cry' in the sense of
'utter its characteristic cry' is elaborated by two pages of material
designed solely to show that in English one uses a large number of
different verbs to translate /rɔ́ɔŋ/ depending on the bird or animal
being described, e.g., the cow <u>lows</u>, the crow <u>caws</u>, the cat <u>mews</u>,
the horse <u>neighs</u>, the lion <u>roars</u>, the elephant <u>trumpets</u>, etc. Now
this kind of information is no doubt useful to the Thai speaker who
wishes to find the proper English word to express his thought, but to
the native speaker of English such a listing is nothing short of tire-
some. And worse yet, from the standpoint of the speaker of English,
nothing is included to warn him that in spite of its broad coverage the
Thai word cannot be used in place of English <u>cry</u> (in the sense of <u>weep</u>)
— for this meaning the term /rɔ́ɔŋhâj/ must be used.

　　In Prachachang's <u>English-Thai Dictionary</u> we find again that
the orientation is toward the speaker of Thai, not of English. The
English pronoun <u>me</u>, for example, is glossed /chǎn/, /phǒm/,
/khâaphacâw/, etc., with no hint to the unwary that /chǎn/ is used
in speaking to inferiors and intimates, /phǒm/ is used only by men,
/khâaphacâw/ is most commonly used in speeches and editorials.
And of course only the native speaker of Thai would have any idea of
what is included under 'etc.'

　　Since both of these dictionaries are actually intended for native speakers of Thai, not of English, no criticism is intended in these
examples. They are cited to show why dictionaries intended for native
speakers of one language are likely to be inadequate for speakers of
another language.

　　4. There is another desideratum for a good dictionary, monolingual or bilingual, which can be stated very simply. A good dictionary is one in which you can find the information you are looking for —
preferably in the very first place you look. Nothing could be sillier
than the tacit assumption, far too commonly encountered, that it is
somehow good for the soul of the user if he has to work hard to find
what he is looking for. This means that everything will have to be in
strict alphabetical order. It is 'no fair' to list some words in alphabetical order while others are to be found only in groups or sets. Followed out to its logical conclusion, this means that in an English-X

dictionary, geese will be separately listed from goose (though cross-
referenced), sang will be separately listed from sing, etc.[3] It is perfectly true, of course, that a foreign student studying English will have
to learn our irregular plurals and past tenses. It is not true, however,
that he derives any benefit from wasting even as much as five minutes
finding out what geese means if, by chance, he has not yet learned that
particular irregular plural.

        Experience has shown me, however, that the definition of a
good dictionary as stated above (one in which you can find what you are
looking for — preferably on the first try) is one which is extremely
difficult to adhere to at all times. This is not necessarily because of
any intrinsic difficulty but rather because limitations of space sooner
or later make themselves strongly felt even in the most ambitious
project. Furthermore, each different language tends to have its own
brand of difficulties, and in some instances the difficulties even seem
to be intrinsic. I should like to give a couple of examples of some
kinds of difficulties that may be encountered.

        In the compilation of the Thai-English dictionaries I have at-
tempted to adhere to this dictum. This means that everything in the
files has been completely cross-referenced. But when the files are
used as the basis for the actual dictionaries, we find that there would
be a great many instances of multiple listing if the dictum were always
carried out to its strict logical conclusion. Thai is a language which
is rich in composite expressions of all sorts. It is not at all uncommon
for such expressions to contain a sequence of four or more morphemes
which must be translated as a unit into English, e.g.,

        / chêŋchág hàgkradùug/ 'to curse roundly,' composed of
        / chɛ̌ŋ/ 'to curse, revile,' / chág/ 'to pull,' / hàg/ 'to break,'
        / kradùug/ 'bones.'

Since Thai is conventionally written without any spaces between words,
the English-speaking student has no clue as to which elements form a
semantic unit and which do not. Following our dictum that it should be
possible to find what one in looking for in the first place one looks, the
above Thai expression would have to be placed under all four of its constituent parts. But when this instance is multiplied by hundreds of other
instances, we find that a staggering amount of space is required. Still,

how are we going to decide which composites should be given the preferential (multiple listing) treatment and which should not?

There is, however, an even more intractible type of language, so far as our dictum is concerned. This is the type of language which has a multiplicity of prefixes and infixes, such as Tagalog or other Malayo-Polynesian language. It is customary to make dictionaries of such languages in terms of stems only. Expansions containing prefixes and/or infixes must be searched for under the appropriate stem. But this requires considerably more grammatical sophistication on the part of the user than is ever required, for example, on the part of the user of the ordinary English or French dictionary. Words found in actual texts would have to be analyzed before they could be looked up. The human dictionary-user might proceed by trial and error, but how could a machine be programmed to cope with this kind of dictionary? On the other hand, if we try to follow our dictum and list everything in strict alphabetical order, the number of entries becomes enormous. It would almost seem to be necessary to make a separate dictionary for every text.

In spite of special types of difficulties that may be encountered from time to time, and from language to language, the dictum remains a highly useful one which can profitably be much more widely followed to improve the quality of bilingual dictionaries in general.

NOTES

[1] In the realm of monolingual dictionaries, however, Random House's ACD contains more of these features than any other dictionary I know.

[2] Danish-English dictionaries printed in Denmark are the only dictionaries I know which use English 'four-letter words' to translate their Danish counterparts. The result is not obscene — it is simply straightforward and accurate translation.

[3] In the realm of monolingual dictionaries, on the other hand, we again find that Random House's ACD provides exactly what is here recommended. If it has proven desirable to provide this information even for the native speaker, think how much more useful it would be in a bilingual dictionary.

15 | The Study of American Indian Languages:
A Brief Historical Sketch

The study of the languages of the American Indian has
spanned a period of nearly five centuries. During the course of these
centuries different reasons for their study and different approaches to
their study have been paramount at different times. In connection
with the Spanish Conquest, especially in Mexico and Peru, we find
that much attention was given to the preparation of grammars and dictionaries of the new languages that were encountered, often enough
with the devoted efforts of converts who knew the languages being
described or else who worked in close collaboration with the missionaries who were engaged in making converts. In the 1500s scholars were ignorant of the great diversity among languages; they knew
Latin, Greek, and sometimes Hebrew and tended to describe a new
language in terms of concepts familiar to them from these languages.

Early grammars were very early indeed and were being composed and printed both in Mexico and Peru. We need only mention a
grammar of Nahuatl by Andrés de Olmos which appeared in 1547
(McQuown 1967:3), one of Tarascan by Maturino Gilberti in 1558, and
one of Inca by Domingo de Santo Tomás in 1560 (Rowe 1974). Many
others appeared in increasing volume throughout the succeeding
decades. Although we may regret the extensive use of the Latin model
for the grammatical studies of the early missionaries, we owe a great
debt to them. In more than one instance an early missionary grammar or translation, say of a religious treatise, is the only record we
have of a language now extinct. Thus Timucua, an extinct language of
central Florida, was preserved for us by Francisco Pareja whose
Arte de la lengua timuquana is dated 1614. Other famous early works
on North American languages came along in the seventeenth century.
These include Roger Williams' A key into the language of America,

an extensive vocabulary of Narragansett published in London in 1643, John Eliot's translation of the Bible into Natick or the language of the Massachuset which appeared in 1663, and Eliot's The Indian grammar begun; or, an essay to bring the Indian language into rules, published in 1666. Timucua is not closely related to any other known language, but Narragansett and Natick belong to the widespread Algonkian linguistic family and even though these particular languages are now no longer spoken, we can learn a great deal about them through comparison with other Algonkian languages.

But grammars, dictionaries, and translations are written by men who are able to dwell long in the place where the language is spoken. Other kinds of activities by men of more mobile habits, were also taking place in the New World in these early centuries. For example, in the more northerly reaches of North America we have the voyages of Jacques Cartier in the Gulf of Saint Lawrence in 1534 and 1535-36. We learn that as a result of these voyages, captives from the area were taken back to France. There an unknown man of education (Cartier was presumably illiterate) elicited vocabularies from these captives which were included in publications describing the voyages. The language belongs to the Iroquoian family; it is sometimes called Laurentian since it is not identical with any of the present-day Iroquoian languages (Chafe 1973:1169). Among other famous early vocabulary collections may be mentioned the Virginia Algonkian vocabulary of Captain John Smith (1612). And at about the same time William Strachey collected a similar vocabulary which was not published until 1849 (Siebert 1975:291).

Throughout the seventeenth century the two kinds of activity, (1) the missionaries' writing of grammars and associated materials and (2) the explorers' collection of vocabularies, continued unabated. By the eighteenth century the age of exploration was in full swing and explorers of many nations were in keen competition with one another. They wanted to know about the raw materials of the new places and so collected plant and animal specimens, mineral specimens and all other things which attracted their attention. In this context there developed what might be called the 'natural history' approach to languages and it first took the form of a mania for collection. If it had been as easy to collect languages as it was to collect botanical and mineral specimens, this would have been a very fruitful period in the history of linguistics. Travellers and explorers filled their notebooks with word lists, and while these have not been without value, they represented far less of a language than a leaf represents of a plant. Still such efforts were unquestionably better than failure to obtain any linguistic information at all.

Interestingly enough, a further impetus toward the collection of vocabularies came toward the end of the eighteenth century when a new discovery was made about language. It was found that by comparing the vocabularies and grammatical forms of various languages, some of them could be seen to have striking resemblances so that (as it was finally determined) they could be assumed to have derived from the same ancestral language. This was a revolutionary discovery when compared to the belief previously held by many that Hebrew, the language of the Old Testament, was the ancestor of all languages.

Although this discovery pertained primarily to the languages of Europe, i.e., their relationship or lack of it to each other and the relationship of some of them to languages in India, it was almost immediately realized that the discovery had applicability to American languages also. In 1787 Thomas Jefferson, concerned that the languages of the American Indian would disappear before their history and origin was understood, declared that it was of the utmost importance for vocabularies to be made of as many American Indian languages as possible in order to preserve them so that future scholars might be enabled to determine their interrelationships even if the languages themselves were no longer spoken. Even though his notion of the value of vocabularies in this endeavour was exaggerated, his notion that material on as many languages as possible was needed was admirable.

In the Old World, Catherine the Great ordered a compilation of as many vocabularies of the world as possible. Some of the results were published in Adelung and Vater's Mithradates (1806-17). In the New World somewhat similar efforts were being made by Benjamin Smith Barton (1797) who hoped in this way to be able to show that the languages of the American Indian were related to the languages of Asia. Out of these and similar efforts scholars were beginning to gain some notion of the number and variety of the linguistic families of the world.

The beginning of the nineteenth century saw an increase in American scholarly interest in American Indian languages. Not only were more and more vocabularies being collected, in accordance with Jefferson's advice, but other kinds of collection were also being pursued. Peter S. Duponceau, as corresponding secretary of the newly organized American Philosophical Society, was making efforts to obtain manuscripts of materials on American Indian languages to be deposited in the Library of the Society. In the course of this interest he corresponded with the Moravian missionary John Heckwelder and learned about the peculiarities of Delaware, an Algonkian language (Duponceau 1819). Duponceau was also well familiar with the early Spanish grammars of South American and Mexican languages. John Pickering, who was also working at about the same time, was likewise familiar with these early works. This is of interest because it marks a watershed in American Indian linguistics. After Duponceau and Pickering, North American linguists (except for those who specialized in Latin America) tended to neglect these earlier works or even denigrate them as being virtually useless. Duponceau of course was an armchair linguist; in fact he little understood the nature of field work. But when anthropological linguistics became largely a field discipline, the interest in works of earlier centuries disappeared.

John Pickering performed many valuable services in the form of editing earlier unpublished works on Northeastern languages. For example, he edited the famous Abnaki Dictionary by Father Rasles (1883), the original manuscript of which is in the Harvard Library. This work, with glosses in French, was composed in 1699, more than a century and a half before it was published. But Pickering was not solely an armchair linguist. He also had direct contact with an unwritten language. He worked on Cherokee with the help of a young Cherokee boy who was attending school in Worcester. In fact he prepared a grammar of Cherokee (1830) and had hoped that his orthography for the language might be adopted by the Cherokee Indians for their own use. Unfortunately for this idea, however, Sequoyah, the inventor of the Cherokee syllabary, had just succeeded in teaching many of his fellow tribesmen in North Carolina how to write their language through the use of his syllabary. So Pickering abandoned his idea of promulgating the use of his Latin-based alphabet for Cherokee. Still, Pickering's efforts in this direction were not entirely wasted. He had developed a phonetic alphabet, one of the most important

features of which was the use of the Italian values for the vowels, and
this was intended to be used in writing down unwritten languages. It
was used by missionaries in Fiji, for instance, as well as in North
America.

We have now hinted at two important things which engaged
the attention of persons interested in unwritten languages throughout
most of the rest of the nineteenth century, namely, (1) the collection
of vocabularies and other linguistic materials and (2) finding a way of
writing down these languages so that all sounds, including the unusual
ones, could be adequately represented.

The collection of vocabularies, which was greatly facilitated
by development of ways of writing the languages down, led to one of
the most important achievements of the century, namely a careful and
systematic comparison of these vocabularies with one another and a
satisfactory determination of which languages were alike and which
were different. Though the work of Barton and Jefferson and others
should not be overlooked, a turning-point leading to real progress in
the problem of the relationships of these languages came almost by
accident. In 1823, the great German naturalist and explorer, Baron
Alexander von Humboldt asked Albert Gallatin (who had been
Jefferson's Secretary of the Treasury) for a classification of the languages of America. Gallatin prepared one and then sent off his only
copy. Later on, when the American Antiquarian Society asked for a
copy with a view to publication, he had to make another compilation.
This was fortunately based on much fuller materials than the first one
and, in fact, served to provide the first real breakthrough in the classification problems of the eastern part of North America. It was published in 1836. He realized, however, that adequate materials to
classify the languages of the western part of the continent were lacking. Then the publication of Horatio Hale's vocabularies containing,
among other things, materials collected in California and the Northwest (1968 [reprint]) made it possible for Gallatin to publish a revised and greatly expanded classification in 1848.

Gallatin's work provided the essential background for what
was perhaps the major accomplishment in the field of American Indian languages in the nineteenth century, namely, the definitive classification of the languages of North America north of Mexico by Major

John Wesley Powell in a publication which appeared in 1891. (In contrast with this observe that a similarly satisfactory classification of the languages of South America has not yet been achieved, though a good foundation for this was laid by Powell's contemporary, Daniel G. Brinton, in a work published in the same year). Some years earlier Powell had become director of the Bureau of Ethnology as well as of the Geological Survey and in connection with this he directed that as many vocabularies as possible should be compiled for North America. In order to ease the way for such compilations he prepared schedules of words and paradigms which he expected the investigators to fill out (1880). The kinship schedules were especially full. He also recognized the need for an adequate orthography and in connection with his schedules he gave suggestions for ways in which the investigators could handle the various sounds they were likely to meet. The work done at the Bureau of American Ethnology under the direction of Powell constituted a new era in anthropological linguistics. For the first time it could be said to have become professionalized. Of course Powell himself was an explorer and acquired his interest in this kind of work in connection with his own collection of vocabularies among the Ute Indians. And some of the workers had been missionaries, but by and large it could be said that this was the era in which professionalism developed. In particular, a new kind of linguistic scholar could be said to have appeared, namely the field linguist. While much earlier work had been collected from native speakers wherever they might happen to be, such work, whether the preparation of a grammar or the collection of a vocabulary, had been done as an adjunct to some other kind of work. But now we saw scholars being sent into the field for the sole purpose of collecting material on the Indian languages. They wisely saw also that it was important to record the folklore in the native language. In other words, to collect texts. This was entirely different from the translation of Biblical passages or missionary treatises into the native languages. Text collection reflected an attitude which focused upon the Indian language itself rather than making use of the language for some ulterior purpose. The Bureau thus set the tone for this kind of work for the future. Grammars were written and dictionaries and volumes of texts were compiled (Sapir 1917b). The task was an endless one, though, and the Bureau also encouraged the accumulation of more material by its willingness, on occasion, to purchase manuscripts containing materials of this kind.

Much progress had been made in the study of American Indian linguistics in the nineteenth century, but another new era was about to begin. Powell, with his genius for organization, was the right man to solve the major classification problems, but some of his ideas about language in general were highly idiosyncratic and were therefore not suitable for a theoretical model. Thus in one place he said (1891:112):

> He who studies only one Indian language and learns its manifold curious grammatic devices, its wealth of words, its capacity of expression, is speedily convinced of its superiority to all other Indian tongues, and not infrequently to all languages by whomsoever spoken. If like admirable characteristics are asserted for other tongues he is apt to view them as derivatives from one original. Thus he is led to overlook the great truth that the mind of man is everywhere practically the same, and that the innumerable differences of its products are indices merely of different stages of growth or are the results of different conditions of environment. In its development the human mind is limited by no boundaries of tribe or race.

The next stage in the development of linguistic theory was destined to take a point of view almost diametrically opposed in several respects to that expressed by Powell. It was introduced by Franz Boas, who dominated the field of American Indian linguistics (as well as the other branches of anthropology) through most of the first half of the twentieth century. His approach came to be known as 'linguistic relativism' (or 'cultural relativism' when applied to culture in general). In his great essay on language, written as the 'Introduction' to the Handbook of American Indian Languages (1911) he nowhere mentions Powell's name, but a careful reading of what he has to say indicates that he was at pains to refute some of the latter's most cherished ideas. Boas was very fortunate in having some of his early experiences with such difficult languages as Eskimo and Kwakiutl. These languages were so totally different from the usual European languages that he was forced to consider a new approach to the problem of describing languages. He saw that the imposition of the usual categories of European grammar on an American Indian language, as was all too often done in missionary grammars, could only result in distortion.

If each language was to be described in its own terms, then it was clear that the new emphasis had to be on internal analysis, not history. In referring to the first volume of grammatical sketches which he edited, he said (1911:77):

> The following grammatical sketches have been contributed by investigators, each of whom has made a special study of the linguistic stock of which he treats. . . . Moreover, the method of treatment has been throughout an analytical one. No attempt has been made to compare the forms of the Indian grammars with the grammars of English, Latin, or even among themselves; but in each case the psychological groupings which are given depend entirely upon the inner form of each language. In other words, the grammar has been treated as though an intelligent Indian was going to develop the forms of his own thoughts by an analysis of his own form of speech.

This might be called the Boasian manifesto and it became the basis of the later-to-be-named 'structuralist school' of linguistics, and by the 1940s and 1950s it was the basis of much linguistic work on European languages as well as on American and other so-called preliterate languages.

Following Boas, the great leaders in the study of anthropological linguistics were Edward Sapir, one of Boas's students, and Leonard Bloomfield, who had been trained in Germanic philology. Other students of Boas, whose primary focus was cultural anthropology, also made contributions to linguistics. Among these were John R. Swanton, Alfred L. Kroeber, and Paul Radin.

Sapir's impact on the field was manifested in several important ways. First of all, he undertook to describe American Indian languages in accordance with the Boasian dictum. He wrote brilliant analytical grammars of Takelma (Oregon) and Southern Paiute (Utah) and collected extensive materials on many other important languages, including Nootka (Vancouver Island), Yana (California), Hupa (California), and Navajo (Arizona and New Mexico), which can be used as the basis for the writing of grammars by others as has already been done for Navajo by Harry Hoijer (Sapir and Hoijer 1967),

At one period in his life Sapir was also extremely interested in the problem of the classification of the American Indian languages. After Powell, interest in this matter had skipped a generation, so to speak. But gradually, many scholars were beginning to feel that the Powell scheme was too conservative, that there must be connections between at least some of the families that Powell had kept separated. As a consequence, a period of reductionism set in, and scholars competed with one another in proposing new amalgamations of formerly separated families. Roland B. Dixon and Alfred L. Kroeber (1919), faced with twenty-two distinct Powellian families in California alone, gradually reduced the number in several stages, and Sapir (1913, 1917a) participated in this also. John R. Swanton (1915, 1919, 1924), working in the Southeast, introduced a number of reductions there and Paul Radin (1919) made many suggestions about even greater reductions for North America as a whole. But the greatest reductionist of them all was Sapir, who finally classified the immense diversity of North American languages into six superstocks (1929). Although he is best known among cultural historians and archaeologists for this, he probably never intended for the scheme to be taken as seriously as it was. Indeed, his intention was to break the tyrannical hold of the Powell classification for as he said in 1917b: 81:

> While nothing is further from my mind than to minimize the
> great usefulness of Powell's classification, I may be par-
> doned for regretting the too definitive and dogmatic form in
> which it was presented. This has had the effect until recent-
> ly of discouraging further researches into the problem of lin-
> guistic groupings in America.

Perhaps with the hope of avoiding a similar judgment for his own classification he warns that it is "suggestive but far from demonstrable in all its features at the present time" (1929: 129).

Unlike some language classifiers, Sapir was also intensely interested in promulgating the use of the methods of comparative linguistics, as developed in the Indo-European field, to the comparison of languages within several of the American Indian linguistic families, particularly Uto-Aztecan and Athapaskan. This was an interest he shared with Leonard Bloomfield (Sapir 1931: 297-306). In addition, Sapir was interested in comparing more distantly related languages,

as was done in his highly controversial comparison of Wiyot and
Yurok (Ritwan) of Northern California with the Algonkian family which
lay entirely east of the Rocky Mountains. An even more controversial comparison was that which he made among Haida and Tlingit and
Athapaskan (the socalled Na-Déné hypothesis). His search for more
distant congeners of American Indian languages led him even further
into the study of a possible connection between his hypothetical and
controversial Na-Déné stock and the Sino-Tibetan stock of Asia. This
material was never published. In attempting to make these wider connections, Sapir raised problems and issues which are still far from
solution. An exception must be made to the Algonkian-Ritwan or Algonkian-Wiyot-Yurok relationship which is now generally accepted
(Haas 1958). The other suggestions remain unestablished.

        Another important student of American Indian languages who
belonged to this period was Leonard Bloomfield. He worked most of
his life on the description and comparison of several Algonkian languages. But his descriptive results in the form of grammars of Eastern Ojibwa (1957) and Menomini (1962) were only published posthumously under the editorship of Charles F. Hockett. His comparative work on Algonkian had an equally important result. He demonstrated in a way that none could doubt or refute that it is possible to
reconstruct proto-morphemes by the comparison of related unwritten
languages with as much precision and accuracy as had been done in
the comparison of European languages with their long written traditions. This he accomplished in his reconstruction of Proto-Algonkian.
In my opinion his grammatical sketch "Algonquian" (1946) is his
greatest work.

        By mid-twentieth century Boas, Sapir and Bloomfield were
all dead. In the meantime many of their students had attained positions at major universities throughout the country. Some of these
still had a primary interest in the study of American Indian languages,
though others had had their attention diverted to unwritten and written languages of other parts of the world. Of especial importance to
the continuing growth of American Indian linguistics was the founding,
in 1953, of the Survey of California Indian Languages (later Survey of
California and Other Indian Languages) at the University of California,
Berkeley, under the direction of Murray B. Emeneau and later Mary
R. Haas. This provided a great boost in the study of the languages of

California and nearby parts of the West. Several years after the
founding of the Survey of California Indian Languages, Laurence C.
Thompson of the University of Washington (and later of the University
of Hawaii) set up the Northwest Survey of Languages in 1962 under a
grant from the National Science Foundation. Many other universities
have encouraged field work on American Indian languages by individual students; for example, Floyd Lounsbury of Yale University, who
has been prominent in fostering the study of Iroquoian languages,
Charles F. Voegelin of Indiana University, who has encouraged students to work on some of the Yuman, Uto-Aztecan, and Tanoan languages, Norman A. McQuown of the University of Chicago, who has
fostered the study of Mayan languages, and others.

It is remarkable that interest in doing field work on unwritten
languages has thrived during the past thirty years in spite of very important changes that have taken place in the theoretical approach to
linguistics. During the ascendancy of the Bloomfieldian tradition
(from approximately 1930-60) there was a tendency to downplay the
importance of many of the broader aspects of linguistics that were so
interesting to Sapir and his students. Even in the narrower confines
of synchronic description, process had to be eliminated because it
was considered historical and history (in linguistic description) had
to be eschewed at all costs. And in the end the cost was very high
indeed.

Toward the end of the Bloomfieldian era Zellig Harris published Structural Linguistics (1951) which hinted at trouble to come.
With the publication in 1957 of Syntactic Structures by Noam Chomsky,
a student of Harris's, a new era had clearly set in. The Chomskyans
proceeded to throw out almost everything the Bloomfieldians had so
painstakingly constructed, even the most cherished artifact of all,
the phoneme. (The word is still used but in a different sense.) Field
work was of little interest to either Harris or Chomsky. Consequently, what is of interest to us here is what kinds of effects the Chomskyan revolution had upon the study of American Indian languages.
Well, in truth, the effects were both good and bad. The chief good
effect was that it freed linguistics from some of the too narrow constrictions of the Bloomfieldian methodology and particularly, of many
post-Bloomfieldian encumbrances. Many of the facets of language
which had so fascinated Sapir again took on importance in the overall

linguistic picture. One thinks particularly of his interest in the relations between psychology and language, society and language, culture and language, and the like. Indeed we now have such subdisciplines as psycholinguistics, sociolinguistics, and language acquisition, to mention only a few. And along with this has come the establishment of several new journals to treat of such subjects.

On the other hand, the bad effects of the Chomskyan revolution were in the beginning quite devastating. One of their principles is that only a native speaker knows his language well enough to work out its grammar. On its face the principle may seem reasonable but it had an especially dampening effect on American Indian linguistics because we have had so often to work on languages with only a few speakers left, too old to be made into linguists even if they should so desire. Consequently, young graduate students, many of whom in the past would have looked forward to carrying out field work on an unwritten language of North or South America, Africa, Australia, or Southeast Asia, were now confronted with the fact that they themselves were native speakers only of English. Those who were required to adhere to this principle by their teachers therefore worked only on English. Interest in doing field work went into a serious decline in many graduate centers. But this difficulty has by now been largely overcome in two ways, both with fortunate results. Within the terms of the dictum that only a native speaker can work out the grammar of his language, unwritten languages would be forever neglected unless a speaker of such a language was trained in linguistics. But by now some native speakers have been trained in linguistics, a few quite successfully by Kenneth Hale of the Massachusetts Institute of Technology. And there are sure to be many further successes along these lines. But lest it be thought that this is something entirely new, it should be remembered that Boas also trained native speakers whenever he could — a notable case is that of Ella Deloria and her work on the Dakota language (Boas and Deloria 1941).

But training native speakers to be linguists cannot even begin to take care of the whole problem. There are still hundreds of unwritten languages — what are we to do about them? At this point another principle has come to the rescue. Concentration on one's own language somehow seems to lead to the conclusion that there is a universal grammar that can be deduced from one's own language.

Now this is certainly not a new idea but the very one that Boas and his followers had been at such pains to dispel. Fortunately it has not become necessary for us to fall back into the beliefs of the pre-Boasian period. Instead in recent years there has been another kind of linguistic activity, standing somewhat aside from both the Bloomfieldian and the Chomskyan paradigms, which has come to the rescue in this impasse. The activity referred to has been the work of Joseph H. Greenberg and his staff at Stanford University on language typology and language universals. Clearly such a project cannot be pursued by limiting it to the perusal of grammars of languages written by authors who are native speakers thereof. Indeed for the purposes of a universal project, the more languages for which information can be obtained the better. Happily, then, there is now a renewed interest in all kinds of languages spoken near and far and it is by necessity accepted that information on most of them may have to be supplied through field work done by nonnative speakers. Consequently, there has been a renewal of interest in field work. Nevertheless, this renewal of interest has not always been an unmitigated blessing. In their search for universal tendencies in as large a number of languages as possible, some scholars have taken an atomistic approach. In other words, they have obtained examples of relative clauses, auxiliary verbs, the copula, and so on, from speakers (or grammars) of as many languages as possible without regard to anything else in the language.

At this point it may be instructive to return to Boas and his approach to language. As I review the various theoretical upheavals of the past six or seven decades, I am struck by the fact that we can still learn much from Boas. In the present climate of interest in the problem of language universals, we must not overlook the importance of the holistic approach so emphatically endorsed by Boas. A language must be understood and described as a whole. It is not a thing of bits and pieces, haphazardly strung together. It must be seen and described as a whole. But once that is done, its parts can be compared with parts of other holistically described languages, though it may turn out that the comparable parts are embedded in rather different matrices. Hence the results may not seem so pat as when done by the present piecemeal process. But if that is so then some theoretical modification may be required. In any event the integrity of a language as a unified whole must be protected.

There remains another aspect of Boas's thought that deserves attention in the light of some of our present-day activities. It will be remembered that he had little interest in classificatory linguistics, not because he did not believe in the genetic classification of languages, but because he deplored the grand reductionism of Dixon and Kroeber, of Swanton, and particularly of Radin and Sapir. His stance was completely misunderstood by his famous students. Kroeber even took the position that Boas was uninterested in history, a criticism that Boas explicitly denied. I think he was right in doing so. Since he accepted the Powellian classification of North American languages and felt that we were not yet ready to go much beyond that, he had little interest in classificatory problems per se. And since little had been done on unwritten languages in what is technically, though confusingly, known as 'comparative linguistics', he did not give much attention to this problem. It was later developed by others, particularly Sapir and Bloomfield, as has been mentioned. Nevertheless, he was aware of the problem, for he said (1911:77):

> There is not the slightest doubt that, in all Indian languages processes have occurred analagous to those processes which are historically known and to which the modern Indo-European languages owe their present form.

And further (1911:78):

> The results of our investigation [of the present state of each language] must be supplemented at a later time by a thorough analysis and comparison of all the dialects of each linguistic stock.

In his repudiation of the extremes of reductionism practiced by Sapir and others he was ahead of his time again.

Sapir's classification of the stocks of North America into six superstocks stood for several decades. In the 1950s Morris Swadesh (1959) introduced even further reductions, eventually on a worldwide scale, and combined this with his innovative ideas about glottochronology, or lexicostatistics, and the possibility of dating the length of time two languages had been separated (Hymes 1960). Joseph Greenberg has also been engaged in postulating distant relationships and in proposing new broad classifications, particularly in Africa (1966) and South America (1960). Others, however, were beginning to proceed in the opposite direction, namely the splitting up of some of Sapir's superstocks, at first usually to put the parts together in new combinations. Several people have participated in making proposals for new combinations and not a few are still engaged in this activity. However, the pendulum seems now to be swinging gradually toward an increase in the amount of splitting being done. So we now have the classic opposition of lumpers vs. splitters. In our proposals about the classification of North American languages we have clearly moved in cycles of splitting and lumping, more or less successively. We have not gone back completely to the basic Powellian classification but we are closer to it now than at any time since 1890. Nevertheless some of Sapir's insights have stood the test of time, particularly in the matter of the relationship of Wiyot and Yurok to Algonkian, which was, ironically, one of the two of his reductions which Boas objected to most strenuously.

While splitting appears to be in the ascendancy now, there will in the future be more lumping, but in a different way and after a fresh look at all the proposed components.

There is one more aspect of Boas's interest in history which deserves more than passing mention. One of Boas's strongest arguments against lumping was his clear recognition that all kinds of traits are shared across genetic boundaries. Borrowed words were not at issue. He was impressed by the broad areal traits of phonology and morphology with which he was so familiar in his work on Northwest Coast languages. But in spite of this the problems of genetic linguistics received more attention than areal linguistics. Then came Murray Emeneau's seminal article "India as a Linguistic Area" (1956). And about the same time Charles F. Voegelin and others were stressing the need for such studies in regard to American Indian languages.

By now we are ready to agree that Boas was right when he perceived the distribution of areal traits as a historical process. In other words, history does not reside in genetic relationship alone but is equally important in areal distributions. Now, half a century after Boas's insistence on this point and twenty years after Emeneau's

article appeared, one of the most exciting fields in anthropological
linguistics is areal linguistics. In fact genetic and areal studies are
no longer considered antithetical, but are frequently carried on and
discussed side by side.

There are literally hundreds of things that I have failed to
discuss in my attempt to give a brief history of nearly five hundred
years of American Indian linguistics. Perhaps I have spent too much
time on the early centuries of our discipline. On the other hand, we
are usually far too negligent of our historical antecedents. Duponceau
and Pickering had the knowledge they did in part from their perusal of
sixteenth and seventeenth century grammars. In spite of the fact that
these early works were written in the Latin mold — a device that was
so deplored by Boas and Bloomfield and their followers — these grammars are not entirely valueless. Every so often we 'rediscover'
something that was already well known centuries ago. Scholars as
learned as Bloomfield and Franklin Edgerton (Edgerton 1943) thought
that Schoolcraft had invented the terms 'inclusive' and 'exclusive' for
a common division of the first person dual and plural. But these categories were first discovered by the early grammarians of the Inca and
Aymara languages and these terms or near synonyms appear in sixteenth century grammars (Haas 1969). Another very early interest
was in the multiplicity of 'verbs for eating' which fascinated the earliest grammarians as much as it does Herbert Landar (1964) and
Brent Berlin (1967) today.

But in spite of all the things that we have failed to do, major
accomplishments are vast, particularly in the study of North American and Mexican languages. In the nearly five centuries that the languages of the Americas have been under study, we have acquired a
deeper understanding of both the differences and the similarities of
these languages to one another.

In order to reach this understanding, we have had to prepare
dozens of grammars, dictionaries, and volumes of texts. At the same
time we have made much progress in establishing genetic relationships, especially at the family level (as opposed to the phylum level,
which remains controversial), and we are on our way to a better understanding of the linguistic areas which so often cut across the genetic boundaries. It will not be an exaggeration to say that the

continuing study of American Indian languages remains one of the
great challenges to linguistic scholarship.

NOTE

This paper is based in part on lectures on the history of the study of
American Indian languages given at Barnard College in 1971 and at
Northwestern University in 1975, and in part on a paper presented at
the meetings of the American Anthropological Association in November 1976 entitled "Anthropological Linguistics: History" and published
in Perspectives on Anthropology 1976, ed. by Anthony F. C. Wallace
et al., Special Publication of the American Anthropological Association No. 10, pp. 33-47 (1977).

REFERENCES

Adelung and Vater. 1806-17. Mithradates.

Barton, Benjamin Smith. 1797. New Views of the Origin of the
        Tribes and Nations of North America.

Berlin, Brent. 1967. Categories of Eating in Tseltal and Navaho.
        IJAL 33.1-6.

Bloomfield, Leonard. 1933. Language. New York: Henry Holt.

_____ 1946. Algonquian. Linguistic Structures of Native America,
        by Harry Hoijer and others. VPFA 6.

_____ 1957. Eastern Ojibwa. Ann Arbor: University of Michigan
        Press.

_____ 1962. The Menomini Language. New Haven and London:
        Yale University Press.

Boas, Franz. 1911. Introduction. Handbook of American Indian Lan-
        guages. BAE-B 40/1.1-83. Washington.

Boas, Franz and Ella Deloria. 1941. Dakota Grammar. Memoirs
        of the National Academy of Sciences, vol. XXIII, Second
        Memoir. Washington.

Brinton, Daniel G. 1891. The American Race. New York.

Chafe, Wallace L. 1973. Siouan, Iroquoian, and Caddoan. Current
        Trends in Linguistics, ed. by Thomas A. Sebeok. 10(2).
        1164-209. The Hague: Mouton.

Chomsky, Noam. 1957. Syntactic Structures. The Hague: Mouton.

Dixon, Roland B. and A. L. Kroeber. 1919. Linguistic Families of
        California. UCPAAE 16.47-118.

Duponceau, Peter S. 1819. Report of the Historical and Literary
Committee of the American Philosophical Society. Transactions of the Historical and Literary Committee of the American Philosophical Society, Vol. I, xi-xvi.

Edgerton, Franklin. 1943. Notes on Early American Work in Linguistics. Proceedings of the American Philosophical Society 87.25-34. Philadelphia.

Eliot, John. 1666. The Indian Grammar Begun: or, An Essay to
Bring the Indian Languages into Rules. Cambridge: Marma-
duke Johnson.

Emeneau, Murray B. 1956. India as a Linguistic Area. Language
32.3-16.

Gallatin, Albert. 1836. A Synopsis of the Indian Tribes within the
United States East of the Rocky Mountains and in the British
and Russian Possessions of North America. Trans. and
Coll. American Antiquarian Society. 2.1-422. Cambridge.
_____ 1848. Hale's Indians of North-west America, and Vocabu-
laries of North America, with an Introduction. Trans. of the
American Ethnological Society. 2.xxiii-clxxx, 1-130. New
York.

Greenberg, Joseph H. 1960. The General Classification of Central
and South American Languages. Selected Papers of the 5th
International Congress of Anthropological and Ethnological
Sciences, pp. 791-794.
_____ 1966. The Languages of Africa. The Hague: Mouton.
_____ , ed. 1963. Universals of Language. Cambridge: M.I.T.
Press.

Haas, Mary R. 1958. Algonkian-Ritwan: The End of a Controversy.
IJAL 24.159-73.
_____ 1969. 'Exclusive' and 'Inclusive': A Look at Early Usage.
IJAL. 35.1-6.

Hale, Horatio. 1968. Ethnography and Philology. U.S. Exploring
Expedition 1838-1842. Ridgewood, N.J.: The Gregg Press.

Harris, Zellig. 1951. Structural Linguistics. Chicago: University
of Chicago Press.

Hoijer, Harry. 1973. History of American Indian Linguistics. Current Trends in Linguistics. 10(2). 651-67.

Hymes, Dell. 1960. Lexicostatistics so Far. Current Anthropology
1.(1).3-44.

Hymes, Dell, ed. 1974. Studies in the History of Linguistics.
Bloomington: Indiana University Press.

Landar, Herbert. 1964. Seven Navaho Verbs of Eating, IJAL 30.
        94-6.
McQuown, Norman A. 1967. History of Studies in Middle American
        Linguistics. Handbook of Middle American Indians, vol. 5:
        Linguistics, ed. by Norman A. McQuown, pp. 3-7. Austin:
        University of Texas Press.
Mandelbaum, David G., ed. 1949. Selected Writings of Edward Sapir.
        Berkeley and Los Angeles: University of California Press.
Pareja, Francisco. 1886. Arte de la lengua timuquana, compuesta
        en 1614. Bibliothèque Linguistique Américaine, vol. 11.
        Edited by Lucien Adam and Julien Vinson. Paris.
Pickering, John. 1830. A Grammar of the Cherokee Language.
        Boston.
Powell, John W. 1880. Introduction to the Study of Indian Languages
        with words, phrases and sentences to be collected. Washing-
        ton.
_____ 1891. Indian Linguistic Families of America North of Mexi-
        co. Seventh Annual Report of the Bureau of [American]
        Ethnology, 7.7-142. Washington.
Radin, Paul. 1919. The Genetic Relationship of the North American
        Indian Languages. UCPAAE 14(5). 489-502.
Rasles, Father Sebastian. 1883. A Dictionary of the Abnaki Lan-
        guage. Memoirs, American Academy of Arts and Sciences
        1.370-574.
Rowe, John Howland. 1974. Sixteenth and Seventeenth Century Gram-
        mars. In Hymes 1974, pp. 361-379.
Sapir, Edward. 1913. Wiyot and Yurok, Algonkin Languages of Cali-
        fornia. AA 15.617-46.
_____ 1917a. The Position of Yana in the Hokan Stock. UCPAAE
        13.1-34.
_____ 1917b. Linguistic Publications of the Bureau of American
        Ethnology, a General Review. IJAL 1.76-81.
_____ 1921. Language: An Introduction to the Study of Speech. New
        York: Harcourt, Brace.
_____ 1929. Central and North American Indian Languages. Ency-
        clopaedia Britannica[14], 5.128-41. Reprinted in Mandelbaum
        (1949).
_____ 1931. The Concept of Phonetic Law as Tested in Primitive
        Languages by Leonard Bloomfield. Methods in Social
        Science: A Case Book, ed. by Stuart A. Rice, pp. 297-306.
        Chicago. Reprinted in Mandelbaum (1949).

Sapir, Edward and Harry Hoijer. 1967. The Phonology and Mor-
       phology of the Navaho Language. UCPL 50. Berkeley and
       Los Angeles: University of California Press.
Siebert, Frank T., Jr. 1975. Resurrecting Virginia Algonquian from
       the Dead: The Reconstituted and Historical Phonology of
       Powhatan. In James M. Crawford, ed., Studies in South-
       eastern Indian Languages, pp. 285-453. Athens: The Uni-
       versity of Georgia Press.
Smith, John. 1612. A Map of Virginia, with a Description of the
       Country. Oxford: Joseph Barnes.
Swadesh, Morris. 1959. Linguistics as an Instrument of Prehistory.
       Southwestern Journal of Anthropology 15. 20-35.
Swanton, John R. 1915. Linguistic Postion of the Tribes of Southern
       Texas and Northeastern Mexico. AA 13.17-40.
_____ 1919. A Structural and Lexical Comparison of the Tunica,
       Chitimacha, and Atakapa Languages. BAE-B 68. Washing-
       ton.
_____ 1924. The Mushkogean Connection of the Natchez Language.
       IJAL. 3.46-75.
Williams, Roger. 1643. A Key into the Language of America.
       London.

16 The Problem of Classifying American Indian Languages: From Duponceau to Powell

1. Introduction

Throughout the nineteenth century the most critical problem in regard to the American Indian languages was to find some method of classifying them. When the century opened, not even the constituency of the Indo-European stock was fully known, so it is not surprising that at first the problem of classifying the languages of the New World was not specifically or solely their genetic classification. Often enough what interest there was in genetic classification was motivated by attempts to prove kinship with languages of the Old World— sometimes with Hebrew, sometimes with other languages, especially those of Asia. A new focus of attention was emerging in the problem of the overall structural classification of these languages as differentiated from languages in other parts of the world, i.e. their typological classification, and, in consequence, their ranking in terms of higher and lower. At the same time it is apparent that the separation between the two types of classification, genetic and typological, was not always altogether clear in the minds of classifiers. It is interesting to observe that it was in this context that discussion of the problem Grammar or Lexicon? first emerged. It is also interesting to discover that while this problem remained something of an issue throughout the century, the actual context in which it was debated gradually shifted.

By the end of the century the basic genealogical classification of the North American languages was almost completely settled by the appearance of J. W. Powell's Linguistic families of North America north of Mexico.[1] At the beginning of the century, on the other hand, the necessity of setting the genealogical classification of the various languages as a major goal in itself had not yet emerged as a critical problem. In this period much of the interest that was developing in

these languages was focused in another direction. Let us trace something of the history of these differing approaches.

2. Duponceau

2.1. It was in 1819, in a report of the Historical and Literary Committee to the American Philosophical Society, that (Peter)
Stephen Duponceau first promulgated a theory about the nature of
American Indian languages that was to be echoed throughout the century. He proclaimed that there seems to be "a wonderful organization,
which distinguishes the languages of the aborigines of this country
from all other idioms of the known world."[2] And later in the same
paragraph he refers to "those comprehensive grammatical forms
which appear to prevail with little variation among the aboriginal natives of America, from Greenland to Cape Horn." He named this
wonderful organization 'polysynthesis', and described it as follows:[3]

> A polysynthetic or syntactic construction of language is that
> in which the greatest number of ideas are comprised in the
> least number of words. This is done principally in two ways.
> 1. By a mode of compounding locutions which is not con-
> fined to joining two words together,. . .but by interweaving
> together the most significant sounds or syllables of each
> simple word, so as to form a compound that will awaken in the
> mind at once all the ideas singly expressed by the words
> from which they are taken. 2. By an analogous combination
> [of] the various parts of speech, particularly by means of the
> verb, so that its various forms and inflections will express
> not only the principal action, but the greatest possible num-
> ber of the moral ideas and physical objects connected with
> it, and will combine itself to the greatest extent with those
> conceptions which are the subject of other parts of speech,
> and in other languages require to be expressed by separate
> and distinct words. Such I take to be the general character
> of the Indian languages.

In the years that followed he examined the grammars of many
American languages but all seemed to him to reaffirm his earlier hypothesis. Nearly twenty years later he made it the basis of his

prize-winning essay, Mémoire sur le système grammatical des langues du quelques nations indiennes de l'Amérique du nord, where he
says:[4]

> Le caractère général des langues américaines consiste en
> ce qu'elles réunissent un grand nombre d'idées sous la forme
> d'un seul mot; c'est ce qui leur a fait donner par les philo-
> logues américains le nom de langues polysynthétiques. Ce
> nom leur convient à toutes (au moins à celles que nous con-
> naissons), depuis de Groenland jusqu'au Chili, sans qu'il
> nous ait été possible d'y découvrir une seule exception, de
> sorte que nous nous croyons en droit de présumer qu'il n'en
> existe point.

Some version of this statement, frequently enough identifiable even to
the phrase from Greenland to Chili or from Greenland to Cape Horn,
as in the earlier quotation, is repeated time and again throughout
most of the rest of the century by various writers on American Indian
languages. Some of these instances will be noted in other sections of
this paper.

Daniel Brinton, in an essay on Some Characteristics of
American Languages (first read in 1885) tells us that "Duponceau's
opinion found an able supporter in Wilhelm von Humboldt."[5] Humboldt,
who had proposed that there are four plans "on which languages combine words into sentences" (isolating, agglutinative, incorporative,
and inflective)[6]

> placed the American languages among those acting on the in-
> corporative plan. . . . The spirit of this system he defines to
> be, "to impress the unity of the sentence on the understanding
> by treating it, not as a whole composed of various words, but
> as one word."

2.2. But Duponceau did not confine himself to observations
on the uniformity of structure to be found in the Americas; he was also well aware of vocabulary differences. As an illustration of this
point he provides as Appendix A in his Mémoire a comparative vocabulary of an Algonkian language (Delaware) and of an Iroquoian

language (Onandaga) "a l'effet de demontrer <u>la difference totale</u> qui existe entre elles, quant à l'étymologie des mots." [Emphasis supplied.][7] In Appendix B he provides a comparative vocabulary of Algonkian languages and while he notes some differences he finds that "la ressemblance, dans le plus grand nombre, demontre une origine commune." Moreover, "aucun de ces mots ne paraît appartenir aux langues de la famille iroquoise."[8]

It is important to note that Duponceau was able to make the correct identification of many Algonkian cognates even though he had no real understanding of the nature of the sound correspondences. However, he used forty-five basic glosses and cited forms from thirty languages and dialects and this gave him enough scope so that, even without an understanding of sound correspondences, he came very close to being the first scholar to recognize that Gros Ventre (Atsina) is an Algonkian language.[9]

It should also be mentioned that Duponceau provided a list of stocks for much of the eastern part of the continent. We may quote Pickering, in English:[10]

> According to Mr. Du Ponceau,. . .the various Indian dialects on the Northern Atlantic side of America may be classed under four principal stocks or families: 1. The Karalit, or language of Greenland and the Esquimaux; 2. The Iroquois, called by some of the early French writers the <u>Huron</u>; 3. The Lenni-Lenápe, called by the French Canadians, Lénôpé, and by us, the Delaware; 4. The Floridian, or Southern stock.

Although correct in most of its main essentials, the deficiences are more appropriately discussed in 3 in connection with some of Pickering's ideas.

3. Pickering

John Pickering, another dedicated American Indian linguist of the period, accepted Duponceau's theory and described it in some

detail in a lengthy encyclopaedia artical published in 1831.[11] He
points out that since 1819

> all the observations which have been made on Indian lan-
> guages, at that time unknown, have confirmed his theory.
> . . . This result has shown that the astonishing variety of
> forms of human speech, which exists in the Eastern hemis-
> phere, is not to be found in the Western. Here we find no
> monosyllabic language, like the Chinese and its cognate id-
> ioms; no analytical language, like those of the North of Eur-
> ope, with their numerous expletive and auxiliary monosyl-
> lables, no such contrast is exhibited as that which is so
> striking to the most superficial observer, between the com-
> plication of the forms of the Basque language and the com-
> parative simplicity of its neighbors, the French and Spanish;
> but a <u>uniform system</u>, with such differences only as consti-
> tute varieties in natural objects, seems to pervade them all;
> and <u>this genus</u> of human languages has been called (by Mr. Du
> Ponceau) polysynthetic, from the numerous combinations of
> ideas which it presents in the form of words. [Emphasis
> supplied.]

At this time languages of Western America were only beginning to be known. As Pickering says, "We are not yet possessed of
sufficient data for determining how many principal stocks, or families of languages there are in North America."[12] But in spite of this
deficiency in knowledge he is at some pains to express his disagreement with Jefferson, who[13]

> in his Notes on Virginia [1787]. . .has hazarded an opinion,
> that they are very numerous; and then he proceeds. . .to
> draw an inference in contradiction of the received opinion of
> the Christian world as to the age of the earth. His reasoning
> . . .[included the following inference]: ". . .A separation
> into dialects may be the work of a few ages only; but for two
> dialects to recede from one another till they have lost all
> vestiges of their common origin, must require an immense
> course of time, perhaps not less than many people give to
> the age of the earth. . . ." This celebrated writer, however,
> was in great error as to what he assumes to be a "remarkable

fact." The "radical" languages of this continent. . .will be
found, so far as we may judge from the actual, not assumed,
facts of which we are now possessed, to be very few in number: The various dialects of North America, for example,
eastward of the course of the river Mississippi, appear to be
all reducible to three, or at most, four principal stocks. . . .

The list of stocks given corresponds to that quoted in the section on
Duponceau (2. 2).

The above quotation is of great interest for two reasons.
First, it gives us a hint about the chronological bind imposed on early
nineteenth century thinking through adherence to 'the received opinion
of the Christian world as to the age of the earth' (in contradistinction
to Jefferson's more enlightened late eighteenth century view) and we
shall hear more of this in the section on Gallatin. But of equal interest is the fact that Pickering, in his disagreement with Jefferson a-
bout the probable quantity of stocks in North America, was partly
right, but mostly wrong.

It is true that that part of eastern North America which had
been subjected to careful study turned out to have very few stocks.
The first three enumerated are correct except that 'Iroquois' was not
then known to include Cherokee. Moreover, the Floridian stock was
actually something of a catchall. It was believed to include the Cherokee omitted from Iroquois as well as Choctaw and Muskogee (not then
known to be members of a single stock), and some others.[14] Thus
far from there being only three stocks in the east, as he hoped ('three,
or at most, four') it turned out in fact that there were several more
than four.

But not only did Pickering underestimate the complexity of
the picture in the east, he had no inkling of the great diversity that
was soon to become known in the rest of the continent. As explorers,
travelers, and missionaries pushed farther and farther west, the existence of more and more languages became known. It soon became
clear that the linguistic diversity of the west was greater than that of
the east, so in point of fact Jefferson turns out to have guessed far
more accurately than Pickering.

4. Gallatin

4.1. Gallatin produced two important works on the classification of the North American Indian languages. The first, A Synopsis
of the Indian Tribes within the United States East of the Rocky Mountains and in the British and Russian Possessions in North America,
appeared in 1836.[15] But an earlier, unpublished attempt at classification "was made in the year 1823, at the request of. . .Baron
Alexander Humboldt."[16] But, he continues, when the American Antiquarian Society later asked for a copy, it turned out he "had not kept
any, but had in the meanwhile collected and obtained access to many
important materials." His classification of 1836 was therefore more
adequate than his earlier one. He described the methodology he used
as follows:[17]

> The form of a comparative vocabulary was adopted as far as
> practicable; and, in preparing it, every source of informa-
> tion, whether in manuscript or in works already published,
> was resorted to. The selection of the words was necessarily
> controlled by the materials. Those and no others could be
> admitted, but such as were found in a number of the existing
> vocabularies, sufficient for the purpose intended.

His intention in regard to the term 'family of languages' is also significant in this connection:[18]

> . . .the expression "family," applied to the Indian languages,
> has been taken in its most extensive sense, and as embrac-
> ing all those which contained a number of <u>similar primitive
> words</u>, <u>sufficient to show that they must</u>, at some remote ep-
> och, <u>have had a common origin</u>.

He appears to have expected, by means of such vocabulary inspection,
to arrive at connections of some depth, for he continues:

> It ["family"] is not used in that limited sense in which we des-
> ignate the Italian, Spanish, and French as languages of the
> Latin stock, or the German, Scandinavian, Netherlands, and
> English as branches of the Teutonic; <u>but in the same way</u>

> as we consider the Slavonic, the Teutonic, the Latin and
> Greek, the Sanscrit, and. . .the ancient Persian, <u>as retain-</u>
> <u>ing in their vocabularies conclusive proofs of their having</u>
> <u>originally sprung from the same stock</u>. [Emphasis supplied.]

He further states, quite reasonably (especially since California was
not included), that[19]

> The number of families, of distinct languages, and of dia-
> lects, does not appear to be greater in North America, than
> is found amongst uncivilized nations in other quarters of the
> globe. . ..Insulated remnants of ancient languages are also
> found, not only in Asia, as in the Caucasian mountains, but
> even in Europe, such as the Basque. The difficulty of ac-
> counting for that diversity, is the same here as in the other
> continent;

But we are brought up short when he concludes the paragraph:

> and <u>there is nothing</u> that I can perceive, in the number of the
> American languages and in the great differences between
> them, <u>inconsistent with the mosaic chronology</u>.[!] [Empha-
> sis supplied.]

This echoes beautifully, of course, the chronological bind in which
Pickering found himself, as mentioned in the preceding section (3).

When Gallatin takes up the discussion of grammar, he starts
out by echoing Duponceau and Pickering:[20]

> Amidst that great diversity of American languages, consid-
> ered only in reference to their vocabularies, <u>the similarity</u>
> <u>of their structure and grammatical forms</u> has been observed
> and pointed out by the American philologists.... The result
> appears to confirm the opinions already entertained on that
> subject by Mr. Du Ponceau, Mr. Pickering, and others; and
> to prove that all the languages, not only of our own Indians,
> but of the native inhabitants of America <u>from the Arctic</u>
> <u>Ocean to Cape Horn</u>, <u>have</u>, as far as they have been investi-
> gated, <u>a distinct character common to all</u>, and apparently

> differing from any of those of the other continent, with which
> we are most familiar. [Emphasis supplied.]

He goes a few steps beyond his predecessors, however, when he
makes the following important observations. First,

> It is not. . . asserted that there may not be some American
> languages, differing in their structure from those already
> known; or that a similarity of character may not be discov-
> ered between the grammatical forms of the languages of
> America, and those of some of the languages of the other
> hemisphere.

Secondly,

> Although the materials already collected appear sufficient
> to justify the general inference of a similar character, they
> are as yet too scanty to enable us to point out, with preci-
> sion, those features which are common to all the American
> languages, and those particulars in which they differ; or even
> to deduce, in those best known to us, the rules of their gram-
> mar from the languages, such as they are spoken.

But his inability to shake off the constrictions of the Mosaic chronology wins over in the end and colors his inferences about origins:

> [The languages] of America seem to me to bear the impress
> of primitive languages, to have assumed their form from
> natural causes, and to afford no proof of their being derived
> from a nation in a more advanced state of civilization than
> our Indians. Whilst the unity of structure and of grammati-
> cal forms proves a common origin, it may be inferred from
> this, combined with the great diversity and entire difference
> in the words of the several languages of America, that this
> continent received its first inhabitants at a very remote epoch,
> probably not much posterior to that of the dispersion of man-
> kind. [Emphasis supplied.]

4.2. In 1948 Gallatin published a new classification of the
languages of North America under the title of Hale's Indians of

North-west America, and Vocabularies of North America, with an Introduction.[21] As suggested in the title, this was occasioned in large part by the wealth of new material that had become available through the labors of Horatio Hale. (See 8.) His general outlook remains the same:[22]

> The only object I had in view. . .was to ascertain, by their vocabularies alone, the different languages of the Indians within the United States; and, amongst these, to discover the affinities sufficient to distinguish those belonging to the same family. . . .
> The word "family" must, in the Indian languages, be taken in its most enlarged sense. Those have been considered as belonging to the same family which had affinities similar to those found amongst the various European languages, designated by the generic term, "Indo-European." But. . .this has been done without any reference to their grammar or structure; for it will be seen. . .that, however entirely differing in their words, the most striking uniformity, in their grammatical forms and structure, appears to exist in all the American languages, from Greenland to Cape Horn, which have been examined. [Emphasis supplied.]

His substantive contribution in this later work was that he "succeeded in ascertaining thirty-two distinct families, in and north of the United States."[23] This was a landmark in the history of the genealogical classification of North American languages and was not superseded until the work of Powell and his coworkers completed what Gallatin had begun. (See 11.)

5. Latham

Robert Gordon Latham, a British philologist who wrote on a variety of subjects, including American ethnography, was also among those who operated on the theory of grammatical similarity for these languages. Like others who were making contributions to linguistic classification at this time, he used vocabulary similarities for determining his closer groupings. But he also assigned to vocabulary a somewhat broader significance than many, for he believed that the

American languages taken as a whole had lexical as well as grammatical similarities. The chief point of interest for our present purposes is that he accepted the fact of grammatical similarity but felt constrained to present some proof of lexical similarity. In a brief paper entitled Miscellaneous contributions to the ethnography of North America, originally read in 1845, he clearly expounds his view. His contributions are, he says,[24]

> mainly intended to serve as isolated points of evidence towards the two following statements:
> 1. That no American language has an isolated position when compared with the other tongues en masse, rather than with the languages of any particular class.
> 2. That the affinity between the languages of the New World, as determined by their vocabularies, is not less real than that inferred from the analogies of their grammatical structure.

Thus while he accepts 'the analogies of their grammatical structure' he is also looking for 'affinities' in their vocabularies.

6. Whitney

In the second half of the nineteenth century the man who easily ranked as the most distinguished American linguist was William Dwight Whitney of Yale. His distinction, as is well known, was not in the field of American Indian languages but in Sanskrit and Indo-European comparative philology. He wrote one of the first of what was to become a famous list of books called Language.[25] This had its beginning in a series of lectures on The Principles of Linguistic Science which he delivered at the Smithsonian Institution in Washington, D. C. in March, 1864.[26] Both in his original series of lectures and in his later expanded version, he felt called upon to make some comment about the languages of America. He echoes Duponceau, Pickering, and Gallatin, and, in addition, reveals a bias of his own:[27]

> Yet it is the confident opinion of linguistic scholars that a fundamental unity lies at the base of all these infinitely varying forms of speech [in America]; that they may be, and

> probably are, <u>all descended from a single parent language</u>.
> For, whatever their differences of material, <u>there is a sin-</u>
> <u>gle type or plan upon which their forms are developed and</u>
> <u>their constructions made</u>, <u>from the Arctic Ocean to Cape</u>
> <u>Horn</u>; and one sufficiently peculiar and distinctive to consti-
> tute a genuine indication of relationship. This type is called
> the incorporative or polysynthetic. It tends to the excessive
> and abnormal agglomeration of significant elements in its
> words; whereby, on the one hand, cumbrous compounds are
> formed as the names of objects and a character of tedious
> and time-wasting polysyllabism is given to the language.
> [Emphasis supplied.]

It is of considerable interest to note that in spite of Whitney's
acceptance of Duponceau's 'fundamental unity' theory and his uneasi-
ness about 'time-wasting polysyllabism', he was nevertheless among
the first to urge the use of 'sound method', i.e. that developed by
Indo-European scholars, in the study of American Indian languages.[28]

> To enter upon a bare and direct comparison of modern Amer-
> ican with modern Asiatic dialects, for the purpose of dis-
> covering signs of genetic connection between them, would be
> a proceeding utterly at variance with all the principles of lin-
> guistic science, and could lead to no results possessing any
> significance or value.... Sound method. . .requires that we
> study each dialect, group, branch, and family by itself, be-
> fore we venture to examine and pronounce upon its more dis-
> tant connections. <u>What we have to do</u> at present, then, <u>is</u>
> <u>simply to learn all that we possibly can of the Indian lan-</u>
> <u>guages themselves</u>; <u>to settle their internal relations</u>, <u>elicit</u>
> <u>their laws of growth</u>, <u>reconstruct their older forms</u>, <u>and as-</u>
> <u>cend toward their original condition</u> as far as the material
> within our reach, and the state in which it is presented, will
> allow. [Emphasis supplied.]

This is a very interesting statement in more than one respect. In particular, it shows no shred of the prejudice that developed
in other quarters to the effect that unwritten languages could not be
subjected to the same type of rigorous methodology that was applied
so successfully to the written Indo-European languages.[29] At the

same time it is clearly a reaction against the efforts on the part of
some scholars of the time to search for farflung relationships; Whitney
himself seems to have closed his mind to any hope of finding linguistic
evidence for Asian connections of the American Indians, for he continues: [30]

> If our studies shall at length put us in a position to deal with
> the question of their Asiatic derivation, we will rejoice at it.
> I do not myself expect that valuable light will ever be shed
> upon the subject by linguistic evidence.

7. Trumbull

7.1. Like Pickering before him (whose general paper was
published in 1831), J. Hammond Trumbull wrote an encyclopaedia
article entitled Indian Languages of America which appeared in 1876.[31]
In some ways it almost seems as though no progress has been made
in the intervening half century. There are still strong echoes of
Duponceau in his first sentence: [32]

> In a general view of the languages of the Western World their
> number and variety are at first more remarkable than is that
> approach to <u>uniformity in plan of thought and verbal struc-
> ture which establishes something like a family likeness a-
> mong them all</u>. [Emphasis supplied.]

But as a matter of fact it is beginning to become clear that the picture
is more complicated than had been earlier believed. More material
in more detail had become available and it was possible to begin to
raise some doubts: [33]

> Is there any bond of union between these numerous families
> of languages radically distinct? any characteristic features
> common to them all which testify to the original unity of all,
> or at least distinguish them as a class from languages of the
> Eastern hemisphere? <u>The answer must be given less confi-
> dently now than it might have been fifty years ago</u>, when the
> attention of scholars had been directed to only a few of the
> American families of speech, and it was easy to assume

that the structural and grammatical characteristics of these
were common to all Indian languages. At present, broad
generalizations are felt to be hazardous. As the range of observation has widened, . . .it has been discovered not only
that American tongues differ among themselves in some of
the features which formerly were regarded as distinctive of
the class, but that no one of these features is, in kind if in
degree, peculiarly American. No morphological classification which has yet been proposed provides a place for American languages exclusively, nor in fact can their separation as
a class be established by morphological characteristics or
external peculiarities of structure. [Emphasis supplied.]

In spite of this, the chief premise of the Duponceau hypothesis is still
upheld, for he continues: [34]

Their common likeness is their plan of thought, rather than
in their methods of combining elements of words or annexing
formatives to roots. Mr. Duponceau was the first to suggest
this. . . .

There are, however, many points at issue in regard to the
American Indian languages, besides the chief topic of the present article, and on these Trumbull usually acquits himself very well and in
a manner showing considerable progress since the time of Duponceau
and Pickering.

It is also worthy of note that Trumbull has an entirely modern
view about the possibility of applying the 'comparative method' to
American Indian linguistic families. His arguments about the need
for such work are similar to those of Whitney, already quoted, but if
anything he has stated them more felicitously: [35]

Till the comparative grammar of the languages of each of the
principal American families shall have been investigated,
and the laws and limits of phonetic changes are better understood than at present, questions as to the genetic relation of
one of these families to another must remain unanswered.
As yet, philology has no sufficient data for determining either
the fact or the degree of such relationship. Still less is the

philologist competent to decide, on evidence now supplied by
language, that any family of American speech is, or is not,
of Asiatic, European, or African derivation.

7.2. There are other points, too, on which Trumbull begins
to sound a more modern note. The success achieved by Gallatin in
the solution of many classificatory problems through the use of a list
of words having similar glosses led the Smithsonian Institution to a-
dopt in 1863 a Standard Vocabulary for the use of 'officers of the
government, travellers, and others'.[36] Its chief purpose was to ascertain 'the more obvious relations between the various members of
existing families'. A plethora of material was gathered along these
lines in the ensuing years leading Trumbull to complain in his 1871
paper On the best Method of Studying the North American Languages
that:[37]

> An erroneous impression appears to have been very generally
> received, that real progress in the knowledge of a language
> has been made when one or two hundred words taken from its
> vocabulary have been set over against certain words of our
> language which have meanings not very dissimilar.

Thus a reaction against vocabulary-gathering, at least as an end in
itself, was beginning to set in.[38] One reason for Trumbull's distrust
of exercises in vocabulary-matching was the difficulty of determining
reasonably exact equivalences:[39]

> Every standard vocabulary includes the verb 'to eat,' yet this
> verb has not, so far as I can discover, its equivalent in any
> American language. The Algonkin has four or five primary
> and a great many composite verbs of eating, but none of
> these expresses the simple act of taking food. . . . One verb
> . . . signifies 'to eat animal food' (or that which has or has
> had life); another, 'to eat vegetable food;' another, 'to eat
> soft food' (that which may be dipped up, spoon-victuals, such
> as samp, succotash, and the like); others, 'to eat ravenously,
> to devour like beasts of prey,' — 'to graze,' or take food
> from the ground as cattle do, — and so on.

Moreover,[40]

> in view of the fundamental differences in grammatical struc-
> ture and in plan of thought between the American and the Indo-
> European languages, it is nearly impossible to find an Indian
> name or verb which admits of exact translation by an English
> name or verb. But the standard vocabularies. . .assume
> that equivalents of English generic names may be found among
> Indian specific and individual, — that English analysis may be
> adequately represented by Indian synthesis.

He is therefore led to make some recommendations for the improvement in the method of studying American languages, namely,[41]

> That a constant aim of the student of any of the American lan-
> guages should be the resolution of synthesis by analysis.
> What the Indian has so skillfully put together — 'agglutinated'
> or 'incorporated' — must be carefully taken to pieces, and
> the materials of the structure be examined separately. . . .

And,[42]

> To single out and fix the primary meanings of the verbal roots
> should be the ultimate aim in the study of every Indian lan-
> guage. What excessive synthesis has done, searching analy-
> sis must undo.

Valuable as these recommendations are, it is still possible to recognize that they rest on Duponceau's original assumption of the polysynthetic character of American languages.[43] Nevertheless, a new era
in American linguistics has begun with Trumbull's programmatic
statement. This is an early and clear formulation of the methodology
which dominated American linguistic work until well into the second
half of the twentieth century. It is, of course, the 'atomistic' approach which Chomsky labels as characteristic of what he calls the
'taxonomic model' as opposed to the transformational model.[44]

8. Hale

As a very young man, Horatio Hale had served as ethnologist
and philologist of the Wilkes Exploring Expedition to the South

Pacific.[45] In this connection he carried out an extensive comparison
of Polynesian languages. Then, "in 1841, when the expedition stopped
at Oregon Territory, Hale left it to spend several months in the pursuit of a more intensive study of the varied languages and customs of
the Northwest,"[46] This latter work formed the basis of Gallatin's
1948 opus, Hale's Indians of Northwest America, already discussed
(4. 2). After this promising beginning, personal affairs kept Hale out
of scholarly pursuits for nearly a quarter of a century. In his later
life, applying the kinds of comparison he had used in his Polynesian
work, he undertook to prepare for Iroquoian[47]

> a pretty extensive comparative vocabulary (procured by my-
> self directly from native speakers) of all the languages of
> this stock, viz. the Huron (or Wyandot) and the Mohawk,
> Oneida, Onondaga, Cayuga, Seneca, and Tuscarora.

This was never completed but some of the results were published in
1883 when he had carried his work far enough to include Cherokee also among the Iroquoian languages.[48] It is fair to say, I think, that in
the Grammar or lexicon? issue, he gave the edge to grammar, though
he preferred them to be neatly balanced. Thus he says,[49]

> When the languages of the two nations or tribes show a
> close resembalnce in grammar and vocabulary, we may at
> once infer a common descent, if not of the whole, at least
> of some portion of the two communities. [Emphasis sup-
> plied.]

But in the specific issue of the relationship of Cherokee to Iroquois,
he points out that[50]

> The similarity of the two tongues, apparent enough in many
> of their words, is most strikingly shown, as might be expec-
> ted in their grammatical structure, and especially in the af-
> fixed pronouns, which in both languages play so important
> a part.

But he is troubled by the instances in which "Cherokee words differ
utterly from those of the Huron-Iroquois languages,"[51] and concludes,

> There seems, in fact, to be no doubt that the Cherokee is a mixed language, in which, as is usual in such languages, the grammatical skeleton belongs to one stock, while many of the words are supplied by another.

A few years earlier, though not published until about the same time, Hale had made another discovery of affiliation among the tribes of the eastern United States. In connection with his work among the Six Nations, he discovered that the Tuteloes who also lived among them, were not of Iroquoian linguistic affiliation, as had previously been supposed, but were clearly Siouan.[52] No vocabulary of the language existed prior to Hale's work, but in this case vocabulary alone was sufficient to make the initial identification:[53]

> A vocabulary which I took down from his [a Tutelo's] lips showed beyond question that his people belonged to the Dakotan [Siouan] stock.

Later, as he obtained more information on the language, he was able

> to compare it, not merely in its phonology and its vocabulary, but also in its grammatical structure, with the Dakotan languages spoken west of the Mississippi.

9. Gatschet

Like Hale, Albert S. Gatschet also made some linguistic identifications that had previously been uncertain. And like Hale, he gave the edge to grammar. When Hale published his material on the affiliation of Cherokee and Iroquois (8.1), Gatschet expressed his agreement,[54] for

> [Hale] established this connection, not on lexical data only, but also, and more firmly, on grammatic grounds.

At the same time, he also set forth his own corroborative evidence which included instances of both lexical affinity and 'affinity in grammatic elements'. He is careful to add that "in investigations of this kind grammatic affinity is of greater weight, however, than resemblances of words."[55]

Somewhat earlier Gatschet published a short article on The
Test of Linguistic Affinity.[56] Here he emphasized that[57]

> The investigation is of a double character, for it extends over
> the <u>words</u> or the lexical part of the languages, and over their
> grammatic <u>forms</u>, inflections, etc. , especially over the af-
> fixes.

He also makes, but does not elaborate on, the important point that
"All these comparisons must be made under the guidance of the <u>pho-
netic laws</u> traceable in both idioms to be compared."[58]

10.   Brinton

10.1.   Daniel G. Brinton was a contemporary of Powell's
and the two men were in keen competition to present a definitive classification of American Indian languages.   Each had a high degree of
success but in very different ways.

Brinton's The American Race, first published in 1891,[59] was
largely a presentation of his classification of all the languages of the
western hemisphere.   His presentation for North America was almost
simultaneously superseded by Powell's but his classification of South
American languages became the starting-point for all subsequent
classifications.[60]   Brinton of course recognized his inadequacies in
regard to North America but he acknowledged his indebtedness to
H. W. Henshaw (who was working under Powell) 'for revising the list
of North Pacific Coast Stocks, and various suggestions'.[61] For a
number of years Powell had stimulated the collection of large amounts
of material for the Bureau of American Ethnology but Brinton was unable to make use of this, for[62]

> access to this was denied me except under the condition that
> I should not use in any published work information thus ob-
> tained; a proviso scarcely so liberal as I had expected.

Brinton, in his Preface, asserts his preference for grammar
over lexicon:[63]

Whenever the material permitted it, I have ranked the grammatic structure of a language superior to its lexical elements
in deciding upon relationship. In this I follow the precepts
and examples of students of the Aryan and Semitic stocks; although their methods have been rejected by some who have
written on American tongues. As for myself, I am abidingly
convinced that <u>the morphology of any language whatever is</u>
<u>its most permanent and characteristic feature</u>. [Emphasis
supplied.]

The reference to 'some who have written on American tongues' is
doubtless aimed at Powell.[64] Rowe, on the basis of the remarks
quoted here, maintains that "Brinton took exactly the opposite theoretical position from Powell's."[65] But Brinton appears to have over-
stated his position, perhaps out of pique at Powell, for later on, when
he himself wishes to draw conclusions on the basis of vocabulary, he
takes a broader approach to the problem:[66]

A proper comparison of languages or dialects includes not
merely the vocabulary, but the grammatical forms and the
phonetic variations which the vocal elements undergo in passing from one form of speech to another. In some respects,
the morphology is more indicative of relationship than the
lexicon of tongues; and it is in these grammatical aspects
that we are peculiarly poorly off when we approach American
dialects. Yet it is also likely that <u>the tendency of late years</u>
<u>has been to underestimate the significance of merely lexical</u>
<u>analogies</u>. <u>The vocabulary</u>, after all, <u>must be our main</u>
<u>stand-by</u> in such an undertaking. [Emphasis supplied.]

In view of the nature of the materials at his disposal, and for other
reasons, it is clear that his position is very little different from that
of Powell's (see 11) after all.

10.2. In spite of the very large number of independent stocks
or families to be found in the Americas ("of such there are about
eighty in North and as many in South America"),[67] Brinton's view regarding the 'prevailing unity of grammatic schemes in American
tongues'[68] does not differ too much from that of Duponceau, its

originator. That his modification is slight is seen in the following remarks: [69]

> Another characteristic, which at one time was supposed to
> be universal on this continent, is what Mr. Peter Du Ponceau
> named polysynthesis. . . .
> Another trait, however, which was confounded with this by
> Mr. Du Ponceau, but really belongs in a different category
> of grammatical structure, is truly distinctive of the lan-
> guages of the continent, and I am not sure that any one of
> them has been shown to be wholly devoid of it. This is what
> is called incorporation. [Emphasis supplied.]

In The American Race, Brinton describes the same tendency
in Humboltian terms: [70]

> The psychic identity of the Americans is well illustrated in
> their languages. There are indeed indefinite discrepancies
> in their lexicography and in their surface morphology; but in
> their logical substructure, in what Wilhelm von Humboldt
> called the "inner form," they are strikingly alike. The points
> in which this is especially apparent are in the development of
> pronominal forms, in the abundance of generic particles, in
> the overweening preference for concepts of action (verbs),
> rather than concepts of existence (nouns), and in the conse-
> quent subordination of the latter to the former in the propo-
> sition. This last mentioned trait is the source of that char-
> acteristic called incorporation. The American languages as
> a rule are essentially incorporative languages, that is, they
> formally include both subject and object in the transitive con-
> cept, and its oral expression. . . . I have yet to find one
> [American language], of which we possess ample means of
> analysis, in which it does not appear in one or another of its
> forms, thus revealing the same linguistic impulse. [Empha-
> sis supplied.]

11.1. Powell's Linguistic Families of North America north
of Mexico, which appeared in 1890, definitively settled most of the
classificatory problems for the languages included in his survey. Like

most of those who preceded him, he based his classification on lexical evidence. In his underlying theoretical approach to these languages, however, he held certain views which differed from those of most of his predecessors.

Lewis Henry Morgan, a Rochester, New York lawyer who, as a cultivated man of his time, was deeply impressed by the revolutionary new information that was being painstakingly uncovered by geologists and biologists as to 'the great antiquity of mankind upon the earth'[71] was attracted to the study of the social organization of the Iroquois Indians of his native state. After years of study of these Indians and other peoples of the world, he published his major work, Ancient Society, in 1877 and it is here that he developed his theory of social evolution:[72]

> It can now be asserted upon convincing evidence that <u>savagery</u> preceded barbarism in all the tribes of mankind, as <u>barbarism</u> is known to have preceded <u>civilization</u>. The history of the human race is one in source, one in experience, one in progress. [Emphasis supplied.]

Powell, himself a geologist and explorer of no mean accomplishment, was well-disposed toward Morgan's theories and, in his own way, he adapted them to the theory of language development as well. At the same time he did not free himself entirely from the implications of Duponceau's theory. One is able to see this because Powell is more generous than most classifiers in explaining the principles he used in making his classification.[73]

> Languages are said to be cognate when such relations between them are found that they are supposed to have descended from a common ancestral speech. The evidence of cognation is derived <u>exclusively from the vocabulary</u>. Grammatic similarities are not supposed to furnish evidence of cognation, but to be phenomena, in part relating to stage of culture and in part adventitious. [Emphasis supplied.]

His explanation of why he thinks "grammatic similarities are not supposed to furnish evidence of cognation" is, however, frequently overlooked:[74]

It must be remembered that extreme peculiarities of grammar, like the vowel mutations of the Hebrew or the monosyllabic separation of the Chinese, have not been discovered
among Indian tongues. It therefore becomes necessary in the
classification of Indian languages into families to neglect
grammatic structure, and to consider lexical elements only.

The first sentence of this excerpt is highly reminiscent of Pickering's
paraphrase of Duponceau, already quoted, to the effect that "we find
no monosyllabic language, like the Chinese and its cognate idioms,"
etc. (See 3.) So Powell did not entirely free himself from the grip
of Duponceau when he adopted Morgan's evolutionary theory.

But returning to Powell's assertion in the second sentence of
the above excerpt that it is necessary 'to neglect grammatic structure', we find he defends this position in the following way: [75]

But this statement must be clearly understood. It is postulated that in the growth of languages new words are formed
by combination, and that these new words change by attrition
to secure economy of utterance, and also by assimilation
(analogy) for economy of thought. ... The paradigmatic words
considered in grammatic treatises may often be the very
words which should be dissected to discover in their elements primary affinities. But the comparison is still lexic,
not grammatic.

He then proceeds to define the difference between lexical and grammatical comparison: [76]

A lexic comparison is between vocal elements; a grammatic
comparison is between grammatic methods, such, for example,
as gender systems. The classes into which things are rele-
gated by distinction of gender, may be animate and inanimate,
and the animate may subsequently be divided into male and
female, and these two classes may ultimately absorb, in part
at least, inanimate things. ... All of these characteristics are
in part adventitious, but to a large extent the gender is a phenomenon of growth, indicating the stage to which the language
has attained. A proper case system may not have been

> established in a language by the fixing of case particles, or,
> having been established, it may change by the increase or
> diminution of the number of cases. A tense system also has
> a beginning, a growth, and a decadence.... All of these
> things are held to belong to the grammar of a language and
> to be grammatic methods, distinct from lexical elements.
> [Emphasis supplied.]

But Powell did not rule grammar out entirely. In his own mind he is
clear about the point at which grammatical considerations are to be
admitted:[77]

> With terms thus defined, languages are supposed to be cog-
> nate when fundamental similarities are discovered in their
> lexical elements. When members of a family of languages
> are to be classed in subdivisions and the history of such lan-
> guages investigated, grammatic characteristics become of
> primary importance. [Emphasis supplied.]

In other words, grammatical features are of use in determining subgroupings but not major groupings. Powell's reason for making this
assertion is clear. He believes that grammar changes much more
rapidly than lexicon and it is this which makes a difference in their
relative utility for classification:[78]

> The words of a language change by the methods described,
> but the fundamental elements or roots are more enduring.
> Grammatic methods also change, perhaps even more rapidly
> than words, and the changes may go on to such an extent that
> primitive methods are entirely lost, there being no radical
> grammatic elements to be preserved. Grammatic structure
> is but a phase or accident of growth, and not a primordial
> element of language. The roots of a language are its most
> permanent characteristic.... The grammatic structure or
> plan of a language is forever changing, and in this respect
> the language may become entirely transformed. [Emphasis
> supplied.]

11.2. In the course of his study of the vocabulary and other
materials which provided the basis for his classification, Powell's

views underwent some change, and this is set forth in his Concluding
Remarks. [79] In particular he is troubled by the extent of borrowed
materials. His 'general conclusion' on this topic is[80]

> That borrowed materials exist in all the languages; and that
> some of these borrowed materials can be traced to original
> sources, while the larger part of such acquisitions cannot be
> thus relegated to known families. In fact, it is believed that
> the existing languages, great in number though they are, give
> evidence of a more primitive condition, when a far greater
> number were spoken. When there are two or more languages
> of the same stock, it appears that this differentiation into di-
> verse tongues is due mainly to the absorption of other ma-
> terial, and that thus the multiplication of dialects and lan-
> guages of the same group furnishes evidence that at some
> prior time there existed other languages which are now lost
> except as they are partially preserved in the divergent ele-
> ments of the group. [Emphasis supplied.]

This conclusion has led him to change the hypothesis he held at the
beginning of the investigation,

> namely, that common elements would be discovered in all
> these languages, for the longer the study has proceeded the
> more clear it has been made to appear that the grand pro-
> cess of linguistic development among the tribes of North
> America has been toward unification rather than toward mul-
> tiplication, that is, that the multiplied languages of the same
> stock owe their origin very largely to absorbed languages
> that are lost. [Emphasis supplied.]

Although even in his own judgment his classificatory scheme is very
conservative, [81] he is now beginning to wonder whether he was conservative enough. [82]

> The opinion that the differentiation of languages within a sin-
> gle stock is mainly due to the absorption of materials from
> other stocks, often to the extinguishment of the latter, has
> grown from year to year as the investigation has proceeded.
> Wherever the material has been sufficient to warrant a

conclusion on this subject, no language has been found to be simple in its origin, but every language has been found to be composed of diverse elements. [Emphasis supplied.]

Powell's classification has stood the test of time remarkably well. Proposed changes have been overwhelmingly in the direction of combination rather than division, except for one or two problems in the languages of Oregon. But Powell himself anticipated the contrary development in keeping with his changing views about the causes of differentiation among languages:[83]

> Migration introduces a potent agency of mutation, but a new environment impresses its characteristics upon a language more by a change in the. . .meaning of words than by a change in their forms. There is another agency of change of profound influence, namely, association with other tongues. . . .In the presence of opinions that have slowly grown in this direction, the author is inclined to think that some of the groups herein recognized as families will ultimately be divided, as the common materials of such languages, when they are more thoroughly studied, will be seen to have been borrowed. [Emphasis supplied.]

We can be grateful, then, that Powell saw fit to publish his classification when he did. We should perhaps also be grateful to Brinton whose intention to include his own scheme for North America in his larger one for the whole of the Western hemisphere seems likely to have had some effect on Powell's timing.

12. Conclusion

12.1. Prior to the nineteeenth century what little had been done on the classification of the American languages had been done on the basis of vocabulary, all too often on the basis of a few words. But the primary object was to determine the origin of the inhabitants of the New World. Thomas Jefferson who, in his Notes on the State of Virginia (1787),[84] was one of the first to urge that "vocabularies [be] formed of all the languages spoken in North and South America" had it in mind for the material to be used to determine 'the derivation of

this part of the human race'.[85] A few years later Benjamin Smith
Barton presented some of his ideas on classification in New Views of
the Origin of the Tribes and Nations of America (1797)[86] which he
dedicated to Jefferson. But more than anything else he wanted to con-
nect the American Indians with the peoples of Asia and so he mixed
in a scattering of words in Asian languages as well.

        An entirely new dimension was added early in the nineteenth
century when Duponceau announced his conviction that the languages
of the Americas were structurally very much alike, i.e. all were
chararacterized by 'polysynthesis', and that this structural type was,
moreover, unique to the Americas. This constituted a comprehensive
typological classification for the whole hemisphere, and W. Humboldt,
who proposed that all the languages of the world could be divided into
four types (isolating, agglutinative, incorporative, and inflective) included the American languages among those of the incorporative plan.

        During this period, typology was not clearly separated from
grammar. And as long as Duponceau's premise was accepted, it is
obvious that it would appear fruitless to attempt to classify the American languages on the basis of grammar, so the only method left open
was by means of lexicon. Excellent and lasting results were achieved
in just this way by the labors of Gallatin.

        By mid-century the remarkable achievements of the Indo-
Europeanists were widely acclaimed by all linguistic scholars. Some
of their most brilliant discoveries were made by careful attention to
grammatical detail so it became fashionable in many quarters to urge
the supremacy of grammar over lexicon in matters of classification.
And thus it happens that Whitney, who confuses typology and grammar
in so far as the American languages are concerned, infers that they
'are all descended from a single parent language'. (See 6.) But he
was also among the first to urge that we study these languages intensely and 'reconstruct their older forms', an undertaking which was
as yet inconceivable to most of those who were actually in contact
with the data. Some of the latter, in fact, were still searching for a
living parent language. Thus some who knew the Algonkian languages
believed that Delaware was the parent while others argued the merits
of Ojibwa for this honor.

The approach to American Indian languages became more sophisticated in the writings of Trumbull. Trumbull was not a field
worker, but he was a competent Algonkianist and was also knowledge-
able about what had been written on the languages of other families.
He urged the investigation of the 'comparative grammar of the languages of each of the principal American families' (7.1) and also the
thorough-going synchronic analysis of each language (7.2).

By this time there were some professional field workers engaged in the study of American Indian languages and scholars like
Hale, Gatschet, and J. O. Dorsey set a new tone. Hale's comparative Iroquoian studies were never completed, but at least he was able
to prove that Cherokee was an Iroquoian language.[87] He did not con-
fuse typology with grammar and when he spoke of the similarity of
grammatic structure between Cherokee and the other Iroquoian languages, he had in mind the same niceties of detail that had impressed
Indo-Europeanists in their comparisons of Sanskrit with other Indo-
European languages.

But a definitive classification of the languages of North and
South America had not yet been made. Brinton, with his broad command of the literature on the languages of both continents, wished to
make just such a classification. However, he did not have access to
the copious materials on the languages of North America which had
been diligently collected under the auspices of the Smithsonian Institution for nearly forty years. Therefore while Brinton actually published a classification of the scope he had in mind, he was aware of
his shortcomings and the reasons therefor. Although he is almost
always quoted as one who gave grammar priority over lexicon in
making his classifications, the truth of the matter is that he was
rarely able to do so because of the scarcity of grammatical material
on most of the languages of the hemisphere. His practice is better
characterized by his declaration that "the vocabulary, after all, must
be our main stand-by in such an undertaking." (See 10.)

Powell, having access to the unpublished manuscripts of the
Bureau of American Ethnology, material collected, for the most part,
by his specific direction, was able, with the help of his coworkers in
the Bureau, to make the definitive classification of the languages of

North America north of Mexico. He declared lexicon to be the critical measure of relationship and he succeeded in presenting to the
world a basic classification that has stood the test of time.

It is well he published his classification when he did. He was
beginning to be troubled by the undoubted presence of borrowed material in the lexicons of all languages, and he was tending, not in the
direction of more combination, but of greater division. His evolutionary theories were also not working out quite the way he had anticipated. In part he is satisfied with what he has observed: [88]

> From the materials which have been and may be gathered in
> this field the evolution of language can be studied from an
> early form, wherein words are usually not parts of speech,
> to a form where parts of speech are somewhat differentiated.
> . . . The evolution of mind in the endeavor to express thought,
> by coining, combining, and contracting words and by organ-
> izing logical sentences through the development of parts of
> speech and their syntactic arrangement, is abundantly illus-
> trated.

But within some of the given languages the situation appears full of
incongruities:

> The languages are very unequally developed in their several
> parts. Low gender systems appear with high tense systems,
> highly evolved case systems with slightly developed mode sys-
> tems; and there is scarcely any one of these languages. . .
> which does not exhibit archaic devices in its grammar.

Throughout the century one investigator after another finds
that lexicon provides a higher yield in reliability than any of the other
devices that are available for use. Duponceau's 'uniform system' of
structure for the whole hemisphere leaves lexicon as the primary cri-
terion of differentiation. Powell's evolutionary scheme, which he himself did not attempt to use for classificatory purposes, was also seen
to be full of ambiguity whenever it is applied to any particular language. In some recalcitrant cases, however, grammar turned out to
be very helpful; in particular, we find Hale and Gatschet making good
use of it in identifying Cherokee as Iroquoian. In general, however,

the type of grammatical information that would be most useful, was
lacking. The taxonomists of the nineteenth century were fortunate
that the wealth of lexical material collected during that period proved
as effective as it did in setting up a viable classification.

12.2. This paper should be taken as a first attempt to trace
the history of some of the ideas with which American linguists were
concerned during the nineteenth century. An assessment of these
ideas in terms of their interaction with related intellectual currents,
especially those pertaining to biological taxonomy (e.g. the Linnean
classification) has not been undertaken here.[89] But several promising leads for further investigation lie in this area, from Pickering's
observation that Duponceau's term 'polysynthetic' can be taken as
descriptive of a 'genus of human languages' (see 3) all the way to
Powell's insistence on a rigorous nomenclature for his linguistic
families which he based on the model of the Linnean classification
though with a different set of rules.[90]

NOTES

An abbreviated version of this paper was read at the Forty-first Annual Meeting of the Linguistic Society of America in December, 1966.
It has undergone several revisions since that time. The final one was
completed while I was concurrently a Senior Fellow of the National
Endowment for the Humanities and Fellow in residence at the Center
for Advanced Study in the Behavioral Sciences, Stanford, in 1967-68.

[1]Seventh Annual Report, Bureau of [American] Ethnology,
pp. 1-142. Washington (1892).

[2][Peter S. Duponceau], Report of the historical and literary
committee to the American Philosophical Society. —Read, 9th January, 1818. Transactions of the Historical and Literary Committee of
the American Philosophical Society, Vol. I. xi-xvi, Philadelphia
(1819). The quoted material is found on p. xiv.

[3]Report of the corresponding secretary to the Committee, of
his progress in the investigation committed to him of the general
character and forms of the languages of the American Indians. Read
12th January, 1819. Trans. of the Historical and Literary Committee
. . ., vol. I, Philadelphia (1819).

[4] Paris, 1838. Quotation on p. 89.

[5] D. G. Brinton, Some characteristics of American languages, p. 353, in Essays of an Americanist, Philadelphia (1890).

[6] D. G. Brinton, Wilhelm von Humboldt's Researches in American languages, pp. 339-40, in Essays. . . .

[7] Duponceau, Mémoire, p. 259.

[8] Ibid., p. 314.

[9] Mary R. Haas, Roger Williams's sound shift: A study in Algonkian, in To Honor Roman Jakobson: Essays on the occasion of his seventieth birthday, 1.819, The Hague-Paris (1967).

[10] John Pickering, Introductory memoir, pp. 371-72, in Father Sebastian Rasles, A dictionary of the Abnaki language, Memoirs, Amer. Acad. of Arts and Sciences 1.370-574 (1833).

[11] [John Pickering], Indian languages of America, Encyclopaedia Americana, Vol. IV (Appendix): 581-900. The quotation is from p. 581.

[12] Ibid., p. 584.

[13] Ibid., pp. 584-585.

[14] The term 'Floridian', then, is not to be equated with Muskogean, as is sometimes implied. This corrects, for instance, the statement by Clark Wissler in The American Indian and the American Philosophical Society, Proc. of the Amer. Philosophical Soc. 86.193 (1942).

[15] Trans. and Coll. Amer. Antiquarian Soc., 2.1-422, Cambridge (1836).

[16] Ibid., p. 1.

[17] Ibid., p. 2.

[18] Ibid., p. 4.

[19] Ibid., p. 5.

[20] Ibid., pp. 5-6 for this and the following quoted passages.

[21] Albert Gallatin, Hale's Indians of north-west America, and vocabularies of North America, with an introduction, Trans. of the Amer. Ethnological Soc. 2. xxiii-clxxx, 1-130, New York (1848).

[22] Ibid., p. cxix.

[23] Ibid., p. xcviii.

[24] Robert Gordon Latham, Opuscula. Essays chiefly philological and ethnographical, p. 275, London and Edinburgh (1860). Powell also quotes the two main points made by Latham in Linguistic Families, p. 14.

[25] William Dwight Whitney, Language and the study of language, 5 New York (1889).

[26]William Dwight Whitney, Brief abstract of a series of six lectures on the principles of linguistic science, Appendix to the Annual Report of the Board of Regents of the Smithsonian Institution, Washington (1864), pp. 95-116.

[27]Whitney, Language, p. 348.

[28]Op. cit., p. 351.

[29]Mary R. Haas, Historical linguistics and the genetic relationship of languages, in Thomas A. Sebeok (ed.), Current Trends in Linguistics, Vol. III. 113-153, The Hague (1966). See the discussion on pp. 120-21.

[30]Whitney, Language, p. 351.

[31]Johnson's New Universal Cyclopaedia, 2. 1155-1161, New York (1876).

[32]Op. cit., p. 1155.

[33]Op. cit., p. 1157.

[34]Op. cit., p. 1158.

[35]Op. cit., p. 1161.

[36]George Gibbs, Instructions for research relative to the ethnology and philology of America, Smithsonian Misc. Collections 160, Washington (1863). Reference is to p. 13.

[37]J. Hammond Trumbull, On the best method of studying the North American languages, Transactions of the American Philological Association, 1869-70, 1. 55-79, Hartford (1871).

[38]It must not be overlooked, however, that he readily conceded the usefulness of the Standard Vocabulary for the purposes for which it was originally intended: "The standard vocabulary continues to be useful to inexperienced collectors and as a guide in provisional classification. Next to the satisfaction of learning a new language is that of learning something about it — of ascertaining by means of a comparative vocabulary that it is or is not like some other language which we know...." Ibid., p. 58.

[39]Ibid., p. 61.

[40]Ibid., p. 63.

[41]Ibid., p. 64.

[42]Ibid., p. 65.

[43]See ibid., p. 59.

[44]Noam Chomsky, Current issues in linguistic theory, The Hague (1966). Reference is to p. 11.

[45]Jacob W. Gruber, Horatio Hale and the development of American anthropology, Proc. of the American Philosophical Society, 111. 5-37 (1967). See p. 9.

[46]Ibid.

[47]Quotation from a letter of Hale's to Powell in 1881, Gruber, op. cit., p. 35.

[48]Horatio Hale, Indian migrations, as evidenced by language, Part I. The Huron-Cherokee stock, The American Antiquarian 5.18-28 (1883).

[49]Ibid., p. 18.

[50]Ibid., p. 26.

[51]Ibid., p. 27.

[52]Horatio Hale, The Tutelo tribe and language, Proc. of the American Philosophical Society 21.1-47 (1884). Also Hale, Indian migrations as evidenced by language, Part II, The American Antiquarian 5.108-124 (1883).

[53]Hale, The Tutelo tribe, p. 13.

[54]Albert S. Gatschet, On the affinity of the Cheroki to the Iroquois dialects, Trans. of the American Philological Association 16.xl-xlv (1886). The quotation is from p. xli.

[55]Ibid., p. xlii.

[56]Albert S. Gatschet, The test of linguistic affinity, The American Antiquarian 2.163-165 (1879-80).

[57]Ibid., pp. 163-164.

[58]Ibid., p. 165.

[59]Daniel G. Brinton, The American Race, New York (1891). The edition I have seen is Philadelphia (1901).

[60]John Howland Rowe, Linguistic classification problems in South America, in Papers from the Symposium on American Indian Linguistics, UCPL 10.1-68, Berkeley and Los Angeles (1954). Reference is to p. 19.

[61]Op. cit., p. xii.

[62]Ibid.

[63]Ibid., p. x.

[64]Brinton did this not infrequently, sometimes indirectly as here, and sometimes by referring to him directly.

[65]Rowe, Linguistic classification problems, p. 19.

[66]Brinton, op. cit., p. 333.

[67]Ibid., p. 57.

[68]Daniel G. Brinton, Some characteristics of American languages, in Essays of an Americanist, Philadelphia (1890), p. 352.

[69]See Brinton, American languages and why we should study them, in Essays of an Americanist, p. 321.

⁷⁰See p. 56. This passage, with its reference to 'surface morphology' and 'logical substructure' finds a clear echo in the phrases 'surface structure' and 'deep structure' used by the transformational generative grammarians of the 1960s who have also been influenced by Humboltian thinking.

⁷¹Lewis Henry Morgan, Ancient Society (1877), p. 1.

⁷²Ibid.

⁷³Powell, Linguistic families, p. 11.

⁷⁴Ibid.

⁷⁵Powell, Linguistic families, p. 11.

⁷⁶Ibid.

⁷⁷Ibid., p. 12.

⁷⁸Ibid.

⁷⁹Ibid., pp. 139–142.

⁸⁰Ibid., p. 140.

⁸¹"In arranging the scheme of linguistic families the author has proceeded very conservatively." (Ibid.)

⁸²Ibid., p. 141.

⁸³Ibid.

⁸⁴Thomas Jefferson, Notes on the State of Virginia, ed. by William Peden, Chapel Hill (1955). p. v.

⁸⁵Ibid., p. 101.

⁸⁶Philadelphia.

⁸⁷Barton had postulated the relationship of Cherokee to the Iroquoian languages in 1797, but his evidence was too sparse to be convincing. Besides other guesses of his had been disproven, so this one was discounted also.

⁸⁸Powell, op. cit., p. 139.

⁸⁹I am indebted to Jacob W. Gruber for some insightful comments on a prepublication copy of this paper. These have to do in particular with some of the hints I set forth in this section.

⁹⁰Powell, Linguistic families. . ., pp. 2–5.

17 | 'Exclusive' and 'Inclusive': A Look at Early Usage

1. How old is the usage?

'Exclusive' and 'inclusive' are now widely accepted as convenient labels to distinguish the two kinds of first person duals and/or
plurals found in various languages around the world. The distinction
is based on whether the second person is excluded ('exclusive') or included ('inclusive').

The only attempt I know of to trace something of the history
of the use of these terms is found in a paper by Franklin Edgerton entitled Notes on Early American Work in Linguistics.[1] Since several
of his surmises turn out to be mistaken, the attempt is made here to
trace the matter a bit further back into the past. There are at least
four points on which Edgerton's account[2] requires some correction,
viz.

(1) He thinks Henry Rowe Schoolcraft may have originated
these terms, first using them in a work published in 1834.

(2) Or, if he did not originate them (see the fourth item), then
"it seems, at any rate, certain that Schoolcraft was the first even to
identify and clearly define the usage in any American language, viz.
in Ojibwa, in 1834 (Narrative of an expedition through the Upper Mississippi: 173)."[3]

(3) The second assumption rests in part on Edgerton's belief
that "European linguists seem to have first met the formal distinction
in the Malayo-Polynesian languages, where it is common."

(4) Although aware that the terms were also used by Wilhelm von Humboldt, Edgerton believes that that scholar's first published use was in Über die Kawi Sprache, published in 1838, where the German equivalents 'einschliessender' and 'ausschliessender Plural' occur.

2. Humboldt's use

It turns out that Humboldt had used the terms in a paper published in English (An Essay on the Best Means of Ascertaining the Affinities of Oriental Languages) which appeared in 1828, [4] ten years before the publication of Über die Kawi Sprache and six years before Schoolcraft's use. The discovery of Humboldt's earlier use and the context in which he uses the terms suffices to refute all four of Edgerton's points. The particular passage is as follows: [5]

> Several American languages have two plural forms in the first person, an _exclusive_ and an _inclusive_ form, according as we would include or exclude the person addressed. It has been thought that this peculiarity belonged exclusively to the American languages; but it is also found in the Mantchu, the Tamul, and in all the dialects of the South Sea Islands. [Emphasis supplied.]

It is clear from the offhand way in which Humboldt uses the terms that he was not the first one so to use them. Moreover, since he mentions it was once thought that the distinction was a 'peculiarity' of the American languages, Edgerton's surmise that European scholars first became acquainted with it in the Malayo-Polynesian languages will also not stand up.

3. Duponceau's 'particular' and 'general' plural

Both Duponceau and Pickering had written of this peculiarity of American languages a few years earlier, but Duponceau preferred the terminology _particular_ and _general_ for exclusive and inclusive, respectively. In Duponceau's commentary on Eliot's Indian Grammar, [6] written at the request of Pickering in 1820, he tells us that Pickering called the particular plural ' The _American_ plural.' In The Indian Grammar Begun [p. 7][7] Eliot lists two words for _we_, but he does not describe or mention the distinction between them. Duponceau correctly distinguished them. [8]

> The same difference is found in the <u>Massachusetts</u> [as in the Delaware], where <u>we</u> is expressed in two modes, <u>neenawun</u> and <u>kenawun</u>; the one. . .beginning with the affix of the <u>first</u> person. . .and the other with that of the <u>second</u> person; from whence, and the great affinity of the two languages, I strongly conjecture, that <u>neenawun</u> means the particular, and <u>kenawun</u> the general plural.

There is a gap in the knowledge of this period, however, for the exclusive-inclusive distinction was partly confused with a dual-plural distinction (see 5). Duponceau conjectures:[9]

> The question whether all the Indian languages have the <u>particular plural</u>, or some of them the <u>dual</u> in lieu of it is an interesting one. I at first inclined to the former opinion; but recent inquiries make the latter seem the most probable. In one of them, at least, (the Cherokee), it appears that there is a <u>dual</u> number. Mr. <u>Pickering</u>. . .was led to conjecture, that what had been called the <u>dual</u> in the Cherokee was in fact only the <u>particular</u> or <u>limited</u> plural.... But he has since informed me. . .he has ascertained that the Cherokee language has a proper <u>dual number</u>, like the languages of antiquity.

4. Pickering's 'American' plural

Pickering's opinions in regard to the exclusive plural are to be found in his commentary on Edwards' description of Mohegan in the section devoted to a general discussion of number in the American languages. [10]

> One of the most remarkable features of the American languages is, the variety and mode of using the <u>Numbers</u> of the nouns and pronouns. Some of them (the <u>Guaranese</u>, for example) have only a <u>singular</u> number, and are destitute of a distinct form for the <u>plural</u>. Some, on the other hand, have not only the singular and plural, but a <u>dual</u> also, like the

Greek and various other languages of the eastern continent; while a third class of them has not only a singular, dual, and plural (that is the common unlimited plural of the European languages) but also an additional plural, which is denominated by some writers the exclusive plural, by others the particular plural; and by others the limited plural; but which, if it should prove to be peculiar to the languages of this continent, might very properly be called the American plural.

Pickering then adds some remarks on what he has found in the writings on the South American languages. Although he is not concerned with tracing the origin of the terms 'exclusive' and 'inclusive' — after all he seems to have no particular preference for them — he does cite sources that enable us to trace them back to 1782, and possibly even to 1754. He tells us that Gilij[11] describes this type of number distinction in Tamanacan, Inca, and Chiquito and he gives quotations from this source at some length. For our purposes the following brief excerpts will suffice:[12]

In my MS. Grammar of the Tamanacan language, I have called this mode of speech the determinate plural.

But of greater interest is the fact that in another passage the very terms 'inclusive' and 'exclusive' appear:[13]

[In Cichitto, i.e. Chiquito] there is, in the first person plural, the inclusive number, as it is called, and the exclusive number, exactly as in the language of the Incas.

Gilij's work was published in 1782, but Pickering adds, "See also Torres Rubio's Arte, &c. pp. 6 and 52." This latter work was published in 1754.[14]

5. Gallatin's remarks

Gallatin's famous work, entitled A Synopsis of the Indian Tribes within the United States East of the Rocky Mountains, and in the British and Russian Possessions in North America,[15] is most often consulted as the first basic work on the classification of the

languages of North America. But the work is also notable for its
discussion of the grammatical features of the North American languages tolerably well known at the time. He first mentions the topic
of exclusive-inclusive in the following terms:[16]

> In all the languages which have been investigated, with the
> exception of those of the Sioux family, concerning which the
> information is not sufficient, there is, besides the singular
> and general or indefinite plural, a third number, which is
> sometimes a dual, more generally a definite or special plural,
> occasionally assuming both forms.

We learn further that:[17]

> In the various dialects of the Algonkin-Lenape, and in the
> Choctaw, it is a definite plural; but, although including al-
> ways, in every dialect, a definite number of persons, it is
> not applied precisely in the same manner in all.
>   In the Delaware, according to Mr. Heckewelder, it em-
> braces our family, nation, select body. . .; and including
> therefore, at least when he, or they belong to the nation or
> select body, the person or persons spoken to. But in the
> Chippeway [Ojibwa], as we are informed by Mr. Schoolcraft,
> it always excludes the person or persons thus spoken to; and
> it is used in the same manner in the Micmac.

Gallatin uses the same terminology, 'definite' for 'exclusive,' and in
addition, 'indefinite' for 'inclusive' when describing Choctaw usage:[18]

> In the Choctaw, where pishno [/pišnŭ/] is the pronoun of
> the first person for the definite, and hupishno [/hapišnŭ/]
> that for the indefinite; according to Mr. Wright, "hupishno
> is used, when speaking of an action in which all the hearers
> are concerned. But if all the hearers are not concerned in
> it, but only the speaker and some other persons (understood
> or designated), pishno is used."

A few pages later he adopts Schoolcraft's terminology when talking
again about Algonkin-Lenape:[19]

The exclusive or special plural is that which excludes the
person spoken to. The inclusive or indefinite includes that
person.

6. Conclusion

Table 1 has been prepared to show the synonymy of the various terms that have been used to describe the notions exclusive and
inclusive. I make no claim to have traced the terms back to their
original source. However, two points appear to have been established
with a reasonable degree of firmness: (1) The terms have been in use
for at least two centuries and probably more. (2) They may very well
have been first used to describe a seeming peculiarity of American
languages — not North American languages, to be sure, but South
American.[20]

It should also be pointed out that, while Schoolcraft did not
originate the terms, there is a growing tendency after his time to use
them in preference to competing terms. Duponceau, in his earlier
work, and Pickering seem to have preferred Duponceau's somewhat
less felicitous terms 'particular' and 'general'. Gallatin uses several
terms but includes among them 'exclusive' and 'inclusive'. Duponceau,
in his Memoire sur le système grammatical des langues de quelques
nations indiennes de l'Amérique du nord,[21] quotes Schoolcraft and
uses 'exclusif' and 'inclusif' as well as 'particulier' and 'général'.

Trumbull, writing four decades later, clearly indicates his
preference for 'exclusive' and 'inclusive' by italicizing them in his
text:[22]

In many [Indian languages] there are two pronouns of the first
person plural, which, combining with nouns and verbs, form
the inclusive and exclusive, or "general" and "limited", plurals, the former including both the speaker and those to whom
he speaks ("you and I"), the latter including only the speaker
and those for whom he speaks, and excluding all others ("we,
not you").

TABLE 1

		Exclusive	Inclusive
1560	Domingo de Santo Tomás	(forms which exclude)	(forms which include)
1607	González Holguin	exclusiuo	inclusiuo
1619	Torres Rubio	excluyendo	incluyendo
1782	Gilij	escludente	includente
1782	Gilij	determinate	
1820	Duponceau	particular, limited	general
1823	Pickering	exclusive = particular = limited; American	(general)
1829	Humboldt	exclusive	inclusive
1834	Schoolcraft	exclusive	inclusive
1836	Gallatin	definite or special = exclusive	indefinite = inclusive
1838	Humboldt	ausschliessend	einschliessend
1838	Duponceau	particulier; exclusif	général (illimité); inclusif
1876	Trumbull	exclusive (limited)	inclusive (general)
1911	Boas	exclusive	inclusive

He also mentions the distribution of the use of such pronominal ideas and, incidentally, clarifies the Cherokee situation which was not fully described by Duponceau:[23]

> The double first person plural (inclusive and exclusive) belongs to all Algonkin languages, to the Iroquois, Cherokee,

Choctaw, Sahaptin (Nez Percé), Quichua, and others. It is found also in the Dravidian languages of Southern India, in the Manchu, in Polynesian and some Australian dialects, and in those of Hottentot tribes of South Africa.... In the Cherokee. . .the dual as well as the plural has inclusive and exclusive forms for the first person — "we two" (i. e. "he and I"), and "we two" (i. e. "thou and I, and not he").

As might be expected, the details of specification differ from language family to language family. The Siouan languages, for example, have a special inclusive form but no contrasting exclusive form. In other words, the inclusive is simply you and I and aside from this the dual is generally not distinctive. Except for the Choctaw branch, the known Muskogean languages do not have an exclusive-inclusive distinction. On the other hand, there are the Algonkian languages, which have exclusive and inclusive plurals, and the Iroquoian languages, including Cherokee (as mentioned by Trumbull),[24] which have a full set of duals as well as plurals and make the exclusive-inclusive distinction in both.

Although 'exclusive' and 'inclusive' have been shown to have a history of at least two centuries, the terms were generally used in competition with other terms in descriptions of North American languages up until the publication in 1911 of the first volume of the Handbook of American Indian Languages.[25] In his famous 'Introduction' Boas uses the terms in his general discussion of the principles of classification in pronouns[26] and makes no mention of competing terms. The terms are also used in the grammatical sketches contained in the book wherever pertinent. Thus we find both terms used in Kwakiutl, Chinook, and Fox (Algonkian), and the inclusive alone in Dakota (Siouan).[27] In the second volume of the Handbook, Coos is described as having the exclusive-inclusive distinction in the dual but not in the plural, while Siuslaw has it in both the dual and the plural.[28] Yuchi, described in the third volume, lacks a dual, but has the exclusive-inclusive distinction in the plural.[29]

The present study has been limited to a history of the usage adopted for languages of the Western hemisphere. It is hoped that others may be encouraged to trace out the usage applied to the Malayo-Polynesian languages and the languages of Asia and Africa.

7. Addendum: Comments by John H. Rowe

John H. Rowe, who did not see the prepublication copy of
this paper until his return from Peru in late September, immediately
sent me some comments that clear up several points about early usage that are left hanging in my remarks. This is so interesting that
I quote it here in Rowe's own words with his permission.[30]

> The trail you followed in asking how old the usage is leads
> right to some authors that I know quite well, and you might
> be interested in some comments and supplementary notes.
> Pickering's translation of Gilij's Italian is not quite ac-
> curate. What Gilij says in the original (I own a copy) is:
> "in questa lingua avvi nella prima persona del numero plurale
> il numero detto _includente_, e quello che chiamasi _escludente_
> nè più nè meno, che nella lingua degl'Inchi." (p. 246). (Ital-
> ics in the original.) "Includente" and "escludente" mean
> literally "including" and "excluding," not "inclusive" and "ex-
> clusive."
> The equivalent Spanish terms are used by Torres Rubio:
> "incluyendo" and "excluyendo." It should be noted that the
> 1754 edition of Torres Rubio's work (I have a copy of that,
> too) is a reprint of a work originally published in 1619 (Lima).
> The earliest use of "inclusive" and "exclusive" that I
> know of is in the Inca grammar by Diego González Holguin,
> published in 1607. He speaks consistently of "plural inclu-
> siuo y exclusiuo" (first on f. 11r).
> The first Inca grammar, that of Domingo de Santo Tomás
> (1560), uses a verbal rather than an adjectival terminology;
> he speaks of forms which include or exclude. I do not have
> access to the second grammar of 1586, so cannot tell you
> whether González Holguin was anticipated exactly in the 16th
> century or not. In any case, it is evident that the inclusive-
> exclusive contrast was noted in Inca from the very beginnings,
> and the Inca grammatical tradition is a very good candidate
> for the source of the concept in North America, through Gilij
> and Pickering and Humboldt.

NOTES

It is a pleasure to acknowledge that this paper was written while I was holding concurrently a Senior Fellowship of the National Endowment for the Arts and Humanities and a fellowship in residence at the Center for Advanced Study in the Behavioral Sciences, Stanford.

[1] In Proceedings of the American Philosophical Society, 87. 25-34 (1943).

[2] Edgerton, op. cit., p. 31, footnote 29.

[3] I have not seen the edition referred to by Edgerton. In 1855 a new addition with appendices appeared under the title, Summary Narrative of an Exploratory Expedition to the Sources of the Mississippi River, in 1820: Resumed and Completed by Discovery of its Origin in Itasca Lake, in 1832 (Philadelphia: Lippincott, Grambo, and Co.). One of the appendices includes a section on Observations on the Grammatical Structure and Flexibility of the Ojibwa Substantive. On p. 458 he states that "there is, in the pronoun, an inclusive and an exclusive plural," and adds:

> the plural we, and us, and our — for they are rendered by the same form — admit of a change to indicate whether the objective person be included or excluded. This principle . . . forms a single and anomalous instance of the use of particular plurals. [Emphasis in thicker underlining added.]

[4] In Transactions of the Royal Asiatic Society of Great Britain and Ireland, 2.3-11 (1828). The paper is stated to be by Baron William Humboldt and "contained in a letter addressed to Sir Alexander Johnston, knt., V.P.R.A.S."

[5] Ibid., p. 7.

[6] Peter S. Duponceau, Notes and observations on Eliot's Indian grammar. Addressed to John Pickering, Esq., Collections of the Massachusetts Historical Society, Series 2, 9. i-xxix (Boston, first printing 1822, reprinting 1832).

[7] John Eliot, The Indian grammar begun: or, an essay to bring the Indian language into rules, Collections of the Massachusetts Historical Society, Series 2, 9. 243-312 (Boston, 1832) (a reprinting of the original edition, Cambridge 1666).

[8] Duponceau, op. cit., p. xxix.

[9] Ibid., p. xx.

[10] John Pickering, Notes by the editor [to Edwards' observations on the Mohegan language], Collections of the Massachusetts

Historical Society, Ser. 2, 10.98-134 (Boston, first printing 1823, reprinting 1843).

[11]F. S. Gilij, Saggio di Storia Americana, vol. iii (Roma, 1782). Pickering refers to pp. 163 and 181; also 236, 237, and 246.

[12]Pickering, op. cit., p. 107, quoting from Gilij.

[13]Ibid., pp. 107-108, quoting from Gilij.

[14]Father Torres Rubio, Arte y vocabulario de la lengua Quichua general de los Indios de el Peru (Lima, 1754). Pickering refers to pp. 6 and 52. See also fn. 29.

[15]Trans. and Coll. Amer. Antiquarian Soc., 2.1-422 (Cambridge, 1836).

[16]Ibid., p. 171.

[17]Ibid.

[18]Ibid., p. 172.

[19]Ibid., p. 179.

[20]Since this was written comments received from John H. Rowe (see 7) have cleared up all these points and Table 1 has been emended to show the story back to 1560.

[21]Paris, 1838.

[22]J. Hammond Trumbull, Indian languages of America, Johnson's New Universal Cyclopaedia 2.1160 (New York, 1876).

[23]Ibid.

[24]Cherokee was not known to be Iroquoian in Trumbull's time. It was even thought it might turn out to be Muskogean; Trumbull, op. cit., p. 1156.

[25]Franz Boas, ed., Handbook of American Indian Languages, Part I (= BAE-B 40, Part I, Washington, 1911).

[26]Ibid., pp. 39-40.

[27]Ibid., p. 529 (Kwakiutl), p. 580 (Chinook), p. 851 (Fox), and p. 908 (Dakota).

[28]Franz Boas, ed., Handbook of American Indian Languages, Part 2 (= BAE-B 40, Part 2, Washington, 1922). The Coos forms are given on p. 395 and the Siuslaw on pp. 468-475.

[29]Franz Boas, ed., Handbook of American Indian Languages, Part 3 (Glückstadt-Hamburg-New York, 1933-38).

[30]For the references cited in Rowe's comments see Paul Rivet and Georges de Créqui-Montfort, Bibliographie des langues aymará et kičua. Université de Paris. Travaux et Mémoires de l'Institut d'Ethnologie. — LI. Paris (1951-56) 4 vols. Vol. I of this work, dated 1951, covers the years 1540-1875, and the works listed

are provided with running catalogue numbers. These numbers are
given below in connection with the following authors in the order they
are mentioned by Rowe:

Gilij, 1780-84, no. 141.

Torres Rubio, 1754, no. 124.

Torres Rubio, 1619 (the first edition), no. 53.

González Holguin, 1607, no. 35.

Domingo de Santo Tomás, 1560, no. 3 (there are two modern facsimile editions).

Anonymous Inca grammar of 1586, no. 9.

18 | Problems of American Indian Philology

1. Introduction

The study of American Indian languages is a pursuit that has been going on for more than four centuries. Within a few decades after Columbus's landing in the West Indies, the Spanish had penetrated into Mexico and Peru, and basic works on Inca (Quichua), Aymara, Nahuatl, and Tarascan — to mention only some of the earliest — were already under way. The work was done by priests, who were usually the best-educated men of their day. Far from being monolingual, they all knew Latin and Greek and many were also versed in Hebrew. They were thus as well prepared for their task as any men could be in the early part of the sixteenth century.

Throughout the intervening centuries the work of priests and missionaries, Protestant as well as Catholic, has accounted for over ninety percent of the material available on American Indian languages. This is as true of work in the twentieth century as in earlier times. But in spite of the prominent role of missionaries in this work, many other materials were collected by travellers and explorers, especially in the 17th, 18th, and 19th centuries. Some of these men had very little education of any kind, while others had more sophistication in navigation, geography, and botany than in letters. But the explorer, even though he was often mainly an advance man for the exploiter, had a serious obligation to record all the information he could about rivers and mountains, flora and fauna, minerals, and other matters of possible economic importance. And included in this array of data-gathering was the obligation to provide some information about the inhabitants and their customs and languages.

By the nineteenth century some exploring expeditions were well-equipped with trained scientists to provide information on their specialty. It was unusual for linguistics, or 'philology', as it was then often called, to be represented on an expedition; but it did happen on rare occasions. A notable instance is the case of Horatio Hale. At the age of twenty, having just been graduated from Harvard, he was appointed philologist and ethnographer to the United States Exploring Expedition, commanded by Charles Wilkes, which circumnavigated the globe from 1838 to 1842. In 1841 the Expedition stopped at the Oregon Territory and Hale departed in order to conduct a survey of the languages and peoples of Northwestern America, and he collected materials from Central California to Vancouver Island.

With the work of Hale we have come to an important turning point in the study of American Indian languages. Although his appointment was as 'philologist', this term had a broader implication than it came to have later. He was in fact a field linguist, i.e., a scholar who wrote down linguistic information from the lips of the native speakers solely for scholarly purposes. Prior to his time (and frequently after) those who worked directly with native speakers were generally missionaries with the practical intent of translating catechisms and con- fesionarios or the Bible; while those whose interests were solely of a scholarly nature tended to rely on vocabularies, grammars, and dictionaries collected and written up by others. But Hale's work, published in 1846,[1] was not given wide circulation by the Government and did not have the impact it might otherwise have had, much to Hale's disappointment. However, Albert Gallatin, who had in 1836 published a classification of the American Indian languages of as much of North America as he had material for,[2] made good use of Hale's material in his 1848 classification which he published under the title Hale's Indians of north-west America, and vocabularies of North America, with an introduction.[3]

The almost complete shift from what might be called armchair philology, as practised by Peter S. Duponceau, Albert Gallatin, and Robert Latham,[4] to field linguistics, as begun in the same period by men like Horatio Hale, was spurred by another exploring expedition a half century later — namely, the Jesup North Pacific Expedition of 1883-84, which initiated Franz Boas as a field anthropologist and linguist. The eventual influence of Boas was so great that through the better part of the 20th century scholarly work on American Indian languages was conducted almost entirely by the field approach. In many cases this approach became so extreme that the work of early missionaries and travellers, even where pertinent, was neglected in favor of whatever the investigator could obtain from contemporary speakers. Hence Truman Michelson, even though he had been trained in Indo-European philology in Germany under Brugmann, took the view as a field worker that "It is simply a waste of time to attempt to unravel the vagaries of the orthography of the older writers in the case of dialects existing today."[5]

This shift of emphasis had another important impact. Direct field work on American Indian languages gave rise to the descriptive method in linguistics as promulgated by Edward Sapir and Leonard Bloomfield and their immediate followers. This method finally came to be associated with what might be called an 'antiphilological' stance. This was justified on the basis of the fact that traditional orthographies often obscured the actual sounds of a language, while the use of a phonetic alphabet more often than not clarified many grammatical as well as phonological features of a language.

2. Renewed Interest in Philology

Now, as we approach the last quarter of the 20th century, a new attitude in regard to the records of the past is gaining ascendance. The American Indian linguist is no longer exclusively a descriptive and/or comparative linguist, he is often a philologist as well; and articles are beginning to be written with this approach in mind. Indeed the volume on Linguistics in North America (Current Trends in Linguistics, vol. X) which has just appeared signals this new interest with an article by Ives Goddard entitled "Philological Approaches to the Study of North American Indian Languages: Documents and Documentation."[6]

American Indian philology poses all the problems of philology in general plus a few that are rather special to it. The following problems are especially deserving of study: (1) orthographies, (2) the interpretation of orthographies, (3) theoretical orientation from century to century, (4) translation, (5) extinct and unidentified languages.

Within the scope of this paper most of the discussion is concerned
with the first two points.

3.1. Orthographies

The development of the idea of a phonetic alphabet which could
be adapted to a variety of languages came rather late. Vast quantities
of material on and in languages of the New World have been written in
one or the other of the Euronational orthographies — including Spanish,
English, French, Portuguese, Swedish, Dutch, and German (as deriv-
atives of the Latin alphabet), as well as Greek and Russian. Indeed
for three centuries only Euronational orthographies were used, though
special adaptations were of course often necessary. As might be expected, Spanish, and, more rarely, Portuguese orthographies were
used in Latin America and in Florida; French, in Canada and Louisiana; while English was used in most other parts of North America, including Canada. Overlapping was common and of course travellers
might make use of their national orthographies anywhere. Russian was
employed in Alaska and for a few vocabularies on the coast of California. German was used by Moravian missionaries in Pennsylvania and
parts of the South; and for at least one language (Creek, a Muskogean
language) the Moravians are said to have adapted the Greek alphabet.
Before the advent of the idea of a phonetic alphabet these orthographies
were utilized, as nearly as possible, with the values they had in the
language of the recorder; when new sounds had to be transcribed various kinds of adaptation had to be made and such adaptations might vary
from recorder to recorder. Sometimes a recorder might borrow a
letter or two from some other orthography known to him, as when
Greek letters were sometimes employed.

In addition to the various adaptations of Euronational orthographies in various parts of the New World, there also arose some post-
Columbian native or partially native orthographies and syllabaries.
Perhaps the most celebrated native syllabary is the one invented by
Sequoiah for his native Cherokee. He did not understand the values of
the letters of the Latin alphabet, but he was aware that white men could
read by the use of such written letters. He copied letters and figures
from a spelling book, sometimes backwards or upside down, and he
also invented many letters. He gave each of them a syllabic value and

it took him considerable time to determine how many he would need.
In the end he used six symbols for each consonant sound in order to
accommodate six different vowels, e.g., /ya/ /ye/ /yi/ /yo/ /yu/
/yə/. The invention of the Cherokee syllabary was an outstanding
achievement.[7] It was accepted by the Cherokee leaders in 1821 and
was quickly learned by dozens of previously nonliterate monolingual
speakers. A weekly newspaper, The Cherokee Phoenix, began to appear in 1828. Over the years many materials on myths, medicines,
and other lore were written down by numerous Indians. Some of these
have been collected and are on deposit in the Smithsonian Institution
National Anthropological Archives and some have been interpreted and
translated. Some have been published. But many more remain un-
worked and it would be hard to estimate how much material has never
even been collected.

        Although Moravian missionaries of the 18th century are said
to have adapted the Greek alphabet for the writing of Creek, a Muskogean language of Alabama and Georgia (later Oklahoma), this method
apparently did not catch on with the speakers. In the middle of the
nineteenth century a collaboration between a missionary and a Creek
convert led to the development of the Creek alphabet through adaptation of certain letters of the Latin alphabet. Since there are only
thirteen consonants, little change was required. However, each consonant was always written with the same letter, unlike the practice in
most European languages, and digraphs for consonants were also a-
voided. In addition two well-chosen adaptations were made. The letter c was used for the ch sound; and r, which did not occur as a phoneme of the language, was adapted for /ɬ/, the voiceless lateral spirant. The English values of the vowels and diphthongs were used, however, and this has resulted in inconsistency and ambiguity. Nevertheless, the alphabet was learned and used by large numbers of Creeks,
and at one time there was a newspaper. The Bible has been written in
this alphabet and there are also hymns and religious tracts. In addition there is a Creek-English and English-Creek dictionary as well as
other works, such as the Constitution and Laws of the Creek Nation.

        The Creek alphabet could also be adopted for use in writing
some other Indian languages, and those who spoke Creek and some
other Indian language often wrote both languages in the Creek alphabet. I have seen Hitchiti, another Muskogean language, and Natchez,
a language isolate distantly related to Muskogean, written in this way.

Early in the nineteenth century there developed a great interest in comparing as many American Indian languages as possible in order to determine something of their interrelationships. Prominent among those who were interested in this endeavor were Benjamin Smith Barton, Thomas Jefferson, and John Pickering. But their efforts were far too often hampered in an exasperating fashion by the lack of a consistent orthography. The solution of the problem was not easy. Throughout the 19th century and on into the 20th, all kinds of recommendations were made to achieve an orthography suitable for representing the sounds of all languages. John Pickering may have been the first to tackle the problem head-on, in his essay "On the adoption of a uniform orthography for the Indian languages of North America."[8] It was successful enough to be used not only by many missionaries to the Indians but also in the Sandwich Islands. But many facts about the wide variety of sounds, especially consonants, were not yet known. Interestingly enough, vowels seemed at first to be the greatest problem, not because of any great vocalic subtleties in the Indian languages, but because of the great discrepancies in the use of the familiar a e i o u of the Latin alphabet, especially among the English, the French, and the Germans. Pickering, recognizing the severity of this problem, recommended that these letters by used with their Italian values.

As time went on, other recommendations and modifications were made by Albert Gallatin,[9] Horatio Hale,[10] George Gibbs,[11] William Dwight Whitney,[12] and John W. Powell.[13] In spite of the great effort expended, none of these was completely satisfactory. The Powell recommendations, however, were widely used, since he required their use among the many missionaries, explorers, field workers, and Indians whom he called upon to fill out the blank Schedules he had prepared in his Introduction to the Study of Indian Languages.[14] The Powell alphabet, with an occasional modification, was also employed by the various field workers who were affiliated with the Bureau of American Ethnology of the Smithsonian Institution, the Bureau having been founded by Powell. These workers accumulated vast quantities of material, much of which has never been published but remains as a valuable source of information in the archives of the Bureau (now the National Anthropological Archives).

When the Handbook of American Indian Languages, Part I,[15] appeared under the editorship of Franz Boas, Boas described his own orthography, which was a modification of Powell's, in his "Introduction."[16]

By and large, the contributors to the volume used the same general
system; but if another orthography was already in use for a particular
language, the editor permitted that usage, with modification if needed
for phonetic accuracy. If more than one orthography was in use,
equivalences might be given, as was the case for Dakota where the
orthography devised by Stephen R. Riggs was preferred but the equivalents in the system devised by James O. Dorsey are also presented.[17]

But there was a growing dissatisfaction with some of the de-
ficiencies of the system as well as with some of the more awkward
symbols being used, such as the exclamation point to mark glottalized
consonants (e.g., p! t! k!) or the raised epsilon ᵋ to indicate the
glottal stop. Consequently some of the members of the American Anthropological Association, among them Franz Boas and Edward Sapir,
sponsored a revised orthography. This was explained and illustrated
in "Phonetic Transcription of Indian Languages," published in 1916.[18]
This system of transcription rather quickly superseded earlier systems. This means, for instance, that Sapir's transcription of a particular language would be given in one system of transcription before
1916 and in the revised system after that date. Many linguists gave no
more clue as to the change than to say after 1916, "The alphabet is
that now in general use in America."[19]

As will be readily understood, the problems encountered in
finding an orthography for American Indian languages are no different
from those encountered with other unwritten languages. But the orthographic traditions of North America were little affected by what
went on in other parts of the world. About this time a group of European scholars founded the International Phonetic Association, and one
of the first things they did was to devise a standardized orthography
which they called the International Phonetic Alphabet, or IPA.[20] Although this alphabet would have been useful for American Indian languages, its use did not catch on among American linguists who seemed
inclined to stick with their own system. One of the few field workers
who did use it (other than an occasional visiting European) was John P.
Harrington, who in spite of having been taken on as an ethnologist in
the Bureau of American Ethnology, which had usually been rather conservative in its orthographic usage, made some use of the IPA in some
of his work. However, he also used many idiosyncratic signs of his
own invention, as in his Kiowa Vocabulary.[21]

So, except for a few deviants like Harrington, the A.A.A. system was more or less consistently applied for the next quarter of a century. By the early 1930's, however, certain ideas about the theory of the phoneme were developing and some changes were again in order. In 1934, a group of six Yale linguists published a note in the American Anthropologist entitled "Some Orthographic Recommendations"[22] which set forth some very important changes. These were accepted more readily and more widely than any previous recommendations among American Indian linguists. Some influence of the IPA could be seen but in general the system retained many important distinctions. After forty years this orthographic system is still widely used though quite a few individual variations have crept in, particularly in the last decade.

These 1934 orthographic recommendations had a strong impact in two ways. The first was the dictum that "A suitable orthography for representing the sounds of a given language should provide a unit symbol for each phoneme, i.e., for each psychologically unitary sound...."[23] The second impact was the abandonment of certain idiosyncrasies that had characterized the Americanist system for many decades. The most perturbing of these was the use of c for the sound of the English sh. I do not know who first used this letter in this way but it has been found in the writings of missionaries of French Canada belonging to the middle of the 19th century. It is undeniable that the selection of a proper symbol for this sound has almost always been controversial and the proper interpretation of the multiplicity of representations that are or have been in use requires not a little esoteric knowledge. The 1934 recommendation was to use [š]. Most of the other changes involved the adaptation or invention of unitary symbols for the former digraphs; e.g., [c] for ts, [č] for tc, [λ] for dl [ƛ] for ʈɫ. The general adoption of these recommendations was rather swift. Articles employing them began to appear in the International Journal of American Linguistics, in Language, and elsewhere. Languages like Nootka (Vancouver Island), which had been worked on by Edward Sapir from the early part of the century, were written in one orthography before 1916, in another orthography after 1916, and in still another after 1934. The change in the value of the letter c has been a particular source of misunderstanding, especially since c is often also used for [č] if only one affricate occurs in a given language.

Within the last decade or so there has come to be less uniformity among linguists in orthographic use than formerly, but for

the most part the variations are individual. Thus in writing his Athapaskan materials Harry Hoijer used the digraph ƚ prior to 1934, ƛ for
a couple of decades after 1934, and then readopted the old Boasian ꓡ
in an article in 1960, [24] and has also sometimes returned to the digraph ƚ. Similar vacillations could be cited for other writers.

The major change that has taken place in the last decade is
the influence of recent phonological theory. Here the phoneme of the
1930's is bypassed; an underlying form is formulated and a sequence
of rules derives the phonetic output. The actual phonetic symbols
used for this last stage, however, have not necessarily undergone
much change. But when words are written morphophonemically rather than phonetically, a particular language can present an utterly different appearance from what it had when written according to classical
phonemic theory.

3.2. Problems with the Interpretation of the Writing System

With four centuries of accumulated materials, with numerous
Euronational orthographies and specially adapted orthographies (such
as for Creek), and the even more numerous phonetic orthographies,
any would-be philologist who wishes to make use of a given document
(even a short vocabulary) soon realizes that he must have a great deal
of information before he can make a phonetic interpretation of it. The
chief kinds of additional information needed can be summarized as
follows:

Up to 1800 it is necessary to know the nationality of
the recorder in order to interpret his orthographic usage.
Contrast, for example, the value of ch in Spanish and English,
in French, and in German; or the value of j in Spanish, in
English, in French, and in German; etc.

From 1800 on it is still often necessary to know the
nationality of the recorder, but it is also necessary to know
whether he has adopted one of the standardized phonetic orthographies that begin to appear every generation or so. And
after 1900 it may be very important to know whether the document was written before or after 1916, before or after 1934,
and so on. For example, if a student working on Algonkian

equates c̱ written by Bloomfield in 1925[25] with c̱ written by
him in 1946[26] (as has been done in more than one instance),
he has made a serious error.

The orthography of the document may be one especially invented or adapted for the particular language, and
the letters may very well have quite idosyncratic values;
e.g., ṟ for [ɬ] in Creek.

The occupation of the recorder may also be very important since it may give a clue to his degree of education or
to the amount of time he may have spent listening to the language. Thus vocabularies written down by travellers, explorers, or surveyors may be based on just a few hours'
work — not enough time to grasp the sounds of a strange language other than superficially, even for a linguist. Anthropologists may also spend very little time on the language,
while those who do spend considerable time can probably be
counted as linguists. Then we have missionaries and linguists
who generally spend a considerable amount of time with a language and we can thus hope we have a more reliable document.

The preceding points are based on the assumption
that the recorder is a foreigner. We also have many documents written by native speakers (e.g., Cherokees, Creeks,
Choctaws, Dakotas, and many others), where a certain a-
mount of literacy may have become rather general in the tribe.
A somewhat different situation exists when a single native
speaker has been taught to write his language in order to provide material for the linguist, as when Sapir taught Alex
Thomas to write Nootka. In either of these cases careless-
ness in regard to certain features, especially diacritics, may
develop, as when most Creeks dropped the macron on ē (to
be read [i·]) and it could not be distinguished from e̱ (to be
read [i]).

It is also necessary to know the theoretical orientation of the period in which the document was written; in
times of fluctuation it is even necessary to know the theoretical orientation of the person writing the document. A

document prepared in terms of classical phonemic theory
will require a very different interpretation from one written
prior to the development of the theory. Sapir's early Nootka
materials contain a wealth of phonetic detail, including whis-
pered vowels and consonantal timbres as well as variant re-
cordings of one and the same word; but the phonemically
transcribed materials published later lack these details and
variations. [27]

If the language of the document is extinct but has
living relatives, guidance in the phonetic interpretation of the
document can be gained (though not without pitfalls) through
comparison with modern dialects.

If the language of the document is extinct and has
no known relatives, the chances of making some determination of the sounds represented range from very poor to reasonable, depending upon the various factors mentioned above.

Examples of some of the problems mentioned above may help
clarify some points. Not all of the priests who followed the Spanish
conquerors into Mexico and Peru were Spanish-born — some may have
been Italian or Portuguese. And even though they might still adopt
Spanish orthography in writing an Indian language, their hearing of the
new sounds would be influenced by their native language.

There is an even more serious problem in regard to documents written in Spanish possessions in the 16th century. Spanish of
this period was undergoing some sound changes and for this reason, if
the value of the Indian sound is unknown, the interpretation can be extremely troublesome since it may be impossible to determine which
side of the sound shift the recorder's speech is on. This problem
causes difficulties in the interpretation of the many 16th century documents of Mexico and Peru. Fortunately many of these languages are
still spoken so it is usually possible to make plausible deductions.
However, it is not all smooth sailing even then, and this for two reasons: (1) the modern dialect may not be a direct descendant of the
16th century recorded dialect; and (2) in four hundred years the Indian
language may have undergone some sound shifts.

There is a tremendous amount of philological work that could
be done in comparing these early recorded languages with their modern descendants and/or relatives, but the surface has scarcely been
scratched, largely because the philological frame of reference has
been so widely neglected by American Indian linguists, as I have mentioned earlier.

In 1950 John H. Rowe made a preliminary attack on such a
problem in his article "Sound Patterns in Three Inca Dialects,"[28] by
using the modern Cuzco and Ayacucho dialects to make a detailed determination of the sounds of Classic Inca. The problem of the sibilants, however, was not completely solved, as he explains:

> Examining the distributions of the letters, s, ss, c,
> and z in our documents we find that they fall easily into pairs
> ....It seems likely, then, that these four letters represent a
> maximum of two phonemes; the question is whether there
> really were two such phonemes in the Classic dialect or wheth-
> er the four letters represent merely an extension of obsolete
> spelling conventions to Inca. In the latter case we might have
> only one s phoneme as in modern Cuzco and Ayacucho. [29]

Now we are faced here with a most remarkable set of circumstances.
Clearly we need more Spanish philological studies to determine more
about the 16th century variant spellings and pronunciations. At the
same time there is a considerable amount of 16th century material
written in Aymara and several languages of Mexico which could be
subjected to the same kind of philological analysis as has been applied to Inca by Rowe. Moreover, I venture to say that if this were
properly done, American Indian philology might possibly throw some
light on 16th century Spanish philology. In this way important new
possibilities could be opened up in the future. The chief difficulty is
that a great many Indian specialists would have to get involved and
then their work would have to be made known to and understood by His-
panic philologists. [30]

Similar philological problems exist in the interpretation of
all of the other Euronational orthographies. Indeed most of them pose
even more problems than the Spanish. The worst of all is probably
the English, though French can be pretty exasperating, and while the

chief use of these two orthographies was in the 17th, 18th and early
19th centuries, some use has continued to the present. French missionaries of the 17th and 18th centuries prepared a large volume of
material on the Iroquoian and Algonkian languages, and much of this
material remains unpublished. Victor E. Hanzeli provides much
valuable information in "Missionary Linguistics in New France,"[31]
including a discussion of the way in which the missionaries worked
and a list of many of the unpublished manuscripts.

Many more examples could be adduced but these will suffice
for the present. There remain a few more points in regard to writing which deserve some discussion.

3.3. Miscopying

Miscopying is as serious a problem in American Indian philology as it is elsewhere. It is especially critical in the case of extinct languages. When handwritten vocabularies are published in
printed form, all sorts of errors creep in. Even an experienced linguist may have no way of figuring out whether a particular squiggle is
to be interpreted as wi, we, mi, me, nu, un, im, iin, or whatever,
and it is not hard to find examples of this. And when an amateur pre-
pares a handwritten vocabulary for publication, the results can be almost useless. This would not be too bad if users would only remember the high likelihood of error, but there is a tendency to overlook
this. I know of no way around this except by publishing a facsimile of
the original manuscript alongside the printed interpretation. The
reader then has a chance to make his own interpretation of the handwriting and to make corrections accordingly. A good example of this
having been done is seen in John P. Harrington's "The original Strachey vocabulary of the Virginia Indian language."[32] Although Harrington
had considerable familiarity with Algonkian languages, he has made
some errors of interpretation. These can often be corrected by referring to the facsimile, particularly if the word has cognates. For
example, where Harrington reads Quautamu, I read Quantamu, which
is from Proto-Algonkian *kwantamwa 'he swallows it.' In place of
Racaioh 'sand,' I read Racawh, which is from PA *le·kawi. But to
publish all such things in facsimile would be very expensive, so it
must be emphasized that when a facsimile is not given the original
should be checked by the user whenever possible.

There is another kind of miscopying which can very easily be overlooked by the American Indian philologist. This arises from the copying and recopying of the same document through many hands. In this case it may even be very difficult to determine which is the original. This problem can arise at any time, of course, but it is particularly to be remembered in connection with materials from the first half of the nineteenth century. This was the time when interest was high in obtaining vocabularies of as many American Indian languages as possible in order to attempt to classify them. Interested persons traded copies of such vocabularies and there is often no knowing how many handwritten copies exist, with no one knows how many errors in each. Thomas Jefferson, Peter S. Duponceau, Albert Gallatin, Robert Latham, and many others were engaged in this activity.

There is still another kind of miscopying which arises to plague us. This is when a field worker makes a mistake in copying his own notes, either because he is unable at times to read his own handwriting or through an occasional lapse. Many of the field workers of the Bureau of American Ethnology would make a 'fair copy' of their original field notes. Sometimes the original was then destroyed, but at other times both copies are still extant. After the typewriter came into use, the fair copy was often made on the typewriter. If the type-written copy had no errors, it was an improvement since it eliminated undecipherable squiggles. But the greatest chance for error arises when a field worker transcribes his original notes into another phonetic system. Since phonetic orthographies tend to change every twenty or thirty years, there is scarcely a field worker who has not had to do just this. When the same letter is used with different values in succeeding systems, the chances for error are very great.

3.4. Rewriting

By 'rewriting' I mean not simply transcribing a document from one phonetic system into another, but a reinterpretation of the writing system of the original document. This problem arose particularly during the time when many linguists wished to reinterpret older works in terms of phonemic theory. In many cases this simply cannot be done with satisfactory results. But the temptation can be very strong, especially in the case of materials written with a plethora of phonetic niceties which are so difficult to print and awkward to quote. It is really not possible to be dogmatic about whether rewriting should be done or not be done. There may be occasions when it can serve a useful purpose. But it is always risky, especially in the case of extinct languages, and so probably should be avoided if possible. A good example occurs in the case of Ofo, a Siouan language of the Southeast. The only vocabulary we have of the language was taken down by John R. Swanton early in this century.[33] He frequently wrote x̱, x̱, or ẖ after certain consonants but sometimes he wrote the same word without such indication. Although he himself was at pains to point out that "x̱, x̱, and ẖ all usually stand for the aspirate which follows several Siouan consonants and is particularly prominent in the Ofo language,"[34] several Siouanists have chosen to rewrite his words without any indication of aspiration. But careful comparison with Siouan languages west of the Mississippi shows this to be a mistake. Ofo aspirated consonants must be recognized as phonemes distinct from unaspirated consonants even though Biloxi and Tutelo, its nearest relatives, lack the distinction, for the Ofo aspirated consonants correspond to both aspirated and glottalized consonants of Dakota. In terms of Proto-Siouan we discover that Ofo ṯ is from PS *t or *ṟ while Ofo ṯh (or ṯx, ṯx) is from PS *th or *t?. Thus we have PS *topa 'four,' Ofo tó pa; PS *thá 'ruminant,' Ofo i'txa 'deer'; PS *t?čhi 'to die,' Ofo aṯhě.[35]

4. Conclusion

Although I have tried to sketch out the multiplicity of orthographic problems through four centuries and a wide variety of languages of the New World, there are doubtless many things that have not been touched upon. As the awareness of philological problems among these languages grows we shall see many kinds of specialties arise. With some languages there is enough material to concentrate on one language (including perhaps its dialects) through several centuries, as could be done with Kechua (Quichua or Inca), Aymara, Nahuatl, or Yucatec, for example. In other cases there is material for specialization in a language family, such as Algonkian, which has many living representatives but also great quantities of older materials on languages which have long disappeared, as well as some which are still spoken. Or one could specialize in a certain tradition, such as Spanish missionaries in the 16th century or French

missionaries in the 17th century, or Moravian missionaries of the
18th century, or even Summer Institute of Linguistics missionaries of the 20th century. Clearly a wealth of possibilities lies
ahead and the whole field of the study of American Indian languages
will profit.

NOTES

[1]Horatio Hale, Ethnography and philology. United States exploring expedition during the years 1838, 1839, 1840, 1841, 1842,
Vol. 6, ed. by Charles Wilkes. Philadelphia, 1846. Reprinted in
1968 by The Gregg Press, Inc., Ridgewood, N. J.
    [2]Albert Gallatin, "A synopsis of the Indian tribes within the
United States east of the Rocky Mountains and in the British and Russian possessions in North America." Transactions and Collections
of the American Antiquarian Society 2.1-422 (1836).
    [3]Albert Gallatin, Transactions of the American Ethnological
Society 2.xxiii-clxxviii, 1-130 (1848).
    [4]Cf. Mary R. Haas, "Grammar or lexicon? The American
Indian side of the question from Duponceau to Powell." IJAL 35.239-
255 (1969).
    [5]Truman Michelson, "Preliminary report of the linguistic
classification of Algonquian tribes." BAE-R (1906-07) 28.221-290b
(1912). The quotation is from p. 280.
    [6]Ives Goddard, Current Trends in Linguistics: X: Linguistics
in North America, ed. by Thomas A. Sebeok, 727-745. The Hague:
Mouton, 1973.
    [7]A plate showing the characters of the Cherokee syllabary is
to be found opposite p. 112 in James Mooney, "Myths of the Cherokee,"
BAE-R (1897-98) 19 (pt. 1) (1900).
    [8]John Pickering, American Academy of Arts and Sciences —
Memoirs o.s. 4.319-360 (1818).
    [9]Cf. notes 2 and 3.
    [10]Cf. note 1.
    [11]George Gibbs, "Instructions for research relative to the eth-
nology and philology of America." Smithsonian Miscellaneous Collections 7, article 11 (= Publication 160) (1863).
    [12]W. D. Whitney, "On the alphabet." Introduction to the study
of Indian languages, by John W. Powell, 3-6. Washington, D.C., 1877.

[13]John W. Powell, Introduction to the study of Indian languages. 2nd ed. Washington, D.C., 1880. Contains Powell's revision of Whitney's alphabet, pp. 1-16 (see note 12).

[14]Ibid.

[15]Franz Boas, ed., Handbook of American Indian languages, parts 1 and 2. BAE-B 40 (1911).

[16]Franz Boas, "Introduction." Handbook of American Indian languages, part 1. BAE-B 40.1-83 (1911). Reprinted (with J. W. Powell, Indian linguistic families of America north of Mexico), Lincoln, University of Nebraska Press, 1966. Parts reprinted in Language in culture and society: A reader in linguistics and anthropology, ed. by Dell Hymes, 15-26, 121-123, New York, Evanston and London: Harper and Row, 1964.

[17]Franz Boas and John R. Swanton, "Siouan (Dakota)." Handbook of American Indian languages, part 1. BAE-B 40.875-965 (1911).

[18]Franz Boas, E. Sapir, P.E. Goddard, and A.L. Kroeber, "Phonetic transcription of Indian languages." Smithsonian Miscellaneous Collections 66(6) (1916).

[19]Pliny F. Goddard, "Wailaki texts." IJAL 2.77-137 (1921). The quotation is on p. 77.

[20]See, for example, The principles of the International Phonetic Association. London: International Phonetic Association, 1949.

[21]John P. Harrington, "Vocabulary of the Kiowa language." BAE-B 84 (1928).

[22]George Herzog, Stanley S. Newman, Edward Sapir, Mary Haas Swadesh, Morris Swadesh and Charles F. Voegelin, "Some orthographic recommendations arising out of discussions by a group of six American linguists." AA 36.629-631 (1934).

[23]Ibid., p. 629.

[24]Harry Hoijer, "Athapaskan languages of the Pacific coast." Culture in history: Essays in honor of Paul Radin, ed. by Stanley Diamond, 960-976. New York: Columbia University Press, 1960.

[25]Leonard Bloomfield, "On the sound system of Central Algonquian." Language 1.130-156 (1925).

[26]Leonard Bloomfield, "Algonquian." Linguistic structures of native America, by Harry Hoijer and others (Viking Fund Publications in Anthropology 6), 85-129 (1946). Reprinted with corrections, A Leonard Bloomfield anthology, ed. by Charles F. Hockett, 440-488. Bloomington and London: Indiana University Press, 1970.

[27] Edward Sapir, "The rival whalers, a Nitinat story (Nootka text with translation and grammatical analysis)." IJAL 3.76-102 (1924-25); Edward Sapir and Morris Swadesh, Nootka texts: Tales and ethnological narratives with grammatical notes and lexical materials. Special Publication of the Linguistic Society of America. Philadelphia, 1939.

[28] John H. Rowe, IJAL 16.137-148 (1950).

[29] Ibid., p. 146.

[30] John Rowe has informed me of some work done along these lines. See, for example, William J. Entwistle, The Spanish language, together with Portuguese, Catalan and Basque. London: Faber and Faber, 1936. The section on pp. 246-7 is titled "American Indian evidence for the evolution of Spanish."

[31] Victor E. Hanzeli, Janua Linguarum, series major 29. The Hague: Mouton, 1969.

[32] John P. Harrington, BAE-B 167.189-202 (= Anthropological Paper 46) (1955).

[33] J. O. Dorsey and John R. Swanton, "A dictionary of the Biloxi and Ofo languages." BAE-B 47 (1912).

[34] Ibid., p. 319.

[35] Mary R. Haas, "Swanton and the Biloxi and Ofo dictionaries." IJAL 35.286-290 (1969).

Franz Boas (1858-1942), Edward Sapir (1884-1939) and
Leonard Bloomfield (1887-1949), taken together, dominated the field
of American Indian linguistics for nearly half a century. Boas was
the first and was the teacher of Edward Sapir. Leonard Bloomfield
came into the field from a different route, but was also influenced by
Boas through personal contact. If one recalls that American Indian
languages had been studied in one fashion or another for nearly four
centuries before Boas began his work, it is difficult to see at first
why his impact was so great and why, indeed, many people seem to
think that almost nothing was done before Boas. The difference was
in approach and in the insistence on field work. Boas was trained as
a physicist, [1] but he also had strong influences from the field of geography and he began his work among Eskimos and Indians in connection
with that interest. Boas had his own unique way of doing field work.
This consisted of writing out voluminous texts and then proceeding to
translate and analyze them word by word and sentence by sentence in
so far as possible. [2] When Boas began his work among the Northwest
Coast Indians, almost all of them were still monolingual, or at least
spoke no European language. The lingua franca of the area was the
Chinook jargon and for this reason Boas learned to speak that. [3]

It must not be overlooked that linguistics was only one of the
fields that Boas was interested in. More than anyone else he was a
master of all fields of anthropology, and in his studies of the American
Indian he was as interested in physical anthropology, archaeology,
mythology, and ethnology, as in linguistics. [4] When one recalls this
it is even harder to understand how he managed to accumulate such a
large body of material of a linguistic nature. However, he believed
that the culture could be understood through the language and not

otherwise and, since so many Indians were unable to express themselves in any language other than their own, he was forced to acquire
his material through the language.

As is well known, Boas's most important theoretical contribution to the study of linguistics was his promulgation of the concept
of linguistic relativism, that is, that each language had to be studied
in and for itself. It was not to be forced into a mold that was more
appropriate to some other language. Side by side with this was his
insistence on seeing the language as a whole. He was not concerned
merely with phonetics, or merely with morphology, or merely with
lexicography. Instead he placed equal emphasis on all these facets.
He set forth these ideas clearly and concisely in his "Introduction" to
Part I of the Handbook of American Indian Languages, of which he was
editor (Boas 1911). This Introduction became the leading statement
of linguistic principles and methodology for decades to follow. Indeed
it is still a most important piece of work to read. Here he set forth
the various ways in which languages could differ from each other. Previously the emphasis had been on taking the categories of some familiar language and then showing how these were expressed in the language under study. [5] In addition, Boas's Introduction set forth a-pro-
gram of what was to be accomplished in the way of providing grammars for the languages of North America. He listed the families and
language isolates that he felt should be included in his Handbook. Many
of these grammars did appear. There were Parts I (1911) and 2
(1922) and finally 3 (1933-38) and then a single grammar comprised
the beginning of Part 4 (1941) which was never completed. It was an
ambitious program, one that perhaps could never have been completed
in the form in which he envisaged it. Nevertheless it set the wheels
in motion and the work that has followed in a steady stream ever since
then owes more than can possibly be expressed to Boas's penetrating
vision.

As one goes through the Handbook today one is likely to find
some of the early grammars difficult to read. The degree of sophistication that has been arrived at at present is of course the direct
beneficiary of these early struggles. The early pieces have strange
phonetic symbols and long and difficult descriptions of many features
that can be handled today with considerably more ease. Still if these
pioneering grammars had not been written we certainly would not be
able to do what we can do today.

Although Boas from time to time mentioned that certain languages might be related to one another, he was not primarily interested in the field of linguistic classification. I think he recognized that Powell's 1891 classification was adequate for general purposes, [6] and only now and then did he venture any suggestions beyond that. He was early intrigued by structural similarities between Tlingit and Haida and the Athapaskan languages, a subject which even today is controversial. Moreover, in his later years he felt that attempts to place such difficult languages in a larger schema was an idle exercise. Later this became something of a bone of contention between Boas on the one hand and Sapir and Kroeber on the other.

Edward Sapir was the student of Franz Boas. Boas dominated the whole field of American anthropology for half a century and, with his strong personality, he also dominated those who studied under him. No one dared to cross him in any significant way and they all looked for the master's approval. Of course there is no question but that Sapir would have been a great scholar even if he had never met Boas, but the direction of his talents would have been other than it was. Although he was already something of a Germanic scholar at the time he met Boas, Boas made him feel that he still had everything to learn about language.

Sapir had a very keen ear and was able to record the difficult languages of the West with great facility. He espoused the relativistic and holistic approaches of Boas. He recorded and analyzed a voluminous amount of material on Takelma, a language of Oregon which has since passed into oblivion. As his doctoral dissertation, he prepared a lengthy grammar of Takelma (Sapir 1912) which Boas published in Part 2 of the Handbook; he also published texts and a vocabulary (Sapir 1909). In his concluding section of the grammar he presents a sort of thumb-nail sketch of the language, contrasting it with some of the neighboring languages and enumerating some of its more 'typical American' traits (Sapir 1912: 282):

> Some of the more important of these typical or at any rate
> widespread American traits, that are found in Takelma, are:
> the incorporation of the pronominal (and nominal) object in
> the verb; the incorporation of the possessive pronouns in the
> noun; the closer association with the verb-form of the object

than the subject; the inclusion of a considerable number of
instrumental and local modifications in the verb-complex; the
weak development of differences of tense in the verb and of
number in the verb and noun; and the impossibility of drawing
a sharp line between mode and tense.

He clearly savored every nuance of every language that he worked on
and the wonder of it all is that he worked on so many. As an aside, at
this point it is of interest to point out that Sapir frequently required
students in his seminar to prepare a thumb-nail sketch of each of the
languages we had been analyzing. Such a sketch had to be written by
making only the most minimal use of actual linguistic forms. [7]

Sapir spent fifteen years in Ottawa, where he became Chief
Ethnologist in the Division of Anthropology, Geological Survey of the
Canadian National Museum. He had the occasion to do considerable
field work — it was at this time that he undertook his lengthy work on
the Nootka language. In addition he turned his attention very seriously
to working out a revised classification of the American Indian languages north of Mexico. The standard classification was Powell's,
which set up fifty-five linguistic families north of Mexico. The area
of California alone had twenty-two. Sapir had previously started some
work on the California languages, particularly on Yana, which he carried out during a year spent here. He became familiar with the work
of Dixon and Kroeber who were trying to reduce the twenty-two families to a smaller number. Sapir was interested in their efforts and
also made his own contributions to them. It may have been this that
set him to thinking about the continent as a whole. He eventually compressed the fifty-five Powellian families into six superstocks. This
involved him in a variety of classificatory and comparative endeavors.
He carried out comparative linguistic studies within certain families,
for example Uto-Aztecan and Athapaskan, and published important
contributions to both of these. But when it came to putting larger
groups together, this could not be carried out with the same kind of
rigorous comparison but entailed making use of other kinds of devices,
including rather specific types of structural and morphological similarities. Perhaps the grandest scheme that Sapir came up with was
the Hokan-Siouan, which included many of the languages of California,
of Texas, and of the Northeast and Southeast as well as some of Mexico and Central America. The typological characteristics that he as-
signs to the superstock are stated by him to be:

> The Hokan-Siouan languages are prevailingly agglutinative,
> tend to use prefixes rather than suffixes for the more formal
> elements, particularly the pronominal elements of the verbs;
> distinguish active and static verbs; and make free use of com-
> pounding of stems and of nominal incorporation. (Sapir 1929).

His ultimate classification into six superstocks finally appeared in the
Encyclopaedia Britannica of 1929. By that time he was teaching at the
University of Chicago and was soon to go to Yale. At Yale his interests moved on in other directions and he seems not to have cared too
much about continuing his classificatory activities, at least not in
North America. However, several of his students became interested
and were inspired by his work to carry on similar activities later on
in their lives.

As was hinted earlier, Sapir's ambitious projects in regard
to the classification of American Indian languages were not viewed
with approval by Boas. One of the controversies that ensued arose
from Sapir's attempt to set up a superstock, Nadené, consisting of
the Athapaskan languages plus Tlingit and Haida. Pliny Earle Goddard,
a former missionary who had studied Hupa and a number of other
Athapaskan languages, did not accept this relationship and published
an article refuting Sapir's claims. Boas concurred in Goddard's position. This particular problem is still not completely amenable to
solution. While there are strong structural similarities between
Tlingit and Haida and the Athapaskan languages, the kind of cognates
that one would like to find to clinch the matter are not easy to come
by and so the matter remains controversial to this day. Perhaps the
most remarkable of Sapir's discoveries about distant or previously
unsuspected relationships was the case of the connection that he postulated between the Algonkian family of languages and Yurok and Wiyot, small language communities of northwestern California. The
latter two languages had been placed together by Dixon and Kroeber,
since they displayed certain similarities, but no one had previously
dreamed that they could possibly be related to the Algonkian family
of languages lying far to the East. When Sapir set forth his evidence
he was attacked by Truman Michelson, the leading Algonkianist of the
time. And Boas concurred in Michelson's position. Sapir never lost
his belief in this particular relationship, but since it had been a matter of such severe controversy it was not generally accepted. Even

European scholars, such as C. C. Uhlenbeck, viewed it with skepticism. As it turns out, this was probably one of the best of Sapir's amalgamations and today there is general agreement with Sapir's position that Algonkian, Yurok, and Wiyot are indeed genetically related (Haas 1958). Many of the far-reaching schemes that he set up other than this, however, still open up enormous vistas for future work and will not be solved for a long time to come.

Sapir was not only an inspiring teacher, he was also an unusually gifted writer who also tried his hand at poetry. His linguistic and cultural papers are often gems of exposition and can be read for their style with as much pleasure as for their content. Among other activities of the Ottawa period was the production of a general book called Language (Sapir 1921), which still remains a classic.

Bloomfield entered the field of American Indian languages not through training in anthropology but from another direction, namely the study of foreign languages and Germanic and Indo-European philology.[8] Nevertheless, Bloomfield recognized the value of culture and ethnology for the study of linguistics. Moreover, he was influenced by Boas even though he was not a student of Boas. He himself recognized his indebtedness in his obituary of Boas when he says: "He taught William Jones, Truman Michelson, Edward Sapir, and others now living, and with unfailing kindness he helped many who were not formally his pupils." (Bloomfield 1943:198). I think Bloomfield included himself in the latter category. He also acclaims Boas as one who had contributed so very much to the development of descriptive language study, saying, in this same obituary: "The native languages of our country had been studied by some very gifted men, but none had succeeded in putting this study upon a scientific basis. The scientific equipment of linguists, on the other hand, contained few keen tools except the comparative method and this could not yet be here applied." I suspect he also appreciated Boas because of the latter's insistence on a large body of textual material.

Bloomfield's thoughts about doing field work are expressed in a review of one of Michelson's works (Bloomfield 1922:276):

One can imagine few more fascinating experiences in the study of mankind than to hear an Algonquian language spoken

and to appreciate upon closer study the marvellous complexity of what one has heard. The scientific problem is
correspondingly difficut. I believe that the solution, short
of giving linguistic training to a native speaker, lies in the
way of sich einleben — the notation of everyday speech and
the attempt to become, to whatever extent is possible, a
member of the speech-community.

Bloomfield's most important contributions to the study of American
Indian languages are, first, his descriptive studies of Fox (on the
basis of William Jones's work) and Cree, Menomini, and Ojibwa (on
the basis of his own field work), and secondly, his very careful comparative studies of these four languages. He insisted that the descriptive studies had to precede the comparative studies and he set
out to provide an outstanding example of this principle. When he undertook his comparative work on these languages, he was motivated
by a strong desire to refute the idea, common among European linguists, that unwritten languages did not lend themselves to the kind
of rigorous comparative study that could be applied to written languages. His admirable article "On the Sound System of Central Algonquian" (1925) successfully refuted this notion, and in a footnote to
the article he makes it clear that this was an important reason for
preparing it. He says (Bloomfield 1925: 130):

> I hope, also, to help dispose of the notion that the usual pro-
> cesses of linguistic change are suspended on the American
> continent (Meillet and Cohen, Les langues du monde, Paris
> 1924, p. 9). If there exists anywhere a language in which
> these processes do not occur (sound-change independent of
> meaning, analogic change, etc.), then they will not explain
> the history of Indo-European or of any other language. A
> principle such as the regularity of phonetic change is not
> part of the specific tradition handed on to each new speaker
> of a given language, but is either a universal trait of human
> speech or nothing at all, an error.

Later, in his "Algonquian" sketch (1946), he provided a fuller exposition of the character of Proto-Algonkian, including morphology as
well as phonology.

Unlike Sapir, Bloomfield had no interest in deeper comparative studies and so he did not enter into any of the controversies in
this area. In his Algonkian sketch he mentions that Wiyot and Yurok are
are alleged to be related to Algonkian, but he himself does not make
any commitment on this score. I suspect he felt that such studies
would be premature, that one needed to progress step by step and
amass all the necessary material on Proto-Algonkian before proceeding to make deeper studies.

In 1914 Bloomfield published a book called <u>An Introduction
to the Study of Language</u> and this was a great improvement on anything
that was then available on general language study. It is interesting
that one of the reviewers complains that he quotes too often from unusual or lesser known languages, among which the reviewer includes
Russian! In 1933 Bloomfield published a book called <u>Language</u> which
was a complete revision, indeed a new writing, of his earlier book.
This book became the basis of a school of linguistics which later came
to be known as 'structural linguistics'. Bloomfield himself seems to
have used the word 'descriptive linguistics', or sometimes 'synchronic linguistics' (Saussure's term), for a careful study of any individual
language without regard to its history and further, of course, to distinguish this from contrastive and comparative linguistics.

Through this book Bloomfield became a leader in the field of
general linguistics quite apart from his important contributions to the
study of American Indian languages. At the same time, because of this
book and also because of the general works of Boas and Sapir, the field
of American Indian languages began to have an impact upon general linguistic studies that it had not previously had. Consequently, it can be
said that the study of American Indian languages had an impact on
American linguistic theory in the first half of this century which was
almost as great as that which the study of Indo-European and classical
languages had had in the nineteenth century. The work of Boas, Sapir,
and Bloomfield on languages that previously had not been written down
by anyone opened up a whole new era of linguistic study. Techniques of
field methods had to be developed, phonetic systems had to be developed, and this very struggle with ways to write down previously unwritten languages led to the development of the American version of
classical phonemic theory. Certainly this whole notion would never
have emerged as a problem if linguists had continued to work only on

written languages. American Indian languages opened up other vistas as well. These included the possibility of testing the applicability of the comparative method to unwritten languages. Both Bloomfield and Sapir rose to this challange and Sapir presented some of their results in a fascinating article entitled "The Concept of Phonetic Law as Tested in Primitive Languages by Leonard Bloomfield" (1931) in which he presented results obtained by Bloomfield in respect to Algonkian and by himself in respect to Athapaskan.

Other problems did not receive equal attention among the three great minds. Sapir in particular was interested in what should properly be called classificatory linguistics, because while ideally it should rest on comparative linguistics, practically it often does not. Neither Boas nor Bloomfield were interested in building up larger groupings of languages of the type proposed by Sapir. Unlike Sapir and Bloomfield, Boas did not make any significant contributions to comparative linguistics, although he set out some of the sound correspondences of the Salishan languages in collaboration with his student Haeberlin. But the one thing that Boas emphasized more than anyone else was what has more recently come to be known as areal linguistics. Perhaps it was his early interest in geography that led him in this direction. He was interested in the distribution of traits in mythology, in culture and in languages. He returned to this problem again and again, and his position was for the most part not properly understood by Sapir or by Kroeber, who felt that he was using this as a weapon against their classificatory schemes. Kroeber even accused Boas of being 'antihistorical' in his attitude. This puzzled Boas because, as he saw it, these interests were as validly historical as were classificatory interests. He even went so far as to say (Boas 1920: 375):

> If these observations regarding the influence of acculturation
> upon language should be correct, then the whole history of
> American languages must not be treated on the assumption
> that all languages which show similarities must be considered as branches of the same linguistic family. . . . In other
> words, the whole theory of an Ursprache for every group of
> modern languages must be held in abeyance until we can
> prove that these languages go back to a single stock and that
> they have not originated, to a large extent, by the process
> of acculturation.

Boas's position in turn both puzzled and infuriated people like Sapir and Kroeber, who wished to make genetic classifications of these languages in so far as they possibly could. I think it's fair to say that today there is much more sympathy and understanding for Boas's point of view than there was in the past. His programmatic statement of 1920 can be readily accepted today because we no longer view it as opposition to genetic classification (Boas 1920:376):

> Firstly, we must study the differentiation of dialects like those of the Siouan, Muskhogean, Algonquian, Shoshonean, Salishan, and Athapascan. Secondly, we must make a detailed study of the distribution of phonetic, grammatical, and lexicographical phenomena, the latter including also particularly the principles upon which the grouping of concepts is based [e.g. shape, as in classificatory verbs]. Finally, our study ought to be directed not only to an investigation of the similarities of the languages, but equally intensively toward their dissimilarities. Only on this basis can we hope to solve the general historical problem. [Emphasis added.]

But I should not leave the impression that Sapir was unaware of or uninterested in borrowings and diffusion and the like. He saw their significance too, and in part he needed some of his larger groupings in order to highlight the differences between what he considered to be genetic and what might be considered diffused. He gives some examples of this in his famous paper on "Time Perspective" (1916), where he finds that certain traits, such as the use of instrumental verb prefixes, appear both in Maidu and in nearby Washo and Shasta-Achomawi (also Shoshonean), and he is interested in the fact that on the basis of the Dixon and Kroeber classification Maidu belongs to Penutian, while the neighboring Washo and Shasta-Achomawi are Hokan.

In summing up, I should say that Boas will be remembered for his editing of the Handbook of American Indian Languages, for the founding of the International Journal of American Linguistics, for his work on Kwakiutl, Dakota, and many other languages, and for his insistence on the study of areal phenomena. (Boas was also probably the first to train American Indians as linguists)[9]. Sapir will be

remembered for his seminal work on Uto-Aztecan, Athapaskan, and
Hokan-Coahuiltecan, for his grand classificatory schemes which we
are still in the process of testing, for his meticulous grammars of
Takelma, Southern Paiute, and other languages, and also for his book
Language. Bloomfield in turn will be remembered for his work on
Proto-Algonkian, in which he demonstrated the way in which unwritten
languages can be reconstructed both as to their phonology and their
morphology, for his synchronic studies of Fox, Cree, Menomini, and
Ojibwa, and of course for his influential book Language.

In his poignant dedication for Linguistic Structures of Native
America Bloomfield spoke of Boas as "the teacher, in one or another
sense, of us all" (Hoijer et. al. 1946:5). Here it is fitting to make
the same statement in regard to all three of these great men as the
teachers, in one or another sense, of all who are working in the field
today.

NOTES

[1]He received the Ph. D. at the University of Kiel in 1881. His
dissertation was Contributions to the understanding of the color of sea
water.

[2]He also relied on native speakers to write out texts for him,
both materials of their own and materials from other Indians. Among
the Kwakiutl, George Hunt furnished texts to Boas for over forty years.

[3]One cannot help but wonder how adequate the jargon was to
translate the many texts he was obtaining. However, he appears to
have relied on his own ability to fill in those things that were not adequately expressed in the jargon.

[4]None who followed him ever achieved his stature in all of
these fields. However, he expected his students to learn something
of all of them. Many of them rebelled. Sapir, for example, refused
to take up physical anthropology.

[5]This approach resulted in such ridiculous statements as
"This language has no gender. In order to indicate gender it is necessary to add the word 'man' to indicate the masculine and 'woman'
to indicate the feminine. " Unfortunately this kind of nonsense was
not uncommon and usually resulted in overlooking the actually existing
categories of the particular language.

[6]However, he was aware of its limitations: "Much of the material on which Major Powell's work is based is exceedingly scanty, and it is obvious that more accurate studies will show relationships which at the time could not be safely inferred" (Boas 1920).

[7]The above quotation is only a part of such a thumb-nail of Takelma.

[8]See his doctoral dissertation on Germanic Secondary Ablaut (Bloomfield 1909-10).

[9]Prominent among American Indians whom he trained as linguists were William Jones, a Fox Indian, and Ella Deloria, a Dakota Sioux. See also note 2.

REFERENCES

Bloomfield, L. 1909-10. A semasiological differentiation in Germanic Ablaut. Modern Philology 7.245-382.

_____.1914. An introduction to the study of language. New York: Henry Holt and Company/London: G. Bell.

_____.1922. Review of The Owl Sacred Pack of the Fox Indians by T. Michelson. American Journal of Philology 43.276-81.

_____.1925. On the sound System of Central Algonquian. Language 1.130-56.

_____.1933. Language. New York: Henry Holt and Company.

_____.1943. [Obituary of Boas]. Language 19.198.

_____.1946. Algonquian. Linguistic structures of Native America, by H. Hoijer et al., 85-129. New York: Viking Fund Publications in Anthropology 6.

Boas, F. ed. 1911. Handbook of American Indian languages Part 1. Bureau of American Ethnology Bulletin 40. Washington, D.C. "Introduction" reprinted by Georgetown University Press, n.d.

_____.1920. The classification of American Indian languages. American Anthropologist 22.367-76. Reprinted in Boas 1940: 211-18.

_____.ed. 1922. Handbook of American Indian languages Part 2. Bureau of American Ethnology Bulletin 40. Washington, D.C.

_____.ed. 1933-38. Handbook of American Indian languages Part 3. Columbia University Press. (J.J. Augustin: Glückstadt-Hamburg-New York.)

_____. 1940. Race, language, and culture. New York: Macmillan.

_____. ed. 1941. Handbook of American Indian languages Part 4.
New York: J. J. Augustin.

Haas, M. R. 1958. Algonkian-Ritwan: The end of a controversy.
International Journal of American Linguistics 24.159-73.

Hoijer, H. et. al. 1946. Linguistic structures of Native America.
New York: Viking Fund Publications in Anthropology 6.

Powell, J. W. 1891. Linguistic families of North America North of
Mexico. Washington D. C.: Bureau of [American] Ethnology
Annual Report 7 (1885-86).

Sapir, E. 1909. Takelma texts. University of Pennsylvania, Anthropological Publications 2:1.1-263.

_____. 1912. The Takelma language of Southwestern Oregon. First
issued as an extract from the Handbook of American Indian
languages Part 2, ed. by F. Boas. Washington D. C.: Bureau of American Ethnology Bulletin 40.

_____. 1916. Time perspective in aboriginal American culture: A
study in method. Canada, Department of Mines, Geological
Survey Memoir 90, Anthropological Series no. 13. Ottawa:
Government Printing Bureau. Reprinted in Selected Writings
of Edward Sapir, ed. by D. G. Mandelbaum, 389-467. Berkeley and Los Angeles: University of California Press, 1949.

_____. 1921. Language: An introduction to the study of speech. New
York: Harcourt, Brace.

_____. 1929. Central and North American languages. Encyclopaedia
Britannica 14th edition 5.138-41. Reprinted in Selected
Writings of Edward Sapir, ed. by D. G. Mandelbaum, 169-
78. Berkeley and Los Angeles: University of California
Press, 1949.

_____. 1931. The concept of phonetic law as tested in primitive lan-
guages by Leonard Bloomfield. Methods in Social Science: A
Case Book, ed. by S. A. Rice, 297-306. Reprinted in Selected Writings of Edward Sapir, ed. by D. G. Mandelbaum, 73-
82. Berkeley and Los Angeles: University of California
Press, 1949.

1. During the nineteenth century, as science achieved greater and greater success in the realm of discovery and explanation of the so-called "laws" of nature, more and more disciplines strove for increased prestige by claiming to be sciences. Linguistics was no exception. "Linguistic science" has been an elegant term for linguistics through much of the present century, sometimes as a translation of German "sprachwissenschaft" or the Danish "sprogvidenskab," as in John Spargo's translation (1931) of Holger Pedersen's work <u>Linguistic Science in the 19th Century</u>, at other times as an independently preferred term, as in Edgar Sturtevant's <u>An Introduction to Linguistic Science</u> (1949). Today the preferred term appears to be "linguistics" and only rarely does one encounter the term "linguistic science". Nevertheless, most linguists are as anxious as ever to lay claim to being scientists, and one of the ways in which they show this is to follow the lead of the physical and biological scientists in describing their aims and goals. For this reason they often take over terminology in vogue among the supposedly more rigorous disciplines. Today one of the most prominent catchwords is "model" and since models are not entirely new in linguistics, it may be interesting to consider some of the models that have been used in the past and to look more searchingly into the affect they have had on the development of linguistic theory.

2. In discussing the developmental history of American linguistics, most present day linguists completely ignore the man who was perhaps the most powerful influence toward the end of the nineteenth century. This man was Major John Wesley Powell, at present known among linguists almost exclusively for his excellent classification of the American Indian languages north of Mexico (1891).

Perhaps no other man has done so much to stimulate the collection and publication of basic materials in American Indian languages. For this, as well as his important classification, he is deservedly known and honored. But his theoretical orientation in regard to language is never mentioned. It was silenced completely by another powerful genius, Franz Boas, in his remarkable "Introduction" to the Handbook of American Indian Languages (1911), a work which was itself a part of the grand publication plan envisaged in Powell's linguistic program for the Bureau of American Ethnology (Smithsonian Institution).

Powell had no training in philology or linguistics.[1] He was, among other things, a Civil War veteran who had lost an arm and acquired a military title in the course of that tragic episode. But more importantly for our purposes he was, in the terminology of the day, a natural historian or natural scientist (among other things a geologist), and it was to be expected that the scientific theories of his time would influence him greatly. This was the time of the ascendancy of the Darwinian theory of evolution. The remarkable success this theory had in explaining the known facts of biology stimulated many theoreticians to attempt to apply it in explanations of the growth and development of social institutions as well. Lewis Henry Morgan was the foremost American in this attempt[2] and his work made a tremendous impression on Powell who accepted the evolutionary model of Morgan for the field of linguistics as well. When he prepared the second edition of his book, Introduction to the Study of Indian Languages (1880),[3] Powell included a remarkable new chapter entitled "The Rank of Indian Languages." On this subject he says:

> Students of Indian languages have sometimes fallen into error about their rank or value as instruments for the expression of thought. . . . The assumed superiority of the Greek and Latin languages to the English and other modern civilized tongues, has in part been the cause of the many erroneous conceptions of the rank of Indian tongues. When the student discovers that many of the characteristics of the classic languages appear in the Indian which are to a greater or less extent lost in the modern civilized languages, he has at once assumed the superiority of the Indian tongue; and when he has further discovered that some of these characteristics are even more highly developed than in the classic ones he has been led to still further exalt them. (1880: 69-70)

It is his aim to counteract this tendency and so he proceeds, in his own words, "to set forth the rank of the Indian languages by briefly comparing them with the English and incidentally with some other languages". (1880:70) To do this he brings in Morgan's theory which involves, among other things, the thesis that social development proceeds through three stages, savagery, barbarism, and civilization. Transferring this schematicization to language, Powell maintains that languages which have highly developed inflectional systems belong at the stage of barbarism. On the other hand, a largely analytic language like English, with its reliance on principles of word order rather than concord and inflection, is to be placed at the highest stage of civilization. He expounds this in the following terms:

> It is worthy of remark that all paradigmatic inflection in a civilized tongue is a relic of its barbaric condition. When the parts of speech are fully differentiated and the process of placement fully specialized, so that the order of words in sentences has its full significance, no useful purpose is served by inflection. (1880:74b)

In arriving at his ranking of languages, Powell relies very heavily on the principle of economy.

> Economy in speech is the force by which its development has been accomplished, and it divides itself properly into economy of utterance and economy of thought. Economy of utterance has had to do with the phonic constitution of words; economy of thought has developed the sentence. (1880:74b)

His relegation of highly developed inflectional languages to a low rank in his evolutionary heirarchy is justified in the following terms:

> All paradigmatic inflection requires unnecessary thought. In the clause 'if he was here', 'if' fully expresses the subjunctive condition, and it is quite unnecessary to express it a second time by using another form of the verb 'to be', and so the people who are using the English language are deciding, for the subjunctive form is rapidly becoming obsolete. (1880: 74b)

The pièce de resistance of Powell's argument in favor of "economy of thought" comes when he cites Ponca (a Siouan language) as an example of the antithesis of such economy:

> A Ponca Indian, in saying that a man killed a rabbit, would have to say the man, he, one, animate, standing, in the nominative case, purposely killed, by shooting an arrow, the rabbit, he, the one, sitting, in the objective case; for the form of a verb to kill would have to be selected, and the verb changes its form by inflection and incorporated particles to denote person, number, and gender as animate or inanimate, and position as standing, sitting, or lying, and case; and the form of the verb would also express whether the killing was done accidentally or puposely, and whether it was by shooting or some other process, and, if by shooting, whether by bow and arrow, or with a gun; and the form of the verb would in like manner have to express all of the things relating to the object; that is, the person, gender, and case of the object; and from the multiplicity of paradigmatic forms of the verb to kill this particular one would have to be selected. Perhaps one time in a million it would be the purpose to express all of these particulars, and in that case the Indian would have the whole expression in one compact word, but in the nine hundred and ninety-nine thousand nine hundred and ninety-nine cases all of these particulars would have to be thought of in the selection of the form of the verb, when no valuable purpose would be accomplished thereby. (1880: 74c) [Emphasis mine.]

In the light of all this, his conclusion as to the proper ranking of languages[4] should come as no surprise:

> In the development of the English, as well as the French and German, linguistic evolution has not been in vain. Judged by these criteria, the English stands alone in the highest rank; but as a written language, in the way in which its alphabet is used, the English has but emerged from a barbaric condition. (1880: 74c)

3. Although Powell himself clearly recognized the importance of studying the American Indian languages — after all the

purpose of his book was to encourage their study — still his remarks
on their ranking, if taken seriously, would certainly have hampered
their proper investigation.[5]

Therefore the time had come for a reevaluation and it was almost to be expected that there would be a complete turnaround. This
was accomplished by Boas who completely silenced Powell's grand
theoretical concept in his excellent "Introduction" to the Handbook of
American Indian Languages (1911). Moreover, he does it entirely by
indirection without even mentioning Powell's construct. He even de-
molished the Ponca example, quietly and unobtrusively, in the following words:

> We find that, in the Ponca dialect of the Siouan languages,
> nouns are classified according to form, and that there is a
> clear formal distinction between the subject and the object
> of the sentence. These important features have disappeared
> entirely in the Dakota dialect of the same group of languages.
> (1911: 81)

One of the most important facts to discover when a scholar
takes a very positive and definite stand on some theoretical point is
simply, "What (or who) is he trying to refute?" More often than not,
he does not give his readers an explicit answer to this question. In
large part this seems to be because he assumes that his readers are
already familiar with the current theory and it is therefore a needless
waste of time to spell it out. That readers of a later generation will
misinterpret or misunderstand the reasons for the stand he has taken
is something that he does not foresee. Consequently, Boas's espousal
of what is today sometimes referred to as "extreme relativism" has
been all too frequently misunderstood as a reaction against ethnocentrism, including glottocentrism. However, what he was really re-
acting against and what he was completely successful in eradicating
from American anthropological theory was the powerfully attractive
evolutionary model as an explanation of the development of social institutions and languages. This becomes quite clear, I think, when we
recognize that he silenced not only any would-be supporters of Powell's
crude evolutionary scheme for languages, but, even more importantly
(and also more explicitly), the much more sophisticated model for
social institutions developed by Lewis Henry Morgan in Ancient

Society. Glottocentrism and ethnocentrism were in it, of course, but only incidentally. No one would think of denying or opposing the evolutionary model for biology simply because man is the most highly developed species in the mammalian class!

4. Evolutionary theory (actually of a pre-Darwinian variety) has also influenced the construction of another model commonly used by linguists. This is the so-called "family tree" model, first proposed by August Schleicher. [6] Most historical linguists today readily admit the shortcomings of this model for their purposes but are hard-pressed to find a better model to take its place. Since this model is normally used to show subgroupings among languages known to be related, it performs a much more modest task than the aims Powell had in mind in his evolutionary model, since the latter was an attempt to rank languages into lower and higher stages in accordance with what we would now call their typologies and was not intended to show anything about the historical relationships among them.

Implicit in the use of the family tree model is the concomitant use of the biological family model to describe the genetic relationships among languages. This model has furnished us with so much of our terminology in historical linguistics that we are not likely to be able to eradicate its influence from our thinking any time soon. The very term "genetic relationship" is one of such terms and along with this go such well-established usages as "parent language", "daughter language", "sister language", and the like — terms which we continue to use in spite of the oft-repeated disclaimers regarding the adequacy of the family model when dealing with related languages.

The models described above are historical in so far as what they represent could not be postulated without assuming that time has elapsed. In the Powell scheme of evolutionary stages time is necessary for the transition from a lower stage to a higher stage. In the Schleicher model time is necessary in order to account for the emergence of many present-day languages out of a single parent language of the past. Nevertheless both types of model are essentially static. Even though time is an essential assumption in each case, time itself lies outside the model and is in no way represented as part of the model. It is worth mentioning that only a dynamic model could do

justice to the inevitable temporal nature of historical development
and no one seems to have come up with any suggestions for a dynamic
model.

    5. The nineteenth century, spilling over into the early twen-
tieth, had as its greatest achievement the development of the historical and comparative study of the Indo-European languages. A point
was finally reached, however, when further development was less and
less possible without greater attention to the construction of a descriptive or synchronic model for the study of a language. For one
thing, there are hundreds of languages in the world whose history is
unknown and these were being neglected because of this fact. This
almost meant that descriptive or synchronic linguistics was sometimes treated as if it was the antithesis of historical-comparative or
diachronic linguistics. Leonard Bloomfield took a clear stand about
the difference in the two approaches and the necessity, as he saw it,
for their strict separation. A strong statement of this point of view
is seen in the following passage from his Language (1933):

> All historical study of language is based upon the comparison
> of two or more sets of descriptive data. It can be only as ac-
> curate and only as complete as these data permit it to be. In
> order to describe a language one needs no historical know-
> ledge whatsoever; in fact, the observer who allows such
> knowledge to affect his description, is bound to distort his
> data. Our descriptions must be unprejudiced [by history],
> if they are to give a sound basis for comparative work. (1933:
> 19-20)

Although Ferdinand de Saussure had, before Bloomfield, defined the
difference between descriptive and historical linguistics (in terms of
"synchronic" vs. "diachronic"), still Bloomfield's model of descriptive linguistics was the most influential one in America because his
book gave a clear exposition of the principles to be followed in working
out the description of a language, any language.

    Bloomfield's model held sway for nearly three decades and
was further developed by many followers. This model is a static one
and the basic tenet is that of a strict ahistoricity. Moreover, in the
hands of the post-Bloomfieldians the model became increasingly

inelastic in a way that would not have been at all congenial either to
Boas or to his distinguished student, Edward Sapir. In the case of
Boas this is all the more remarkable in view of the fact that among
anthropologists, at least, he has generally been considered antihistorical.

Sapir's approach was also descriptive but not to the exclusion of a dynamic point of view. What kind of descriptivism Sapir's
theoretical approach might have led to had it been fully developed remains something of a mystery. The proper flowering of the Sapirian
approach was rather suddenly arrested by the publication of
Bloomfield's revised Language in 1933. [7] Sapir had planned to revise
his own book Language (1921), but his untimely death in 1939 made
this forever impossible. At any rate, I doubt that his approach would
ever have led to quite such an extreme of ahistoricism as the Bloomfieldian approach did. The "why" of things in a language became
strictly taboo in the Bloomfieldian approach and Sapir would never
have been satisfied with this. Although he appreciated as well as
anyone the desirability of maintaining a proper distinction between
descriptive and historical linguistics, he was always fascinated by
the "why". This included not only the historical "why" but also the
psychological "why". And this is what gives Sapir his essentially
unique place among linguistic theoreticians.

With the rise of synchronic-descriptive linguistics, there was
for a time a waning of interest in historical linguistics. This was especially pronounced during the thirties and forties of this century. In
a sense this was a good thing because it allowed time for the collection and description of materials on a variety of languages, not only
American Indian languages but a number of Asian and European languages as well, a development that was triggered in large part by
World War II.

But let us return again to the impact of the rise of descriptive linguistics on linguistic theory. What is the basic minimum model used by the descriptive linguist? I can think of no better analogy
than the cross-section, the cross-section of a log, if you like. This
is a highly compressed model. It has no time, no depth, no fluidity.
It is entirely static. In some of its more extreme applications, it
compresses idiolects, sometimes even dialects. [8] But this static

model did not achieve this rigidity (sometimes called rigor) without
encountering difficulties.   The continual pushing and pulling in regard
to morphophonemics is an excellent example of this.[9] It is also a
very important part of the reason why in recent years there has developed at M.I.T. and other places what might be called an 'anti-
phonemic' school of linguistics.

This is not the place to enlarge upon other difficulties with
this particular static model. What is of interest here is how this
model has been adapted by some to historical linguistics as well, a
feat which might at first glance seem well nigh impossible. How is
it done? Historically related languages known in a time sequence are
compared as so many cross-sections, each of which is to be equally
rigorously described in so far as this is possible. This is similar to
but not identical with earlier formulations which spoke of 'stages' of
a language. Change in language, by this model, is seen as a total replacement of each cross-section (stage) by the next successive one.
Replacement is postulated even if no significant difference exists between the two stages at any one or two points up to all points in the
next succeeding stages. This view is not entirely without interest or
advantages and by no means all of its advantages have been exploited.
Nevertheless, a cross-section is only a cross-section. Think how
absurd it would be if a tree could be described only by cutting it down
and sawing it up into dozens of cross-sections, each of which theo-
rectically lacks thickness. It becomes clear that the cross-section
model has its severe limitations. There should, in fact, be some way
to devise a longitudinal section to describe much that is inevitably
overlooked when the point of view is limited to the examination of successive cross-sections. Although this too would be a static model, it
would clearly give a vastly different view.

In addition to our highly developed static models we very
much need to search for dynamic models. These are needed both for
the proper description of a single language at a given point in time
and even more particularly for the proper understanding of historical
developments.

In synchronic linguistics the individual speaker is of great
importance and the model must somehow take this into consideration.
One way in which this has been done is to speak of the idiolect (but to

allow also for the fact that an individual may speak more than one).
But it is not enough to recognize the importance of the individual
speaker. The reason is simple. Language is a social phenomenon,
not a phenomenon of the individual. In other words, it exists for the
purposes of interaction between individuals and it might be better to
say that each individual speaks several sociolects. The sociolect is
what is spoken when interacting with other individuals, i.e., communi-
cating, in a given social situation. In highly stratified societies of the
type found in India, one or more of these sociolects may actually be a
distinct and different language (e.g., English, Kannada, and Hindi).
In a somewhat more fluid society, such as ours, most of the sociolects are what are sometimes called 'varieties' of the same language
and the upward mobility often encountered in our society frequently requires that a new sociolect be acquired as one moves upward. Moreover, the total synchronic description of a language must recognize
these sociolects as having some fluidity and also as being intermingled
in a variety of ways, e.g., as wires in a cable.

Turning once more to historical linguistics, I should like to
suggest that we need to look for some kind of a flow model. Physicists
have developed some, such as those for fluids and gases. There may
be others of which I am unaware. In order properly to cope with linguistic change we need to think of it as dynamic, as flowing, as having
movement, in particular, as passing through time. At the present
stage of our science we are not really coping with this fact at all. But
promise for progress in the future surely lies in this direction.

6. I have briefly reviewed some of the linguistic theories
that have competed for attention in America in the past century. They
show a certain interesting shift in emphasis in our way of looking at
language. Questions that motivated searchers of one era are forgot-
ten and replaced by quite different questions in the next era. This
leads me to introduce still one more model, an epicyclical model, [10]
which might be applied to fashions in theory, including linguistic
theory. As one theory wanes in influence, another develops and
flowers, soon, supposedly, to decline and be replaced by something
new. But not all theories go through full cycle. Some are cut off
abruptly at one of the developing stages. Powell's theory of the

ranking of languages is one which was abruptly cut off, probably deservedly so. We find it amusing now. I wonder which of the theories
that we are espousing now will most amuse our successors in the middle of the twenty-first century!

NOTES

Presidential address to the Linguistic Society of America, December,
1963, Chicago, Illinois. This written rendition is essentially the same
as the orally delivered address except for some minor deletions, occasional modification of phraseology, and abbreviation of the final
paragraphs. The notes, of course, have been added.

[1] Powell's life has received the attention of more than one
biographer. Among others, see Wallace Stegner's Beyond the Hundredth Meridian (Boston, 1954) and William Culp Darrah's Powell of
the Colorado (Princeton, 1951).
[2] See Ancient Society; or Researches in the Lines of Human
Progress from Savagery, through Barbarism to Civilization (New
York, 1877).
[3] The first edition, published three years prior to the second
edition, was different in several respects. Both editions were intended to be practical manuals for fieldworkers, but the first edition has
little more than the bare essentials, e.g., the alphabet to be used in
writing down the words, phrases, and sentences which were to be
collected and also "explanatory notes" accompanying some of the subdivisions of the materials to be collected. Powell solicited the aid of
William Dwight Whitney, noted Indo-European scholar and Sanskritist
of Yale University, in preparing the "alphabet" of the first edition.
But in the second edition he went ahead on his own, saying, "For the
alphabet as it is now presented, Professor Whitney is not responsible,
but the writer is greatly indebted to him for laying the foundation of
the chapter as it appeared in the previous edition." (1880: vi)
[4] It is not without interest that William Dwight Whitney in his
Language and the Study of Language (New York, 1875) also accords
English a high rating when he says:

So the English language, starting in that monosyllabism which
the Chinese has never quitted, has made the whole round of

possible development, till its most advanced portions have
almost come back again to their original state [in accordance
with Whitney's theory about the nature of Proto-Indo-Euro-
pean]. . . . It is therefore in its essential character as far
removed from the Chinese as is the Greek. Its resources
for the expressions of relations. . .are hardly inferior to
those of the tongues of highest inflective character. . . .

Our general conclusion must be that, if the English is
not entitled to all the exaggerated enconiums which are sometimes heaped upon it, if it has no right to be set at the head
of all languages, living or extinct, it is at least worthy of all
our love and admiration, and will not be found unequal to anything which the future shall require of it — even should circumstances make it the leading tongue of civilized humanity.
(1875: 472-473)

But Whitney's evaluation is not part of any Morganian evolutionary
scheme. However, it is a clear statement of what might be called
Linguistic Manifest Destiny!

[5]In his preface, for example, he points out that "Hundreds of
languages are to be studied." (1880: viii)

[6]See, for example, John Webster Spargo's translation of
Holger Pedersen's Linguistic Science in the Nineteenth Century (reprinted under the title The Discovery of Language, Bloomington,
1962), p. 312.

[7]The earlier version was entitled An Introduction to the Study
of Language (New York, 1914).

[8]The Smith-Trager phonology of English is an outstanding example of this.

[9]The pushing and pulling in regard to morphophonemics were
inevitable because of the strong ahistoric stance. Statements implying
priority were thought to imply history and were therefore to be avoided.

[10]See Charles Edward Gray, "An Analysis of Graeco-Roman
Development: The Epicyclical Evolution of Graeco-Roman Civilization," American Anthropologist 60.13-31 (1958).

REFERENCES

Bloomfield, Leonard. An introduction to the study of language. New
York: Holt, 1914.

Bloomfield, Leonard. Language. New York: Holt, 1933.

Boas, Franz. Introduction. Handbook of American Indian languages.
      (BAE-B 40, Part I.) Washington, D.C.: Smithsonian In-
      stitution, 1911.

Darrah, William Culp. Powell of the Colorado. Princeton, N.J.:
      Princeton University Press, 1951.

Gray, Charles Edward. An analysis of Graeco-Roman development:
      The epicyclical evolution of Graeco-Roman civilization.
      American Anthropologist 60. 13–31 (1958).

Morgan, Lewis Henry. Ancient society; or, Researches in the lines
      of human progress from savagery through barbarism to civi-
      lization. New York: Holt, 1877.

Pedersen, Holger. Linguistic science in the 19th century. Trans-
      lated by John Spargo. Cambridge, Massachusetts: Harvard
      University Press, 1931. (Reprinted under the title The dis-
      covery of language. Bloomington: Indiana University Press,
      1962.)

Powell, John Wesley. Introduction to the study of Indian languages,
      with words, phrases and sentences to be collected. 2nd ed.
      Washington, D.C.: Government Printing Office, 1880.

Sapir, Edward. Language: An introduction to the study of speech.
      New York: Harcourt, Brace, 1921.

Stegner, Wallace. Beyond the hundredth meridian. Boston: Houghton
      Mifflin, 1954.

Sturtevant, Edgar H. An introduction to linguistic science. New
      Haven: Yale University Press, 1949.

Whitney, William Dwight. The life and growth of language. New
      York: Appleton, 1875.

Part III. Historical and Areal Linguistics in North America

21 | Historical Linguistics and the Genetic Relationship of Languages

1. Introductory Remarks

1.1 The most widely acclaimed theoretical approaches in the field of linguistics during the past thirty years have been directed toward the development of methodologies for dealing with the structures of languages in a nonhistorical sense. We have had, among many others, Sapir, Bloomfield, Hjelmslev, Jakobson, Martinet, Harris, and Chomsky. Whatever differences may exist between their approaches (especially as developed by their followers), they have in common the desire to expose, in the most precise and elegant fashion, the structure of language. In the view of many students today linguistics can lay claim to being a science only to the extent that it can demonstrate success in this aim.

For a contrast to this view it is instructive to take a look at the predominant attitude of the nineteenth century. In that period it was <u>Comparative and Historical</u> linguistics that was held up for admiration as being 'scientific'. In a late essay Bloomfield[1] made no bones about this fact:

> . . . a new mastery of historical perspective brought about, at the beginning of the nineteenth century, the development of comparative and historical linguistics. The method of this study may fairly be called one of the triumphs of nineteenth century <u>science</u>. In a survey of <u>scientific method it should serve as a model</u> of one type of investigation, since <u>no other historical discipline has equalled it</u>. (p. 2) [Emphasis mine.]

Indeed the very term 'linguistic science', so commonly used in this period, seems more often than not to have meant 'historical and

comparative linguistics'. Moreover, the discipline was generally acknowledged to be the most rigorous and hence most 'scientific' of all
those branches of knowledge commonly subsumed under such terms
as the humanities and the social sciences, or, as Sapir[2] has pointed
out: "In the course of their detailed researches Indo-European linguists have gradually developed a technique which is <u>more nearly perfect than that of any other science dealing with man's institutions.</u> "
(p. 207) [Emphasis mine.] In that same period anthropology, for example, was struggling to achieve the status of a scientific discipline,
whereas linguistics, even though being claimed as a branch of anthropology,[3] had already achieved recognition as a scientific discipline
of the highest order. The success of linguistics thus served as a spur
to many other disciplines, particularly those concerned with 'man's
institutions'.

1.2 What was it that linguistics had that other disciplines sought to
emulate ? Clyde Kluckhohn[4] has expressed it this way:

> In a period when even some natural scientists considered the
> systematic study of humanity as fruitless because of the com-
> plexities involved or actually denounced it as contravening
> the conception of God-given free will, <u>the success of com-
> parative philology</u>, perhaps more than any other single fact,
> <u>encouraged students of man to seek for regularities in human
> behavior.</u> (p. 110) [Emphasis mine.]

Linguistics had a rigorous method of demonstrating the genetic relationship of languages. Moreover, it had amassed a great amount of
material that was more than sufficient to prove the genetic relationship of what is now known as the Indo-European family of languages.
The key to success in this demonstration can be summed up in two
simple statements:

> (1) Phonetic 'laws'[5] are regular provided it is recognized
> that
> (2) certain seemingly aberrant forms can be shown to be the
> results of analogy.

The discovery of these truths was crucial in establishing linguistics as a scientific discipline. Though they may seem simple

enough now — as all great truths do, once they are formulated — they
did not take form overnight and they were not arrived at without many
a false start and wrong assumption. Moreover — and this may come
as a surprise to many — their power has not yet been fully exploited.
There are dozens and dozens of linguistic families in the world but
few indeed can lay claim to having been as thoroughly studied and as
adequately reconstructed as Indo-European. [6] If we can convince ourselves of the necessity of applying the rigorous methodology already
developed for Indo-European to as many other families as possible,
we can hope to achieve many highly rewarding advances in our knowledge of farflung genetic relationships among the languages of the
world. But if we are unable to convince ourselves of this necessity,
our handbooks will continue to be filled with highly speculative and all
too often plainly dubious or misleading information.

1.3 Although scholars in the eighteenth century were already fumbling
around with notions of language relationship, their efforts were on the
whole crude. It was not until Sanskrit became known to scholars of
the West that real progress began to be made. Sanskrit was much older than the oldest languages of Europe then known, and the transpar-
ency of much of its structure soon revealed answers to problems that
had previously vexed scholars. Nevertheless, even this great treasure
house did not provide ready-made solutions to all problems. The
proper evaluation and interpretation of the material was acquired only
gradually. For example, it was thought at first that since Sanskrit
was older than other then known Indo-European languages everything
about it was to be considered a more accurate reflection of an earlier
state of affairs than anything found in more recent languages. Scholars tended to feel that if Sanskrit was not itself the 'ancestor' of
Greek, Latin and most other languages of Europe, it was nonetheless
chronologically so much closer to it that its testimony should take precedence over the testimony of the younger languages. [7] The numerous
errors that were engendered by this approach were eventually corrected, however, and this in itself was one of the triumphs of Indo-
European scholarship. That much the same kinds of problems had to
be tackled all over again with the discovery of the still older Hittite in
the early part of the twentieth century means only that it takes time to
assess the evidence from a previously unknown cognate language and
that chronological readjustments are not easy to make on short notice.

Today it is commonplace for students to take 'field methods' courses and it is taken for granted that a well-trained student will be able to cope with any language in the world whether or not it has ever been written down. Indeed, one of the most beneficial aspects of modern applied linguistics is the devising of alphabets for unwritten languages as an aid in combatting illiteracy. In view of our present sophistication in this regard, it is hard to realize how enslaved the minds of scholars of only a few decades ago were to writing and to the written forms of language. It comes as something of a shock to realize that most of the great advances in Indo-European studies were made under the illusion that the written language was the language. The rationale of this unquestioned assumption is not hard to find. The fact that Sanskrit, for example, was a written language is the reason that we know it well today. If it had not been written we should certainly never be able to know what we do know about it. Even with all our hard-earned skill in the reconstruction of protolanguages, we would not quite be able to 'reconstruct' Sanskrit by comparing the modern Indic vernaculars. So even though we are no longer dependent upon the discovery of written documents in advancing our knowledge of linguistic relationship (in the case of unwritten languages, for example), it would be a serious mistake not to recognize the great value of written languages. In particular there is the historical consideration that we might never have arrived at the point of being able to reconstruct great numbers of the morphs of an unwritten language we call Proto-Indo-European if we had not had written documents of many Indo-European languages at different time levels to help us verify our results and thus give us confidence in our methods. With written languages of different time levels scholars can check their hypotheses in two directions because they have documented verification which provides relative chronology. Scholars who work with unwritten languages cannot do this in quite the same way since they have only one documented time-point, namely the present.

But the earlier reliance on written languages needs to be noted in order to see how it eventually threatened to become an impediment to the further development of linguistic science. Since the existence of written languages, particularly those long extinct whose age can be calculated not only in centuries but millennia, was of great strategic importance in the development of our knowledge of Indo-European, some scholars came to believe that the historical and

comparative study of languages was impossible without written records of earlier stages of the same or related languages. This view,
as expressed in the first edition of Les langues du monde, [8] aroused
the ire of Leonard Bloomfield and thus gave rise to an interesting and
important chapter in the development of comparative linguistics.

1.4 Bloomfield, usually celebrated for the prominent role he played
in the development of descriptive (as opposed to historical) linguistics
after 1933, the year of the appearance of his epoch-making book Language, [9] was actually one of the greatest historical linguists of this
century. A fine Germanic and Indo-European scholar, he also became interested in the Algonkian languages of North America and soon
recognized the feasibility of reconstructing Proto-Algonkian. That the
task imposed problems and difficulties of a type not likely to be encountered by the Indo-European comparativist made it all the more in-
triguing.

      The Algonkian languages were of course not 'written' lan-
guages in the ordinary sense of the term, and of course there were no
written records of any earlier stages of any of the languages. On the
other hand, many of them had been written down, in one fashion or
another, by nonnatives of several nationalities, particularly missionaries and travelers, and there was a far greater amount of material
in existence on these languages than on any other language family of
North America. [10] Brief vocabularies and other materials on one or
another Algonkian form of speech began appearing as early as 1609, [11]
and by 1663 Eliot had completed his monumental task of translating
the Bible into Natick (or Massachusetts). [12] A few years later Eliot
published The Indian grammar begun, or an essay to bring the Indian
language into rules, [13] but this language was unfortunately one of those
which became extinct before modern firsthand studies could be made
of it.

      From these beginnings the stream of materials on Algonkian
languages became a virtual flood. There were many dictionaries,
some bilingual for French, English, or German, some for more than
one of these. There were grammars[14] and etymological studies and
numerous other works. Moreover, the resemblances among the languages were such that it had long been recognized that they were

genetically related and that this remarkable family had a geographical spread greater than that of any other family in North America.
So there were even scholars who had commenced comparative work
on these languages, the most notable of whom was Truman Michelson,[15]
but the results, though considerable, had been only haphazardly presented when Bloomfield entered the field. In order to give a rigorous
demonstration of the genetic relationship of these languages, it was
obvious to Bloomfield that he would have to reconstruct the protolanguage, and he proposed to do so by using exactly the same techniques
that had been so successfully applied by the neogrammarians in the reconstruction of Proto-Indo-European.[16] Furthermore, since many
Indo-European scholars thought such a task could not be successfully
accomplished in the absence of written records of earlier stages of
the languages, Bloomfield set out quite deliberately to disprove this
thesis. The result was his masterly paper "On the sound-system of
Central Algonquian"[17] which paved the way for all future work in comparative Algonkian. Furthermore, to make sure that the nature of
his accomplishment, with its important implications for similar work
on all unwritten languages, would not be lost on his Indo-European
confreres in Europe, and especially the editors of Les langues du
monde, he appended the following footnote:

> I hope, also, to help dispose of the notion that the usual pro-
> cesses of linguistic change are suspended on the American
> continent (Meillet and Cohen, Les langues du monde, Paris,
> 1924, p. 9). If there exists anywhere a language in which
> these processes do not occur (sound-change independent of
> meaning, analogic change, etc.), then they will not explain
> the history of Indo-European or any other language. A prin-
> ciple such as the regularity of phonetic change is not part of
> the specific tradition handed on to each new speaker of a
> given language, but is either a universal trait of human
> speech or nothing at all, an error. (p. 130)

1.5 Bloomfield's success in reconstructing Proto-Algonkian is so
significant in the development of historical linguistics that it deserves
closer scrutiny and will be discussed in somewhat more detail later.
Bloomfield's intention was to demonstrate that the 'sounds' of the protolanguage of a set of unwritten related languages could be reconstructed with the same degree of rigor and reliability as had been achieved

for the Indo-European languages. Before he could do this, however,
he had to have a completely accurate and reliable 'description' of each
unwritten language that was to be used in the demonstration. All too
frequently nonnatively written materials were entirely inadequate for
his purposes. [18] He therefore seems to have developed his theories of
descriptive linguistics in large part in order to tackle his problems
of historical linguistics. But this had a result which he perhaps did
not anticipate, namely, that in many quarters a schism developed between descriptive linguistics and historical linguistics. Although
other factors and other persons were also involved in the movement,
it remains true that Bloomfield helped to crystallize a theory of descriptive linguistics, particularly the theory of the phoneme, at exactly the moment in history at which it was most needed in the rapidly
developing studies of American Indian and other unwritten languages.
The repercussions quickly affected even the study of written European
languages which came more and more to be studied as if they were unwritten languages. This was, needless to say, a shocking approach
at the time and one which did not, of course, go unchallenged.

        The important point here is that the development of a rigor-
ous methodology in comparative linguistics in the nineteenth century
led to the development of a rigorous methodology of descriptive linguistics in the twentieth century. The thread of continuity is therefore rigor. Moreover, Bloomfield is probably properly credited with
being the first American linguist to exercise the utmost scrupulous-
ness in maintaining the separateness of history and description. His
deep concern with reconstructing the phonological and grammatical
structure of Proto-Algonkian made him realize he would first have to
have adequate descriptions of the languages to be used in making the
reconstruction. And it was to this end he was so interested in shar-
pening the tools of descriptive linguistics. This was no idle or sterile
interest. It culminated in the tightly-knit paper entitled simply "Algonquian" which was the only comparative sketch in Linguistic structures of native America. [19]

1.6 The greatness of Bloomfield's treatment of Algonkian can be ascribed to a variety of reasons. [20] A very important point of methodology lies in his limitation of the problem to the comparison of four
languages[21] for which he had adequate (though often less than abundant)

descriptive materials, namely Fox, Cree, Menominee, and Ojibwa.
This method had both advantages and disadvantages, though for an
initial comprehensive statement of Algonkian comparative grammar
the advantages seem far to outweigh the disadvantages. The languages
chosen are all so-called Central languages and do not comprise even
these in toto. To have attempted to use all available materials on the
dozens of Algonkian languages for which some kind of information was
available[22] would have rendered the task so unwieldy and unmanageable
that he would not have been able to complete it in a lifetime. By limiting himself to those languages over which he had good control he was
able (1) to work out the phonological system for Proto-Algonkian as
reflected in those particular four Central languages, [23] and (2) to reconstruct large numbers of fully inflected words rather than being confined solely to the reconstruction of roots. [24] The second result had
the further advantage of enabling him to write what was essentially an
outline descriptive grammar of the protolanguage. He had also begun
work on a comparative dictionary of his four selected Algonkian languages, and to this end had assembled extensive slip files on each of
them. He did not live to complete the task himself but progress toward achieving this goal is now being made by a younger scholar. [25]

1.7 It would be a great satisfaction to be able to say that the work of
Bloomfield on Algonkian, together with that of Sapir on Uto-Aztecan,[26]
Athapaskan, [27] and other linguistic families, not to speak of the vast
amount of work currently being done on the reconstruction and classification of unwritten languages, has succeeded in allaying the doubts
of all Indo-Europeanists about the type of results that can be achieved
without the aid of documentary materials from earlier periods when
these are by definition unobtainable. But in a recent textbook on historical linguistics we find that the old prejudices, though slightly modified perhaps, have not been entirely banished. The following quotation, for example, has a familiar ring: [28]

> Genealogical classification was admirably suited to deter-
> mine the interrelationships of languages such as the Indo-
> European for which we have many records from several mil-
> lennia. For languages attested only today we may be limited
> to classification based on typology. (p. 49)

Typological classifications are of value in their own right, and can, needless to say, be applied to anciently recorded languages as well as to 'languages attested only today'. To imply that genealogical classification is possible only for linguistic families having written records of varying chronology while typological classification belongs to contemporary languages is to sell both types of classification short. Languages are languages, whether written or unwritten, living or dead, and whatever type of classification can be applied to one can also be applied to any other. The best answer, I think, is to paraphrase a statement of Sapir's[29] about the discovery of phonetic laws in unwritten languages:

> If these laws are more difficult to discover in primitive [unwritten] languages, this is not due to any special characteristic which these languages possess but merely to the inadequate technique of some who have tried to study them. (p. 74)

In the same way, if genealogical classification is more difficult of achievement in unwritten languages, this is again due to the 'inadequate technique of some who have tried to study them' [emphasis mine]. Indeed we might better paraphrase Bloomfield's famous footnote, quoted earlier, and say that the possibility of both genealogical and typological classification 'is either a universal trait of human speech or nothing at all, an error' [emphasis mine].

    There is also still current an even more flagrant misunderstanding of the nature of unwritten languages. Although the error has been refuted innumerable times in the literature, there are still some who believe that unwritten languages change with a rapidity that soon renders reconstruction so tenuous as to be meaningless. A recently expressed version[30] of this view is seen in the following fantastic statement:

> In some linguistic families, notably Amerindian and African, prehistory is but a few decades distant. Any thrust into the past will involve the linguist in reconstruction. . . . By the time the Amerindian or African linguist has reached, speaking in terms of the genealogical tree. . ., the third or fourth generation, which perhaps carries him backward no farther than a century [!], he faces a proto-language of his own

> making that has an exceedingly small degree of verisimili-
> tude.... (p. 32) [Emphasis mine.]

Indeed one might almost say, would that it _were_ true! For if among
American Indian and African linguistic families, prehistory were
'but a few decades distant', comparative linguists would have a field
day. They could take a large 'live' sample every ten years and thus
have an actual check on linguistic change that would bid fair to equal
the short-lived fruit fly in studying genetic change in biology. Unfortunately for the prospects of any such check, languages change in
much the same ways the world over, and writing per se neither retards nor accelerates the change.[31] When sister languages, both written and unwritten, are seen again and again to have diverged in phonology, morphology, and lexicology in remarkably similar ways, then
we can be sure that the lapse of time needed to accomplish this has
been comparable too. No, among unwritten as well as written languages prehistory is written in millennia, not decades.

We have already seen in section 1.4 that the Algonkian languages (whose divergence is comparable to that of the Romance or
Germanic languages) have been written down since the early 1600's,
i.e. starting over three and a half centuries ago. If Pulgram's thesis
had a grain of truth, then Eliot's Natick Bible of 1663, now three centuries old, would be written in a language far more archaic than
Proto-Algonkian itself; indeed it would be a kind of 'Hittite' of Algonkian. Instead Natick is as close to Penobscot and other nearby Algonkian languages as Swedish is to Danish, and Proto-Algonkian cannot
by any manner of means be reckoned as any less ancient than Proto-
Germanic. In innumerable instances where American Indian linguists
have checked words in early vocabularies (100-300 or more years old)
with the same words in languages still spoken — Natick is no longer
spoken — they have discovered no appreciable change whatsoever. In
other instances, minor sound changes appear to have taken place, but
in no instance are these more drastic than those known to have taken
place in European (written) languages in a comparable period of time.
One very interesting example of such minor sound changes has been
called to my attention by my student, Allan Taylor, who collected a
vocabulary of Atsina (a Plains Algonkian language varying only dia-
lectically from Arapaho) and compared this with a vocabulary of the
same language (same dialect) written down nearly 200 years ago, in

1790 to be exact. The first four numerals are sufficient to illustrate
the nature of these changes. Moreover, we also know the reconstructions of the Proto-Algonkian forms of these words and can thus compare both varieties of Atsina with these much older forms: [32]

	Atsina (1960)	Atsina (1790)	Proto-Algon.
one	čέɛθiy	kar-ci [kɛɛsay]	*pe·šik-
two	níɪθ	neece [niis]	*ni·š-
three	nέɛθ	narce [nɛɛs]	*ne ʔθ-
four	yέɛn	ne-an [ni(y)ɛɛn]	*nye·w-

Early Atsina k̲ > modern č̲ (before front vowels), early Ats. s̲ > modern θ̲, and the initial syllable of 'four' has dropped. But the changes
that have taken place between PA and early Atsina are far more drastic: PA *p > early Ats. k̲ everywhere (modern k̲ before back vowels,
č̲ before front vowels); PA *š̲ > early Ats. s̲ (> θ̲); PA *-ʔθ- > early
Ats. s̲ (> θ̲); PA *w̲ > n̲ (in 'four' and many other words).

2. Protolanguages and Problems of Reconstruction

2.1 What is a protolanguage? The answer, quite simply, is that any
language is an actual or potential protolanguage. Two or three thousand years hence — barring catastrophic changes — a variety of languages stemming from English will be spoken in wide areas of the
globe, areas more or less delineating those in which English is now
spoken as a first language. The same can be said, with appropriate
modifications in regard to size of area, of Spanish, Portuguese, Russian, and Chinese, not to speak of Hindi, Tamil, Kikuyu, and a host
of others.

Given the lapse of a sufficient amount of time, this means (1)
that the descendants of these languages, if still spoken, will have diverged enough to be compared and used in the reconstruction of their
respective parent languages, and (2) that the result of such reconstruction will provide a body of material that is recognizably like the
the English, Spanish, Portuguese, etc. spoken today. It will not, however, be identical with what appears in written records. Linguistic
change takes place in the spoken language and the written language always lags far behind in recording this change, in large part, of course

to retain the tremendous advantages of the fiction of cohesiveness in the linguistic community as long as possible, in spite of ever-increasing differences in the spoken language. The word 'mayor' is spelled m-a-y-o-r from London to Vancouver and from Atlanta to Brisbane, even though the actual pronunciation of the word may vary so widely as to be unrecognizable out of context (or possibly even in context) if persons of different areas chance to meet. Furthermore, dozens of words and turns of expression having only local provenience may never chance to be recorded anywhere but will persist in their own areas completely uninfluenced by the fact that they did not find a place in the written language of today. Still more important, there are many things which will inevitably be lost in all the daughter languages and thus be unrecoverable by the comparative method. These are the reasons why Proto-Romance is not in all details identical with recorded Latin. But this fact, far from being an indictment of the comparative method is an elegant example of its tremendous power.

Every protolanguage was in the same way once a real language, whether or not we are fortunate enough to have written records of it. Furthermore, even when we do have written records, we find that what we are able to reconstruct of a given protolanguage always falls short of giving us the full picture of the real language it stands for. But written records fall short, too, as we have seen in the case of local pronunciation variations, lexical items, and turns of expression, and reconstruction methods can and do, in fact, give us information about parent languages not to be found in written records. We are of course twice blessed when we have both, as in the case of Proto-Romance and Latin. When we have only the reconstructed protolanguage, however, we still have a glorious artifact, one which is far more precious than anything an archeologist can ever hope to unearth.

A protolanguage, then, is reconstructed out of the evidence that is acquired by the careful comparison of the daughter languages and, in the beginning of the work, what is reconstructed reflects what can be discovered by working backwards in those cases where all or most of the daughter languages point to the same conclusion. This provides the initial framework. Once this is established, the principle of analogy can be drawn upon, and by its use instances in which there are aberrations, statistically speaking, can often also be plausibly accounted for. Deductive as well as inductive hypotheses must

be constructed and checked. Then when all the comparisons that can
reasonably be made have been made, and when all the reconstructions
that can reasonably be made have been made, the result is a prototypical model of the daughter languages, or, what we normally call a
protolanguage.

     If we turn the whole thing round and look at it from the other
direction we see that the daughter languages are not only different
from each other but also from the protolanguage. We describe this
differentiation by calling it 'linguistic change'. In phonology, linguistic change normally shows such regularity that it is possible to formulate what the nineteenth century linguists proudly called 'phonetic
laws' on the analogy of what their fellow natural scientists were with
equal pride referring to as 'laws of nature', [33] even though, as Sapir
once remarked, ". . .phonetic laws are by no means comparable to
the laws of physics or chemistry or any other of the natural sciences.
They are merely general statements of a series of changes characteristic of a given language at a particular time."[34] The most impressive
characteristic of phonetic laws, or statements of phonetic correspondences, is their power to predict.[35] Other types of linguistic change
do not operate with the same kind of predictable regularity; perhaps
it would be better to say that we have not yet arrived at the point of
being able to make statements about other types of linguistic change
in such a way as to reveal such a power. Change can occur in inflection and in other parts of morphology. It can occur in meaning and in
vocabulary. But since it has not yet become possible to make predictable statements about any of these kinds of changes, the verifiable
regularity of sound correspondences is seen to be even more precious
than it may have seemed at first.

     In the sections which follow problems of both phonological
and morphological reconstruction are discussed, with examples taken
largely from the Muskogean family of languages.

2.20 The Muskogean family of languages[36] formerly flourished in the
southeastern part of what is now the United States. There are four
distinct languages still extant, so by accident we have a neat workable
set of languages without being constrained to choose among them.
They are Choctaw (Ch), Koasati (K), Hitchiti (H), and Creek (C). As
an aid to the understanding of the illustrative sound changes, Table I

Table I

Combined chart of the consonants and vowels of four Muskogean languages

	Bilabial	Dental	Alveolar	Palatal	Velar	Faucal
Voiceless Stops	p p p p	t t t t		č c c c	k k k k	
Voiced Stops	b b b -					
Voiceless Spirants	f f f f	ɬ ɬ ɬ ɬ	s - - -	š s s s		h h h h
Voiced Nasal Continuants	m m m m	n n n n				
Voiced Nonnasal Continuants	w w w w	l l l l		y y y y		· · · ·
Vowels	u u u u			i i i i		a a a a

shows the combined consonant and vowel charts[37] of the four languages arranged in quadrant form (in each box) for convenience, viz.

Ch	K
H	C

In Table II[38] several sets of items having the same gloss are taken from these four Muskogean languages and the illustrations used in the sections which follow are based on this material.

2.21 Sound change is often characterized as being of two types, (1) regular and (2) sporadic, and the first is sometimes further described as 'gradual' and the second as 'sudden'. Since the second type is usually said to include such phenomena as assimilation and dissimilation as well as metathesis, it is clear that the regular vs. sporadic

Table II

Sample sets of cognates in four Muskogean languages

	1. sun	2. sleep	3. arrow	4. night	5. day	6. mulberry
Ch	haši	nusi	naki	ninak	nittak	bihi
K	hasi	nuci	łaki	niła(hasi) 'moon'	nihta	bihi(cuba) 'fig'
H	ha·s(i)	nu·c(í·ki)	(in)łak(i·)	ni·łak(i)	nihtak(i)	bi[h]–(Sn)
C	hási	nuc(ita)	łi.	nłłi.	nittł.	kf.
PM	*hasi	*nuci	*Naki	*niNaki	*nihtaka	*kʷihi

	7. fish	8. squirrel	9. two	10. go through	11. snake	12. wide
Ch	nani	fani	tuklu	łupul(li)	sinti	patha
K	łału	ipłu	tuklu	łuput(li)	cintu	patha
H	ła·ł(i)	hłʔ·ł(i)	tukl(an)	———	cint(i)	———
C	łału	łu	hukkul(ita)	łupu·t(t–)	cittu	tałph(i·)
PM	*NaNi/u	*ixʷaNi/u	*hutukulu	*łupu(·)t–	*cinti/u	*patha

dichotomy cannot be fitted exactly with the gradual vs. sudden one, for some types of assimilation may very well take place gradually while metathesis cannot occur in any fashion other than suddenly.

It seems to me that it might be more revealing to show phonological change on two axes, the syntagmatic (horizontal) and the paradigmatic (vertical). According to this model, assimilation, dissimilation, and metathesis are arranged on the syntagmatic axis while so-called vowel and consonant 'shifts' or correspondences are placed on the paradigmatic axis.

Illustrations of Muskogean sound correspondences, i.e. the paradigmatic axis, are taken up first. The items for 'fish', no. 7 (Table II), comprise a perfect set of cognates. The sound correspondences are as follows:

(1) Ch n̠ : K, H, C ł̠. See also 'arrow', no. 3; 'night', no. 4 (second cons.); and 'squirrel', no. 8. The symbol *N̠ has been chosen as the reconstruction for the n̠ : ł̠ correspondence. The symbol *n̠ is needed when all the languages show n̠, e.g. 'sleep', no. 2; 'night', no. 4 (first cons.). Similarly, *ł̠ is needed when all have ł̠, e.g. 'go through', no. 10.

(2) Ch, K, and C short vowel in initial open syllable : H long vowel. See also 'sun', no. 1; 'sleep', no. 2; 'night', no. 4. This is reconstructed as a short vowel.

(3) Ch final i̠ : K, H, C final u̠. See also 'squirrel', no. 8; 'snake', no. 11. This correspondence is found only in final syllables and is symbolized in reconstruction as *i̠/u̠. Some final syllables show i̠ in all languages and for these *i̠ is reconstructed; see 'sun', no. 1. Similarly for *u̠; see, in part, 'two', no. 9, where Ch and K both have u̠.

In terms of these correspondences and the symbols chosen to represent them, the full PM reconstruction for 'fish' is *NaNi/u.

Other sets of cognates shown in Table II illustrate still other regularities in correspondences. Choctaw has two sibilant spirants,

s̱ and š̱, where the other principal languages have only s̱ (ranging
from [s] to [š] but often closer to [š̱]; see Table I). The usual correspondences for these two Choctaw sounds are:

Ch š̱ : K, H, C s̱; see 'sun', no. 1.
Ch s̱ : K, H, C c̱ (affricate); see 'sleep', no. 2; 'snake',
  no. 11.

2.22 Turning now to the sound changes that are best shown on the syntagmatic axis, we can illustrate assimilation, dissimilation and metathesis. Assimilation is shown horizontally by the use of a straight
arrow; it is directed to the right (→) for assimilation to what follows
and to the left (←) for assimilation to what precedes. Dissimilation
is shown by a bar; it is placed on the right (⊣) or on the left (⊢) in accordance with the same principle. Finally, metathesis is shown by
a looped arrow, to the right (↻) or to the left (↺). In Table II examples
of consonantic assimilation resulting in gemination are seen in 'day'
(both Ch and C), no. 5; 'two' (C), no. 9 (see also Table IV); and
'snake' (C), no. 11. Thus for 'snake' we have:

PM *c̱inti/u : pre-C *c̱in → tu : C c̱íttu.

Dissimilation is rare. An example is seen in 'squirrel' (K), no. 8,
more fully discussed in 2.24:

PM *ix^waNi/u : pre-K *if⊣ łu : K ipłu.

Metathesis, on the other hand, is fairly common, particularly between subdialects of Choctaw and Creek. In Table II there is one example, viz. 'wide' (C), no. 12:

PM *patha : pre-C *p↻a th(i·) : C táph(i·)

2.23 Sometimes it is necessary to employ considerable ingenuity to
obtain the reconstruction which will account for all the differences
among the daughter languages. In addition to different articulatory
features associated with the various vowels and consonants, as when
ṉ corresponds to ł, it is often necessary to reckon with other kinds of

phonological change. For example, even though the stems of all the
daughter languages show two syllables for a certain item it may turn
out that the prototype language had three (or even more) syllables. As
a case in point, let us look at the word for 'night', no. 4 in Table II.
Although no problem is encountered in comparing V_1 in all four languages, a first glance at V_2 seems to show a special correspondence,
viz. Ch, K, H a̲ : C i̲· . But a look at the word for 'day', no. 5, reveals that there is also a correspondence of Ch, K, H a̲ : C a̲· . An
examination of the environment in which both correspondences appear
(i. e. stem final position) enables us to make a somewhat improved
statement that Ch, H a̲k̲, K a̲ : C i̲· or a̲· . The proper solution, however, does not become clear until we study the word for 'arrow', no.
3, a disyllable. Here the correspondence is:

      Ch, K a̲k̲i̲, H a̲k̲ : C i̲·

and we see that when Creek has i̲· the prototype must have been *a̲k̲i̲,
as in Choctaw. Choctaw and Koasati final i̲ appear for prototype
final *i̲ in disyllabic words only; in words of more than two syllables,
Choctaw lacks final i̲ and Koasati lacks not only final i̲ but the preceding k̲ as well. Using the disyllabic word 'arrow', no. 3, as a
model we can then assume that the prototype for 'night', no. 4, also
ended in *a̲k̲i̲ even though in this instance Creek provides our only clue
to the identity of the final vowel. [39] This leads to the proper reconstruction of the word for 'night' as a trisyllabic *ni̲N̲aki̲, even though
all the daughter languages have reduced it to a disyllabic word.

      But what about the word for 'day', no. 5, which has Creek
a̲· ? In this case no disyllabic word has been turned up as an aid in
the solution of our problem. But we do not need it. If Creek i̲· is the
reduction (contraction) of *a̲k̲i̲ in 'night', then Creek a̲· must be the
reduction of *a̲k̲a̲ in 'day'. We can then confidently reconstruct the
prototype for 'day' as *ni̲h̲t̲a̲k̲a̲.

2. 24 A more complex problem is posed by the word for 'squirrel',
no 8. If we had only Choctaw fa̲n̲i̲ and Creek ɫu̲ we might be tempted
to dismiss the forms as noncognate except for the nagging fact that Ch
n̲ : C ɫ and Ch final i̲ : C final u̲ are both well-attested correspondences. Even so it would probably be very difficult to make a satisfactory full reconstruction without the neat evidence supplied by

Koasati ip*u. This allows us to make a hypothesis about the sound
correspondences among the three which can best be shown in a vertical arrangement, as in the lefthand column of Table III. Again we
seem to have a trisyllabic word as the prototype even though all the

Table III

PM 'squirrel'

Ch	f a n i			* x^W a N i / u
K	i p ł u	*i f	ł u	*i x^W ø N i / u
H	h ī ł-	*i	ł-	*i x^W ø N i / u
C	f ł u	i	ł u	*i x^W ø N i / u
PM	*i x^W a N i / u			*i x^W a N i / u

daughter languages have a disyllabic word, but the reduction rules
needed are quite different from those for 'night', no. 4, and 'day', no.
5. Choctaw has lost the vowel of the first syllable (symbolized by ø
in the righthand column) and Koasati, Hitchiti and Creek have lost
that of the second syllable. The loss of the second vowel leaves a
cluster of two spirants, f and ł (as shown in the middle column). Koasati shows dissimilation in manner of articulation and replaces f with
the homorganic stop p; Hitchiti and Creek have dropped it. [40] The
prototype word for 'squirrel' is *ix^WaNi/u.

    Solving the problem of the reconstruction of the word for
'squirrel' turns out to provide a clue to the problem of the reconstruction of the word for 'two'. If Choctaw has lost the first vowel and Koasati, Hitchiti, and Creek the second vowel in the trisyllabic prototype
for 'squirrel', is it possible that longer words might show the loss of
odd-numbered vowels in some languages as against the loss of even-
numbered vowels in others? In other words, is the vocalic syncope
in 'squirrel' actually an instance of alternative syncope? [41] If we show
the probable sound correspondences among the words for 'two' in a
vertical fashion, we have the arrangement shown in the lefthand column of Table IV. Choctaw, Koasati, and Hitchiti have syncopated the
first and third vowels, Creek the second, as is shown by ø in the
righthand column of the table. Pre-Creek had a two-stop cluster *tk,
as shown in the middle column, and *t has assimilated to *k in position of articulation giving the geminate cluster kk in modern Creek.

The reconstruction which most adequately accounts for all the modern
attested forms for 'two' is *hutukulu.

Table IV

PM 'two'

Ch, K	t u k l u		*Ø t u k Ø l u
H	t u k l-		*Ø t u k Ø l-
C	h u k k u l-	*h u t → k u l-	*h u t Ø k u l-
PM	*h u t u k u l u		*h u t u k u l u

2.31 The examples from Muskogean given in the preceding section illustrate the same regularity of phonological change that has now become familiar in Indo-European, Algonkian, and many other language
families. They also serve to illustrate two important differences between a <u>real</u> language and a reconstructed protolanguage.

(1) If I could hear Proto-Muskogean spoken I would know the
precise phonetic quality of the consonant I can now only
symbolize as *<u>N</u>, or in full as Ch <u>n</u> : K, H, C <u>ł</u>. This
lack of precision, however, is trivial because there can
be no doubt that there was a distinctive protoconsonant
characterized by some feature of <u>n</u> and some feature of
<u>ł</u>. The symbol used reflects this.

(2) If I could hear Proto-Muskogean spoken I would also
know the precise nature of the final syllable or syllables
of the words for 'fish', no. 7, and 'squirrel', no. 8 (in
Table II) which can now be symbolized only awkwardly
as *<u>i/u</u>. But with more evidence from some direction I
could make a change in the reconstruction in a nontrivial
fashion, e.g. by adding something to it.

A reconstructed protolanguage is an approximation to a real language
but it always falls short of being identical with the actual prototype
language. The phones of a real language and the morphs of a real language <u>are</u> as they have been recorded at a given moment of time, whether that moment was the record made by a trained fieldworker yes-
terday or by a scribe in ancient times. The reconstructed phones and

the reconstructed morphs of a protolanguage are of course expected
to represent the best efforts of scholars in approximating the reality
of these entities. But more evidence, or different evidence — the discovery of a new daughter language, for instance — can bring new insights which may at any time make it necessary to change the reconstruction of a phone or of a morph. And when this happens the reconstruction <u>must</u> be changed. In this way the approximation to the reality can be increased even if never reached. What can be reconstructed of a protolanguage is thus comparable to the visible part of an ice-
berg; only a greater or lesser percentage is recoverable in spite of
the certainty that the reality was both quantitatively and qualitatively
much richer. In this respect historical linguistics is like archeology.
In the one case it is impossible to recover the living flesh of the spoken language that was the prototype, in the other it is impossible to
reify the processes of social interaction that belonged to the particular horizon.

2.32 It was mentioned above that reconstructions can be changed on
the basis of new insights. But where are these new insights to come
from? Some of the most likely possibilities are discussed in the following paragraphs.

2.321 (1) <u>A new interpretation of the material on hand.</u> — a new hypothesis about the interpretation of some recalcitrant facets of the
material already available can be developed. The most celebrated
example of this is Saussure's postulation in 1879 of a schwa (ǝ) to help
regularize the statements about the development of certain Indo-European vowels. It was nearly fifty years later that Kuryłowicz[42] proposed to identify this with the transcribed <u>h</u> of Hittite, on which materials, unknown to Saussure of course, had only recently been discovered.

          A less spectacular example can be taken from Table II in
connection with the Muskogean word for 'mulberry', no. 6. Because
of a very limited number of examples (many of which had other problems) the cognation of Choctaw <u>bihi</u> and Creek <u>kí</u>· was not immediately
recognized. But the postulation of a PM labiovelar consonant $*k^W$(>
Ch, K, and H <u>b</u>, C <u>k</u>) provided an entirely satisfactory solution to the

problem.[43] A glance at Table I shows that b̲, as the only voiced stop,
skews the configuration of stops in Choctaw, Koasati, and Hitchiti.
But the postulation of *k̲ᵂ for PM completely eliminates the necessity
of retaining that skewing in the protolanguage:

PM voiceless stops and affricates: *p̲ *t̲ *c̲ *č̲ *k̲ *k̲ᵂ

In this case we can never hope to recover documentary evidence to
confirm the hypothesis, though we may some day be fortunate enough
to find support through extrafamilial comparison; see 2.323 below.

2.322 (2) The discovery of a new daughter language. — The discovery of a new daughter language signals the need to reexamine all previous work in the light of the new evidence. Unbelievable as it may
seem, this is all too seldom done. If the body of reconstructed material already in existence is extensive, the attempt will be made to
fit the new language into the already established scheme in so far as
it is possible to do so. There will be a strong temptation to explain
away the things that do not fit the old scheme as aberrations of the
newly discovered language. It is of course always possible that they
are, but this should never be taken for granted. The new language
must be studied not only in relation to the reconstructed material but
also in relation to all of the previously known daughter languages. If
this is done, it may very well turn out that some reconstructions will
be seen to be faulty or some phases of the morphology of the protolanguage will be defective or biased in the direction of certain daughter
languages. In all such circumstances changes in the reconstructed
scheme will have to be made. To put it in other words, instead of
trimming the new material to fit the old scheme, one must modify the
old scheme to accommodate the new material. Even in Indo-European,
the best studied family of them all, scholars are lagging far behind in
their exploitation of the important new material that has become available to them in the twentieth century. Tocharian, for example, "has
contributed little to our knowledge of Indo-European", according to
Lehmann, because "most of the basic research. . .has been undertaken only recently".[44] But until Tocharian, and Hittite, and all the
other unexploited Indo-European language materials, have been ex-
haustively studied for all the information they can yield, we are
obliged to confess that our knowledge of Proto-Indo-European is far

less adequate than it would need to be. Indeed this lag in the articulation of newly discovered materials (often chronologically older) with
the more thoroughly worked materials (often chronologically younger)
explains the persistent uncertainty about the meaning of the aberran-
cies of Hittite which have ranged from the hypothesis that Hittite was
a sister language of Indo-European (the so-called 'Indo-Hittite hypothesis')[45] to "speculation that Hittite may be Creole, i.e., the descendant of a Pidgin originally used for communication between
speakers of Indo-European and non-Indo-European languages in Ana-
tolia".[46]

2.323 (3) <u>The comparison of one protolanguage with another</u>. — The
most challenging way in which new insight into reconstruction can be
achieved comes about when one protolanguage is compared with another protolanguage, or, as often happens, when a protolanguage is
compared with a single language lacking near relatives.[47] This type
of comparison can truly be said to be one of the most important new
frontiers of historical and comparative linguistics.

　　　　Even in the nineteenth century, Indo-Europeanists were already aware that this was likely to be the next step — witness the suggestions of a genetic relationship between Indo-European and Hamito-
Semitic, or between Indo-European and Finno-Ugric — but Indo-Europeanists have not really led the way in this field. An important early
piece of work was the Whorf-Trager comparison of reconstructed Uto-
Aztecan forms with reconstructed Tanoan forms.[48] More recently it
is probable that more has been done in comparing some of the protolanguages of Mexico than those anywhere else.[49]

　　　　When two or more protolanguages are compared (or when one
or more protolanguages and one or more 'language isolates' are compared) they are treated like daughter languages of a still earlier protolanguage. In other words, the investigator is seeking to establish an
earlier 'common horizon'.[50] Little work of this kind has been done
among families north of Mexico since the aforementioned effort of
Whorf and Trager. However, a small beginning has been made in the
comparison of Proto-Algonkian and Proto-Muskogean,[51] and Table V
shows a comparison of a certain type of final in the two protolanguages
together with a possible modification of the PM reconstruction in the

light of the PA evidence. The hypothesis is only a hypothesis, however, and has not yet been verified.[50] It is shown as an example of
the way in which a new insight in regard to the reconstruction in one
protolanguage may be gained through comparison with another language.

Table V

'Fish', 'squirrel', and 'tree' in
Proto-Algonkian and Proto-Muskogean

	fish	squirrel	tree
PA	*n a m e· k w-	*a n i k w-	*m e ʔ t e k w-
PM	*N a N i / u	*i x^{w}a n i / u	*i t t i / u
PM (modi-fied)	*N a N i k u	*i x^{w}a n i k u	*i t t i k u

2.4 Each time the reconstruction of a new linguistic family is undertaken, the comparativist is struck anew with the beautiful regularity
of the phonological correspondences to be found among the daughter
languages. Even though there are almost always some phonological
loose ends, the over-all consistency of the system is generally sufficient to give him renewed confidence in the comparative method. But
once he turns his attention to the problems of morphological reconstruction, the terrain becomes much more difficult and he is well-
advised to proceed with the utmost caution. It is here that he will
find whole systems (say the paradigmatic structure of the verb) being
simplified in one language, elaborated in another language, and completely rearranged in still another language. While it is true that he
will still follow the same basic ground rule, namely to set up as the
prototype system the simplest one adequate to explain the divergent
developments of the daughter languages, the whole process is much
more complicated than the setting up of a phonological system which
can be verified with multiple examples of the same sound correspondence, or, frequently enough, patterned sets of sound correspondences
(e. g. 'Grimm's law'). Phonological systems can be set up by working
backwards to the protolanguage and checked by working forward to the
daughter languages. Paradigmatic and inflectional systems, however,

are often affected first by phonological change and then by analogic
loss or re-formation (leveling) so that the end results in the various
daughter languages may give the impression of having very little in
common. If the analogical leveling has been extensive enough, it will
not be possible to find the solution by making a conventional phonological reconstruction of each term in a paradigm.[53] Instead it may be
necessary to make a series of bold hypotheses about the structure of
the paradigm as a whole until a model is arrived at which comes nearest to explaining what is actually found in each of the daughter languages.

        The prototype verbal paradigm of the Muskogean languages
provides an interesting example.[54] In all of the Muskogean languages
the third person subject of the verbal paradigm is an unmarked category. The marked categories are first and second person singular
and plural (symbolized as 1S, 2S, 1P, and 2P). In Choctaw the 1S
element is a suffix and the other three elements are prefixes, whereas in Hitchiti and Creek all the elements are suffixes; see Table VI.

        If these were the only three Muskogean languages for which
materials were available, we could, on the basis of the evidence
shown in Table VI, construct three hypotheses: (1) the protosystem
was like Choctaw, but Hitchiti and Creek have leveled out the position
of the affixes to agree with the suffixed first person; (2) the protosystem was like Hitchiti and Creek, but Choctaw has 'innovated' a prefixed position for the 2S, 1P, and 2P affixes; (3) the protosystem had
two classes of paradigms, one like Choctaw, the other like Hitchiti
and Creek. Without further evidence, many workers would probably
prefer the first hypothesis, since it seems somehow 'simpler'. The
third hypothesis would probably be least favored since it is, on the
face of it, simply additive and, in this form at least, does not seem
to 'explain' anything. As will be brought out in the ensuing discussion,
the third hypothesis is best on the Proto-Muskogean level and the
first hypothesis can only be made workable at the pre-Proto-Muskogean level.

        Fortunately, Choctaw, Hitchiti, and Creek are not the only
Muskogean languages for which paradigmatic material is available,
and still more fortunately, the material from the additional source
is of such a nature as to solve the problem. Whereas Choctaw,

Table VI

Subject affixes of Choctaw, Hitchiti, and Creek

	Choctaw Prefix	Choctaw Suffix	Hitchiti Suffix	Creek Suffix
S 1		-li	- li	-ay-
2	iš-		-icka	-ick-
P1	il-; i·-/C		-i·ka	-iy-; -i·-/C
2	haš-		-a·cka	-a·ck-

Hitichiti, and Creek have a single paradigmatic class each, Koasati
has a total of three paradigmatic classes, the first of which is identical with the single Choctaw paradigm, and the third of which closely
resembles the single Hitchiti paradigm, while Creek shows only slight
phonological variations of the latter; see Table VII. That the three-
class system of Koasati is a reflection of certain important features
of the Proto-Muskogean system is attested by the fact that it shows
the framework within which the difference between the Choctaw system, on the one hand, and the Hitchiti and Creek systems, on the
other, could have originated; see Table VIII. Furthermore, a careful study of the various uses of Classes II and III in Koasait helps

Table VII

Koasati subject affixes

	Class I Prefix	Class I Suffix	Class IIA, B Infix(suff.)	Class IIA, B Suffix	Class IIC Infix	Class IIC Suffix	Class III Suffix
S 1		-li		-li		-li	-li
2	is-		-ci(-)		-ci-		-(h)iska
P1	il-		-hili(-)		-li-		-(h)ilka
2	has-		-haci(-)		-haci-		-(h)aska

provide the clue to the probable origin of these classes. Even
though the chief evidence comes entirely from Koasati, it is possible
to construct a model of the pre-Proto-Muskogean paradigm[55] which
requires only one set of subject affixes (basically those of Class I,
Table VIII, with slightly varying allomorphs for some affixes) and two
classes of verb stems, [56] (1) those to which the subject affixes are

Table VIII

Proto-Muskogean Subject affixes

	Class I		Class II		Class III
	Prefix	Suffix	Infix(suff.)	Suffix	Suffix
S 1		*-li		*-li	*-kali
2	*iš-		*-ši-		*-iška
P1	*il(i)-		*-hili-		*-(h)ilika
2	*haš(i)-		*-haši-		*-(h)aš(i)ka

attached directly, and (2) those which are conjugated only periphras-
tically with the subject affixes being attached to the auxiliary verb
stem and the whole thing added to the main verb stem; see Table
IX.[57]

Table IX

Model of pre-Proto-Muskogean verbal conjugation

Direct conjugation of verb stem (VS)		Conjugation of auxiliaries	
		Aux. 1 (LI)	Aux. 2 (KA)
S 1	VS li	VS + LI li	VS + KA li
2	iš VS	VS + ši LI	VS + (h)iš KA
3	VS	VS + LI	VS + KA
P1	ili VS	VS + (hi)liLI	VS + (h)ili KA
2	haš VS	VS + haši LI	VS + (h)aš KA

It might reasonably be asked why the model shown in Table IX is assigned to the pre-Proto-Muskogean period rather than to the Proto-
Muskogean period. In the Proto-Muskogean period the auxiliaries
symbolized as LI and KA in Table IX had already developed into classifying suffixes, *-li as a transitivizer and *-ka as a mediopassive.
Analogical leveling in Choctaw resulted in a simple conjugational system wherein subject affixes descended from PM Class I (Table VIII)
were used with all verb stems, including those containing -li and -a
(the Choctaw equivalents of PM *-li and *-ka, respectively). Hitchiti
and Creek, on the other hand, use as their only subject affixes only
those forms (Class III of Table VIII) which have originated from a
complete amalgamation of the prototype subject affixes with Auxiliary

Verb 2 (KA in Table IX). This means that all verb stems, including those containing descendants of *-li (H -li, C -y-) and *-ka (H -ka, C -k-) are conjugated with what originally belonged only to *-ka verbs. Hitchiti verbs in -ka and Creek verbs in -k- thus contain two morphs -ka or -k-; both are ultimately from the same source (i.e. were identical) but through reinterpretation and analogical leveling they now have completely different functions. Choctaw, Hitchiti, and Creek paradigms illustrating this are shown in Table X.[58] Koasati is the

Table X

Choctaw, Hitchiti, and Creek paradigms of *-li and *-ka verbs

		Choctaw	Hitchiti	Creek
*-li		kul. li 'to dig'	patap. li- 'to hit'	wana. y- 'to tie'
verbs	S 1	KUL. LI li	PATAP. LI li-	WANA. Y ay-
	2	iš KUL. LI	PATAP. L icka-	WANA. Y ick-
	3	KUL. LI	PATAP. LI	WANA. Y-
	P1	i· KUL. LI	PATAP. L i·ka-	WANA. Y iy-(~ i· /C
	2	haš KUL. LI	PATAP. L a·cka-	WANA. Y a·ck-
*-ka		pũ· f. a 'to blow'	pu·f. ka- 'to blow'	pu·f. k- 'to blow'
verbs	S 1	PŨ· F. A li	PU·F.KA li-	PU·F.K ay-
	2	iš PŨ· F. A	PU·F.K icka-	PU·F.K ick-
	3	PŨ· F. A	PU·F.KA-	PU·F.K-
	P1	PŨ· F. A	PU·F.K i·ka-	PU·F.K iy-(~ i· /C
	2	haš PŨ· F. A	PU·F.K a·cka-	PU·F.K a·ck-

one language which has reflexes of all three Proto-Muskogean classes of Table VIII (from the three conjugation types of Table IX), but it too has undergone some very special kinds of development. These are shown in Table XI and may be described as follows: (1) Some, but not all, plain Koasati verb stems (i.e. those lacking the classifying suffixes -li and -ka or the causative suffix -ci) which end in ..V(·)CV belong to Class I. (2) Class II includes all verbs with the classifying suffix -li (or an allomorph), but the suffix appears only before 1S -li and in the third person, which is unmarked for subject. In addition Class II includes all stems ending in .. VCCV (e.g. huhcá 'to dig').[59] (3) Class III includes all stems ending in ..kV, i.e. ..ka, ..ki, and ..ku, but the -kV appears only before 1S -li and in the third person, which is unmarked for subject. This means that all Koasati verbs ending in ..kV are conjugated as if they were old *-ka verbs (see 'to chew' in Table XI as the model with KA in capital letters), but the simplest synchronic interpretation is that the 2S, 1P, and 2P prefixes have been amalgamated with the old *-ka to give Class III affixes (see 'to pay', 'to drink', and 'to teach' in Table XI). That this is indeed the simplest synchronic interpretation is seen in the fact that Class III also includes certain stems lacking ..kV, viz. all those ending in the causative suffix -ci (except when -ci is preceded by transitivizing -li which automatically places them in Class II).

Table XI

Koasati paradigms of Classes I, II, and III
including *-li and *-ka verbs

Class I		(-li verbs) Class IIA	Class IIB	Class IIC
	hica 'to see'	kalas.li 'to scratch'	buk.li.ci 'to thresh'	huhca 'to dig'
S1	HICA li	KALAS LI li	BUK LI CI li	HU HCA li
2	is HICA	KALAS ci Ø	BUK ci Ø CI	HU ci HCA
3	HICA	KALAS LI	BUK LI CI	HU HCA
P1	il HICA	KALAS hili Ø	BUK hili Ø CI	HU li HCA
2	has HICA	KALAS haci Ø	BUK haci Ø CI	HU haci HCA

Class IIIA				Class IIIB
(-ka verb)		(other -kV verbs)		
	yas.ka 'to chew'		isku 'to drink'	impunna.ci 'to teach'
S1	YAS KAli	IMFI·KI li	ISKU li	IMPUNNA.CI li
2	YAS is KA	IMFI· hiska	IS iska	IMPUNNA.C iska
3	YAS KA	IMFI·KI	ISKU	IMPUNNA.CI
P1	YAS il KA	IMFI· hilka	IS ilka	IMPUNNA.C ilka
2	YAS as KA	IMFI· haska	IS aska	IMPUNNA.C aska

This concludes the discussion of the development of the Proto-Muskogean conjugational system of the active verb in the extant daughter languages. The pre-Proto-Muskogean model in Table IX provides an example of 'internal reconstruction' within a protolanguage and its value

as a means of explaining the extant systems has been well demonstrated. Its further value as a model to be used in deeper comparisons is discussed in 3.2.

3. The Ranking of Protolanguages and Problems
     of Comparison at Deeper Levels

3.1 When phonological reconstructions of a large number of etyma
are available in two or more protolanguages it is possible to compare
these to determine whether or not the protolanguages may be sister
languages and hence daughter languages of a still earlier protolanguage. This type of comparison is of crucial importance for scholars
working on languages which lack ancient written records. Since we
do not have and shall never have records of ancient Algonkian, Muskogean, Siouan, Iroquoian, Athapaskan, and a host of others, we have
no choice but first to compare sister languages in order to reconstruct the protolanguage for each family. If this is properly done
these protolanguages can serve us almost as well in our attempts to
make deeper comparisons as ancient written languages like Latin,
Greek, Sanskrit, and Hittite have served our Indo-European confreres.
Anyone who denigrates the work of reconstructing such protolanguages
is actually expressing distrust of the comparative method itself. [60]
The fact that Proto-Romance turns out to be a kind of Latin is precisely the sort of thing that serves as a check on the validity of our
methods. I have not heard of anyone wanting to throw out Proto-Germanic because there are no written records of the Germanic of the
time to substantiate it. Nor do I believe for a moment that scholars
would have found themselves unable to reconstruct Proto-Indo-European without written records. In view of the large numbers of living
languages belonging to this family, one cannot believe that the interrelationships would have gone undetected and that methods to deal with
them would have remained undeveloped. Or, for those who can think
of the discovery of the interrelationship of the Indo-European languages only in terms of the way in which it actually took place, let
us put it this way. If the comparative method had been developed in
respect to another family of languages (say Semitic or Sino-Tibetan),
comparativists would have by now been able to work out the interrelationships of living Indo-European languages even if there were no
records earlier than 1800 A.D. The possibility of discovering genetic

relationships, then, does not stand or fall on the basis of the presence or absence of ancient documents. Reconstructed protolanguages can and do take the place of ancient records when the latter are unavailable.

As we continue to refine our methods of comparing protolanguages,[61] it may turn out to be desirable to use a special terminology to describe different ranks of protolanguages. Elsewhere I have proposed that we speak of protolanguages of the First Order and of the Second Order.[62] A protolanguage of the first order is one reconstructed from natural languages, written or unwritten. A protolanguage of the second order is then one reconstructed on the basis of two or more protolanguages of the first order. Deeper ranks, as of the third order or more, can be added as needed.

It turns out that some natural languages are orphans, that is, they have no known sister languages with which they can be compared in order to participate in the reconstruction of a protolanguage of the first order. I propose to call such languages Language Isolates.[63] Their genealogical classification can be determined, if at all, only by comparing them with protolanguages of the first order or even of the second order or more. When this has been done and a body of reconstructions has been painstakingly worked out, what we have is not an expanded or stretched out protolanguage of the first order, but a protolanguage of the second order. This is a point of considerable methodological significance and one which is again and again misunderstood, even by linguists. For example, the Natchez language (formerly spoken near the present Natchez, Mississippi) is a language isolate. It has been suggested that it is related to the Muskogean languages.[64] If this is so, Natchez is not the sister language of Choctaw, Koasati, Hitchiti, and Creek but is a collateral[65] of Proto-Muskogean itself and possibly of other protolanguages and language isolates (see Table XII).[66] Further refinements of the interrelationships among languages included in a construct such as that shown in Table XII cannot be stated until a vast amount of phonological and morphological comparison has been carried out. The methods of phonological comparison are more or less the traditional ones; some of these are illustrated in section 3.3. More challenging is the problem of finding methods of undertaking morphological comparison. This is discussed in the immediately following section.

Table XII

A preliminary model of Wiyot-Yurok-
Algonkian-Gulf interrrelationships

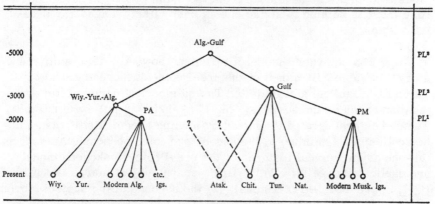

3.2 It has already been demonstrated that even within such a close-
knit family as the Muskogean it is not possible to reconstruct the
prototype paradigmatic structure of the active verb by means of ordinary phonological reconstruction alone. But the problem need not
be abandoned on this account. Instead, as has been shown for Proto-
Muskogean and pre-Proto-Muskogean, one can attempt to construct
a deductive model of the protosystem and if the end results found in
the daughter languages can be successfully explained by its use, its
utility will have been demonstrated.

      The question then arises: Can anything significant ever be
observed by comparing a paradigmatic model constructed for one protolanguage with that of another protolanguage, or with that of a language isolate suspected of being a collateral language ? The answer
would seem to depend on whether or not the two models being compared can be seen to share some unique or unexpected feature, or
perhaps some asymmetrical feature which might be considered diagnostic of possible genetic relationship. As shown in Table XII, there
are four language isolates which are thought to be related to Proto-
Muskogean, namely, Natchez, Tunica, Chitimacha, and Atakapa.[67]
Of these both Natchez and Tunica can combine active verb stems with
conjugated auxiliaries to form periphrastic paradigms. Natchez con-
jugates its auxiliaries by means of subject prefixes for the first, second, and third persons, and the third person is a marked, not an un-

marked category. The resemblance between the Natchez model and
the pre-Proto-Muskogean model of Table IX is thus general and on
the whole rather vague. There is nothing here to indicate that the
models could not be developed from the same prototype but at the same
time there is nothing to strike one as particularly diagnostic of relationship.

The equivalent model for Tunica, however, tells a different
story. In Table XIII a part of the pre-Proto-Muskogean model of
Table IX is laid out alongside the Tunica model of periphrastic conjugation based on the auxiliary -hki (~ ?ahki- ~ ?aki) meaning 'is'.
Tunica has proliferated the model by making gender distinctions (M,
masculine; F, feminine) in the second and third persons. Aside from
this the asymmetrical features of the pre-Proto-Muskogean model
are duplicated exactly: (1) the first person subject morph is suffixed
(* -li in pre-PM, -ni in Tunica), (2) the second person subject morph
is prefixed, and (3) the third person is an unmarked category (provided the Tunica third person singular feminine form is taken as being
older). [68]

Table XIII

Comparison of pre-Muskogean and Tunica models of
periphrastic conjugation with an auxiliary and its subject affixes

Pre-Proto-Muskogean Periphrastic conjugation with *-ka Aux.				Tunica Periphrastic conjugation with -hki Aux.			
		Prefix	Suffix			Prefix	Suffix
S1	VS +	KA	li	S1	VS +	?AHKI	ni
2	VS +	(h)iš KA		2M	VS +	wi HKI	
				2F	VS +	hi HKI	
3				3M	VS +	?u HKI	
	VS +	KA		3F	VS +	?AKI	

This example of the comparison of paradigmatic models has
been given, not to 'prove' that Tunica and Proto-Muskogean are genetically related, but to show the utility of models of this sort for morphological comparison and reconstruction. 'Proof' of relationship,
on the other hand, needs not only this kind of evidence but lexical evidence as well. Moreover, one cannot expect that the comparison of

morphological models will always be as rewarding as it is in the case of Proto-Muskogean and Tunica. The functionally equivalent Natchez model, even though it could very easily be a derivative of, say, a model like the Tunica one,[69] has, if related, leveled out (or 'regularized') its conjugational system until it no longer contains any special feature or combination of features of diagnostic usefulness. However, whenever special features are uncovered by the use of such models, their utility is not to be doubted. In the case of unwritten languages, such as those illustrated, such evidence can be priceless, but so far as I know this type of comparison among unwritten languages has been almost entirely unexploited. It is to be hoped that the Muskogean and Tunica example will serve as an incentive to others to try out the method in other language families.

3.3 When Sapir presented materials in 1913 intended to show that Wiyot and Yurok are genetically related to the Algonkian family (see the lefthand portion of Table XII), his hypothesis received acceptance in some quarters but in general was met with disbelief.[70] Among the factors contributing to the lack of acceptance were several which could be expected to be mitigated or remedied with the passage of time, viz., (1) many people were not yet ready to accept any deeper relationships among the chronologically shallow linguistic families of North America as set up by Powell,[71] (2) the available records of both Wiyot and Yurok were not only scanty but poor, and (3) the sound correspondences among the Algonkian languages themselves were either unknown or inadequately understood.[72] A few cultural anthropologists like Dixon and Kroeber were themselves engaged in postulating deeper relationships and hence were inclined to be favorably disposed toward Sapir's proposal.[73] The leading Algonkianists of the time, on the other hand, had been trained in the rigorous methodology of Indo-European linguistics (as had Sapir) and they could not accept Sapir's conclusion without a stricter marshalling of sound correspondences than Sapir could manage with the type of material at his disposal.[74] Complete acceptance of the hypothesis was consequently withheld for almost fifty years since it was obvious that there would always be a lingering doubt until the Algonkianists were brought around.

The major difficulty lay in having to treat Wiyot and Yurok as sister languages of Cree, Ojibwa, Fox, Natick, Micmac, etc., for

Table XIV

Algonkian and Yurok cognates

	1. his brain	2. his mouth	3. his tooth	4. knee	5. winter
Sh	hotep-i	hoto·n-i	wi·pit-i /wi·pici/	——	pepo·n
C	otihp-i	oto·n	wi·pit	-kitik	pipo·n
O	wi(ni)ntip	oto·n	wi·pit; -a·pit- (med.)	-kitikw-	pepo·n
D	wtʒmp-	wtʃ·n	wipit	kɛɬkw-	——
PA	*wetemp-i ~ *wentep-i	*weto·n-i	*wi·pit-i; *-a·pit-(med.)	*-ketekw-	*pepo·n-
Y	'his hair' weʔlep	weluɬ	warpeɬ	(ʔʒ)kɛɬ	kipu·n

	6. turn	7. long (sg.)	8. long (pl.)	9. bone	10. his liver	11. his tail (bird)
Sh	piyem-	kinw-	kaka·nw-	hoʔkan-i	——	——
C	pi·m̥	kin-	kaka·n-	oskan	oskon	otani
O	pi·m-	ken-	——	ikkan	okko·n	——; M wana·ny
D	pim-	——	——	waxkan	oxkwən-	——
PA	*pyem-	*kenw-	*kaka·nw-	*waθkan-i	*weθkwan-i	*waθany-i
Y	kelom-	knew-	kokonew	weɬkeʔ	wəɬkun	weɬey 'tail' (not bird)

it is now clear that the best way of tackling the problem is to operate
with Proto-Algonkian as a protolanguage of the first order and to compare Wiyot and Yurok with this rather than with the various Algonkian
daughter languages individually as Sapir had been obliged to do.[75]

I have chosen Yurok and Proto-Algonkian to serve as an illustration of the comparison of a collateral language and a protolanguage.[76] Proto-Algonkian probably has a time depth of around two
millennia and when we compare it (rather than Cree, Ojibwa, etc.)
with Yurok we have advantages of almost the same quality as when we
compare Latin (rather than French, Portuguese, etc.) with say,
Gothic (assuming we did not yet have Proto-Germanic). It is maintained (3.1) that a protolanguage reconstructed on the basis of a group
of contemporary unwritten languages can serve us almost as well in
arriving at deeper relationships as can an ancient written language of
comparable antiquity. In corroboration of this contention we present
in Table XIV a sample set of eleven cognates between Proto-Algonkian
and Yurok.[77]

The examples illustrate sound correspondences of the same
type that would be found in comparing any two cognate languages.
Aside from identical correspondences (*p̲ : p̲, *k̲ : k̲, *m̲ : m̲, etc.)
there are several which are nonidentical:

    *t̲ : l̲, ɫ in 'his brain' (Y 'his hair'),'his mouth', 'his tooth',
         'knee'.
    *θ̲ : ɫ in 'his tail'.
    *θ̲k̲ : ɫk in 'bone', 'his liver'. (The symbol *θ̲ in *θ̲k̲ is for-
         mulaic only and is not to be equated with *θ̲ in other po-
         sitions in spite of the seeming similar correspondent
         in Y.)
    *n̲ : ɫ in 'his mouth' (3rd C).
    *y̲ : l̲ in 'turn'.
    *p̲ : k̲ in 'winter' (1st C), 'turn'.
    *a̲n̲ : ə (except after k̲w̲) in 'bone', 'his tail'. Preceding ə̲
         is harmonizing.

Forms from some of the daughter languages of Algonkian are also
shown in Table XIV in order to illustrate the point that it is usually
easier to compare Yurok with PA than it is with one of the daughter

languages. For example, most of the nonidentical correspondences listed above show a Yurok reflex of l̲ or ł̲ and the PA correspondent is *t̲, *θ̲, *n̲, or *y̲. But Cree has t̲ < PA *t̲ and *θ̲ and y̲ < PA *l̲ and *y̲; Ojibwa has n̲ < PA *n̲, *l̲, *θ̲; Shawnee has l̲ < PA *l̲ and *θ̲. Under the circumstances it is simpler to work out the Yurok correspondences in relation to PA. Indeed Sapir ran into difficulties on this account since the PA reconstructions had not been worked out at the time he proposed the Wiyot-Yurok-Algonkian relationship. Observe the following comment:[78]

> . . . Cree sometimes has t̲ where Ojibwa and Fox have n̲. . . in practically all such cases Eastern dialects have l̲, so that what is really involved is not primarily a t̲ — n̲ interchange but a t̲ — l̲ interchange. Here again Wiyot and Yurok are confirmatory, inasmuch as they sometimes have l̲ where Algonkian has t̲ or vice versa.

We now know that when Cree t̲ corresponds to Ojibwa, Fox n̲ and Eastern l̲ the PA reconstruction is *θ̲. But immediately following this remark Sapir gives examples of Wiyot l̲ corresponding to Cree, Ojibwa, Fox, etc. t̲, all of which reflect PA *t̲. One of his examples is Wiyot walul 'his mouth' (see Y and PA in Table XIV). It is obvious that this kind of confusion can be avoided only when reconstructed forms are available. On the other hand, it is important to observe that even though Sapir's examples did not happen to illustrate his comment, he was essentially right. See 'his tail' (Table XIV) where PA *θ̲ : Y ł̲.

4. Problems of Classification

4.1 There has been a significant upsurge of interest in the classificatory and comparative aspects of linguistics in the past 12-15 years. The manifestations of this interest range all the way from attempts to make broad new classifications or reclassifications (as seen in the work of Swadesh and Greenberg)[79] to the rigorous application of the comparative method in new areas (as seen in the work of Longacre, Gudschinsky, and many others).[80] The present ferment of activity in regard to these matters is such that it may seem almost incredible that in 1952 Kroeber could in all seriousness make the following sweeping indictment of linguists for their alleged lack of interest in classificatory problems:[81]

> One of the relations of linguistics with the rest of culture is in. . .the matter of closer and remoter historic classification of languages. <u>To the linguist himself it usually matters very little whether or not two languages are related</u> [!]....
> However, to culture-historical anthropologists such discoveries can be all-important. For instance, let us assume the discovery anywhere in America of an indubitably Indo-European language accepted as such by all Indo-Europeanists, spoken by natives at the time of discovery, and of a degree of divergence indicating that it had branched off from the stock four or five thousand years ago.... The discovery would be of the utmost importance to us for its involvements and implications. That is why, whether we are ethnologists or archeologists, we are constantly looking toward and trying to use these linguistic classifications of relationship.
> Now, <u>if linguists are working on higher problems and do not want to be bothered with this rather elementary sort of classification</u>, that is fair enough. But <u>let them then at least occasionally allow their assistants to assemble the data for a competent classification</u> [!], or aid an ethnologist with basic linguistic grounding to go ahead with it, since it is so important to students of culture. [Emphases mine.]

While it is true that at the time they were made Kroeber's strictures regarding disinterest were not entirely undeserved,[82] still his remarks reveal a failure to grasp the attitudes that were involved in the situation, especially in the 1930's and 1940's. The greatest single achievement in linguistics of the early part of the twentieth century was the clear separation of the descriptive (or synchronic) from the historical (or diachronic) study of languages. But, as pointed out in 1.5, the movement went further than was anticipated and a schism developed between historical linguistics and descriptive linguistics.[83] Descriptive linguists, starting out on the defensive, felt constrained to make broad claims for the superiority of their methods, which were above all ahistorical, in order to show that they were free of the historical methods and interests which dominated the linguistics of the nineteenth century.[84] This affectation of disinterest in historical

linguistics led to a neglect of classificatory problems; this was especially noticeable among the aboriginal languages of America since
these had received so much attention prior to 1930.

But it was not only the rise of descriptive linguistics at the
expense of historical linguistics that brought on a lapse of interest in
classificatory problems among American linguists. An equally important contributing factor was the publication, in 1929, of Sapir's
famous encyclopaedia article on "Central and North American Indian
languages"[85] which presented a grand scheme whereby the fifty-odd
linguistic families of Powell's classification were combined into six
superstocks.[86] Although Sapir himself called his scheme "suggestive but far from demonstrable in all its features",[87] linguists of the
the time could neither prove or disprove the many aspects that had
not already been proven and until this had been done no one seemed
inclined to present a competing scheme. Furthermore, until new and
better descriptions of the American languages became available it was
not likely that Sapir's scheme could be adequately tested and, if necessary, modified. So even among linguists still interested in classificatory problems synchronic studies had the priority, if not from preference, then from necessity. Moreover, an equally pressing need
was for comparative grammars of the numerous families of shallow
time depth. Bloomfield's "Algonquian", discussed in 1.6, was actually a pioneer example of this type of study and, even now, there is
no more urgent need than comparable studies of all the linguistic families of North America.

4.2 The new developments in classificatory linguistics, when they
came in the 1950's, were on the whole disturbing to Kroeber. Whereas
in 1952 he had maintained that "the discovery anywhere in America of
an indubitably Indo-European language. . .would be of the utmost importance [emphasis mine] to us for its involvements and implications",
he protested in 1960 that the discovery of new connections between
Sapir's superstocks (far less spectacular than the discovery of Indo-
European in America!) made the 'overall picture' in America 'chaotic'.[88] Apparently, after three decades in which Sapir's classification had gone unchallenged, Kroeber had come to feel that all parts
of the scheme were or could be backed by the same kind of evidence
that Sapir had presented in his papers on the Algonkian connection of

of Wiyot and Yurok or the Hokan affiliation of Subtiaba[89] — in other
words, that all that was lacking was for younger linguists to fill in the
details. Hence as long as linguists were confirming connections set
up, or at least endorsed, by Sapir, Kroeber felt quite comfortable.
But as soon as the old boundaries began to crumble the picture, quite
understandably, did become 'chaotic'.

Now Sapir, I think, would have been the first to welcome suggestions of new connections across the boundaries he had set. To him
the six superstocks were a set of working hypotheses to be used as a
guide (not as a prison wall) in future work. But linguists were going
to have to amass a great amount of material on languages inadequately
known before they could get on with the work of testing Sapir's ideas.
In the meantime, cultural anthropologists and archeologists, for lack
of any competing scheme, had become accustomed to taking Sapir's
working hypotheses as established connections and had built hypotheses of their own on this basis. Because of the long lapse of time,
they forgot (or ignored) the fact that silence (on the part of linguists)
did not necessarily mean consent — it might mean, because of the un-
believably small number of persons engaged in this work at this critical time, that no new work or thought was being done on vast portions of the scheme.[90]

In 1952 there had as yet been no challenge to boundaries set
by Sapir in North America (north of Mexico) and Kroeber apparently
felt that that job was pretty well done. But in other parts of the world
Kroeber felt that linguists were being negligent in their duties to cultural anthropology and so called for them to "allow their <u>assistants</u>
to assemble the data for a <u>competent</u> classification. . .since it is so
<u>important</u> to students of culture".[91] But it is precisely because it <u>is</u>
so important to students of culture that the making of a 'competent'
classification cannot be casually turned over to assistants or to non-
linguists. In consequence of his inability to appreciate this fact,
Kroeber, by 1960 when the picture in America had come to seem
'chaotic' to him, was ready to throw over genetic classification altogether and now called for linguists to develop other types of taxonomies for languages.[92] He is also ready to abandon "the comparative genetic technique" because he considers that it has failed to give
reliable chronology of great depth (!):[93]

> The century-and-a-half old comparative genetic technique
> . . . is a splendid tool for confirming similarities within di-
> versifications that have been going on for some millennia —
> perhaps up to 5, 000 years, perhaps to 7, 000. But there
> comes a point in the past — perhaps 10, 000 years ago, per-
> haps less — at which the method no longer yields reliable
> results.

There are several misunderstandings and half-truths concealed here
and, because of Kroeber's great prestige (and because he is widely
read not only by cultural anthropologists but also by Indo-Europeanists
and other linguists not specializing in unwritten languages), it is important to clarify some of the points involved.

It must first of all be pointed out that the slow, painstaking
method involving the reconstruction of a protolanguage (the comparative technique par excellence) was something Kroeber admired but
never fully appreciated.[94] Indeed, having had no training in Indo-
European himself (such training at that time being the only way the
comparative technique could be learned), he was often impatient
with those who had, particularly if this training made them reluctant
(as it often did and often still does) to accept any hypotheses of relationship to which the method had not been applied in all its rigor.[95] In
assuming this posture he was both right and wrong. He was right in
that a hypothesis of genetic relationship should not be rejected outright because the proposed succession of comparative techniques cannot yet be applied, but he was wrong, or at any rate neglectful, in
that he did not seem willing to concede that at some point in the investigation of the prehistory of North America (and other areas of the
world) the comparative method could be of great value. And this is
why I believe that he did not fully appreciate the full potential of linguistic reconstruction (in its technical sense) as a tool for recovering
great quantities of historical information of both the diffused and genetic types.[96] This is a pity, for Kroeber was primarily a historian
and for him to have failed to grasp the significance of the great wealth
of historical information waiting to be uncovered by the proper use of
the comparative method in work on unwritten languages is exactly the
same as if an archeologist were to be unable to appreciate the study
of anything but what is on the surface of the site.[97]

4.3 What, then, have we a right to expect from the comparative
method (in the strict sense) and what will we have to do to fulfill these
expectations ?

First of all, it cannot be too vigorously maintained that the
chief value of the comparative method does <u>not</u> lie in its utility for
confirming relationships. Confirmation is merely a by-product. The
really important thing about the use of the comparative method is that
it provides us a means whereby we can reconstruct protolanguages by
comparing sister languages and thus, when the job is fully done, obtain a comparative grammar and dictionary of each protolanguage.
But notwithstanding the fact that we have the necessary methods at
our disposal, we do not yet have a full comparative grammar and dictionary[98] of any American Indian protolanguage. When we have as
many of these as we have linguistic families to work on (I am here
speaking of those of relatively shallow time depths), we shall have a
truly tremendous amount of information about the linguistic situation
in North America as it existed approximately three to four millennia
ago, i.e. c. 2000 B.C. By 'information about the linguistic situation',
I mean rather precise information about the words and ideas expressed in these protolanguages and also the types of grammars they
had. In other words, we would have information much like the linguistic information contained in the ancient written languages of Europe and Asia (e.g. Latin, Greek, Sanskrit, etc.). By far the most
distressing aspect of this rather obvious fact is that such information
is still lacking even though it could be acquired by existing methods.
That we still lack such potentially valuable information seems to be
due to two factors, (1) lack of sufficient motivation to keep at the job
over a long period of time, and (2) lack of sufficient trained manpower.

The achievement of the goal I have in mind would require the
labors of scores of trained scholars. For example, to put it in round
numbers, we need 5-10 people working steadily on the comparison of each
linguistic family; in other words, 5-10 people working on comparative
Algonkian, another 5-10 on comparative Athapaskan, and another 5-10
each on Uto-Aztecan, Tanoan, Iroquoian, Siouan, Muskogean, Caddoan,
Salishan, Wakashan, Yuman, Pomoan, etc.[99] If we could once achieve
a good knowledge of the various protolanguages that were in use around
2000-4000 years ago, we would then be in a proper position to determine whether or not the application of the comparative method to these
protolanguages can carry us back another two to four millennia. The

truth of the matter is that it is completely impossible to say at present what the comparative method can tell us about the linguistic situation in, say North America, at a time reckoned even as much as ten
millennia ago for the simple reason that we still fall far short of being
in a position to make a decent test of the possibility. Before we con-
demn the comparative method as being unreliable beyond 10,000 years
let us find out what it can do for us up to 10,000 years.

Some of us have jumped the gun and made preliminary attempts at the comparison of two or more protolanguages (see 2.323)
but our efforts are hampered by the lack of full comparative dictionaries and by the lack of important information about diffusion and/or
relationship that could be obtained from other protolanguages not yet
reconstructed. All this remains for the future and its accomplishment will be as rewarding and as exciting as would be the discovery
of an assemblage of written documents of previously unknown languages of 2000-4000 B.C.

5. Supplemental Methods

In addition to the traditional comparative method which in
essence involves working backward in time, considerable effort is
now being directed to the development of deductive models in order
to find those which most economically account for the empirical data,
and this in essence involves working forward in time. Such models
are not (or at any rate should not be) intended to replace the comparative method but to supplement it, to add new dimensions, as it were,
to the results presently obtainable. These models, as they are developed, promise to be particularly useful in dealing with subsystems
(or paradigms) of morphology, syntax, and semantic fields, in other
words, precisely those areas of investigation which are particularly
difficult to work with when using only traditional methods.

There is some reason to believe that the more highly for-
malized these models are, the more useful they may in the end turn
out to be. Floyd Lounsbury, in attempting to arrive at new ways of
handling kinship systems, has developed the theory of what he calls
the 'formal account'.[100]

> A 'formal account' of a collection of empirical data has been
> given when there have been specified (1) a set of primitive
> elements, and (2) a set of rules for operating on these, such
> that by the application of the latter to the former, the ele-
> ments of a 'model' are generated; which model in turn comes
> satisfactorily close to being a facsimile or exact replica of
> the empirical data whose interrelatedness and systemic na-
> ture we are trying to understand. A formal account is thus
> an apparatus for predicting back the data at hand, thereby
> making them 'understandable', i.e. showing them to be the
> lawful and expectable consequences of an underlying princi-
> ple that may be presumed to be at work at their source.

His paper on "A formal account of the Crow- and Omaha-type kinship
terminologies", from which the above quotation is taken, was not written as a contribution to linguistics but since a kinship system comprises a semantic field[101] in any language, it would be surprising indeed if the article did not have important implications not only for linguistic theory but more particularly for historical linguistic theory.[102]
There are other semantic fields which will sooner or later yield to a
similar kind of formal analysis. One thinks at once of numeral systems which have been frequently classified (as were kinships systems
prior to Lounsbury's analysis) but a strictly formal account has not,
to my knowledge, been worked out.[103] An experiment is being conducted with quinary systems, particularly with a view to determining
to what extent the logical developments are replicated in actual languages (in this case of the Algonkian family). To say that the logical
steps are the historical steps would be an oversimplification, but to
say that the historical steps bear no relation to the logical steps would
be patently false. The discovery of their interrelatedness (i.e. of the
logical steps and the historical steps) will probably have to be worked
out linguistic family by linguistic family.

Bloomfieldian doctrine emphasized that proper descriptive
statements cover only the what, never the how or the why. But we
should not make the mistake of carrying this doctrine over into historical linguistics as well. For historical linguistics cannot lay claim
to having completed its job until the how and the why can also be rigorously stated. It is not enough to state that linguistic change consists
of phonemic and morphemic replacement.[104] Distinctive feature

analysis and typological phonology have already helped elucidate the
nature of sound change. It is to be hoped that formal models of semantic fields may eventually aid in the understanding of morph replacement within the lexicon. In addition, it is clear that still other
kinds of formal models will be needed in the explanation of morph replacement in the grammatical domain (e.g. inflection and the use of
grammatical operators).

NOTES

[1]Leonard Bloomfield, "Linguistic aspects of science",
Foundations of the unity of science 1.4.1-59 (1939).

[2]Edward Sapir, "The status of linguistics as a science", Lg.
5.207-14 (1929).

[3]The latter part of the nineteenth century was characterized
by an almost feverish desire to classify everything, including scientific disciplines which were subdivided into a variety of branches and
subbranches. Among many others, Daniel G. Brinton proposed a
scheme 'for the nomenclature and classification of the anthropological sciences' which included four main branches: 'I. Somatology:
Physical and Experimental Anthropology'; 'II. Ethnology: Historic
and Analytic Anthropology'; 'III. Ethnography: Geographic and Descriptive Anthropology'; and 'IV. Archeology: Prehistoric and Recon-
structive Anthropology'. 'Linguistics' finds it place as item (e) under
Ethnology. See Daniel G. Brinton, "The nomenclature and teaching
of anthropology", American Anthropologist, o.s. 5.263-71 (1892),
particularly pp. 265-6.

[4]Clyde Kluckhohn, "Patterning as exemplified in Navaho culture", Language, culture and personality, eds. Leslie Spier, A.
Irving Hallowell, and Stanley S. Newman 110 (Menasha, Wisconsin,
1941).

[5]The term 'law' is a misnomer if interpreted as a universal
term. A 'phonetic law' simply states what phone is found in a particular language at a particular time in terms of its correspondent in
an earlier language (attested in writing or reconstructed), or vice
versa.

[6]This is not, of course, intended to imply that the work on
Indo-European is now complete. On the contrary, a reassessment is
urgently needed in order to integrate the vast amount of new material
that has become available to scholars in the twentieth century.

[7]William Dwight Whitney, in an article originally published in 1867, eloquently expresses the situation in the following words:

"The temptation is well-nigh irresistible to set up unduly as an infallible norm a language [Sanskrit] which casts so much light and explains so many difficulties; to exaggerate all its merits and overlook its defects; to defer to its authority in cases where it does not apply; to accept as of universal value its features of local and special growth; to treat it, in short, as if it were the mother of the Indo-European dialects, instead of the eldest sister in the family." [Emphasis mine.] See Whitney, "Indo-European philology and ethnology", Oriental and linguistic studies, 1.198-238 (New York, 1874); pp. 203-4. Of course Sanskrit can no longer even be considered the 'eldest sister'.

[8] A. Meillet and M. Cohen, Les langues du monde[1](Paris, 1924).

[9] Even though the book devotes almost as much space to historical and comparative linguistics as to descriptive linguistics, the strong 'behavioristic' and 'nonmentalistic' orientation of the descriptive section gave it a greater initial impact. Such orientation was in accord with the dominant scientific trends of the time and was motivated, in part at least, by the continuing desire to demonstrate the scientific nature of linguistics as a discipline. Sapir, on the other hand, was never seduced by this particular kind of scientism and that is the reason why his book Language (New York, 1921) still strikes new readers of today as a fresh and lively piece of work.

[10]The remarkable Bibliography of the Algonquian languages by James C. Piling (Washington, 1891) is by far the largest (614 pages) of several bibliographies of important American Indian linguistic families compiled by the same author.

[11]Fide Pilling, op. cit., p. 577. According to this source the earliest material published was a list of numerals of Souriquois, or Etchemin, which appeared in Histoire de la novelle France contenant les navigations, découvertes, et habitations faites par les François . . ., by Marc Lescarbot (Paris, 1609).

[12]John Eliot, The holy Bible, containing the Old Testament and the New (Cambridge, 1663).

[13]Cambridge, 1666.

[14]One of the most famous of these is a nineteenth century one, A grammar of the Cree language, with which is combined an analysis of the Chippeway dialect, by Joseph Howse (London, 1844). The most recent grammar is Bloomfield's own study of Menominee, never

entirely completed and published posthumously: The <u>Menomini language</u> (New Haven-London, 1962).

[15]His first important work on Algonkian was "Preliminary report on the linguistic classification of Algonquian tribes", <u>Annual Report of the Bureau of [American] Ethnology 1906-07</u>, 221-90b (Washington, 1912). Many others followed since the study of these languages remained his principal preoccupation throughout his life.

Sapir and Kroeber also made early contributions to the study of comparative Algonkian, e. g. Edward Sapir, "Algonkin <u>p</u> and <u>s</u> in Cheyenne", <u>American Anthropologist</u>, n. s., 15.538-9 (1913); A. L. Kroeber, "Arapaho dialects", <u>Univ. of Calif. Public. in Amer. Arch. and Ethn.</u> 12/3.71-138 (1916), especially pp. 77-80.

[16]Holger Pedersen, <u>The discovery of language (Linguistic science in the nineteenth century)</u> 277-310 (Bloomington, 1962). This is a reprinting of John W. Spargo's translation (Cambridge, 1931).

[17]<u>Lg.</u> 1.130-56 (1925).

[18]However, he used such materials when he had no other choice. For example, in the paper just cited he says: ". . .for Cree I use Lacombe, <u>Dictionnaire et grammaire de la langue des Cris</u>, Montreal 1874, correcting the forms where necessary, from observations made last summer for the Canadian Bureau of Mines" (130). Later on, when he had more materials of his own on Cree, he relied most heavily on these.

[19]By Harry Hoijer and others (= <u>Viking Fund Publications in Anthropology</u> 6) (New York, 1946).

[20]Some of these reasons are set forth in an appreciation of Bloomfield's work on Algonkian written some years ago by C. F. Hockett; see "Implications of Bloomfield's Algonquian studies", <u>Lg.</u> 24.117-38 (1948) (reprinted in <u>Readings in Linguistics</u>, ed. Martin Joos 281-289, Washington, D. C., 1957).

[21]Otto Dempwolff, working at about the same time on comparative Austronesian, also effectively limited his problem. The principal languages used in his <u>Vergleichende Lautlehre des Austronesischen Wortschatzes</u> (Hamburg, 1934) are Javanese, Toba-Batak, and Tagalog.

[22]Pilling's 614-page bibliography of these languages, already referred to, was published in 1891. In the half century following the Pilling publication a great deal more material had been printed on these languages.

[23]The phonological system reflected in the Central languages will probably turn out to be <u>almost</u> adequate to account for the systems of all the Algonkian languages, and not just the Central ones. However, some minor changes will almost certainly have to be made.

[24]It is interesting to observe that, for reasons extraneous to the present discussion, the work on Indo-European led to the reconstruction of roots. This led at least one famous American linguist of the nineteenth century, William Dwight Whitney, to assume that the protolanguage had no inflection; see <u>Language and the study of language</u> (New York, 1875), especially pp. 357 and 279.

[25]C. F. Hockett, who has been given charge of all of Bloomfield's Algonkian materials by Bloomfield's literary executor, published the first installment of such a dictionary in 1957; see "Central Algonquian vocabulary: stems in /k-/", <u>IJAL</u> 23.247-68 (1957).

[26]Edward Sapir, "Southern Paiute and Nahuatl, a study in Uto-Aztekan", Pt. I and Pt. II, <u>Journal de la Société des Américanistes de Paris</u>, n.s. 10.379-425 (1913) and 11.443-88 (1914).

[27]A discussion of some of his results in comparing the Athapaskan languages is included by Sapir in "The concept of phonetic law as tested in primitive languages by Leonard Bloomfield" 297-306 in <u>Methods in social science: a case book</u>, ed. Stuart A. Rice (Chicago, 1931); reprinted 73-82 in <u>Selected writings of Edward Sapir</u>, ed. David G. Mandelbaum (Berkeley-Los Angeles, 1949).

[28]Winfred P. Lehmann, <u>Historical linguistics</u> (New York,1962).

[29]"The concept of phonetic law. . ." 74 (of reprint).

[30]Ernst Pulgram, "The nature and use of proto-languages", <u>Lingua</u> 10.18-37 (1961).

[31]This is not to be taken to imply that change in language is never retarded or accelerated; rather it is claimed that (1) writing in itself is <u>not necessarily</u> accompanied by significant retardation and, conversely, (2) lack of writing in itself is <u>not necessarily</u> accompanied by great acceleration.

The study of the possible retardation of replacement of items in the lexicon (especially the so-called 'basic list') is receiving some attention from persons interested in glottochronology (e.g., A. Richard Diebold, Jr., "A control case for glottochronology", <u>American Anthropologist</u>, n.s., 66.987-1006 [1964]). An important paper describing one type of condition that could accompany conservatism in lexical replacement is Charles A. Ferguson's "Diglossia", <u>Word</u> 5.325-40 (1959) (reprinted in <u>Language in culture and society</u>, ed. Dell Hymes

429-39, New York, Evanston, and London, 1964). He discusses the
not uncommon situation in which a superposed or 'high' (H) variety of
a language is used, especially by adults, in addition to the regional
or 'low' (L) variety. He limits discussion of the problem, however,
only to instances in which the 'high' variety also has 'a sizeable body
of written literature' (330). In the event that this written literature
in H is an older variety of L, the borrowing of lexemes from H into L
is bound to show up as a seeming retardation in lexical replacement.
Even here, however, I do not believe that writing is a necessary condition for such a situation. A highly venerated oral literature which
is passed from generation to generation by memorization provides an
entirely comparable situation. Similarly a high form of speech used
by privileged persons can exist side by side with a 'lower' form of
speech spoken by common persons. For the Natchez Indians of Mississippi it has been reported that 'the speech of the Nobles differed
from that of the lower orders'; John R. Swanton, Indian tribes of the
lower Mississippi Valley . . .182 (= Bulletin 43, Bureau of American Ethnology) (Washington, 1911). Swanton's information is taken
from Le Page du Pratz, Histoire de la Louisiane, 3 vols. (Paris,
1758) and he adds that "Du Pratz says 'this difference in language exists only in what concerns the persons of the Suns and Nobles in distinction from the people' ". [Emphasis mine.] The decimation of the
tribe at the hands of the French in the early eighteenth century brought
on the breakdown of most of the old culture and it was impossible to
confirm this in the 1930s when I worked with the last fluent speaker
(now deceased). There are, however, a few ideas still expressed by
two distinct terms and it is my guess that these may be all that is left
of this example of preliterate diglossia in North America. Preliterate
diglossia can also exist when the speech of men differs from that of
women, since both sexes usually know both types of speech in order
that male children can be taught by the mother as well as the father
and that men as well as women can speak the proper forms when imitating female characters in telling myths; see, for example, my paper "Men's and women's speech in Koasati", Lg. 20.142-9 (1944) (reprinted in Language in culture and society, ed. Dell Hymes 228-233,
New York, Evanston and London, 1964).

[32]The Atsina forms quoted are taken from a comparative
study of Arapaho and Atsina presented by Allan R. Taylor at the Conference on Algonquian Linguistics held at the National Museum of
Canada, August 24-28, 1964. The bracketed interpretation of the

1790 Atsina forms is my own. — The 1790 forms of Atsina are taken from Edward Umfreville, The present state of the Hudson's Bay 202 (London, 1890). The Proto-Algonkian forms are taken from Bloomfield's "Algonquian" 116-117 with the omission of the numeral suffix *-wi and with the following changes in symbols: ʔ replaces q and vowel length (e.g. i·) replaces double vowels (e.g. ii). In many languages, e.g. Fox, Menominee, Shawnee, Miami, Delaware, Powhatan, and Natick, the usual word for 'one' is a descendant of PA *nekot-, but several other languages, e.g. Ojibwa, Abenaki, Passamaquoddy, and Arapaho-Atsina, have words descended from PA *pe·šik-.

[33] Present-day scientific philosophers are also quick to point out the imprecision, though not necessarily the uselessness, of the term 'law of nature'. Thus Ernest Nagel, in The structure of science (New York-Burlingame, 1960), says: "The label 'law of nature' (or similar labels such as 'scientific law', 'natural law', or simply 'law') is not a technical term defined in any empirical science. . ." (49). [Emphasis mine.]

[34] "The concept of phonetic law. . ." 73 (of reprint).

[35] Sapir stresses this in "The concept of phonetic law. . ." when he says that Bloomfield's "setting-up of phonetic law No. 6 was, by implication, a theoretically possible prediction of a distinct and discoverable phonetic pattern. The prediction was based essentially on the assumption of the regularity of sound change in language" 78 (of reprint). [Emphasis mine.]

[36] See Mary R. Haas, "The classification of the Muskogean languages", Language, culture, and personality, eds. Leslie Spier, A. Irving Hallowell, and Stanley S. Newman 41-56 (Menasha, Wisconsin, 1941). The paper sets forth most of the sound correspondences with examples, but full reconstructions are seldom given. Other extant 'languages' of the Muskogean family are but dialect variants of these, viz. Chickasaw (almost identical with Choctaw, but spoken by a separate political body), Alabama (very close to Koasati but spoken by a separate political body), Mikasuki (very close to Hitchiti but spoken by a separate group), and Seminole (almost identical with Creek but spoken by the descendants of those who fled to the Everglades during the Indian wars).

[37] A dash is used in Table I when a given language lacks a certain sound. Choctaw is the only one of the four languages which distinguishes an alveolar and a palatal sibilant. The other languages

have a single sibilant which may range from alveolar to palatal but is
frequently more palatal and is therefore placed in that column. Vowel
length, symbolized by a raised dot (·) configurates like a voiced non-
nasal continuant in all the languages and for that reason is placed in
that row on the chart.

    [38]The following conventions are used in Table II. A linguistic
item placed in parentheses is a separate morph, not entering into the
comparison, which often or usually co-occurs with the morph being
compared. In Koasati niɬa- is not the usual word for 'night' but occurs
only in certain special combinations, e. g. with hasi 'sun' in the word
quoted; cuba 'big' is combined with bihi-, not recorded separately, in
the quoted word for 'fig'. In Hitchiti -i is a suffix used with all nouns;
-i·ki is the infinitive marker for verbs; in- in the quoted word for 'arrow' is the third person possessive marker in alienable possession;
and -an in 'two' is a numeral suffix. In Creek -ita is the infinitive
marker for verbs. An item placed in square brackets is inferred or
'reconstituted'; thus bi[h]- occurs only in bi hasi 'mulberry month',
taken from ms. materials of John R. Swanton (Sn), and it is assumed
that the single h actually should be two: bi[h]hasi.

    [39]Mary R. Haas, "The historical development of certain long
vowels in Creek", IJAL 16. 122-5 (1950). This solution had not yet
become clear to me at the time "The classification..." was written.

    [40]Hitchiti hĩ·ɬ(i) has the usual lengthened vowel for a proto-
type initial open syllable, but the nasalization is unexplained. The
initial h is common in this language as the onset before a vowel. The
Hitchiti form has thus lost as much of the prototype material as has
Creek.

    [41]Final vowels are not subject to syncope.

    [42]Jerzy Kuryłowicz, "ə Indoeuropéen et h Hittite", Symbolae
grammaticae offertes à J. Rozwadowski 95-104 (1927).

    [43]The most unusual thing about this sound correspondence is
that it splits the Muskogean family along lines which differ from the
split attested in a number of other sound correspondences. The
deepest split is apparently between Choctaw-Chickasaw as the Western
division, on the one hand, and Alabama-Koasati, Hitchiti-Mikasuki,
and Creek-Seminole as the Eastern division, on the other hand. This
is illustrated in nos. 1, 2, 3, 4, 7, and 8 in Table II and is discussed
in more detail in "The classification..." 43-5. The b: k correspondence, however, keeps Alabama-Koasati, and Hitchiti-Mikasuki with

Choctaw-Chickasaw and separates Creek-Seminole from all the rest. See also Mary R. Haas, "Development of Proto-Muskogean *k^W", IJAL 13.135-7 (1947).

[44]Lehmann, Historical linguistics 38.

[45]Edgar H. Sturtevant, The Indo-Hittite laryngeals 23-8 (Baltimore, 1942); "The pronoun *so, *sā, *tod and the Indo-Hittite hypothesis", Lg. 15.11-9 (1939), and other writings. Sturtevant credits Emil Forrer with having first advanced the hypothesis in 1921.

[46]Warren Cowgill, "Universals in Indo-European diachronic morphology", Universals of Language, ed. Joseph H. Greenberg, 91-113 (Cambridge, 1963). The quotation is on p. 101.

[47]In other words, an isolated language or a 'language isolate' (see 3.1).

[48]B. L. Whorf and G. L. Trager, "The relationship of Uto-Aztecan and Tanoan", American Anthropologist 39.609-24 (1937). They describe what they have done in the following terms: "But by reconstructing the ancestral forms of each family, and then by comparative methods delving still deeper into the past, we discover the common ancestor of both. The fundamental matrix of relationships is exposed, and it becomes possible for scholars to proceed on finer and finer lines in order to make historical deductions and reveal time perspectives" (610).

[49]See, for example, Robert E. Longacre, "Amplification of Gudschinsky's Proto-Popolocan-Mixtecan", IJAL 28.227-42 (1962) and the references to work by Stanley Newman, Morris Swadesh, Sarah Gudschinsky, and other scholars cited therein. In his most recent paper ("On linguistic affinities of Amuzgo", IJAL 32.46-9 [1966]). Longacre summarized the results of some of this work in the following terms: "Detailed comparative work has been done within the Mixtecan, Popolocan and Chiapanec-Manguean language families. It has further been demonstrated that these three families are related. Gudschinsky's initial coupling of Mixtecan and Popolocan has been more recently amplified and brought into sharper focus. Amuzgo itself has been worked into the reconstructions. By now we can with considerable confidence offer (1) a sketch of the phonological structure of reconstructed Popolocan-Mixtecan-Amuzgoan (and probably including Chiapanec-Manguean); (2) a phonological characterization of Proto-Mixtecan as a descendant of this earlier layer; and (3) a phonological characterization of Proto-Popolocan as another descendant of this earlier layer."

[50]This is a term used by Longacre and others in the works mentioned.

[51]Mary R. Haas, "A new linguistic relationship in North America: Algonkian and the Gulf languages", Southwestern Journal of Anthropology 14.231-64 (1958).

[52]Verification will include seeing how this gibes with other special developments of *VkV, as discussed in 2.2. Developments of the type there include *aki, *aka, *iki, and *uku; no certain examples of *iku have been found. A caution must be inserted at this point, however. If this new hypothesis is the answer, it has to be a development which is chronologically earlier than the type described in 2.2. Otherwise Choctaw would have final ik and Koas, final i in the words for 'fish', 'squirrel', and 'tree' (see Table II) in parallel fashion with the words for 'day', 'night', etc. Since the development is not parallel, it can be fitted into the scheme only by assuming that it took place before the other changes affecting *VkV. If this hypothesis turns out to be untenable in its present form, this does not invalidate the principal point being illustrated here, namely that the comparison of two protolanguages may suggest a modification of certain reconstructions in one or the other or both of them. It only means that a modification different from that shown in Table V will have to be worked out.

[53]Cf. also Calvert Watkins, "Remarks on reconstruction and historical linguistic method", Indo-European origins of the Celtic verb 1-8 (Dublin, 1962).

[54]Mary R. Haas, "A Proto-Muskogean paradigm", Lg. 22. 326-32 (1946).

[55]The development of this hypothesis, as described here, is new and not to be found in my earlier paper "A Proto-Muskogean paradigm".

[56]Or, alternatively, two methods of conjugating verbs. The hypothesis of two classes of verb stems implies that some verb stems were inflected one way and other verb stems were inflected the other way. This seems the most likely hypothesis, but the other possibility, namely that in the pre-Proto-Muskogean period all, or at least many, verb stems could be conjugated both ways, cannot be ruled out entirely.

[57]In Table IX the following special abbreviations are used: VS, verb stem; LI, stem of the first auxiliary verb (now retained in some languages as -li, classifying suffix of transitive verbs); and KA,

stem of the second auxiliary verb (now retained in some languages as -ka, classifying suffix of certain intransitive verbs). The shape of the third person form, even here an unmarked category, is included in the table in order to show the relationship between verb stem and auxiliary when no subject affix is used. Spaces are used in all three columns of the table to indicate morph boundaries.

[58]In Table X an actual verb stem is used as an example. It is shown in capital letters with a period indicating the boundary between root and classifying suffix. As in Table IX spaces are used to show the boundaries between the verb stem and its subject affixes.

[59]Class II also includes a very few stems, such as tala 'to weave', which do not fit either category and which, by canonical shape, one would expect to belong to Class I. This is a clear example of the arbitrariness of the class system at present.

[60]This is not to say that every body of starred forms has been arrived at in strict accordance with the comparative method. But when it has not it is due either to the ineptitude of the worker or to the fragmentary nature of the material with which he is working. It bears no relationship to the applicability of the method to all groups of related languages, written or unwritten, ancient or modern, living or dead.

[61]Even though it is still the same old comparative method applied at a deeper level, refinements are to be expected in any ongoing science.

[62]"A new linguistic relationship in North America..." 259.

[63]I first used the term in a paper entitled "Is Kutenai related to Algonkian?" read at the Conference on Indigenous Languages in North America held at the University of Alberta in July, 1964. The term is intended to be a technical one and was constructed by inverting the phrase isolated languages, long in use as a descriptive, if not technical, term for such languages. For example, Whitney uses the phrase 'isolated tongues' (in the text) or 'isolated languages' (in the running head) in Language and the study of language[5] 355 (New York, 1875).

[64]This was apparently first discussed in detail by John R. Swanton in "The Muskhogean connection of the Natchez language", IJAL 3.46-75 (1924). A more recent treatment of the problem is by Mary R. Haas in "Natchez and the Muskogean languages", Lg. 32. 61-72 (1956).

[65]It is not correct to say that Natchez is a sister language of
Proto-Muskogean; instead it is the sole known descendant of an ancestor language contemporaneous with Proto-Muskogean. Such an
ancestor language is, however, unknowable and for this reason is also
not to be termed a sister language of Proto-Muskogean. To get
around the difficulty I prefer to say that Natchez, if related, is a
'collateral' of Proto-Muskogean since both would be descended from
the same protolanguage of the second order.

[66]As suggested in my "A new linguistic relationship...".
Special abbreviations used are PL[1], PL[2], and PL[3] for protolanguage
of the first order, second order, and third order. Language abbreviations are: Alg., Algonkian; Wiy., Wiyot; Yur., Yurok; Atak.,
Atakapa; Chit., Chitimacha; Tun., Tunica; Nat., Natchez; Musk.,
Muskogean; PA, Proto-Algonkian; PM, Proto-Muskogean. On the
far left of the table are time estimates. All are impressionistic, but
it should be remembered that PA and PM show a kind of divergence
similar to what is familiar to us in the Romance and Germanic families of languages.

[67]These are the so-called 'Gulf' languages. Tunica was formerly spoken along the Yazoo River in Mississippi (later along the
Red River in central Louisiana); Chitimacha was spoken near the mid
coastal area of Louisiana and Atakapa along the western coastal area
of the same state.

[68]Its lack of symmetry guarantees that the 3FS form is older
while the 3MS is clearly a re-formation on the analogy of the second
person forms.

[69]A complete model of the conjugation of auxiliary verbs in
Natchez would, if placed alongside a similarly complete model of
those in Tunica, show a great many points of similarity.

[70]Edward Sapir, "Wiyot and Yurok, Algonkin languages of
California", American Anthropologist, n.s., 13.617-646 (1913).

[71]John W. Powell, "Indian linguistic families of America
north of Mexico", Seventh Annual Report of the Bureau of [American]
Ethnology, 7.7-142 (1891).

[72]The first complete statement of these sound correspondences was based on a selection of the Central Algonkian languages
only and was presented a dozen years later by Bloomfield in "On the
sound-system of Central Algonquian" (note 17); see also sections 1.4
and 1.5.

[73]Roland B. Dixon and A. L. Kroeber, "Linguistic families of California", UCPAAE 16.47-118 (1919). "The authors therefore accept his [Sapir's] findings in full confidence..." (113). But some felt otherwise. Franz Boas, in particular, was completely skeptical of Sapir's proposal even after Gladys Reichard's fuller material on Wiyot became available. It is well known, of course, that in his later years Boas was skeptical of all attempts to find deeper relationships among the American Indian languages. See, for example, his "The classification of American languages", American Anthropologist, n.s., 22.367-76 (1920).

[74]Truman Michelson attempted to refute Sapir's proposal in "Two alleged Algonquian languages of California", American Anthropologist, n.s., 16.361-67 (1914). C. C. Uhlenbeck also expressed skepticism in several places, e.g. Review of A. Meillet et M. Cohen, Les langues du monde..., 1924, IJAL 4.114-6 (1927).

[75]Sapir was hampered methodologically by the lack of Proto-Algonkian reconstructions. Nevertheless, he recognized the probable nature of the relationship for he said: "Whether Wiyot and Yurok form a group as compared with Algonkin or whether Wiyot, Yurok, and Algonkin proper are three distinct major divisions of the stock remains to be seen"; "Wiyot and Yurok..." 646.

[76]See also my "Algonkian-Ritwan: the end of a controversy", IJAL 24.159-73 (1958) where both Wiyot and Yurok are compared with PA. 'Ritwan' is a term used by Dixon and Kroeber to refer to Wiyot and Yurok as a stock; see "Linguistic families..." 112-3. A recently published paper comparing the two California languages is that of Karl V. Teeter, "Wiyot and Yurok: a preliminary study", Studies in Californian linguistics, ed. William Bright (= UCPL 34) 192-8 (1964).

[77]The abbreviations used in Table XIV are as follows: Sh, Shawnee; C, Cree; O, Ojibwa; D, Delaware; M, Menominee; PA, Proto-Algonkian; Y, Yurok. The inanimate singular suffix -i is always separated by a hyphen in the forms quoted.

The PA vowels are *i *e *a *o (short and long); consonants are *p *t *c *k *s *š *h *θ *l *m *n *w *y. Additional symbols used in Delaware are ə (schwa), u (short and long), and x (voiceless velar spirant). The Yurok vowels are i e ə (retroflex 'er') a o u (short and long); consonants p t c k kᵂ (also glottalized p' etc.) s š ł g (voiced velar spirant) h l r m n w y ʔ; see R. H. Robins, The Yurok language (= UCPL 15) 1-300 (1958).

Some of the comparisons shown in Table XIV appear also in my "Algonkian-Ritwan..." but 'turn' (no. 6) and 'long (pl.)' (no. 8) are new and for 'winter' (no. 5) a better PA cognate has been found.

[78]Sapir, "Wiyot and Yurok..." 641.

[79]For example, Joseph H. Greenberg, "Studies in African linguistic classification", Southwestern Journal of Anthropology 5.79-100, 190-8, 309-17 (1949), 6.47-63, 143-60, 223-37, 388-98 (1950), and 10.405-15 (1954); id., "The general classification of Central and South American languages", Selected Papers 5th Internat. Cong. Anthrop. and Ethnol. Sci. 791-4 (1960); Morris Swadesh, "Linguistics as an instrument of prehistory", Southwestern Journal of Anthropology 15.20-35 (1959); id., "On interhemisphere linguistic connections" 894-924 in Culture in history: essays in honor of Paul Radin, ed. Stanley Diamond (New York, 1960); id., "Linguistic relations across Bering Strait", American Anthropologist 64.262-91 (1962).

[80]For example, Robert E. Longacre, Proto-Mixtecan (= Publication 5, Indiana University PRCAFL) (Bloomington, Indiana, 1957); id., "Amplification of Gudschinsky's Proto-Popolocan-Mixtecan", IJAL 28.227-42 (1962); Sarah C. Gudschinsky, Proto-Popotecan (= Memoir 15, Indiana University Publ. in Anthropology and Linguistics) (Baltimore, 1959).

[81]Alfred L. Kroeber, "Concluding review", An appraisal of anthropology today, eds. Sol Tax, Loren C. Eiseley, Irving Rouse, and Carl F. Voegelin 368 (Chicago, 1953). The symposium at which these words were spoken took place in the Wenner-Gren Foundation headquarters in New York in June, 1952.

[82]However, even at that time the barbs should have been directed to a few, not to all linguists. So far as I know, all of Sapir's students are interested in historical and classificatory problems and have published on them.

[83]The following comment by Lounsbury is also pertinent here: "This is not to imply as sharp a division between structuralists and historians in linguistics, however, as developed at one point between their anthropological counterparts" (Floyd G. Lounsbury, "Language", Biennial review of anthropology 1961, ed. B. J. Siegel 280 (Stanford, 1962).

[84]Lounsbury, ibid., lists the first distinguishing feature of 'the linguistic outlook dominant in this country over the past twenty years' under the rubric 'A strict ahistoricism in descriptive

linguistics' and adds: "In origin this amounted to a declaration of autonomy for synchronic linguistics. Synchronic analysis is to stand on its own feet; it does not depend for its success on any knowledge of earlier historical stages of a language."

[85] Edward Sapir, "Central and North American Indian languages", Encyclopaedia Britannica[14] 5.128-41 (1929). Reprinted in Selected writings of Edward Sapir, ed. David G. Mandelbaum 167-78 (Berkeley-Los Angeles, 1949).

[86] Not the least remarkable feature of the Sapir classification was that there were no loose ends. Everything was tied neatly into one of the six bundles, even such difficult problems as Zuñi (placed in Aztec-Tanoan though with a query) and Beothuk (placed in Algonkin-Wakashan, again with a query). But these problem cases are still not solved. Zuñi is at present thought by some to go into a larger grouping with Penutian, and Beothuk is so poorly recorded and so little studied that it seems best to reserve judgment on its placement.

[87] Emphasis mine; p. 172 of the reprinting.

[88] A. L. Kroeber, "Statistics, Indo-European, and taxonomy", Lg. 36.1-21 (1960), a part of which has been reprinted under the title "The taxonomy of languages and culture", in Language in culture and society, ed. Dell Hymes 654-9 (New York-Evanston-London, 1964). The fuller context of Kroeber's remark is as follows: "...a similar change in viewpoint is now occuring as a by-product of the increase of time-depths claimed to result from application of lexico-statistics, and the accompanying findings, especially by Swadesh and Greenberg, of ancient cross-family relationships in the ancient levels of many established 'families'. ...The whole picture of what is genetic and what is secondarily acquired has become turbid; the genetic units have become few but vast, and undefined at the edges. ...At the same time linguists who do not use the summary comparative methods of Swadesh and Greenberg, but operate with comparisons of the long valid sort, are discovering more limited but perhaps more significant cross-ties between genetic groups heretofore rated as wholly unconnected — such as Mary Haas's Muskogian elements shared with Algonkian and Ritwan (SWJA 14.231-64 [1958]). The overall picture, at least among linguists in America, is fast becoming chaotic. When in 1919 Paul Radin (UC-PAAE 14, No. 5) assembled fifteen pages of evidence to show that all native American languages were probably interrelated, he was shrugged or laughed off. Now it is a group of Sapir-trained linguists who are making

much more voluminous findings by newer methods to the same effect as Radin, and the results of their more conservative colleagues
seem to point in the same direction of <u>overall anarchy</u>" (19). [Empha-
sis mine.]

[89]Sapir, "Wiyot and Yurok..."; id., "The Hokan affinity of
Subtiaba in Nicaragua", <u>American Anthropologist</u>, n.s. 27.402-35,
491-527 (1925).

[90]To be sure, some scholars issued cautions on this, but they
seem to have been largely unheeded. Harry Hoijer, in his dual role
of linguist and cultural anthropologist, was especially well-equipped
to assess the situation. In "Some problems of American Indian linguistic research" (<u>UCPL</u> 10.3-12, 1954) he says (5): "But there still
is no conclusive evidence that even the California Hokan and Penutian
stocks are firmly established, not to mention the broader Hokan and
Penutian groups proposed by Sapir.... As the matter now stands, anthropologists too frequently assume that such groupings as Hokan and
Penutian are well established, and so use them as a springboard to
other historical reconstructions."

[91]"Concluding review" 368.

[92]Having come to despair of a genetic taxonomy of languages
comparable to the taxonomies developed in the various branches of
biology where a "good 'natural' classification regularly proves to be
a genetic one, with true homologues" ("Statistics, Indo-European,
and taxonomy" 20), Kroeber still clung to the belief that "linguistics
is a genuine natural science dealing with intangible phenomena"
("Concluding review" 368) and hoped that some other workable taxonomy or taxonomies for languages would be developed. One sugges-
tion was a typological index of the type worked out by Greenberg
(Joseph H. Greenberg, "A quantitative approach to the morphological typology of language", <u>Method and perspective in anthropology</u>:
<u>papers in honor of Wilson D. Wallis</u>, ed. Robert F. Spencer 192-220,
University of Minnesota Press 1954). As has been pointed out earlier in this paper (1.7), these two types of taxonomy are not mutually
exclusive, but are equally applicable to all languages.

[93]"Statistics, Indo-European and taxonomy" 21.

[94]This is not to say that Kroeber was unaccustomed to making
both phonological and structural comparisons. Perhaps the best example of a set of phonological comparisons made by Kroeber is to be
found in his "Arapaho dialects" (<u>UCPAAE</u> 12.71-138, 1916). In a
section entitled 'External phonetic correspondences of the group'

(77-80) he correctly lists a number of such correspondences for the
Algonkian family as a whole, thus antedating by nearly a decade
Bloomfield's correspondences for the Central languages only ("On
the sound-correspondences..."). The difference — and in the end it
is a big one — is that Kroeber did not proceed from this to the actual setting up of prototypical forms, i.e. did not make phonological
reconstructions of whole morphs. Deeper comparison is never possible until this very important step has been taken.

    [95]He was especially annoyed at Michelson for refusing to ac-
cept (or even seriously consider) Sapir's proposal that Wiyot and
Yurok are genetically related to Algonkian (see 3.3) Note the following passage (almost certainly written by Kroeber) in Dixon and
Kroeber "Linguistic families of California" 113: "Dr. Michelson's
attitude is that of the professional Algonkinist fired with an ambition
to bring his branch of study to the level # of exactness attained in the
Indo-Germanic [Indo-European] field. Forgetful that # Algonkin is of
necessity today where Indo-Germanic philology was a hundred and
fifty years ago, and that its material is perhaps one per cent as abundant, he seems to insist that no judgment can be considered that is
not substantiated by evidence of the quantity, and of the degree that
Brugmann would demand. Such an attitude, if persisted in, cannot
but result in complete barrenness of effort for a long time to come.
American linguistics is a new and an undeveloped field, and pioneer
conditions must continue to prevail in it for some time longer. To
throw out all evidence that does not attain to an arbitrary standard of
fineness is sterile as well as unreasonable." The material enclosed
between # # is misplaced in the publication; it is omitted on p. 113
but is to be found on p. 112, 3rd line from the bottom of the page.

    [96]To the great detriment of the proper development of the
historical linguistics of American Indian languages, the age-old
problem of diffused vs. genetic became an outright either-or propo-
sition. Diffusion was especially champoined by those who were
dubious of proposed deep-seated genetic connections. Consequently,
the importance of the proper study of borrowed words and other types
of diffused material in the unravelling of historical sequences is
rarely mentioned in the literature on North American Indian languages.
The valuable lesson taught by the well-known cognation of German
strasse: Eng. street, even though ultimately descended from an old
borrowing from Latin (via) strāta, has never been made use of in
American Indian studies for the good and sufficient reason that the

reconstruction of protolanguages of shallow time depth is as important for the detection of old loanwords at that level as it is for the
detection of deeper genetic connections. The truth of the matter is
that both cognates and borrowed words have a story to tell about earlier connections.

⁹⁷Perhaps it can also be fairly said that Kroeber was the per-
petual pioneer. The discovery of new and unexplored terrain was
much more exciting than the careful mapping of terrain already
covered, no matter how superficially.

⁹⁸The nearest thing we have to a comparative grammar is
Bloomfield's excellent sketch "Algonquian", but it covers only four
Central languages and these not in their entirety. A full comparative grammar will need to encompass as many other Algonkian languages as possible, not only others of the Central type (such as
Shawnee and Miami-Peoria-Illinois) but also those of the East (especially Delaware, Micmac and Penobscot or closely related dialect)
and those of the West (Arapaho, Cheyenne, and Blackfoot). Hockett's
admirable beginning of a comparative dictionary ("Central Algonquian vocabulary...") suffers from exactly the same limitations and
consequently even in the material already published there are likely
to be many omissions as far as the actual prototypical vacabulary is
concerned, gaps which can some day be filled when other Algonkian
languages are brought into the picture. For example, a vocabulary
item attested only in one of Hockett's chosen Central languages will
not appear in his dictionary even though it may appear in every other
Algonkian language on which we have information.

Sapir spent many years of his life working on the comparative grammar and vocabulary of Athapaskan but did not succeed in
satisfying himself that any part of it was ready to be published. Harry
Hoijer has 'inherited' this material and has added much to it of his
own. When it is ready for publication it will be much more comprehensive than the Algonkian material since no arbitrary limitation of
the languages used has been imposed.

⁹⁹There has been a gratifying upsurge of interest in comparative and other Algonkian studies in recent years (as recently as the
last decade) and there are now almost the proposed number of people
doing some kind of work on comparative Algonkian problems. None,
however, are working 'steadily' in this field and many are doing work
on other North American families as well. Uto-Aztecan has also been
receiving increased attention lately, though the optimum number of

people working has not been reached nor are any of them working 'steadily' on comparative problems within this one family. Of the other language families mentioned most are blessed with no more than one, or at most two, definitely part-time workers.

[100]Floyd G. Lounsbury, "A formal account of the Crow- and Omaha-type kinship terminologies", Explorations in cultural anthropology: Essays in honor of George Peter Murdock, ed. Ward H. Goodenough 351- 93 (New York, 1964).

[101]Floyd G. Lounsbury, "The structural analysis of kinship semantics", Proceedings of the Ninth International Congress of Linguists, ed. Horace G. Lunt 1073-89 (London-The Hague-Paris, 1964).

[102]Lounsbury has presented in lectures (e.g. at the Berkeley Linguistic Group in the spring of 1964) convincing structural evidence on how to fill certain gaps in the Latin kinship system as documented. This clearly constitutes a historical bonus in the use of this kind of formal analysis.

[103]A few years ago Zdeněk Salzmann seems to have been working toward such a formal analysis in "A method for analyzing numerical systems", Word 6.78-83 (1950). A strictly formal account, however, needs to be somewhat more abstract and should fulfill as nearly as possible the conditions set forth in the quotation from Lounsbury.

[104]For a careful discussion of replacement, see Henry M. Hoenigswald, Language change and linguistic reconstruction (Chicago, 1960).

22 | The Position of Apalachee in the Muskogean Family

1. Introduction

      Apalachee is an extinct language of Florida. It has long been known to belong to the Muskogean family of languages, but, so far as I am aware, it has never been assigned to its proper position within the family on the basis of strict phonological considerations. In The Handbook of American Indians, [1] under the heading Apalachee, it is stated that these Indians "are linguistically more nearly related to the Choctaw than to the Creeks." In the same source, under the heading Muskogian, Apalachee is put in the same subgroup with Hitchiti, probably on the strength of Gatschet's opinion, viz., "The Hitchiti, Mikasuki, and Apalachi languages form a dialectic group distinct from Creek and the western dialects [by which he means Choctaw and Chickasaw], and the people speaking them must once have had a common origin." [2] Swanton, on the other hand, holds a different opinion, which he states in speaking of the Apalachicola, a town of the Creek Confederacy not to be confused with Apalachee: "In recent times Apalachicola has always been classed by the Creeks as a Hitchiti-speaking town, while the fragment of Apalachee that has come down to us shows that language to have been an independent dialect." [3]

      Virtually all of the linguistic material on Apalachee that has been preserved is contained in "a letter in the Spanish and Apalachee languages" which "was written for transmission to King Charles II" and bears the date January 21, 1688. [4] Swanton kindly provided me with a copy of this letter a few years ago, but it is only recently that I have had the opportunity to study some of the forms and to draw some conclusions about the proper placing of Apalachee among its sister languages.

2. Reasons for Placing Apalachee in the Eastern Division

In 1941 I published a paper entitled The Classification of the Muskogean Languages[5] which gives the classification of the extant languages only. These are divided into two major divisions, the Western and the Eastern. The Western division contains only Choctaw and Chickasaw while the remaining languages all belong in the Eastern division. This latter division is, in turn, further divided into three subdivisions, viz., (1) Alabama-Koasati, (2) Hitchiti-Mikasuki, and (3) Creek-Seminole.

The first point to be investigated concerning Apalachee, then, is whether it belongs to the Western or Eastern division. The first statement quoted above from the Handbook might lead one to suppose that it belongs with Choctaw. But let us first look at the facts. Two of the major phonological considerations[6] that have led to the setting up of the Western and Eastern divisions are as follows:

I. PM (Proto-Muskogean) *N >Western n, Eastern ł, e.g. Choc., Chick. nani fish; Ala., Koas. łału; Hitch., Mik. ła·ł-i; Cr., Sem. łáłu, all from PM *Nani/u.

II. PM *c >Western s, Eastern c, e.g. Choc. nusi to sleep; Ala., Koas. nuci; Hitch. nu·c-i·ki; Cr., Sem. nuc-íta, all from PM *nuci.

Evidence in Apalachee on both of these points places it in the Eastern division and not with Choctaw. The Apalachee evidence is as follows:

I. PM *N >Apal. ł.

PM *-Nki father > Choc. -nki; Apal. -łki, in piłki our father (pilzqui);[7] Hitch. -łk-i; Cr., Sem. -łki. (The Ala., Koas. term -ta·ta is not cognate.)

II. PM *c >Apal. c.

First set of cognates: PM *p-hica to see > Choc. pisa; Apal. pica (picha); Ala., Koas. hica; Hitch. hic-i·ki; Cr., Sem. hic-íta.

(The p- in Choc. pisa and Apal. pica is an old prefix preserved only in these two languages.)

Second set of cognates: PM *-hakcuk^W <u>ear</u> > Choc. haksubiš; Apal. -hakcup, in pihakcup <u>our ears</u> (pihacchup); Ala., Koas. -hakcu (with loss of final consonant); Hitch., -hakcubi; Cr., Sem. -hácku (with metathesis and loss of final consonant).

Further examples are lacking in the material that has been analyzed so far, but the evidence shown above appears to be conculsive.

3. Reasons for Placing Apalachee in the Alabaman Subdivision

We have now placed Apalachee in the Eastern division of the Muskogean family. The next problem is to place it in one of the sub-divisions of the Eastern division or else give it status as a separate subdivision. The following points seem pertinent on this score:

(1) It seems unlikely that Apalachee belongs in either the Creek-Seminole or the Hitchiti-Mikasuki subdivisions because languages of these two subdivisions always suffix all personal pronominal elements used in the conjugation of active verbs.[8] In Apalachee, on the other hand, we find the form haskahu (hascaho) <u>we say</u> where the pronominal element has- <u>we</u>^{c} is prefixed. Compare this with Koasati haska <u>you said</u> < has- <u>you</u> (pl.) + – ka ~ kaha to <u>say</u>. (Koasati has three main paradigmatic classes, one of which prefixes most of the pronominal elements.) This evidence makes it appear probable that Apalachee belongs in the Alabaman subdivision along with Alabama and Koasati. (Choctaw, too, prefixes certain pronominal elements used with active verbs, but it has already been shown that Apalachee does not belong with Choctaw; see §2 above).

(2) Another bit of evidence showing that Apalachee does not belong in the Creek-Seminole subdivision is found in the fact that PM *k^W >b in Apal.,[10] e.g. PM *abi <u>to kill</u>, *ihtibi <u>to fight</u> (< <u>to kill each other</u>) > Choc. abi <u>to kill</u>, itibi <u>to fight</u>; Apal. ihtibi (yhtibi) <u>to fight</u>; Ala. ibi <u>to kill</u>, ittibi <u>to fight</u>; Koas. ibi <u>to kill</u>; Hitch. itibi-(G)[11] <u>to fight</u>. The Creek-Seminole word is not cognate, but other evidence shows us that PM *k^W >k in Cr. -Sem., e.g. PM *k^{W}ihi <u>mulberry</u> > Choc. bihi, Koas. bihi-cuba <u>fig</u> (< <u>big-mulberry</u>), Hitch.

bi-hasi (Sn)[12] mulberry-month, Cr. ki· mulberry. Hence if Apalachee were in the Creek-Seminole subdivision it would have to show k
instead of the b it shows in the word ihtibi to fight.

(3) The Apalachee reciprocal prefix is usually written ihti-
(ihti-, yhti-), as in ihtibi (yhtibi) to fight, ihtipicahin (yhtipichahin)
seeing each other; occasionally it is written iti- (iti-, yti-), as in
itihkapi (itihcapi, ytihcapi) saying to each other. Assuming that ihti-
is correct, we find that the Apalachee form of this prefix is closer to
Alabama-Koasati itti- (which shows gemination < earlier *ihti-) than
it is to Hitchiti and Creek-Seminole iti-, both of which show ungemination < earlier *itti-. (Choctaw also has iti-, but it has already
been shown that Apal. does not belong with Choc.)

(4) The Apalachee word for to give contains the intransitive
or medio-passive suffix -ka, as in imakat (ymacat) gave < imaka to
give + -t, verb suff. The Ala.-Koas. form of this word is iŋka to
give (< earlier *imaka; ŋ regularly arises < m before k).[13] Hitch.
also has iŋka- (G) to give, but Creek lacks the -ka suffix in the cognate form im-fta to give. (Choc. also lacks -ka in ima to give.)

(5) The Apalachee word hasnu (hasnu) we, independent personal pronoun, is something of a puzzle, since it is identical with the
Ala.-Koas. word hasnu you (pl.). It is even more puzzling since it
exists alongside of another word pihnu (pihnu) we which corresponds
more nearly to the first person plural independent personal pronoun
of the other Muskogean languages, viz., Choc. pišnu, Ala. pusnu,
Koas. kusnu, Hitch. puhn-i, Cr. pu· mi. Moreover, the related Apalachee personal pronominal prefixes (used in showing direct object
and possession) are pi- (pi-) us, our, corresponding to pihnu we, and
haci- (hachi-) you, your (pl.), corresponding to hasnu we. If the
translation we is correct for hasnu,[14] then we must assume some
special semantic development for this word in Apalachee, which is
not reflected in the other Muskogean languages and which is not par-
alleled in the personal pronominal prefixes in Apalachee itself. However, Apal. hasnu we is undoubtedly cognate with Ala.-Koas. hasnu
you (pl.) and differs both from Hitch. cihni-ta· ki you (pl.) and from
Cr.-Sem. ci· mi-ta· ki you (pl.). This would then appear to be another point in favor of the Ala.-Koas. connection of Apal.

The evidence given above, meager though it is, leads me to think that Apalachee probably belongs in the Alabaman subdivision. Point 1 above is the strongest evidence we have for this, but points 3 and 5 also lend some weight to the argument. Points 2 and 4 show us that Apal. does not belong with Creek, but leaves us in doubt as to whether it belongs with Ala.-Koas. or with Hitch.-Mik. However, if point 1 is correct, a close connection with Hitch.-Mik. is thereby ruled out. Moreover, while vocabulary resemblances cannot be used as decisive evidence, they provide, I think, good supporting evidence; and the evidence on this score, too, points to an Ala.-Koas. connection rather than to a connection with Hitch.-Mik. (see 4 below).

It should also be pointed out that it is possible that Apalachee was closer to Alabama proper than to Koasati, but since I lack extensive materials on Alabama, this point cannot be settled definitely in the present paper. Only a small part of the Apalachee material contained in the letter that has been preserved to us has been analyzed. If, as I suspect, it is rather close to Alabama, it should be possible to do more with the Apalachee material when more Alabama material has become available.

4. Additional Apalachee Cognates

In this section I shall present a few additional Apalachee cognates gleaned from the material that has so far been analyzed. These are as follows:

(1) PM *api·la to <u>help</u> > Apal. -pila < *apila (?)[15] in hacipi-lat (hachipilat) <u>will aid you</u> (< haci- <u>you</u> (pl.), personal pron. pref. used as object, + -pila + -t, verb suff.); Ala. im-api·la <u>to help</u>.

(2) PM *čuba <u>big</u>, <u>large</u>, <u>great</u> > Apal. cuba (chuba); Ala., Koas. cuba; Hitch. cu·b-i. (The Choc. čitu and Cr. łắkk-i· <u>big</u> are not cognate.)

(3) PM *haknip <u>body</u>, *nipi/u <u>flesh</u>, <u>meat</u> > Choc. haknip <u>body</u>, nipi <u>meat</u>; Apal. -nip <u>body</u> in apinip (apinip) <u>our bodies</u>; Ala., Koas. nipu <u>meat</u>; Hitch. akn-i <u>body</u>. (Creek is not cognate.)

(4) PM *iksa <u>clan</u> > Choc. iksa (B);[16] Apal. -iksa in iniksa

(ynycsa) his clan; Koas. -iksa clan, ayiksa his clan. (Hitch. and Cr. not cognate.)

(5) PM *ayukpa happy, contented > Choc. yukpa; Apal. ayuk-pa in ayukpat (aiocpat) are contented; Ala., Koas. ayukpa. (Hitch. and Cr. not cognate.) Note that Apal. agrees with Ala. Koas. in re-taining the initial a-vowel which is lost in Choc.

(6) PM *nihtak day > Choc. nitak (B) (<earlier *nittak with un-gemination; *nittak in turn is < *nihtak, the PM form); Apal. nihtaka (nihtaga; also nihtoga, prob. a misprint) days; [17] Ala. -Koas. nihta (with loss of final k); Hitch. nihtak-i (with final k preserved before the Hitch. noun-suff. -i); Cr., Sem. nitta· (geminated < earlier *nihta·; the final long a· is to be interpreted as a lengthening as the result of the lost final k.)

(7) PM *k^W anna to want, wish > Choc. banna, Apal. -bana in inbana (inbana) his wish; [18] Ala., Koas. banna to want. (Hitch. and Cr. not cognate.)

(8) PM *ak^{W}i ~ *aku ~ *uki water[19] > Choc. uka (metathe-sized < *aku); Apal. uk-[20] in uk-cikiti (oc chiquiti) water-port; Ala., Koas. uki; Hitch. uk-i; Cr. -Sem. úy-wa (-wa is a common noun suff. in Cr.; uy- is < *uki with loss of k and subsequent change of i to y).

(9) PM *kustini wise; tame > Choc. kustini (B) wise, tame; Apal. kustini- in kustinika-min san (gustinica-min san) some wise; Ala. kustini sober, Koas. kustini tame. Cf. also Ala., Koas. akus-tinni· ci to remember.

(10) PM *mał-to be scared, frightened > Choc. mał-in mał-al-li to scare; to be scared; Apal. mał-in kumałtacihi (cumalztachihi) not fearing; Ala. mał-at-li wild (< scared), Koas. mał-at-li to get scared; Hitch. mał- (G) to be afraid, frightened.

(11) PM *in-/C, *im-/V to him, her, it; for him, her, it > Choc. in- before dental C, im- before V and labial C, i^n- otherwise; Apal. in-/C, im-/V; Ala., Koas. in- before dental C, im- before V and labial C (with other assimilations before other consonants); Hitch. in- before dental C, im- before V and labial C (with other changes

before other consonants); Cr., Sem. in- before nonlabial C, im- before V and labial C (with other assimilations in various subdialects).

(12) PM *hačin-/C, *hačim-/V <u>to you</u> (pl.), <u>for you</u> (pl.) > Choc. hačin-, hačim-; Apal. hacin- (hachin-); Ala., Koas. hacin-, hacim-. (Hitch. and Cr. not cognate.) (The assimilations for this prefix are the same as for cognate 11 above.)

(13) PM *-či-~ -ič-, causative suff. > Choc. -či; Apal. -ci (-chi) in fihlacit (fihlachit) <u>made good</u>; Ala., Koas. -ci; Hitch. -ci; Cr., Sem. -ic- ~ -yc-.

(14) PM *ik-..-u ~ *-iku <u>not</u> > Choc. ik-..-u (as in iklawu (B) <u>to lack</u>; cf. lawa <u>to be many</u>); Apal. i-..-uki (?), as in nuk-ifihluki (noc-yfihluki) <u>things not good</u>, cf. nuk-fihla (noc-fihla) <u>things good</u>; Koas. -ik-..-u, as in ayukikpu <u>not happy</u> (cf. ayukpa <u>happy</u>); Cr., Sem. -iku·, as in nuɬiku· <u>not cooked</u> (cf. nuɬi· <u>cooked</u>).

Note that in the cognates given above the Apalachee form is generally closer to the Ala.-Koas. form (when the forms in the various subdivisions show differences) than it is to the other forms. An exception is seen in (6) where Apal. appears to be closer to the Hitch. form in retaining the final k of the PM form. However, Ala. and Koas. have lost all stem-final consonants, and this may have been a fairly recent change.

It should also be noted that in cognates (4), (5), (7), and (12) Hitchiti and Creek forms are not cognate where Ala., Koas. forms are. This greater degree of vocabulary resemblance between Apalachee and Ala.-Koas. is also probably significant.

5. Resemblances to Choctaw

Apalachee bears a few special resemblances to Choctaw which merit special attention. One of the most interesting of these is the retention of an old prefix p- in the word <u>to see</u>, viz. Choc. pisa, Apal. pica (picha) as against Ala., Koas. hica, Hitch. hic-i·ki, Cr., Sem. hic-íta.[21] However, as has already been shown (§2), the fact that in this set of cognates PM *c > Choc. s, Apal. c shows us clearly that Apal. belongs with the languages of the Eastern division rather than with Choctaw.

Another interesting resemblance between Apal. and Choc. is seen in the first person plural pronominal prefix (used as direct object and as possessive). The Choc. form is pi- and is, strictly speaking a dual form, the plural form being hapi-. The Apal. form is likewise pi-, but is evidently a true plural. Corresponding forms in the other Muskogean languages always show an u-vowel rather than an i-vowel, viz. Ala., Hitch., Cr. pu- us, our (pl.), and the Koas. form ku- is even more divergent. The corresponding indirective form meaning to us, for us is likewise pin-, pim- in both Choc. and Apal.,[22] whereas again the other languages have an u-vowel, viz., Ala., Hitch., Cr. pun-, pum-, and again the Koas. form kun-, kum- is divergent.

In the group of cognates given in §4 above, Apal. often shows vocabularly resemblances to Choctaw (see 3, 4, 5, 6, 7, 9, 10, 11, 12, and 13), but in all these cases it also resembles Ala. or Koas. or both, sometimes even more closely than it resembles Choc. (see 5). There are also a few other vocabulary resemblances to Choc. which may be listed here:

Apal. huluci to love in hulucit (huluchit) loving; Choc. hulitubli (B) to love.

Apal. finha (finha) much; Choc. fihna much (with metathesis in one or the other language).

Apal. im-abaci to teach in imabacit (imabachit) teaching; Choc. im-abači to teach him.

Apal. anukfili to think in anukfilit (anocfilit) thinking; Choc. anukfilli (B) to think.

Apal. anukfilika (anocfilica) thought (the noun); Choc. anukfila (B) thought. But note that the Apal. form has the suffix -ka, a common suffix in the languages of the Eastern division which is equivalent to the Choc. suffix -a.

When more material is available to me on Alabama, perhaps some of these resemblances will also recur there. As I have already shown in another paper,[23] although Alabama and Koasati belong in the

same subdivision of the Eastern division while Choctaw belongs in the
Western division, still, in many cases of lexical dissimilarity between
Alabama and Koasati, we find that Alabama agrees with Choctaw
whereas Koasati agrees with Creek and sometimes with Hitchiti. If
this is true of Alabama, it may also be true of Apalachee.

6. Conclusions

On the basis of phonological criteria (§2) we have been able
to show that Apalachee belongs in the Eastern division of the Muskogean family. Moreover, it probably belongs in the Alabaman subdivision of the Eastern division (§3 and §4). Gatschet's theory that it
belongs in the Hitchiti subdivision would seem to be ruled out on the
basis of its manner of conjugating active verbs (§3) and its greater
vocabulary resemblance to Ala.-Koas. (§4). There are a number of
very clear-cut criteria which could be used to prove this point one
way or the other (in addition to the point about the manner of conjugating active verbs), but I have not yet discovered any Apalachee
cognates that come under these criteria. Briefly stated these criteria are as follows:[24]

(1) Hitchiti retains -Vk- before a liquid or nasal whereas in
Ala., Koas., Cr., and Sem. -Vk- > -V·- in these circumstances,
e.g. PM *lakna yellow > Hitch. lakn-i, Choc. lakna, Ala., Koas.
la·na, Cr., Sem. lá·n-i·. No Apal. cognates coming in this category have been discovered.

(2) Hitchiti stems lengthen the vowel of an initial open syl-
lable, e.g. PM *kuni/u skunk > Hitch. ku·n-i, Choc. kuni, Ala.,
Koas. kunu, Cr., Sem. kúnu. Long vowels are not indicated in the
Apalachee forms that have come down to us.

(3) Hitchiti frequently ungeminates the geminate clusters of
other Eastern division languages, e.g. Hitch. cis-i rat, Ala., Koas.
cissi mouse, Cr., Sem. císsi rat. We cannot be sure that geminate
consonant clusters were always written in the Apalachee forms that
have come down to us. The Apal. word -bana wish corresponds to
Ala., Koas. banna, but the Apal. form may be incorrectly written
for *-banna. Moreover, the Hitch. word is not cognate so we do not
know definitely that Hitch. would show ungemination here. Note also

that the Apal. form of the reciprocal prefix is ihti- and that this shows
gemination in Ala., Koas. itti (< earlier *ihti-), whereas Hitch.
shows ungemination in iti-.

(4) Hitchiti adjectives frequently form their plurals by means
of an infixed -hu· -, e.g. packi long (s.), pachu·ki (pl.), whereas
Koas. and Choc. (probably also Ala.) form adjective plurals by pre-
fixing hu-, e.g. Koas. ɬimihku smooth (s.), huɬimihku (pl.). No special plural forms of adjectives have been discovered in the Apal. material that has come down to us.

Therefore lacking any test cases under the criteria given
above, I prefer to let the matter stand as already stated, namely,
that Apalachee appears to belong in the Alabaman rather than in the
Hitchiti subdivision.

In my paper on Classification[25] I have given a chart which
summarizes the classification of the Muskogean languages. A revision of this chart, amended so as to include Apalachee, is given
below:

      A. Western division
         Old Choctaw
         New Choctaw subdialects, including Chickasaw

      B. Eastern division
         1. Old Alabama
            a. Apalachee (extinct)
            b. New Alabama
            c. Koasati
         2. Old Hitchiti
            New Hitchiti, including its subdialect Mikasuki
         3. Old Creek
            New Creek subdialects, including Seminole

It should be noted that the Alabaman subdivision contains three separate languages, Apalachee, Alabama, and Koasati, whereas the
other subdivisions contain only slightly variant dialects of one language.

NOTES

[1] BAE-B 30 (1907).

[2] Albert S. Gatschet. A Migration Legend of the Creek Indians, Vol. 1, p. 74, Philadelphia, 1884.

[3] John R. Swanton. Early History of the Creek Indians, BAE-B 73. 130 (1922).

[4] Ibid., p. 120.

[5] In Language, Culture, and Personality, ed. by Leslie Spier, pp. 41-56, Menasha, Wisconsin, 1941. The article is hereinafter referred to simply as Classification.

[6] In all I have discovered six major phonological points separating the two divisions, viz., (1) PM *N > Western n, Eastern ɬ, (2) PM *c > Western s, Eastern c, (3) PM *s > Western š, Eastern s, (4) PM *š > Western š, Eastern c, (5) PM final *i/u > Western i, Eastern u, (6) PM final *i/a > Western i, Eastern a. See Classification, cited above, and my more recent article, The Development of Proto-Muskogean *k^W, IJAL 13.135-137 (1947).

[7] Apalachee forms are quoted in a standardized writing that has been equated to the writing I employ in rendering the forms of the other Muskogean languages. In parentheses following the standardized writing I place the Spanish writing employed in the letter. In the form pilzqui note that lz = ɬ and qu (before i) = k. Other changes are c (not before i) = k, ch = c.

[8] See Haas, A Proto-Muskogean Paradigm, Lg. 22.326-32; Hitchiti and Creek paradigms are shown on p. 330.

[9] On the basis of comparison with other languages one would expect this element to mean you (pl.), but the related independent personal pronoun hasnu (hasnu) is also translated we in the Apalachee text. See point (5) in §3 for further discussion of this matter. Note that has- is used as subject of an active verb, whereas the related prefix haci- (hachi-) is used only as direct object or as a possessive.

[10] See The Development of Proto-Muskogean *k^W, already cited.

[11] Hitchiti forms followed by capital G in parentheses are taken from Gatschet, Tchikilli's Kasi'hta Legend in the Creek and Hitchiti Languages, Transactions of the Academy of Science of St. Louis, Vol. V., pp. 33-239 (also separately numbered pp. 1-207), St. Louis, 1892. A Hitchiti glossary is to be found in pp. 163-211 (also separately numbered pp. 131-179).

[12] Hitchiti forms followed by the abbreviation Sn in parentheses are taken from John R. Swanton, A Sketch of the Hitchiti Language (unpublished ms.).

[13]The Apalachee evidence of a form imaka was not necessary in making the deduction that Ala. -Koas. iŋka developed from earlier *imaka.

[14]See note 9.

[15]Long vowels are not written in the Apalachee text; perhaps this is to be read -pi·la < api·la (?).

[16]Choctaw forms followed by capital B in parentheses are taken from Byington, A Dictionary of the Choctaw Language, BAE-B 46 (1915).

[17]It is not known whether the Apal. nihtaka <u>days</u> is a special plural form or a generalized form which could be used in the singular or the plural. If the former is the case the stem was probably nihtak-; if the latter is the correct interpretation the stem is nihtaka.

[18]It is not known whether the Spanish failed to write a geminate cluster in inbana (in which case the stem would be -banna, as in Ala. -Koas.) or whether Apal. has ungeminated certain geminate clusters. Ungemination occurs rather commonly in Hitchiti, but it also occurs sporadically in other Muskogean languages. Modern Hitchiti lacks a cognate for this stem.

[19]The variant PM reconstructions for this word are all necessary to explain the development of the word in all the Muskogean languages. The form *ak^{W}i develops to *aku through labialization of i to u with subsequent delabialization of k^W; it develops to *uki through labialization of the initial vowel a to u with subsequent delabialization of k^W. But *aku is necessary for the Choctaw development, while *uki is necessary for the development of the Ala. -Koas, Hitch. , and Cr. -Sem. forms. The two forms *aku and *uki cannot be equated except by assuming an earlier *ak^{W}i; this earlier reconstruction is also substantiated by comparison with more distant languages, as will be shown in a later paper.

[20]The Apal. word for <u>water</u> occurs only in the compound ukcikiti <u>water-port</u>; perhaps the independent form of the word was *uki, as in Ala. -Koas.

[21]This and other sporadically occurring prefixes are discussed in Classification, p. 54.

[22]The various assimilations for these forms are the same as those given for in-, im- (cognate 11 in §4).

[23]See Classification, p. 46.

[24]See Classification, pp. 48-49.

[25]See Classification, pp. 54-55.

1. The Muskogean family of languages[1] was formerly spoken throughout most of the territory now comprising the states of Mississippi, Alabama, and Georgia, together with adjoining sections of Tennessee and Florida.[2] For the most part the tribes speaking these languages have now been removed or driven away from their original homes, and some of them have become extinct. The extant languages are Choctaw, Chickasaw, Muskogee (or Creek), Seminole, Alabama, Koasati, Hitchiti, and Mikasuki. The first four of these are now spoken in eastern Oklahoma within the confines, respectively, of the former Choctaw, Chickasaw, Creek, and Seminole Nations. Moreover, Choctaw is spoken by a small group which remained in eastern Mississippi and by a number of scattered remnants in Louisiana, and Seminole is spoken by many of the Seminole Indians of Florida. Alabama and Koasati are now spoken in Eastern Texas and Western Louisiana respectively. Hitchiti, practically extinct, is remembered by less than a half dozen individuals living in the Seminole Nation in Oklahoma. The largest group of Mikasuki speakers comprise a part of the Seminoles of Florida, though a few (mostly recent arrivals from Florida) are also to be found in the Seminole Nation.

With respect to the nomenclature applied to these languages, it should be pointed out that the terms Choctaw and Chickasaw are of political rather than linguistic significance, since the two dialects are but subvarieties of the same language. The same is true of Muskogee and Seminole, and of Hitchiti and Mikasuki.

In working out the genetic classification of the Muskogean languages, it has been found that they may be subdivided into two main groups, Western and Eastern. The first of these contains only Choctaw (and its subvariety Chickasaw); the second comprises all the remaining languages. This second division may in turn be divided into

three subgroups; Alabama-Koasati, Hitchiti (including Mikasuki), and
Muskogee (including Seminole).[3] Most of the illustrative material
provided in this paper is taken from Choctaw, Koasati, and Muskogee,
a sufficiently wide representation to indicate that noun incorporation
was a characteristic of Proto-Muskogean.

2. Noun incorporation, far from being the exotic process it
was once considered, has been shown by Sapir[4] to be but one of several possible varieties of stem composition. Specifically, it is the
formation of a derivative verb stem by compounding a noun stem with
a verb stem.

While the process is reflected to some degree in all of the
groups and subgroups of the Muskogean family, it is not a productive
process in any of the individual languages. In some of them, indeed,
its existence could not be demonstrated (perhaps not even suspected)
without reference to the other languages. The only language which
contains a set of nouns clearly related to the petrified nominal elements found in certain Muskogean verbs is Muskogee.

3. In Muskogee the three most important incorporable nouns
(in their typical incorporating forms) are <u>nok</u>- 'neck', <u>fik</u>- 'heart',
and <u>cok</u>- 'mouth'.[5] These are respectively related to the possessed
noun stems[6] -<u>nókwa</u> 'neck',[7] -<u>fi·ki</u> 'heart', and -<u>cókwa</u> 'mouth'.

The incorporated noun <u>nok</u>- as employed in Muskogee always
refers to the neck or throat. Sometimes the verbal derivative containing the noun can be completely analyzed:

> <u>nokfayyitá</u> 'to wring. . .by the neck', lit. 'to neck-wring'
>   <<u>nok</u>- + <u>fayy-itá</u>[8] 'to wring, crank. . .'
> <u>noksómki·</u> 'hoarse', lit. 'throat-lost' <<u>nok</u>- + <u>sómk-i·</u>[9]
>   'lost' (past participle of <u>somk-itá</u> 'to get lost')

In other cases, however, the verb stem to which <u>nok</u>- has been attached does not have an independent existence in the language:

> <u>nokfipíta</u> 'to seize. . .by the throat'
> <u>nokcipilitá</u> 'to choke. . .'
> <u>nokkaca·kkoycitá</u> 'to strangle. . .'
> <u>nokmilíta</u> 'to swallow a liquid'

The incorporated noun fik- 'heart' is found to occur, appropriately enough, in a number of verbs referring to sorrow, jealousy, and fear. As a general rule such verbs are analyzable:

> fiknokkitá 'to get sad, sorrowful', lit. 'to get heartsick' <
>   fik- + nokk-itá 'to get sick'
> fikcakhitá 'to get jealous', lit. 'to get heart-stuck-in' < fik-
>   + cakh-itá 'to get to be sticking up in'
> fiksomkitá 'to get scared, frightened', lit. 'to get heart-lost'
>   < fik- + somk-itá 'to get lost'
> fikhamkitá 'to become brave', lit. 'to become heart-oned
>   (i.e. singlehearted)' < fik- + hamk-itá 'to get to be one'[10]
> fiktackitá 'to get out of breath', lit. 'to get heart-cut-off'
>   < fik- + tack-itá 'to get cut off'

The same element also occurs in one unanalyzable verb fikhonnitá 'to stop, quit, cease'.

The Muskogee element cok- 'mouth' occurs with less frequency than do the other incorporable nouns. In the examples given below only the first is analyzable:

> cokpaykitá 'to put. . .in the mouth' < cok- + payk-itá 'to put
>   one thing in. . .'
> coksa·kkitá 'to carry. . .in the mouth'
> cokna·hitá 'to talk like one who is demented'

4. The most common incorporated noun is Koasati is nok-, referring to the neck or throat. It is to be derived from a Proto-Muskogean stem *nok- rather than directly from the regular Koas.[11] word -no·bi 'neck',[12] which in turn is derived from PM *-nokkʷi (cf. Hitch. -nokb-i 'neck').[12a] The element nok- is found in several derivative verbs of Koasati, only a part of which are analyzable:

> nokpanayli 'to wring. . .by the neck' < nok- + panayli 'to
>   twist. . .'
> nokpannici 'to wring. . .by the neck'
> noktiłifka 'to grab. . .by the throat' (cf. Choc. noktiłiffi,
>   having the same meaning)
> nokbi·li 'to get choked on food' (the same in Ala.)

nokwoyahli 'to belch'

noksolotka 'to get thirsty', lit. 'to get throat-dry' < nok- +
   solotka 'to get dry'

no·halatka 'to get a crick in the neck', lit. 'to get neck-
   caught' < no·- (var. of nok- before h) + halatka 'to get
   caught'

In the examples given above the reference to the neck or throat is
clear. On the other hand, in a word like noksi·pa 'to get angry' the
reference is somewhat obscure until we discover that in Choctaw (see
§6) a number of words referring to various passions also contain nok-,
e.g. Choc. nokhobi·la 'to get angry'. The Koas. and Ala. word
nokcoba 'to stop, quit' likewise contains nok-; note that the Musk.
word of the same meaning (fikhonnitá, §3) contains fik-.

The incorporated noun cok- 'mouth' is somewhat rare in the
Koas. material, having been found so far in only two words:

cokso·ka 'to kiss. . .' < cok + so·ka 'to suck on. . .', the
   Ala. term is cokso·n-ka < cok- + so·nka 'to suck on. . .'
ili̵co·hokfi 'to put. . .in one's mouth' < ili-, reflexive pref.,
   + co·- (var. of cok- before h) + hokfi 'to put one thing
   in. . .'

There are no independent examples of the incorporated noun
fik- 'heart' in the available Koas. material and it seems likely that
no such examples exist. The word ficcakhi (< earlier *fikcakhi) 'to
be jealous' has been borrowed from Musk. fikcakhitá (§3).[13]

5. In the available Hitchiti material I have found only one
example of an incorporated noun, nok- in nokpafi·ki 'to choke', but
it seems likely that more examples will be found when more material
can be collected.

6. The incorporated nouns of Choctaw show an interesting
situation. Only one noun is so used, namely nok-, but it covers much
the same semantic territory as it is covered in Muskogee by both nok-
'neck, throat' and fik- 'heart'. Most of the examples quoted in this
section are taken from Byington's dictionary.[14] Since the element
nok- is not related to -ko·nla·, the regular Choc. stem for 'neck',
the analysis of Choc. derivative verbs containing this element was not

known to Byington. Nevertheless, because of his long contact with the
tribe, his material is exceptionally rich in verbs of this type.

These verbs fall into two main semantic categories, the first
of which comprises those which contain a clear reference to the neck
or throat: [15]

> noktaka·li 'to have something stuck in the throat', lit. 'to get
>   throat-locked < nok- + taka·li 'to hang, stick, lock'
> noktiłiffi 'to strangle. . ., grab. . .by the throat', lit. 'to
>   throat-squeeze. . .' < nok- + tiłiffi 'to squeeze. . .with
>   the fingers'
> nokšika·nli (B) 'to smart, tingle in the throat' < nok- +
>   šika·nli 'to tingle in the nose'
> nokbiki·li 'to be stifled as from overeating' < nok- + biki·li
>   'to press up against. . .with a point or the end of anything'
> noksakki (B) 'to be choked, strangled in water'
> nokłamalli (B) 'to choke or suffocate'
> nokpowalli (B) 'to feel nauseated' < nok- + *-powalli (cf.
>   powaliči 'to cause the waves to roll high')
> nokšitffi, nokšiniffi (B) 'to hang. . .by the neck'
> noksiti·li (B) ' to choke. . .with a cord', lit. 'to neck-bind'
>   < nok- + siti·li 'to tie, bind. . .'
> nokšila (B) 'to be thirsty', lit. 'to be throat-dry' < nok- +
>   šila 'to be dry'
> nokšammi (B) 'to be hoarse'
> nokfoko·wa 'to hiccough'; also nokfičo·wa, nokfičo·li (B)

The second semantic category of verbs built up by means of
nok- comprises those which contain reference to sorrow, fear, passion, or pain. In contrast to Choctaw, Muskogee verbs of this category are generally built up by means of fik- 'heart' and thus we see
that in Choctaw nok- has taken over the functions of both nok- and
fik- as these are employed in Muskogee:

> nokha·nklo 'to be sorry'
> nokwilo·ha (B) 'to be sad, sorrowful'
> nokwanniči (B) 'to tremble through fear', lit. 'to neck-trem-
>   ble' < nok- + wanniči 'to shake, tremble'; note that nok-
>   adds the notion of fear to the complex.

noktaka·nčiči (B) 'to startle. . .'
nokšobli (B) 'to frighten, terrify, intimidate. . .'
noklibiša (B) 'to be in a passion', lit. 'to be neck-heated'
  < nok- + libiša 'to become heated'
nokpalli (B) 'to be interested, excited, tempted'
noktała 'to be jealous'
nokhobi·la (B) 'to be mad, angry'
noktala·li (B) 'to quiet, appease, soothe. . .', lit. 'to neck-
  set. . .' < nok- + tala·li 'to set, place one thing'
nokhammi (B) 'to ache'

In addition, a number of Choctaw verbs referring to palpitation are
built up by means of nok-:

nokbimikači (B) 'to palpitate'
nokwimikači (B) 'to shake, tremble, palpitate, as after an
  effort at running'
noktimikači (B) 'to beat, pulsate, as the heart or pulse'
noktimiči (B) 'to palpitate quickly'

7. This concludes the evidence for the presence of noun incorporation in Proto-Muskogean. The process is not a free one in
any of the modern languages and in Choctaw, for instance, evidence
for its existence cannot be adduced without comparison with the other
languages. Even in Muskogee, where the process seems to be best
preserved, no new formations of a similar type can be made.

Since the process is no longer a free one, it is not surprising
that it has not been previously reported as a characteristic of the Muskogean family. Other American Indian families and languages definitely known to employ the process include Shoshonean, Iroquoian,
Pawnee, and Kutenai.[16] Muskogean may now be added to this list
with the qualification that here the process is found as a survival only.

NOTES

[1]Except where otherwise indicated, the material on which
this paper is based is taken from my own field notes on these languages. The field work of Muskogee was financed by two grants (in

1936 and 1937) from the Department of Anthropology, Yale University. During the second of these trips certain Choctaw and Hitchiti materials were also collected. The collection of Koasati materials and additional Muskogee materials comprised a part of the work done on the history of the towns of the Creek Confederacy under a grant from the Penrose Fund of the American Philosophical Society in 1938-9.

[2] See the map supplement to Handbook of American Indians, Part I, ed. by Frederick Hodge (Bureau of American Ethnology, Bulletin 30; Washington, 1907).

[3] The reasons for this classification are set forth in my article, The Classification of the Muskogean Languages, in the Sapir Memorial Volume 41-56.

[4] Edward Sapir, Language, An Introduction to the Study of Speech 69-70 (New York, 1921).

[5] For an explanation of the system of orthography employed in Muskogee, see my article, Ablaut and its Function in Muskogee, Lang. 16.141-50 (1940).

[6] A possessed noun stem is one which cannot be used without a personal pronominal prefix referring to the possessor, e.g. canókwa 'my neck'.

[7] Whenever the suffix -wa is preceded by a consonant (as in -nókwa and -cókwa), it is dropped when it would come to stand before an element beginning in a consonant. This accounts for its loss in the incorporating forms nok- and cok-. The same rule applies when such words are compounded with nouns rather than verbs, e.g. -cokhálpi 'lip' < -cókwa + hálpi 'skin, hide'.

[8] The suffix -ita is the regular infinitive ending of Muskogee.

[9] The suffix -i· is a Muskogee participial ending.

[10] Muskogee numerals belong to the verb system; see Lang. 16.148.

[11] The following abbreviations are used for names of languages: Koas. = Koasati; Hitch. = Hitchiti; Choc. = Choctaw; Ala. = Alabama; Musk. = Muskogee.

[12] The Koasati phonemic system may be briefly described as follows: There are four voiceless stops, p, t, k, and c (phonetically [č]); one asymmetrical voiced stop, b; four voiceless spirants, f (bilabial), ł, s, and h; and five voiced sonorants, y, w, m, n, and l. There are three vowels, i, a, and o. When not accompanied by the length phoneme, i is [ɪ] except in word-final position, where it is [e];

a̲ is [ʌ]; o̲ is [ʊ]. When accompanied by the length phoneme, the vowels are lengthened and their qualities undergo a change, thus i̲· is [e·], a̲· is [a·] and o̲· is [o·].

See The Development of Proto-Muskogean *kᵂ, IJAL 13.135-137 (1947) for the change in reconstruction introduced in this paragraph.

[13]The Koasati were one of several independent tribes conquered by the Creeks and incorporated by them into their confederacy.

[14]Cyrus Byington, A Dictionary of the Choctaw Language (Bureau of American Ethnology, Bulletin 46; Washington, 1915). Examples quoted from this source are indicated by a capital B placed in parentheses. Unmarked examples are taken from my own notes.

[15]In quoting the forms from Byington's dictionary certain transliterations have been introduced in order that the orthography might be consistent with that used for the other Muskogean languages. Such transliteration has been facilitated by my own knowledge of the language; the following brief description of Choctaw phonemes is taken from my own notes: There are four voiceless stops, p̲, t̲, k̲, and č̲; one asymmetrical voiced stop, b̲; five voiceless spirants, f̲ (bilabial), ɫ̲, s̲, š̲, and h̲; and five voiced sonorants, y̲, w̲, m̲, n̲, and l̲. The vowel system is the same as that given for Koasati (note 12).

[16]Franz Boas, Race, Language and Culture 213 (New York, 1940).

24 | Classificatory Verbs in Muskogee

1. Introduction

A number of American Indian languages are known to have
fairly elaborate sets of verbs semantically differentiated as to the
form or shape (or some other characteristic) of the entity which
serves as subject (intransitive verbs) or as object (transitive verbs).
Examples of languages known to have this characteristic are Navaho
and Cherokee. Cherokee, for instance, has no single verb corresponding to the English verb to lie; instead, there are several different
verbs distinguished as to the nature of the entity referred to by the
subject, such as, round object lies, long object lies, flexible object
lies, liquid lies, and living being lies. A similar multiplicity exists
with a number of transitive verbs, except that with them it is the
nature of the entity referred to by the object that gives rise to the distinction. Important transitive verbs of this type are those meaning to
give. . ., to put. . .in, to pick up. . ., to bring. . ., etc. A few
sets of Cherokee examples[1] taken from my own field notes may be
given for purposes of illustration and later comparison with Muskogee
classificatory verbs.

Set 1: ʔáàhhą́ it's lying (round obj.), čî́íyą́ it's lying (long
obj.), ką́ʔ́ną́ it's lying (flexible obj.), kàneehą́ it' s lying (liquid),
ką̀hnką́ he's lying (living being).

Set 2: čî́ʔahsį̂ I gave. . .(round obj.), čiitî́îsį̂ I gave. . .
(long obj.), čiiną́hsį̂ I gave. . .(flexible obj.), čiineʔą́hsį̂ I gave. . .
(container with liquid contents), čiiyáàk'áàsį̂ I gave. . .(living being—
nonhuman).

Set 3: čĭkʾ I pick up. . .(round obj.), čĭyʄ I pick up. . .
(long obj.), čĭnåkʾ I pick up. . .(flexible obj.), čĭneekʾ I pick up. . .
(container with liquid contents), čḷḷnakʾ I pick up. . .(living being —
nonhuman), čĭḟnakʾ I pick up. . .(living being—human).

The examples given above are intended to show the categories
distinguished in Cherokee classificatory verbs. It is immaterial to
the present discussion whether these categories are distinguished by
suppletion or by other means.

2.1. Classificatory verbs in Muskogee

So far as I know, Muskogee (or Creek)[2] has not previously
been mentioned as one of the languages having this type of verbal complexity. While the phenomenon is not as highly developed as it is in
Cherokee, it clearly exists. However, in Muskogee the phenomenon
is less transparent than in Cherokee because it is tied up inextricably
with the category of number and operates most frequently in verbs
characterized by having suppletive forms to express a difference in
number. It will be of interest to take up the problem systematically.

2.2. Number in transitive and intransitive verbs

The majority of verbs in Muskogee distinguish only two numbers, singular and plural. A few very important and frequently used
verbs, however, distinguish three numbers, singular, dual, and
plural, and the separate forms are generally suppletive or otherwise
irregular. Typical examples of intransitive verbs are:

S	D	P	
litkitá[3]	tukuɫkitá	pifa·tkitá	to run
ayíta	ahuyitá	api·yitá	to go
leykitá	ka·kitá	apu·kitá	to sit
huyɫitá	sihu·kitá	sapaklitá	to stand
wakkitá	wakhukíta	lumhitá	to lie

Many common transitive verbs are characterized by suppletion to express the number of the object, as in the following:

S obj.	D obj.	P obj.	
aweykitá	aka·yitá	apalatíta	to throw. . .away
takleycitá	takka·yitá	takkapu·yitá	to put. . .down[4]

Most verbs distinguish only singular and plural number. A few of these have suppletive plurals and some transitive verbs indicate plurality of the object by infixed reduplication.[5] Examples:

S	P	
apaykitá	atihkitá	to be inside

S obj.	Ṗ obj.	
apaykitá	atihitá	to put. . .inside
wakicitá	lumheycitá	to lay. . .down
isíta	cawíta	to grasp, hold. . .
halatitá	halatheycitá	to take hold of. . .

2.3. Common vs. special usage of dual verbs

In most instances of usage verbs of the above types are distinguished solely on the basis of number, as shown in the following examples:

Intransitive: hunánwat li·tkís the man is running, hunánwat tuku·łkís (two) men are running, hunánwat pifa·tkís (three or more) men are running.

Transitive: pú·sin takléyhceys I put the cat down, pú·sin takkáhyeys I put (two) cats down, pú·sin takkapúhyeys I put (three or more) cats down.

However, the distinction in usage of such number-defined verb forms is not always solely a matter of number. Certain very special uses of some of these forms also occur, and it is these which remind us of the classificatory verbs already briefly described for Cherokee.

The first of these special uses occurs when cloth and articles made of cloth are referred to; articles of this type are invariably used with dual intransitive verbs when serving as subjects, and dual transitive verbs when serving as objects. Several examples contrasting the ordinary usage of dual verbs with the special usage afforded articles made of cloth are given below.

pʉ́·sit taklέyks (one) cat is on the floor (S); pʉ́·sit takkâ·ks (two) cats are on the floor alongside of: nʉ́·ckat takkâ·ks a handkerchief is on the floor (D); pʉ́·sit takkapʉ̂·ks (several) cats are on the floor (P).

pʉ́·sin taklέyhceys I put the cat down (S); pʉ́·sin takkáhyeys I put (two) cats down alongside of: kǽ·pan takkáhyeys I put the coat down (on the floor) (D); [6] pʉ́·sin takkapʉ́hyeys I put the cats down (P).

In verbs which distinguish only singular and plural number the dual number falls together with the plural and articles made of cloth are then required to be used with plural verbs.

pʉ́·sin î·seys I am holding a cat (in hand, lap) (S); pʉ́·sin câ·weys I am holding (two or more) cats alongside of: nʉ́·ckan câ·weys I am holding a handkerchief (P).

pʉ́·sin halâ·teys I have hold of a cat (S); pʉ́·sin halathêyceys I have hold of (two or more) cats alongside of: nʉ́·ckan halathêyceys I have hold of a handkerchief (P).

2.4. Common vs. special usage of plural verbs

Another special use of number-defined verbs occurs with liquids. These generally take plural verbs, though examples are less numerous than is the case with cloth-like objects. The most typical examples occur with transitive number-defined verbs, as shown below. (Intransitive verbs generally treat liquids as being in the singular number.) The examples quoted below illustrate not only the use of plural transitive verbs with liquids, but also the use of dual or plural (plural when a dual form is lacking) transitive verbs with cloth-like objects. These examples give us, then, a complete picture of the classificatory use of number-defined transitive verbs in Muskogee.

islǽ·fkan awέykeys I threw away the knife (S); islǽ·fkan akáhyeys I threw away (two) knives alongside of: nʉ́·ckan akáhyeys

I threw away a handkerchief (D); islá·fkan apalắhteys I threw away
(three or more) knives and: wa·kapisí·n apalắhteys I poured out the
milk (P).

     pú·sin takkíhseys I picked up the cat (S); pú·sin takcắhweys
I picked up (two or more) cats alongside of: nú·cka takcắhweys I
picked up a handkerchief; úywan sakcắhweys I dipped up some water
(P).[7]

3. Conclusion

     Muskogee clearly represents an incipient stage in the devel-
opment of a set of classificatory verbs which we know in a more highly
developed form in languages like Cherokee. In Muskogee classificatory verbs are number-defined, i.e., in their normal usage they are
either dual or plural verbs. The only categories of classification
that have developed are those which distinguish cloth-like objects from
liquids, and these in turn from all other types of objects. Cloth-like
objects are treated as duals when the verb has a distinctive dual form;
otherwise they are treated as plurals. Liquids are treated as plurals.
All other types of objects are treated as singulars, duals, or plurals
depending upon the actual number of entities involved. It is also interesting to note that the category of cloth-like objects in Muskogee
may be compared with the category of flexible objects in Cherokee
and the category of liquids in Muskogee may be compared with the
category of liquids (or container with liquid contents) in Cherokee.

NOTES

    [1]The system of notation employed in the Cherokee forms
given here is not intended to represent a finished product phonemically
or tonemically. For convenience long vowels are written as double
vowels. Three levels of tones are shown: low, marked by a grave
sign over the vowel (à), mid, by no sign over the vowel (a), high, by
an acute sign over the vowel (á). Voiceless unaspirated stops are
written as t, č, and k; aspirated stops as t', č', and k'.

    [2]Muskogee forms quoted in this paper are taken from the
author's field notes on the language. Grateful acknowledgement for
field grants is made to the Department of Anthropology, Yale

University (1936 and 1937) and to the American Philosophical Society (Penrose Fund) (1938–39).

[3]For a brief discussion of the phonemes of Muskogee, see M. R. Haas, Ablaut and its Function in Muskogee, Lg. 16.149–50 (1940). The only change that has been made here is that the back rounded vowel is symbolized by the use of u (short), u· (long) in place of earlier o, o·.

[4]This set of verbs contains the preverb tak(k)- (tak- before C. takk- before V) meaning down, on the ground, on the floor. Their analysis, then, is: tak- + leycitá, tak- + ka·yita, and takk- + apu·-yitá. Compare the related intransitive verbs leykitá, ka·kitá, apu·-kitá to sit.

[5] Note halatitá vs. halatheycitá. The theme occurring in halatheycitá is halatheyc- < halatha-, reduplicated form of halat- (as in the singular verb halatitá), + -ic- ~ -yc-, causative suffix.

[6]Comment of the informant: "Sounds like it ought to mean I put two coats on the ground, but that's because it's something soft." Informants are well aware that this is a special usage of the dual verb and frequently make such comments on the phenomenon. Another common comment: "I don't know why it's that way, but that's the way it is."

[7]The preverb tak(k)- in takcáhweys is explained in note 4 above. The form sakcáhweys has two preverbs, (i)s- meaning with, by means of and ak(k)- in the water, in liquid. The preverb ak(k)- is required here because a liquid is referred to, and (i)s- must be added to that because liquids are dipped up by means of some instrument, e.g. a cup or dipper.

25 | Prehistory and Diffusion

1. Lexical Borrowing

In previous chapters* emphasis has been placed on the reconstruction of protolanguages as a part of the general problem of genetic relationship. But genetic prehistory is not the only kind of linguistic prehistory. In terms of the overall prehistory of unwritten languages, it is as rewarding to uncover evidence of earlier contact as it is to find evidence of genetic relationship. It should be clear that if languages A and B are now widely separated, the uncovering of evidence of lexical borrowing from A to B or B to A indicates (1) that the two languages were once in contact or (2) that the diffusion has taken place through the medium of an intermediary language or languages. Sometimes the path may be difficult to trace, but at other times it is clear enough. For example, Abnaki, an Algonkian language of the northeastern area, was first written down by Father Rasles, a French missionary, in the late seventeenth century. His records make it clear, however, that these Indians had already been in contact with English because their word for 'hog', an imported animal, was piks (< Eng. 'pigs'), generalized by them as a singular.[1]

While it is relatively easy to determine the donor language when this is a European language, the problem becomes more difficult if both the donor language (DL) and the recipient language (RL) are aboriginal. However, a few general guidelines can be laid out. (1) The phonological evidence must be taken into account. (If the presumed loan has $\underline{l}$ in A and $\underline{n}$ in B, the DL is A if A has both $\underline{l}$ and $\underline{n}$

---

*Mary R. Haas. 1969. The Prehistory of Languages. The Hague: Mouton. [Reprinted in 1978]

and B has only n in their respective phonemic inventories). (2) The
morphological evidence must be taken into account. (If the word has
an etymology in A but not in B, then A is the DL.) (3) If both A and
B have several congeners, the DL is likely to be the one whose congeners also have the term. (But if the term is widely used in both
families, then the DL may be a third language, or the borrowing may
even have taken place between the protolanguages; in this case the true
origin may be difficult to determine). (4) If A has congeners and B
has none, A is likely to be the DL if the term is widespread in the
family, particularly if the regular sound correspondences which should
pertain in the circumstances actually do pertain.

Contact prehistory, then, is of considerable interest and importance, even though it can be approached only through the careful
study of loanwords and other diffused phenomena. Moreover, studies
of language contact have received renewed attention in recent years[2]
and it appears likely that more effort will be expended in this direction in the future. Unfortunately, studies of loanwords from one
American Indian language to another are extremely rare. [3] There are
several factors which have contributed to the neglect of such potentially valuable material. Among these are: (1) the lack of good grammars and dictionaries of adjacent languages in sufficient density for
any given area, (2) a tendency to consider a loanword as somehow
less respectable than a cognate, and (3) a disposition to discount the
possibility of borrowing in certain semantic domains.

One sometimes encounters the statement that we are well-
if not over-supplied with data on various languages of North America
and that now all we need is to make proper use of what is already
available. But the student who is seriously interested in the study
of intertribal loanwords cannot accept this for a moment. All too
often he finds that there are four or five grammatical sketches, a
half dozen bodies of texts, and one or possibly two reasonably adequate dictionaries for an area in which perhaps thirty or forty languages were spoken. But a truly adequate study of the intertribal
loans in such an area cannot be undertaken without full data on most
if not all of the languages.

Problems of remote genetic relationship are also handicapped by derogatory attitudes toward loanwords. Almost every proposal

Table I

Consonant systems of the Pacific Coast area

KUTCHIN (Athapaskan)

ʔ   h

kw	kwh	k'w	xw	γw	
k	k	k'	x	γ	
ç	çh	ç'	š	ž	
č	čh	č'		nč	
cy	cyh	c'y	sy	zy	
c	ch	c'	s	z	
tθ	tθh	t'θ	θ	δ	
ƛ	ƛh	ƛ'	ł	l	
t	th	t'		n	nt
			v	(m)	

TLINGIT (Nadene)

ʔ   h

qw	qwh	q'w	xw	x'w	
q	qh	q'	x	x'	
kw	kwh	k'w	xw	x'w	
k	kh	k'	x	x'	y
č	čh	č'	š		
c	ch	c'	s	s'	
ƛ	ƛh	ƛ'	ł	l'	
t	th	t'		n	
			w		

TSIMSHIAN (Penutian?)

ʔ   h

q	qh	q'	x̣			
k	kh	k'	γ			
ky	kyh	k'y		y	y'	
c	ch	c'	s			
			ł	l	l'	
t	th	t'		n	n'	
p	ph	p'	w	w'	m	m'

BELLA COOLA (Salish)

ʔ   (h)

qw	q'w	xw				
q	q'	x̣				
kw	k'w	xw				
k	k'	x				
			y	y'		
c	c'	s				
ƛ'	ł	l	l'			
t	t'		n	n'		
p	p'	w	w'	m	m'	

Table I (continued)

KWAKIUTL (Wakashan)

ʔ   h,ḥ

| qw qwh | q'w | x̣w |
| q qh | q' | x̣ |

kw kwh k'w xw

ky kyh k'y xy y y'

c ch c' s

ƛ ƛh ƛ' ł l l'

t th t'   n n'

p ph p' w w' m m'

QUILEUTE (Chemakuan)

ʔ   h

qw q'w x̣w

q q' x̣

kw k'w xw

k k' x

č č' š y

c c' s

ƛ ƛ' ł l

t t'   d

p p' w b

KLAMATH (Penutian)

ʔ   h

q qh q'

k kh k'

č čh č' y y'

     s

     l l'

t th t'   n n'

p ph p' w w' m m'

KASHAYA (Pomoan [Hokan])

ʔ   h

q qh q'

k kh k'

ṭ ṭh ṭ'

č čh č' š y

   c' s

      l

t th t'   n d

p ph p' w m b

of a remote tie-up that has ever been made has met with the counter-
assertion that whatever resemblances there may be are due to borrowing. Surely this is just as nonrigorous as to assume prima facie
cognation. The habit would scarcely merit attention, however, if it
were not for the fact that there is almost always the implication that
borrowings are useless artifacts which must be weeded out and thenceforth ignored. But loanwords are as important in tracing historical
contacts as cognates are in tracing historical origins.

As an almost inevitable corollary of this attitude of contempt
for loanwords is the reluctance of some investigators to accept the
fact of borrowing even in cases which seem to be incontrovertible.
Such reluctance, interestingly enough, usually takes the form of some
kind of categorical exclusion. For example, basic numerals, or basic
kin terms, or pronouns are among those categories most often mentioned as being unlikely candidates for this (presumed) inferior status.

All such generalizations and rationalizations are sheer mythology based on insufficient evidence. Let us face the facts of history
squarely and without presuppositions. Let us not lose sight of the
fact that even if languages of a given area are not genetically related
(or at least not indubitably so), they are still very likely to show certain similarities. These similarities demand an explanation and their
study is as much a part of the linguistic history of the area as is the
study of genetic relationship.

In North America, as elsewhere in the world, words of
fairly wide provenience have frequently diffused with the spread of
the item they name. The wide range in the West of similar terms for
'tobacco' is a case in point. Similar examples could be cited for borrowings in a variety of semantic domains. A borrowing may even in-
trude into an existing sequence, such as a numeral system. Thus the
Cherokee (Iroquoian) word for 'seven', kahlkwo·ki, does not resemble
anything in other Iroquoian languages but appears to be borrowed from
the neighboring Creek (Muskogean) kulapâ·kin (< kul- 'two' + apâ·kin
'added on').[4]

When words for flora and fauna are borrowed, it can at least
be suspected the the RL is a later arrival in the area than the DL.
The Creek word acína 'cedar' is virtually identical with Cherokee

atsina, but which is the DL and which the RL is not clear. Both may
have gotten the term from an unknown language. Hitchiti (Muskogean)
acin-i (-i, noun suffix) probably borrowed the term from Creek since
Hitchiti has borrowed many words from Creek. Did Proto-Muskogean
lack a word for 'cedar' ? This cannot be answered with certainty. The
remaining Muskogean languages have a term čuwahla (Choctaw, Alabama, and Koasati) which may reflect the prototype. This word has
in turn been borrowed into Biloxi (a Siouan language) as tcuwấhanấ
/čuwahna/ .[5] It is clear that the isoglosses of the words for 'cedar'
do not follow genetic boundaries in the Southeast. This is fairly typical of the problems regarding terms for many flora and fauna of the
area.

But some words are so widespread in a given area that it is
impossible to pinpoint the original DL. Among the aboriginal languages of the Southeast, for example, phonologically similar words
for 'buffalo' are found throughout most of the area. There is Tunica
yániši, Natchez yanasah, Cherokee yahnsạ, as well as the similar
terms in the several Muskogean languages, e. g. Choctaw yaniš̆, Alabama-Koasati yanasa; Hitchiti yanas-i, Creek yanấsa. The original
DL is unknown and may very well be some language other than those
cited.

Sometimes widespread similarities are probably to be attributed to onomatopoeia. But some resemblances are remarkably precise even if one allows for onomatopoeia. Words for 'goose' from the
Southeast to California are a case in point. In the Southeast we have
Natches la·lak, Tunica lấlahki. In California we have Yana (Hokan)
la·laki, Mutsun (Costanoan) lalak, and Nisenan (Maiduan) la·lak' as
well as the only slightly less similar Chimariko (Hokan) lalo, Pomoan
(Hokan) lala, Luiseño (Uto-Aztecan) laʔla, and Southern Sierra Miwok
(Miwokan) laꞑlaꞑ. Many other bird names show equally uneven but
widespread distribution. They deserve further study.

Calques (or translation-loans) are also common among American aboriginal languages. Here it is somewhat more difficult to rule
out independent invention, at least in noncontiguous areas. But sometimes the evidence is quite persuasive. Kato, an Athapaskan language
of northern California, is the only Athapaskan language known to use
as its word for 'four' a repetition of 'two', namely nakkaʔnakkaʔ

Table II

Yurok and Wiyot consonant systems compared with neighboring
California languages and with Algonkian (Miami)

TOLOWA (Athapaskan)	YUROK	WIYOT
ʔ h	ʔ h	(ʔ) h
kw k'w xw	kw k'w	kw kwh
k k' x γ	k k' γ	k kh γ
ç' ṣ		
č čh č' š y	č č' (š) y	č čh š y
ch s	s	c ch s
ł l	ł l	ł l
t th t' n n'	t t' r n	t th ṛ r n
p w m m'	p p· w m	p ph β w m

KAROK (Hokan)	SHASTA (Hokan)	MIAMI (Algonkian)
ʔ h	ʔ h	(ʔ) h
k x	k k' x	k
č y	č č' y	č š y
s	c c' s	s
t θ r n	t t' r n	t l n
p f v m	p p' w m	p w m

'four' (nakka? 'two'). All other Athapaskan languages, even those which are extremely close to Kato, both genetically and geographically, have separate words for 'four'. But Takelma, a Penutian language of southern Oregon, uses the same method as Kato for expressing 'four': gamgam 'four' (gã?m 'two'). Did Kato borrow this device from Takelma? This is not certain, but no one doubts that the Athapaskans came into northern California from the north and it is conceivable that they were once in contact with the Takelma.

2. Structural Diffusion

2.1. The concept of the diffusion area

Even among genetically unrelated languages striking structural resemblances are often found spread over wide geographical areas. These may encompass phonological resemblances (2.2), morphologico-syntactic resemblances, or semantic resemblances of various types, including classificatory schemes (2.3). Even more interesting is the fact that some rather specific resemblances may also occur in widely separated areas. In searching for an answer to the problem posed by such cases, three alternatives present themselves: (1) The resemblance is a clue to genetic relationship at a deep level, (2) it is a clue to earlier contact other than genetic, or (3) it is fortuitous. Among the languages of North America, unfortunately, there has been a tendency to argue in favor of either (1) or (3). Very little consideration has been given to possibility (2).

Emeneau's concept of a linguistic area[6] is based on well-attested examples of structural diffusion across genetic boundaries. Others have argued for the use of other terms, such as 'convergence area',[7] but the phenomenon is the same. The term 'convergence', however, is not a happy one since it is normally used by anthropologists to refer to "the independent apparently accidental development of similarities between separate cultures"[8] whereas what is wanted is a term which would imply the development of similarities through contact. A much better term would be 'diffusion area',[9] which could then be used for culture areas[10] as well as linguistic areas and which could, moreover, be modified at will ('phonological diffusion area', etc.) for greater specificity.

At a time when others were trying drastically to reduce the number of genetic stocks in North America,[11] Boas was much disturbed by the clear existence of such diffusion areas among American Indian languages and was led to take an extreme position in regard to the problems of genetic relationship.[12]

> If the view expressed here is correct, then it is not possible to group American languages rigidly in a genealogical scheme in which each linguistic family is shown to have developed to modern forms, but we have to recognize that many of the languages have multiple roots. (1929:7)

This of course is a version of the Mischsprache theory and his remarks led him into sharp controversy with some of his most eminent students, Sapir and Kroeber among them. But one does not need to accept all the implications of the Mischsprache theory to recognize that the problems that were disturbing to Boas were genuine problems. Moreover, they are mostly problems of historical[13] significance and should be viewed in that light. Some of these are illustrated in the following sections.

2.2. Phonological diffusion

The Pacific Coast area has long been known as a place of widespread phonological diffusion.[14] It is noted for complex consonantal systems, including glottalized consonants (not only stops but frequently spirants and sonorants as well), lateral spirants and affricates, back velar consonants and labio-velar consonants. Various combinations of these traits are found to persist across genetic boundaries again and again.

Tables I[15] and II[16] show the systems of thirteen languages (omitting Miami in Table II which is from another area) whose geographical range is from Alaska to Central California. At least eight linguistic families are represented: Athapaskan, Nadene (but including Athapaskan if Tlingit is actually related), Penutian, Salishan, Wakashan, Chemakuan, Ritwan (Yurok and Wiyot), and Hokan.

Moving from north to south the languages are Kutchin, Tlingit, Tsimshian, Bella Coola, Kwakiutl, and Quileute in Table I; then Tolowa,

Yurok, and Wiyot with Karok and Shasta to the east of Yurok in Table
II; finally, Klamath to the east of Shasta and Kashaya to the south
again in Table I. The most striking features of the area are set off
in boxes with solid lines. The following have been marked in this way:
(1) Labio-velars (kw and/or qw, etc.) in Kutchin, Tlingit, Bella
Coola, Kwakiutl, Quileute, Tolowa, Yurok, and Wiyot; (2) back velars
(q, etc.)in Tlingit, Tsimshian, Bella Coola, Kwakiutl, Quileute, Klamath, and Kashaya; (3) glottalized stops in Kutchin, Tlingit, Tsimshian,
Bella Coola, Kwakiutl, Quileute, Tolowa, Yurok, Shasta, and Klamath;
(4) glottalized spirants in Tlingit; (5) glottalized sonorants in Tsimshian, Bella Coola, Kwakiutl, and Klamath; (6) lateral affricates and
spirants in Kutchin, Tlingit, Bella Coola, Kwakiutl, and Quileute plus
lateral spirants only (ł and/or l') in Tsimshian, Tolowa, Yurok, and
Wiyot.

In addition a three-way contrast in the stop series (unaspirated, aspirated, and glottalized) is shown by braces and occurs in
Kutchin, Tlingit, Tsimshian, Kwakiutl, Tolowa, Klamath, and Kashaya. Most other languages have a two-way contrast, usually plain
and glottalized, as in Bella Coola, Quileute, Yurok, and Shasta, but
occasionally plain and aspirated, as in Wiyot. Karok is very untypi-
cal of the languages in the area in having only one series of stops.

There are also interesting negative traits in parts of the
area. Shown is the extreme paucity of labials in Kutchin, Tlingit, and
Tolowa. Quileute is notable in lacking nasals (since b and d have replaced m and n of its nearest relative, Chemakum, not shown in the
tables). Absence of nasals is also a feature of Nitinat (a Wakashan
language not shown) which has not only b and d in place of Nootka (not
shown) m and n but also b' and d' in place of Nootka m' and n'. A
similar lack of nasals is also a feature of some Salish languages, e.g.
Snohomish.[17]

Yurok and Wiyot (Table II), languages of northern California,
share some of the special traits of the Pacific Coast area with their
immediate neighbors in marked contrast to the Algonkian languages
(of which Miami has been taken as an example) with which they are
genetically most nearly allied. Yurok has glottalized consonants, Wiyot has aspirated consonants, and both have the lateral spirant (ł). There
is also a small subarea here in which r is a common consonant.

Tables I and II show that languages spoken in contiguous areas can come to share a number of phonological traits without regard for genetic boundaries. But suppose two languages which are geographically far apart and not known to be genetically related turn out to have strong phonological resemblances. Can we assume earlier contact between them, i.e., that they were once part of the same phonological diffusion area? This is a difficult question. However, the possibility of historical connection (genetic and/or contact) should not be ruled out entirely. An especially interesting case is that of Yuchi, a language isolate of the Southeast. It was surrounded by Creek (Muskogean), Cherokee (Iroquoian), Catawba (divergent Siouan), and two other languages (Cusabo and Yamasee) which are not definitely classified because of early extinction.

	Cherokee		Catawba
Creek		YUCHI	Cusabo
	Yamasee		

Yuchi has several rather specialized phonological traits, among them glottalized stops, spirants, and semivowels. Except for the presence of a bilabial f, a marked Muskogean trait, and the lateral spirant ɬ (also in Muskogean and some Cherokee dialects), it does not bear much resemblance to its known recent neighbors. But when we compare it with Dakota (a group of Siouan dialects of the Plains), we find several quite striking resemblances. It has been suggested that Yuchi is a distant relative of the Siouan languages[18] and so the resemblance may possibly be due in some measure to this fact (if true). But this does not rule out much more recent contact (quite apart from possible relationship) with Siouan languages, e.g. Ofo and perhaps others now extinct. The phonological resemblance of Yuchi to Dakota and Ofo as well as the considerable lack of resemblance to Creek and Cherokee is shown in Table III.[19]

The glottalized series of stops and spirants[20] shown in boxes and the three-way contrast of stops shown by braces are particular traits shared by Yuchi and Dakota. The bilabial fricative [φ] is found in both Yuchi and Ofo and both may have been influenced by Muskogean. The fact that Proto-Siouan *x and *s have shifted to Ofo s and f, respectively, does not invalidate this possibility. The presence of a lateral spirant ɬ in Yuchi may also be the result of Muskogean influence. The two-letter combinations in the Cherokee chart are clusters, but some are phonetic units, e. g. hl, which is pronounced [ł], perhaps also the result of Muskogean influence. Another (now extinct) dialect of Cherokee had hr [R] instead.

Gross phonological traits have historical significance not only as clues to genetic relationship (in regard to which phonology can be drastically altered as was illustrated in the Pacific Coast area) but perhaps more often as clues to recent or fairly recent contact. But best results in tracing contact possibilities cannot be obtained unless all of the languages of a given area are carefully plotted. Our records are all too often deficient in crucial data for such purposes. Nevertheless it would be worth while to chart the consonant systems of all of North America. If carefully done it should reveal (1) many features of recent phonological diffusion areas, and (2) the possible outlines of some of the earlier phonological diffusion areas.

2.3. Diffusion of classificatory schemes

Most languages of the world have one or more types of arbitrary classificatory schemes which reflect covert taxonomies of greater or less complexity. Most of these reflect a categorization of entities,[21] and the grammatical devices which reveal the classification are of two main types, (1) those which are appended directly to the noun referring to the entity, and (2) those which are always referential, i.e. form a part of the agreement system. Sometimes the categorization is reflected in both these ways.

Generally speaking, there is a series of binary oppositions involved in these taxonomies[22] and the complexity depends on the manner in which these are combined. Typical oppositions are the following:

Singular	:	plural
Individual	:	mass
Human	:	nonhuman
Animate	:	inanimate
Male	:	female
Vertical	:	horizontal
Rigid	:	flexible
Liquid	:	solid

Table III

The Yuchi consonant system compared to Siouan Languages and to neighboring languages of the Southeast

YUCHI										DAKOTA (Siouan)						
ʔ		h								ʔ		h				
k	kh	k'	x							k	kh	k'	x	x'	γ	
č	čh	č'	š	š'	y	y'				č	čh	č'	š	š'	ž	y
c	ch	c'	s	s'									s	s'	z	
t	th	t'					n	n'		t	th	t'				n
		ł	ł'	l	l'										l	
p	ph	p'	f	f'	w	w'	m	m'		p	ph	p'			w	m

OFO (Siouan)							CREEK (Muskogean)				CHEROKEE (Iroquoian)				
		h						h			ʔ		h		
k	kh						k				k	kh			
č	čh	(š)		y			č		y		č	čh		y	hy
		s	sh					s					s		
t	th					n	t		n		t	th		n	hn
					l		ł	l			λ	λh	l	hl[ł]	
b	p	ph	f	fh	w	m	p	f	w	m			w	hw	(m)

Sometimes a three-way contrast is involved, viz.

Singular	:	dual	:	plural
Male	:	female	:	neuter
Vertical	:	squatting	:	horizontal
Liquid	:	viscuous	:	solid

But if often happens that such two- and three-way oppositions are mixed together in unusual ways. Such mixing is found, for example, in the classificatory verb systems of the Athapaskan languages.[23] These languages have two sets of verbs whose use depends upon the classification of the noun referred to.[24] One is a set of neuter verbs the choice among which depends on the classification of the subject, thus, 'a living being lies', 'a round object lies', etc. The other is a set of active verbs the choice among which depends on the classification of the object, thus, 'to pick up a living being', 'to pick up a round object', etc. Mixing occurs in various ways, but some of it is quite consistent from language to language. In Table IV[25] fourteen of the most usual kinds of categories are shown.

        To highlight their widespread use among the Athapaskan languages an indication of their presence or absence in one of the languages from each of the three main areas is marked in the table. A similar type of categorization is also found in other, nonrelated languages. Two striking examples are Takelma and Klamath, two not very closely related members of the Penutian stock. These languages have semantic classificatory schemes which bear a remarkable resemblance to those of some of their Athapaskan neighbors. Their geographical contiguity or near-contiguity to Athapaskan languages of the Pacific area is shown below.[26]

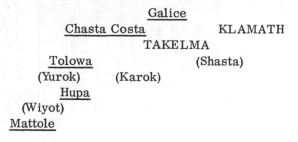

Galice

Chasta Costa   KLAMATH

TAKELMA

Tolowa   (Shasta)

(Yurok)   (Karok)

Hupa

(Wiyot)

Mattole

Table IV

Classificatory schemes in Athapaskan languages and in other non–Athapaskan languages

	CHIPEWYAN (Ath.)	NAVAHO (Ath.)	HUPA (Ath.)	TAKELMA (Pen.)	KLAMATH (Pen.)	CHEROKEE (Iroq.)	CREEK (Musk.)
1. Living being	1	1	1	1		1	
2. Round object	2	2	2	2	2	2	(13)
3. Long rigid object	3	3	3	3	3,3	3	
4. Broad flexible obj. (fabric)	4	4	4	4	4,4	4	
5. Long flexible obj. (rope)	5	5	5	5			
6. Empty container	(3)	(8)		6	6		
7. Container with contents	7,7	7	7		7	7	
8. Bundle or package		8					
9. Liquid		*					(14)
10. Grain, sand, hay	10	10	10	10	10		
11. Mud, dough	11	11	11	**	11		
12. Aggregate or set	c/3	c/3	c/4		c/5		
13. Dual	(5)						13
14. Plural	(5)	c/2	(5)	(5)			14

*Found in the closely related Western Apache, but not in Navaho.

**Categorized in the transitive, but not in the intransitive.

The possibility that the similarity in semantic categories among Takelma, Klamath and the Athapaskan languages is due to diffusion deserves careful consideration.

A more puzzling type of problem, however, exists on the other side of the continent. Cherokee, an Iroquoian language, has a classificatory system identical with the most common Athapaskan categories, viz. 1, 2, 3, 4, and 7 in Table IV. No other Iroquoian language is known to have anything similar to this system. Was it diffused into Cherokee? If so, from what source? Was Cherokee somehow once part of a former diffusion area which also included some of the Athapaskan languages? Again, these questions deserve serious consideration, regardless of the ultimate answers.

One curious feature of all Athapaskan classificatory verb schemes is the mixing in of the category of number. Thus the same verb that is used with rope-like objects in the singular is also used to mark the dual and/or plural of objects of other shapes. Creek, a Muskogean language of the Southeast, contains the remnants (or the beginnings) of a similar system. The language has several sets of suppletive verbs, normally distinguished for three numbers, singular, dual, and plural. But side by side with this number categorization, there is a shape categorization in which a normally dual verb is always used with cloth-like objects (in any number) and a normally plural verb is always used with liquid entities. What is the origin of this mixed categorization? Is it through Cherokee influence? Or do we have here another possible example pointing to a former diffusion area of which both Cherokee and Creek formed a part?

There is another kind of semantic categorization that is much more commonly found in the Southeast. This is a categorization of position, namely, horizontal or lying, indifferent or sitting (squatting), and vertical or standing. It is often mixed with categories like animate vs. inanimate, human vs. nonhuman, male vs. female. It is found with greater or less elaboration in Tunica, Chitimacha, Biloxi (a Siouan language), and Yuchi. It is also reported for Winnebago, a Siouan language of the Midwest. In the related Dakota, however, it is found only in traces but the language appears also to contain traces of a classificatory system which resembles in a vague way the elaborate system of the Athapaskan languages.

The task of tracing out semantic diffusion areas has only just begun. Better studies of classificatory systems are urgently needed, but the possibilities are vast. Serious historical studies will benefit greatly if, along with the more vigorous application of the comparative method to genetic studies, we also begin to devise more rigorous and more effective ways of attacking the vast range of diffusion problems that have been almost completely ignored.

NOTES

[1] They formed the plural through the use of their own animate plural suffix giving piksak 'hogs'. See Father Sebastian Rasles, A dictionary of the Abnaki language (= Memoirs, American Academy of Arts and Sciences, 1.370-574) (1883).

[2] E.g., Uriel Weinreich, Languages in contact (New York, 1953).

[3] Studies of linguistic borrowing in American Indian languages are almost invariably devoted to their adoption of words from European languages. Important as such studies are, they throw little light on intertribal contacts except insofar as European loanwords can be shown to have reached language A through contact with language B (in turn, possibly through language C, etc.) and not directly through contact with European speakers. But even this is rarely attempted.

[4] Floyd G. Lounsbury, "Iroquois-Cherokee linguistic relations", 15, and Mary R. Haas, "Comment on [Lounsbury]", 22, in Symposium on Cherokee-Iroquois Culture (= Bureau of American Ethnology, Bulletin 180) (Washington, 1961).

[5] The direction of borrowing is certain. The Muskogean languages have both l and n as phonemes, but Biloxi has only n.

[6] Murray B. Emeneau, "India as a Linguistic Area", Lg., 32.3-16 (1956).

[7] Uriel Weinreich, "On the compatibility of genetic relationship and convergent development", Word, 14.374-379 (1958). Reference is to p. 379.

[8] Webster's Third New International Dictionary, unabridged. Emphasis added.

[9] Emeneau has also suggested the term 'diffusion area' as being preferable to 'convergence area', but his primary preference is 'linguistic area', his original term. See Murray B. Emeneau,

India and Historical Grammar, 27 (Annamalainagar, 1965).

[10]The term is an old one in anthropology. See, i.a., A.L. Kroeber, Cultural and natural areas of native North America (Berkeley and Los Angeles, 1939).

[11]E.g., Paul Radin, "The genetic relationship of the North American Indian languages", UCPAAE, 14(5). 489-502 (1919) and Edward Sapir, "Central and North American Indian languages", in Encyclopaedia Britannica[14], 5.128-141 (1929).

[12]Franz Boas, "Classification of American Indian languages", Lg., 5.1-7 (1929).

[13]Boas also considered some resemblances, especially those traits distributed unevenly on a world-wide basis, to be 'due to psychological cuases', "The classification of American languages", American Anthropologist, 22.367-376 (1920).

[14]See especially Melville Jacobs, "The areal spread of sound features in the languages north of California", pp. 46-56, in Papers from the Symposium on American Indian Linguistics (= UCPL, 10.1-68) (Berkeley and Los Angeles, 1954).

[15]Plain stops and affricates p, t, k, č, etc. are voiceless unaspirated and h is added to show aspiration. The apostrophe is added to show glottalization of all stops and affricates as well as spirants and sonorants. The sources for the consonantal systems shown in Table I are as follows: Edward Sapir, Unpublished Kutchin materials; Constance Mary Naish, A syntactic study of Tlingit (unpublished doctoral dissertation, 1966) and Gillian Lorraine Story, A morphological study of Tlingit (unpublished doctoral dissertation, 1966); Franz Boas, "Tsimshian", pp. 283-422, in Handbook of American Indian Languages, Part I (= Bureau of American Ethnology, Bulletin 40, Part I) (Washington, 1911); Stanley Newman, "Bella Coola, I: Phonology", IJAL, 13.129-34 (1947); Franz Boas, "Kwakiutl", pp. 423-557, in Handbook of American Indian Languages, Part I; Manuel J. Andrade, "Quileute", pp. 149-292, in Handbook of American Indian Languages, Part 3 (Glückstadt-Hamburg-New York, 1933-38); M. A. R. Barker, Klamath Grammar (= UCPL, 32) (Berkeley and Los Angeles, 1964); Robert L. Oswalt, Kashaya Texts (= UCPL, 36) (Berkeley and Los Angeles, 1966).

[16]The sources for the consonantal systems in Table II are: Jane O. Bright, "The phonology of Smith River Athapaskan (Tolowa)", IJAL, 30.101-107 (1967); R. H. Robins, The Yurok Language (= UCPL, 15) (Berkeley and Los Angeles, 1958); Karl V. Teeter, The Wiyot Language (= UCPL, 37) (Berkeley and Los Angeles, 1964);

William Bright, The Karok Language (= UCPL, 13) (Berkeley and
Los Angeles, 1957); Shirley Silver, The Shasta Language (unpublished
doctoral dissertation, 1966); C. F. Voegelin, Shawnee Stems and the
Jacob P. Dunn Miami Dictionary (Indianapolis, 1937-40).

[17]Thomas M. Hess, "Snohomish chameleon morphology",
IJAL, 32.350-356 (1966).

[18]Edward Sapir, "Central and North American Indian
languages".

[19]Sources for Yuchi, Creek and Cherokee consonant systems
are my own unpublished field notes. Yuchi is also found in Günter
Wagner, "Yuchi", pp. 293-383, in Handbook of American Indian Languages, Part 3, but some features, such as y' and w', are missing
there. Dakota is taken from Franz Boas and Ella Deloria, Dakota
Grammar (= Memoirs of the National Academy of Sciences, vol.
XXIII, Second Memoir) (Washington, 1941) and Ofo has been extracted
from lexical items in James Owen Dorsey and John R. Swanton, A
dictionary of the Biloxi and Ofo languages (= Bureau of American
Ethnology, Bulletin 47) (Washington, 1912).

[20]The glottalized spirants in Dakota are clusters and they
may also be clusters in Yuchi. We are here comparing phonetic traits,
not phonemes.

[21]The study of these is all too often neglected not only in lesser known but in well-known languages as well. The three-way categorization implied in English by the intransitive-transitive pairs, lie-
lay, sit-set, and stand-stand has not, to my knowledge, been worked
out in detail. Observe the noninterchangeability of the noun objects
in the following sentences: (1) Lay the book on the table. (2) Set the
kettle on the stove. (3) Stand the easel by the window. The fact that
there are neutral verbs like 'place', 'put' which can replace the po-
sitional verbs may mean that the categorization is becoming weaker,
but it does not mean that it is lacking.

[22]I owe this insight to a paper by Keith H. Basso, "The Western Apache classificatory verb system: A formal analysis" (1968).

[23]The Athapaskan languages have spread during the past 1500-
2000 years into three main areas, (1) Alaska and western Canada, (2)
the Pacific Coast as far south as northern California, and (3) the
Southwest to beyond the Mexican border.

[24]For a description of the categories involved in several of
these languages, see William Davidson, L. W. Elford, and Harry

Hoijer, "Athapaskan classificatory verbs", in Harry Hoijer and
Others, <u>Studies in the Athapaskan languages</u> (= <u>UCPL</u>, 29) (Berkeley
and Los Angeles, 1963).

[25] Parentheses around a number in Table IV show mixing.
Thus (3) in row 6 means that 6 is expressed by the same verbs as 3.
(The distinction is therefore semantic but not morphological). A repeated number, as 7, 7 in row 7, means there are two separate but
similar categories in the particular language. The device c/3 in row
12 means that category 12 is 'composed of' items classified as 3 in
the singular.

[26] Takelma and Klamath are shown in small capital letters.
The Athapaskan languages are underlined. A few other non-Athapaskan
and non-Penutian languages are shown in parentheses.

Northwestern California has long been noted as an area where tribes of remarkably homogeneous culture speak languages of equally remarkable heterogeneity (Sapir 1921:214). At the core of this area are the Yurok (Algon-Ritwan),[1] Hupa and Smith River (Athapaskan), and Karok (Hokan). In spite of their cultural homogeneity, however, covert taxonomies found in the obligatory categories of Yurok, Hupa, and Karok reveal some important differences. This contrasts sharply with results recently reported by Bright and Bright (1965) in regard to the outer categorization of these languages (with Smith River used as a substitute for Hupa). Since they found "relatively few generic terms, and many terms which do not fall into any hierarchy" (1965: 252), they concluded that "the biotaxonomies of these tribes are much more similar than are their languages" (1965:255).[2]

The important contrasts revealed in the present study are seen particularly clearly in the use of numeral classifiers and classificatory verbs. Yurok has a relatively elaborate set of numeral classifiers (Kroeber 1911, Sapir Ms, Haas Ms, Robins 1958) — which are similar in many respects to those of such Far Eastern languages as Thai (Haas 1942), Burmese (Haas 1951, Pe 1965), Khmer (Jacob 1965), or Vietnamese (Emeneau 1951:93-109; Nguyễn-Đinh-Hòa 1957; Thompson 1965:193-196) — the use of which imposes an arbitrary classification on all objects in the "real" world. Hupa (Golla Ms), like all Athapaskan languages (Davidson, Elford, and Hoijer 1963), has a limited set of classificatory verbs whose use likewise imposes an arbitrary classification on many, though not all, objects in the real world. Aside from classificatory verbs, Hupa also has a classifier used for counting human beings (Goddard 1905:33) in contrast to all other entities. Karok appears to be much less elaborate than either

Table 1.   Yurok Dichotomy of the World (as revealed by classifiers)

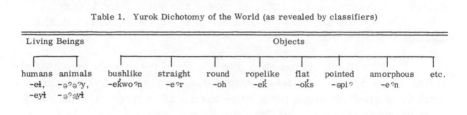

Living Beings		Objects							
humans	animals	bushlike	straight	round	ropelike	flat	pointed	amorphous	etc.
-eɬ,	-ə?ə?y,	-eƙwo?n	-e?r	-oh	-eƙ	-oƙs	-əpi?	-e?n	
-eyɬ	-ə?əyɬ								

Yurok or Hupa, although there is a rudimentary set of numeral classifiers (Bright 1957:70), among which is a special one for human
beings (1957:75).

Yurok Classifiers

The categorization implied by Yurok classifiers[3] reveals a
higher degree of generalization in the treatment of the biosphere than
the Brights found in Yurok generic terminology. The animal kingdom
is divided into two major categories: (1) human beings and (2) all
other animals (mammals, fish, frogs, birds, and insects) except
snakes. The plant kingdom also happens to fall into two major categories: (1) plants and bushes and (2) trees and ferns, but these form
a part of a higher level of abstraction based on classification by shape.
Thus the basic covert dichotomy in Yurok world view, as reflected in
the usage of numeral classifiers, is (1) Living Beings (the animal kingdom), and (2) Objects (everything else) (Table 1).[4]

Living Beings are either Human or Animal, and no nonliving
entities are included in either category. Members of the plant kingdom, on the other hand, are treated like nonliving objects and form
part of a large shape-differentiated and miscellaneous set that includes
the following: (1) Bushlike objects (plants, bushes; the hips; also
songs); (2) Sticklike or Straight objects (trees, ferns, sticks, bridges;
legs); (3) Round objects (rocks, silver dollars, drums, hats; flowers,
berries, nuts; heads, hearts, eyes); (4) Ropelike objects (ropes,
strings; snakes; necks, tongues); (5) Flat objects (boards); (6) Pointed
objects or tools (obsidian blades, knives, men's spoons); (7) Amorphous objects (body parts that are not Bushlike, Straight, Round, or

Ropelike; utensils; streams); and, finally, a number of specialized categories, such as (8) houses, (9) boats and boat-shaped objects, (10) dentalium shells, (11) dentalia strings, (12) woodpecker scalps, and some others.

      Classifiers are combined with adjectives as well as numerals, but as a rule fewer categorical distinctions are made, and the actual forms are often different from those used with numerals. The Yurok classificatory system is not yet fully known, and considerably more field work will be required to remedy this.

      Recent additions to the list of classifiers[5] include -ekin "strand," as in kohcekin "one strand (as of hair)," and possibly -ep', as in kohtep' "one (of a tree)." The informant abstracted -ep' as meaning "it's living and of the tree, brush family" but used kohte?r tepo· "one tree" (koht- "one" + -e?r, classifier for Straight objects) in the actual counting of trees. Perhaps -ep' is not, strictly speaking, a classifier, but simply a concrete suffix that can be used with numeral as well as noun stems, as in ci·sep' "flower, flower bush"; mesterep' "Johnson grass"; pa?a·p' "Woodwardia fern" (literally "water-plant"; cf. pa?ah "water"); pya·p' "manzanita tree" (cf. pyah "manzanita berry"); nəhpəyu·p' "(huckle) berry bush" (cf. nəhpəy "berry (in general)"); me?yk'welu·p' "poison oak"; ne?mu·p' "vetch."

      The Yurok classifier system is one of the most elaborate in North America north of Mexico,[6] and its full functioning cannot be described until the classifier or classifiers that are to be used with each noun are known. In 1950 I elicited a considerable amount of such information, and this, together with that found in Sapir's notes, forms the basis of the following generalizations:

      (1) In some cases different classifiers can be used with the same noun without a difference in referential meaning. Thus, worms are counted with either the Ropelike or the Animal classifier. The difference is entirely taxonomic: in the one case worms are treated as animals and hence living beings, in the other they are shape-differentiated objects. Snakes, on the other hand, are always classified as Ropelike, but there is also a taboo on their mention.

      (2) In other cases, different classifiers are used precisely in order to indicate a difference in referential meaning. Thus, ci·sep'

means "flower bush" when classified as Bushlike, but "flower" when classified as Round: kohteǩwoʔn ci·sep "one flower bush (with flowers)" and kohtoh weci·sep̓ "one flower" or "one of its flowers" (we- is the third-person possessive prefix).

(3) Berries, nuts, acorns, and fruits are classified as Round objects, and the bushes, plants, or trees that bear them are classified as Bushlike (if bushes or plants) or Straight (if trees): kohtoh mahkuɬ "one salal berry"; kohteǩwoʔn mahkeʔw "one salal berry bush."

It is important to observe that whereas the Brights list tree, bush, grass, flower, and berry as the Yurok generic terms in the plant kingdom (1965:252), the classifier system treats these things as shape-differentiated objects belonging to only three categories: Bushlike (flower bushes, berry bushes, strawberry plants), Straight (trees), and Round (flowers, berries).

Hupa Classificatory Verbs

In terms of the number of languages treated, the most comprehensive statement about Athapaskan classificatory verbs is that of Davidson, Elford, and Hoijer (1963), but the categories found in Smith River and Hupa are not included.

Golla, who has done recent field work on Hupa, has found the following categories in that language (Ms): (1) round object, (2) long or sticklike object, (3) living being, human or animal, (4) container with contents, (5) fabriclike object, (6) several objects, or ropelike object, (7) granular mass, (8) doughlike or mudlike object, (9) piled-up fabric (blanket).

Now just as the Yurok system of numeral classifiers cannot be fully understood until its operation with respect to specific lexical items is known, so the full understanding of the Hupa classificatory verb system requires the same kind of information. But comprehensive information of this type is lacking, not only for Hupa but for other Athapaskan languages as well. Consequently, only a few very rough conclusions can be drawn.

We can assume that Hupa category 3 comprises most of the members of the animal kingdom, but we cannot assert that it comprises them all. In Navaho, for example, "some animals, notably frogs" are placed in the category of Mudlike Mass (Davidson, Elford, and Hoijer 1963:32). Does the similar category in Hupa, number 8, also include frogs and other small animals of this type? In word-association tests (Ervin-Tripp Ms), some Navahos associate the snake with verbs of the Ropelike category. This reminds us that the Yurok use the Ropelike classifier for snakes, and we would like to know whether or not Hupa category 6 includes snakes and worms or other "ropelike" animals.

Yurok and Hupa Covert Taxonomies Compared

The Brights found the outer, nonobligatory taxonomies of the tribes of northwestern California to be "quite similar" (1965:257), but my findings reveal important differences in the covert taxonomies of the obligatory categories. As a corollary, I also find that the outer and inner categories of the same tribe show noteworthy differences. Thus, whereas the Brights concluded that among the Yurok "body louse" cannot be subsumed in any class larger than itself, since the outer taxonomy contains no larger class into which it would fit (1965:252-253), the obligatory classification imposed by the use of numeral classifiers puts body lice in the Animal class, along with fleas, flies, mosquitoes, and ticks as well as fish, birds, frogs, and quadruped mammals. Except for the Human class, which the Yurok distinguish from the Animal class, all other objects in the "real" world, including members of the plant kingdom, are classified in one or another of a variety of categories, most of which are shape-differentiated.

Among the Hupa, on the other hand, the situation is entirely different. The obligatory classificatory system, at least as far as it is presently known, falls far short of encompassing all objects of the "real" world. With respect to the biosphere, there is only one pertinent obligatory category, namely the one comprising living beings. But even here, there is an important difference between Hupa and Yurok, for Hupa, unlike Yurok, does not impose a further subclassification into animals and humans. At the same time it is worth noting that the weakly developed classifier system of Hupa does differentiate humans from everything else.

A final point of difference between Hupa and Yurok is that
the Hupa do not concern themselves at all with the plant kingdom insofar as their covert classificatory system is concerned.

Conclusion

Although the linguistic manifestations of the classificatory
systems of Yurok and Hupa are quite different (suffixes added to numerals and adjectives in Yurok, as against special sets of verb-stems
in Hupa), there are some striking similarities in the content of the
classes (Table 2).

It would be important to know whether there are any examples of cross-linguistic influence regarding the membership in these
categories. For example, there is a rather specialized similarity
between the Yurok classification for pairs of blankets and the Apache
(southern Athapaskan) classification for sets of two things. In Sapir's
Yurok notes (Ms), pairs of blankets are enumerated in the Ropelike
class, and in Chiricahua Apache (Hoijer 1945: 21) sets of two objects
are in the comparable class.[7]

However, classifiers are often, though not exclusively,
strongly shape-differentiated wherever they occur, whether in the
Americas (e. g. , Wiyot [Reichard 1925: 84-85; Teeter 1964: 62],
Nootka [Swadesh 1936-1938: 88], Kwakiutl [Boas 1947: 240], Salish,
e. g. , Coeur d'Alene [Reichard 1938: 645], Tzeltal [Berlin and Romney
1964]) or in the Far East, as mentioned earlier. At the same time
classificatory verbs, though apparently much less common than classifiers, also usually include two or three categories of shape-differ-
entiation (e. g. , Cherokee [Haas 1948], Athapaskan [Davidson, Elford,
and Hoijer 1963]).

Both classifiers and classificatory verbs clearly deserve
far more attention than they have received in the past as indicators
of covert taxonomic systems of considerable complexity. It is still
not too late to examine the problem more closely in northwestern
California. Although Wiyot (Algon-Ritwan) and Kato and Mattole

Table 2. Yurok and Hupa Class Constituency

Yurok classifiers	Hupa classificatory verbs
Human beings	Living beings (human and animal)
Animals	
Straight or sticklike objects	Long or sticklike objects
Round objects	Round objects
Ropelike objects	Ropelike objects (or several objects)

(both Athapaskan) are gone, more detailed information could still be obtained for Yurok, Hupa, and Smith River. In view of the unique importance of the area for just this kind of study, the task would be well worth the time and trouble required.

NOTES

[1]Algon-Ritwan is a shortened form of Algonkian-Ritwan used in place of the more cumbersome Algonkian-Wiyot-Yurok. Like the latter, it is not intended to imply or deny a closer relationship between Wiyot and Yurok than either has with Algonkian.

[2]The Brights further conclude that "the Sapir-Whorf hypothesis is not strongly applicable to our data" (1965:255). Sapir's statement "the worlds in which different societies live are distinct worlds, not merely the same world with different labels attached" (1929:209) had a powerful impact in an era of extreme cultural relativism, but was perhaps not intended to be taken with absolute literalness even then. But even more important is the fact that Whorf lumped together in SAE ("Standard Average European") enough different languages (and cultures) actually to invalidate his thesis. He says: "Since with respect to the traits compared, there is little difference between English, French, German, or other European languages with the possible (but doubtful [!]) exception of Balto-Slavic

and non-Indo-European I have lumped these languages into one group labelled SAE" (1941:78). Clearly SAE is nothing more than a label for a specific linguistic area, as defined by Emeneau (1956). What Whorf actually did, then, was to contrast a broad linguistic area (SAE) with a narrow one (Hopi). And if we are willing to accept such a broad definition of SAE, why not set up SANWC ("Standard Average Northwestern California")? After all, it is no more unreasonable to find shared traits in SANWC (Yurok, Karok, and Hupa-Smith River) than in SAE (Romance-Germanic, Balto-Slavic, and Finno-Ugric).

[3]Material from all the sources (Kroeber 1911:423-424, Robins 1958:87-96, Sapir Ms, Haas Ms) was used in arriving at the classificatory system of Yurok, but not all of the minor or rare classes are given here. The information regarding the items that are sub-included in a particular class is taken largely from my own notes. The class labels sometimes differ from those used by Robins. Thus his class labeled "Body Parts, Streams, Utensils" is called "Amorphous" here, since my data indicate that the only body parts included in this class are those that cannot be classified as Straight, Round, Ropelike, etc.

[4]The orthography used in quoting Yurok words is the same as that described by Robins (1958:1-10) with the following exceptions: (1) The strongly retroflexed vowel of Yurok is written /ə/ instead of turned r. (2) The symbol /š/ is not used, since the Yurok sibilant is always more strongly palatalized after /i/ or /y/. (The one minimal contrast between /s/ and /š/ cited by Robins [1958:9] seems to be restricted to the speech of one informant, and in that one instance /š/ can be specially introduced.) (3) The labiovelars /k^W, k̓ ^{W}/ are written /kw, k̓ w/ since they do not seem to differ from other phonologically related clusters, such as /tw, t̓ w, ky, k̓ y/, etc., which are found in initial as well as other positions. (4) There are idiolectal (and probably subdialectal) differences in the pronunciation of some Yurok words, particularly in regard to glottalization; wherever there is a difference, I have used my own data.

[5]This work was done under the auspices of the Survey of California and Other Indian Languages, Department of Linguistics, University of California, Berkeley.

[6]One of the most detailed studies of classifiers in a North American language is devoted to Tseltal (Mayan) (Berlin and Romney 1964), but good descriptions of numeral classifiers in languages north of Mexico are hard to find. They are known to occur in

Wakashan (Nootka, Swadesh 1936-1938:88; Kwakiutl, Boas 1947:
240), Salishan (Coeur d'Alene, Reichard 1938:645), and Wiyot
(Reichard 1925:84-85; Teeter 1964:62) and in a less elaborate form
in a great many other languages.

   [7]It is not stated explicitly that pairs of blankets are included
in the Ropelike class in Apache. What is of interest here is the relationship between "sets of two" and "ropelike objects. "

REFERENCES

Berlin, Brent, and A. Kimball Romney
   1964 Descriptive semantics of Tzeltal numeral classifiers. In
   Transcultural studies in cognition. A. Kimball Romney and Roy
   G. D'Andrade, eds. American Anthropologist 66, no. 3, pt.
   2:79-98.
Boas, Franz
   1947 Kwakiutl grammar. Transactions of the American Philosophical Society, n.s. 37, pt. 3:201-377.
Bright, Jane O., and William Bright
   1965 Semantic structures in northwestern California and the Sapir-
   Whorf hypothesis. In Formal semantic analysis. E. A. Hammel,
   ed. American Anthropologist 67, no. 5, pt. 2:249-258.
Bright, William
   1957 The Karok language. University of California Publications
   in Linguistics 13.
Davidson, William, L. W. Elford, and Harry Hoijer
   1963 Athapaskan classificatory verbs. In Studies in the Athapas-
   kan languages. Harry Hoijer et al. University of California
   Publications in Linguistics 29:30-41.
Emeneau, Murray B.
   1951 Studies in Vietnamese (Annamese) grammar. University of
   California Publications in Linguistics 8.
   1956 India as a linguistic area. Language 32:3-16.
Ervin-Tripp, Susan M.
   Ms   Field notes on word-association tests among the Navaho.
Freeman, John E., ed.
   1966 A guide to manuscripts relating to the American Indian in the
   Library of the American Philosophical Society. Memoirs of the
   American Philosophical Society 65. Philadelphia.

Goddard, Pliny Earle
   1905 Morphology of the Hupa language. University of California
   Publications in American Archaeology and Ethnology 3: 1-143.
Golla, Victor K.
   Ms   A list of classificatory verbs in Hupa [1966].
Haas, Mary R.
   1942 The use of numeral classifiers in Thai. Language 18: 201-
   205.
   1948 Classificatory verbs in Muskogee. International Journal of
   American Linguistics 14: 244-246.
   1951 The use of numeral classifiers in Burmese. In Semitic and
   Oriental studies. University of California Publications in Semitic Philology 9: 191-200.
   Ms   Yurok field notes [1950 and 1966].
Hoijer, Harry
   1945 Classificatory verb stems in the Apachaen languages. International Journal of American Linguistics 11: 13-23.
Jacob, Judith M.
   1965 Notes on the numerals and numeral coefficients in old, middle and modern Khmer. Lingua 15: 143-162.
Kroeber, A. L.
   1911 The languages of the coast of California north of San Francisco. University of California Publications in American Archaeology and Ethnology 9. 3: 273-435.
Nguyễn - Đinh - Hòa
   1957 Classifiers in Vietnamese. Word 13: 124-152.
Pe, Hla
   1965 A re-examination of Burmese "classifiers." Lingua 15: 163-
   185.
Reichard, Gladys A.
   1925 Wiyot grammar and texts. University of California Publications in Archaeology and Ethnology 22: 1-215.
   1938 Coeur d'Alene. Handbook of American Indian Languages,
   pt. 3: 515-707. Glückstadt-Hamburg-New York, J. J. Augustin.
Robins, R. H.
   1958 The Yurok language. University of California Publications
   in Linguistics 15.
Sapir, Edward
   1921 Language: an introduction to the study of speech. New
   York, Harcourt, Brace.

1929   The status of linguistics as a science.   Language 5:207-214.
Ms   Yurok field notes [1927].   (Item no. 3928 in Freeman 1966).
Swadesh, Morris
    1936-1938   Nootka internal syntax.   International Journal of
    American Linguistics 9:77-102.
Teeter, Karl V.
    1964 The Wiyot language.   University of California Publications
    in Linguistics 37.
Thompson, Laurence C.
    1965 A Vietnamese grammar.   Seattle, University of Washington
    Press.
Whorf, Benjamin Lee
    1941 The relation of habitual thought and behavior to language.
    In Language, culture, and personality.   Leslie Spier et al.,
    eds.   Menasha, Wisc., George Banta Co.

1. The Indian tribes of northwestern California have long
been cited as a classic example of cultural homogeneity combined with
extreme linguistic heterogeneity. Sapir's 1921 statement[1] is typical:

> There is the liveliest intertribal intercourse between the
> Hupa, Yurok, and Karok. . . .It is difficult to say what ele-
> ments in their combined culture belong in origin to this tribe
> or that. . . .But their languages are not merely alien to each
> other; they belong to three of the major American linguistic
> groups, each with an immense distribution on the northern
> continent.

Thus Hupa is Athapaskan, Yurok is Algon-Ritwan,[2] and Karok is Hokan. Other tribes of the same subculture area also belong to one of
these three linguistic stocks, e. g. the Tolowa (Athapaskan) to the
north of the Yurok, and Wiyot (Algon-Ritwan) to the south of the Yurok.

In recent years northwestern California has received new attention from field workers, especially linguists,[3] and there has been
a revival of interest in these tribes. Aside from the production of the
essential grammars, texts, and dictionaries[4] and the reaffirmation
of genetic differences, scholars interested in the area are also beginning to recognize that the languages as well as the cultures of these
tribes may have been subjected to interinfluences. Semantic structures, particularly the ethnobiotaxonomy of the several tribes, have
received attention from the Brights,[5] and covert classificatory systems (noun classifiers in Yurok and classificatory verbs in Hupa) are
described in a paper of mine. [6]

In the present paper I wish to call attention to an even more cogent example of interinfluence, namely the presence of consonant symbolism in Karok,[7] Yurok,[8] and Wiyot.[9] The structure of the symbolism and the rules by which it is applied are very similar in the three languages. Since Karok is a Hokan language and Yurok and Wiyot are Algon-Ritwan, it is necessary to postulate diffusion from Karok to Yurok and Wiyot, from Yurok and Wiyot to Karok, or to all of them from still another source. However, a definitive answer to the ultimate source of the trait is beyond the scope of this paper.

2.1. Consonant symbolism is the substitution of one or several specific consonants by one or several different consonants with a consequent change in connotative meaning. Most frequently the change signals the diminutive, the diminutive and the augmentative,[10] or, somewhat analogously, three or four degrees of intensity.[11] But it may also be used to signal status (e.g. a child or a servant) and even abnormalities of persons addressed or referred to.[12] An English example is the substitution of a voiceless postdental th for s in imitation of a person who lisps, as in "Thipping thider through a thtraw."[13]

2.2. In Yurok, Wiyot, and Karok the most prominent use of consonant symbolism is associated with normal vs. diminutive and, in Wiyot, also augmentative. The consonant systems of the three languages are shown in Table I[14] and in Table II the specific symbolic substitutions made in each of the languages are charted. It can be seen at a glance that the three systems of symbolic substitution are very similar. But when one also considers the limitations of the total consonant system in each language (Table I), it turns out that they are even more similar than appears at first glance. For example, the distinction between c and č and between s and š[15] exists only in Wiyot, so substitutions of this type are impossible in Yurok and Karok. Similarly, l is absent in Karok, so r cannot replace l, as in Yurok and Wiyot. Instead, the equivalent replacement in Karok is n for r. Karok has an additional substitution of m for v which is not shown in Table II since it is so extremely rare that Bright considers it an irregularity.[16] Moreover, since v and m as well as r and n are morphophonemically related[17] outside the domain of symbolism, it is at least conceivable that the m for v replacement is an innovation in Karok on the analogy of the n for r replacement.

Table I

Consonant Systems of Yurok, Wiyot, and Karok

Yurok		Wiyot		Karok
p	ṗ'	p	ph (b)	p
t	t'	t	th (d)	t
		c	ch (z)	
č (c)	č'(č)	č	čh (z)	č
k	ḱ	k	kh (g)	k
kw	ḱw	kw	kwh	
		b (β)		f
		d (ṛ)		θ
s (s, ṣ)		s		s (s, ṣ)
		š		
g [γ]		g (γ)		
m		m		m
n		n		n
l		l		
ł		ł		
r		r		r
w		w		v
y		y		y
h		h (h, ʔ)		h
ʔ				ʔ

Table II

Consonant Symbolism in Yurok, Wiyot, and Karok

Yurok		Wiyot			Karok	
Normal	Dim.	Normal	Dim.	Aug.	Normal	Dim.
t	č	t, th	c, ch	č, čh		č
		s		š	θ	
l	r	l	r		r	n

2.3. In Wiyot and Karok the notion of the diminutive (and likewise the augmentative in Wiyot) is not expressed by symbolism alone (connotative meaning) but generally requires the use of a special suffix or suffixes (denotative meaning). The use of these suffixes requires the substitution of each consonant in the normal column by its mate in the diminutive (or augmentative) column.

The Wiyot diminutive suffix is -oc[18] or, rarely, -ic and is used with both nouns and verbs. The Wiyot augmentative suffix is -ačk. Examples without suffix are followed by those with suffix.

Without suffix: (1) dítatk "two roundish objects," dícack "two small roundish objects," díčačk "two large roundish objects."[19]

With suffix: (2) laptóhw "cloud," lapcóhyawac "little cloud," lapčóhyawačk "storm cloud." (3) tawipáhlił "rope," cawipahrołoc "twine," čawiphrółačk "cable" or tawiparóhłačk. (4) dohl- "plate basket," dóhragačk "used plate basket." (5) lóliswił "he sings," rórišwocił "he hums." (6) tak- "spruce," cakíc "young spruce."

The situation in Karok is remarkably similar except that Karok lacks an augmentative suffix. The diminutive suffix is -ič or, rarely, -ač, and there is a second diminutive suffix -is which may also be used separately or in conjunction with the first.[20] The consonant substitutions shown in Table II always take place with the addition of -ič or -ač but not necessarily with -is alone.[21] Examples:

With -ič, -ač: (1) iθári·p "fir tree," ičáni·pič "small fir."[22] (2) θufkírik "great horned owl," čufkínikič "little great horned owl." (3) ʔaʔvárih "high," ʔaʔvánihič "rather high." (4) súruvara "hold," súnuvanač "little hole." (5) ta·t "mother," tátač "mama."

With -is: (6) ʔisra·m "deer lick," ʔisrávis "marshy place." (7) mí·θ "father's sister," mí·čis (dim.).

With -is and -ič: (8) vá·rama "long," vá·namisič "rather long."

2.4. Although the consonant symbolism found in Yurok (Table II) is identical with that of Wiyot (except where Yurok lacks

the critical consonant distinctions) and not too different from that of
Karok, still Yurok does differ from both Wiyot and Karok in that
these symbolic changes are not associated with the use of diminutive
(or augmentative) suffixes. Yurok thus has what amounts to virtually
pure symbolism. Examples, given in terms of the actual consonant
changes, are as follows:

t ~ č: (1) pontet "ashes," pənčəč "dust" and pənčəh "to be
gray (of deer)."²³ (2) tekʷsaʔr "heart of salmon," čekʷs "(human) heart." (3) wentokʷs "female (of animal, bird)," wenčokʷs
"woman." (4) koht- "one" (with certain classifiers) but kohč- "one"
(with certain other classifiers). (5) munt- "white" (with certain classifiers) but munč- "white" (with certain other classifiers).

l ~ r: (6) -ʔlep "hair" but -ʔrep "eyebrow." (7) peloy- "to
be big, old (of humans)," perey "old woman." (8) lohpił- "to gather
(of clouds)," rohpił "to clear (of clouds)." (9) kelomoh "to turn"
(intr.), kelomen- "to turn" (trans.), kelomel "autumn" (i.e.
"turned"), but keromoh "to turn round (of a wheel)," keromekin "to
twist, lock."

If both sets of changeable consonants occur in the same word,
both will be replaced: (10) seʔlet- "to scrape off mud," but seʔreč-
"to whittle wood."

An especially interesting facet of the Yurok situation is the
fact that without overt markers in the form of diminutive and augmentative suffixes, the semantic range of the symbolism is more diffuse.
Thus the "diminutive" column (č and r) is often associated with people
in contrast to animals (examples 2 and 3) and sometimes it appears to
connote the augmentative as well as the diminutive (see example 9 with
keromoh roughly connoting an augmentative and keromekin a diminutive).

Even though the symbolic changes in Yurok are not formally
associated with the use of diminutive suffixes, it is important to note
that a suffix -os, commonly occurring with kinship terms, may represent an archaic diminutive suffix. The following rather long list of
kin terms²⁴ appears to contain such as suffix.

> pičowos "grandfather"
> kučos "grandmother"

totos "father"
kokos "mother"
-čekos "mother"
čimos "uncle"
tulos "aunt"
mičos "male cousin"
pinos "elder sister"
-čnewḱwos "son-in-law"

Eight of the ten words in the list have dental consonants belonging to the changeable set (i.e. t and č). Of these eight, six have č, the expected diminutive change, and only two have t. This lends further credence to the hypothesis that -os is an old diminutive suffix, since we also have clear evidence that it tended to induce the appropriate consonant change as well. Moreover, the two words which do not show change both have a changeable consonant in initial position and it will be recalled that in Wiyot, the initial consonant sometimes resists change. Evidence from the l ~ r set is lacking since the only example that could be affected is tulos "aunt" and since the initial t has resisted change, l might also resist change.

Karok kin terms also frequently take a diminutive suffix and -is seems at least as common in the domain of kin terms as -ič or -ač, whereas outside this domain, the latter suffix is many times the more frequent. However, only a few of the Karok kin terms appear in diminutive form only.

3.1. We are now ready to take a closer look at the problem enunciated in the introductory paragraphs of this paper. What part of the observed similarity in the expression of diminutivism in the three languages is to be ascribed to genetic inheritance and what to diffusion? Obviously we can approach the problem more realistically if we can bring in data from control languages, i.e. from related languages lying outside of the geographical area under consideration. Fortunately this is possible.

3.2. It is now generally agreed that Wiyot and Yurok are related to the Algonkian family, all of whose members lie east of the Rocky Mountains. The diminutive is well developed in these languages and the most common form of the suffix is reconstructed as *-ehs-[25]

but variants, such as *-ʔs-, also occur. However, the cooccurrence of consonant changes when the diminutive suffix is added has been noted only for Cree. In this language "most speakers replace a /t/ anywhere earlier in the word by /c/ [č]" whenever a diminutive suffix is used.[26] Whether the consonant symbolism accompanying the use of the diminutive suffix is archaic or recent,[27] the use of the diminutive suffix is so widespread that there is no justification for doubting its antiquity. The Yurok suffix -os, if truly a diminutive, is possibly cognate with PA *-ehs-, though Wiyot -oc is probably not. This, then, covers the principal features of the Algon-Ritwan side of the story.

3.3. What about Karok and its congeners? Since Hokan is not a closely knit group like Algonkian, Yana, another Hokan sub-family of northern California, has been chosen as a sample. Yana has two diminutive suffixes, -p̓a (singular) and -čeegi ~ -čgi (plural), whose use requires that /l/ anywhere in the word be replaced by /n/,[28] e.g. lal- "foot," but nanǯa "little foot."[29] Thus we see that while the actual Yana suffixes are not cognate with the Karok suffix, they do induce very precisely one of the types of Karok consonant change, viz. Yana l >n, Karok r >n.

Table III
Diminutivism in NW California: Comparison of Special Features

	PA	Y	W	K	Ya
T	(A)	A	A	B	-
L	-	A	A	B	B
Suff.	A	(A)	B	BA	C

4. An attempt is made in Table III to present an analysis of the principal features of diminutivism in Yurok (Y), Wiyot (W), and Karok (K), three neighboring languages of northwestern California, and to compare and contrast these features with those of Proto-Algonkian (PA), related to Yurok and Wiyot, on the one hand, and Yana (Ya), related to Karok, on the other.[30] These two major stocks are separated by a double line. Other special conventions used in the table

are as follows: T covers the change of t to c and/or č (A type) or θ
to č (B type),[31] L covers the change of l to r (A type) or of l(r) to n
(B type), and Suff. covers those containing s (A type), c or č (B type),
or neither (C type).[32] Items placed in parentheses are nonproductive
or limited, e.g. (A) in the T row of the PA column and (A) in the
Suff. row of the Y column.

   An analysis of the table enables us to make some interesting
observations. In terms of number of shared <u>similar</u> features (everything in the same row) the geographically contiguous languages of
northwestern California, namely, Yurok, Wiyot, and Karok are more
like one another than Yurok and Wiyot are like Algonkian or than Karok
is like Yana. In terms of shared <u>identical</u> features (everything with the
same code letter, A, B, or C), however, Karok, the genetically distinct language, tends to be slightly different. Our conclusions, in terms
of what is genetic and what is diffused, can now be stated in the following guarded terms: When the same code letter occurs on the same
side of the double line, the feature is probably genetic, e.g. A and (A)
in the T, L, and Suff. rows. When the same code letter occurs on both
sides of the double line, the feature is probably diffused, e.g. B and A
in the Suff. row of the table. The direction of diffusion, however, still
remains unsolved.

   This and other unsolved problems raised in this paper can be
resolved only by widening the scope of the study to include languages
of Oregon and the Northwest Coast as well as Siouan and additional Algonkian languages lying further east. Important facts needing to be included in such a wider study are the following: Nootka, a Wakashan
language of Vancouver Island, has an s-type diminutive suffix -ʔis
which is widely used in conjunction with various kinds of consonant
changes to connote physical abnormalities.[33] Thus

> people who are abnormally small are spoken of in forms with
> the diminutive suffix; moreover, in such cases, all sibilant
> consonants (s̲, c̲, c̲ʼ; š̲, č̲, č̲ʼ) become palatalized š̲- sounds
> (š́, ć, ćʼ . .), which sound acoustically midway between s̲-
> and š̲ sounds; the diminutive -ʔis itself becomes -ʔiš̲.

This reminds one of the s to š change already described for Wiyot
(see Table II). Since Nootka may very well represent a kind of cultural climax for these features, the problem of diffusion arises again.
There are many reasons for believing that the Wiyot (and Yurok) were

at one time located further to the north and their traits of consonant symbolism might have been acquired at that time. But it must not be overlooked that nearer at hand there is also Wishram, a Penutian language of Oregon, which expresses diminutivism and augmentativism by means of an elaborate series of consonant changes even though diminutive and augmentative suffixes are lacking.[34] Only obstruent consonants are affected by these changes and among these the sibilants are very prominent. Glottalization is also prominent, especially in expressing the diminutive. So, among sibilants, there are these changes to express the diminutive.[35]

> š and its affricative developments č and č̓ become s, c, and c̓ (s seems sometimes to be still further "diminutivized" to c, c to c̓, so that š, s, c, c̓ may be considered as representing a scale of diminishing values). . .

The changes in the sibilants that are used to express the augmentative, on the other hand, are the following:

> s, c, and c̓ become respectively š, č, and č̓ (in some few cases c and č affricatives become ǰ, pronounced as in English judge. . .).

The Wiyot s to š change, which is used for both augmentative and diminutive, is now seen to be similar also to the Wishram expression of the augmentative as well as to one of the Nootka types of diminutive symbolism.

So far our most highly developed examples of consonant symbolism have been taken from western languages. But Dakota, a Siouan language of the Northern Plains, shows "clear evidence of an ancient sound symbolism."[36] [Emphasis supplied] The sounds involved are the voiced and voiceless sets z, ž, γ and s, š, x. The connotation is usually one of increasing intensification, e.g. zí "it is yellow," ží "it is tawny," and γí "it is brown."[37] Sibilants are again prominent and the change from s to š, connoting greater intensity, reminds us of the augmentative connotation of the same change in Wishram. But the same device could also be used to connote affection, as when speaking to children:[38]

When petting children it is customary to pronounce instead
of s and z, the corresponding š̓ [š] and ž̓ [ž], but with half-
closed teeth.

Here it would be important to look for traces of consonant symbolism
in other Siouan languages and to attempt to determine whether or not
it was a characteristic of Proto-Siouan.

Finally, it must be emphasized that the full story in regard
to Proto-Algonkian is not yet known. Although s, as in *-ehs-, *-hs-,
and *-ʔs-, [39] was a common constituent sound in the diminutive suffix, other diminutives probably also existed. In Delaware a common
consonant constituent is T, e.g. -Tət, added to nouns and related
forms added to verbs. [40] It is also very interesting to observe that
Ojibwa has what may be called an ordinary diminutive in -ins (or
-e·ns) or sometimes -iss and also a pejorative diminutive in -išš. [41]
Thus there is anim "dog," animo·ns "little dog," and animošš "dog
(pejorative)." Although this is a change which takes place in the suffix itself rather than in the stems to which it is added, it again reminds us of the s to š change in Wiyot (for diminutive and augmentative) and in Wishram (for augmentative). The Wiyot augmentative is
also a pejorative. Was there possibly a PA *-hš, pejorative suffix,
or is this a late specialization in Ojibwa?

Clearly what started out to be a local problem in diffusion—
in northwestern California—is now seen to have ramifications throughout much of North America. [42] It is urged that others follow through
with studies of diminutivism in other parts of the continent. It is only
in this way that we can hope to reach a better understanding of the
ways in which these features have spread through space and time.

NOTES

[1] Edward Sapir, Language, New York (1921); p. 214.
[2] Algonkian plus Yurok and Wiyot.
[3] Much of the work has been done under the auspices of the
Survey of California Indian Languages, Department of Linguistics,
University of California, Berkeley. Workers include William Bright
on Karok, R. H. Robins on Yurok, Karl V. Teeter on Wiyot,

Victor K. Golla on Hupa, Mary R. Haas on Yurok, and Dale Valory
on Tolowa and Yurok. Some of the recent work of William Bright
and the late Jane O. Bright on Tolowa and Yurok has been subsidized
by the American Philosophical Society (Penrose Fund).

[4]William Bright, The Karok Language, UCPL vol. 13, Berke-
ley, and Los Angeles (1957); R. H. Robins, The Yurok Language,
UCPL vol. 15, Berkeley and Los Angeles (1958); Karl V. Teeter,
The Wiyot Language, UCPL vol. 37, Berkeley and Los Angeles (1964).

[5]Jane O. Bright and William Bright, Semantic Structures in
Northwestern California and the Sapir-Whorf Hypothesis, pp. 249-
258, in Formal Semantic Analysis, ed. by E. A. Hammel, American
Anthropologist, vol. 67, no. 5, pt. 2 (1965).

[6]Mary R. Haas, Language and Taxonomy in Northwestern
California, American Anthropologist 69.358-362 (1967).

[7]William Bright, op. cit., particularly pp. 76-78.

[8]R. H. Robins, op. cit., particularly pp. 13-14.

[9]Karl V. Teeter, op. cit, particularly pp. 21-22 and 68,
and, by the same author, Consonant Harmony in Wiyot (with a note
on Cree), IJAL 25.41-43 (1959).

[10]Edward Sapir, Diminutive and Augmentative consonantism
in Wishram, pp. 638-645, in Handbook of American Indian Languages,
Franz Boas, ed., Bulletin 40, Part I, Bureau of American Ethnology,
Washington, D. C. (1911).

[11]Franz Boas and Ella Deloria, Notes on the Dakota, Teton
dialect, IJAL 7.97-121 (1933). See particularly pp. 112-113.

[12]Edward Sapir, Abnormal Types of Speech in Nootka, Canada Department of Mines, Geological Survey, Memoir 62, Anthropological Series, no. 5, Ottawa (1915). Reprinted in Selected Writings
of Edward Sapir, David Mandelbaum, ed., pp. 179-186, Berkeley
and Los Angeles (1949).

[13]This postdental th is slightly different from ordinary th, as
in "through", since the latter is interdental.

[14]See Robins, op. cit.; Teeter, op. cit.; Bright, op. cit. A
few changes in orthography have been introduced in some cases. In
the Yurok column symbols enclosed in parentheses are those used by
Robins while the one enclosed in square brackets simply clarifies the
pronunciation. In the present paper I use č and č' in order to make it
clear that the Yurok single affricate is like Wiyot č, not like Wiyot c.
In the case of s, the variation between s and š is allophonic, š occurring only after i or y. (There is only one possible counterexample

in Robins' material and for this one š could be specially introduced;
all other counterexamples have been rechecked and appear to have
been typographical errors).

In the Wiyot column items in parentheses are the symbols
used by Teeter in his 1959 article but changed to what immediately
precedes the parenthesized item in his 1964 book.

In the Karok column š is eliminated from the list since it
occurs <u>only</u> after i or y. Hence for the purposes of the present comparison it is best to treat [s] and [š] as allophones of a single phoneme.
Bright separated them on the basis of four or five loanwords and a
deviant reduplicated form in which s rather than š appears after i or
y in a preceding syllable (Bright, op. cit., p. 17).

[15]In Yurok and Karok the difference between these sounds is
subphonemic since it is conditioned by the phonetic environment. See
note 14.

[16]Bright 1957, p. 78.

[17]Bright, pp. 39-40.

[18]There is also a variant -oč.

[19]All examples are taken from Teeter 1959 or 1964, but those
taken from Teeter 1959 are quoted with the orthography changes of
1964 (see Table I). Each set of examples is given a number and the
references are as follows: (1) Teeter 1964, p. 30; (2) Teeter 1959,
p. 41 and note 6 where it is pointed out that expected consonant
changes sometimes fail to affect the initial consonant of the word;
(3) 1959, p. 41 with an alternant from 1964, p. 68; (4) 1964, p. 68;
(5) 1959, p. 41; (6) 1964, p. 68.

[20]Bright 1957, p. 78.

[21]This not specifically mentioned by Bright. However, a good
example is seen in the variants for "black-headed grosbeak" (Bright
1957, p. 331), viz. čurî·pis and čuripisáva·n which have only -is
(and no consonant substitution for r though č may be for θ) as against
čunî·pisič which adds -ič and substitution of n for r. On the other
hand, there are other words which do show the expected consonant
changes when -is is added, e.g. ʔíram "daughter-in-law," ʔínamis
(dim.); mi·θ "father's sister," mî·čis (dim.).

[22]All examples are taken from Bright 1957. Each set of examples is given a number and the references are as follows: (1) p.76;
(2) p. 390; (3) p. 76; (4) p. 77; (5) p. 78; (6) p. 79; (7) p. 367;
(8) p. 79.

[23]All examples are taken from Robins 1958. Some are specifically mentioned on pp. 13-14, others are found scattered throughout the lexicon.

In addition to the consonant symbolism there is sometimes vowel symbolism as well, particularly the replacement of any vowel by ə, as seen in the two examples quoted here.

[24]Robins 1958 gives the list on p. 23 but makes no mention of the common ending or its probable significance. His list is given because these are precisely the words which have special vocative forms, all exhibiting loss of -os and occasionally some other change, chiefly infixation of ʔ. The fact that all these words also occur without -os strengthens the argument for considering -os an archaic suffix.

[25]Leonard Bloomfield, Algonquian, p. 106 (§63), in Linguistic Structures of Native America, by Harry Hoijer and others, VFPA 6 (1946).

[26]Charles F. Hockett, Central Algonquian /t/ and /c/, IJAL 22.202-207 (1956).

[27]Teeter thinks it may be archaic (1959) but Hockett disagrees (p.c.).

[28]Edward Sapir and Morris Swadesh, Yana Dictionary, p. 8, UCPL 22 (1960).

[29]In Northern Yana any syllable-final *n is replaced by d, so we have maaliwal- "wolf," but maaniwadǰa "little wolf, wolf cub."

[30]Mary R. Haas, California Hokan, pp. 73-87, in Studies in Californian Linguistics, William Bright, ed., UCPL 34 (1964).

[31]The s to š change found in Wiyot is not entered on the table since Yurok and Karok could not show such a change because they lack the distinction on the phonemic level.

[32]I have taken the Yana singular diminutive suffix -ṗa as the type rather than the plural -ǰeegi ~ -ǰgi.

[33]Sapir, Abnormal Types of Speech in Nootka. The quotation which follows is found on p. 4. I have modernized the orthography by making the following substitutions, c for ts, c̓ for ts!, š for c, č for tc, and č̓ for tc!.

[34]Sapir, Diminutive and Augmentative Consonantism in Wishram (see note 10), p. 639.

[35]Ibid., p. 638. Modernized phonetic substitutions have been made in the same way as shown in note 33. In addition ǰ is substituted for dj.

[36]Franz Boas and Ella Deloria, Dakota Grammar, Memoirs of the National Academy of Sciences, Vol. XXIII, Second Memoir (1939). The quotation is taken from p. 16.

[37]Ibid., p. 18.

[38]Ibid., p. 18.

[39]Bloomfield, loc. cit.

[40]C. F. Voegelin, Delaware, an Eastern Algonquian Language, p. 155, in Linguistic Structures of Native America, by Harry Hoijer and Others, VFPA 6 (1946).

[41]Leonard Bloomfield, Eastern Ojibwa, Ann Arbor (1957). See pp. 69-70, especially 11.58, 11.59, 11.62, and 11.67.

[42]The use of diminutive suffixes or diminutive and augmentative suffixes occurs much more widely than I have indicated in this paper. Here I was concerned primarily with symbolic changes associated with diminutivism and augmentativism rather than with a derivative process involving suffixes.

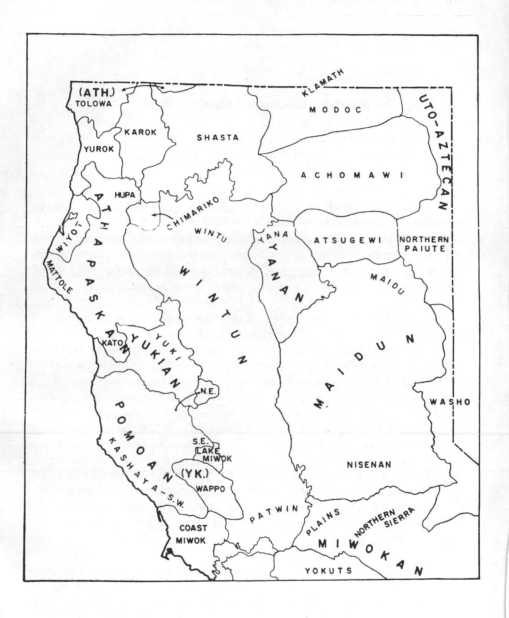

1. Five major linguistic stocks are represented in northern California: Athapaskan, Algonkian-Wiyot-Yurok, Hokan, Penutian, and Uto-Aztecan. Moreover, the Hokan and Penutian stocks are composed of several subfamilies and language isolates whose relationship to each other is not of the easily detectable sort (as is the case with Athapaskan or Uto-Aztecan) but is in fact quite remote.

It is by now well-accepted that languages of the same geographical area may come to resemble each other in a variety of ways and hence it is clear that it is just as important to delineate areal resemblances as it is to depict genetic resemblances. Both types of resemblance provide valuable historical information which can be used in at least two ways. In the first place, once the typical patterns of an area have been described, a language which has deviant traits is seen to require a special historical explanation. In the second place, deviant traits of a particular language can then be compared with typical traits in another area to determine whether or not they bear resemblance to those of the latter. Although the method requires considerable skill and circumspection, it can nevertheless be used to point up the possibility that a language which is deviant in one area may have had historical connections with another area to which it bears resemblance.

In another place (1969, 90-92) I have shown the incongruity of the phonetic traits of Yuchi when examined in the context of the phonetic traits of other Southeastern languages which surround it. At the same time Yuchi phonetic traits show few incongruities when compared with those of languages located west of the Mississippi River. Therefore an earlier connection, genetic or contact, with these latter

languages is strongly suggested. It is situations like this that point
up the value of the areal approach.

Materials are not available in the literature for the kind of
study in depth that a comprehensive areal study of northern California would require. Indeed most areal studies in North America to
date have been confined to phonetic traits since materials on these are
usually available before other things are. In the present paper I will
go somewhat beyond this and include a brief discussion of consonant
symbolism and the diminutive, of numeral systems, and of pronoun
sets, in addition to phonetic traits.

2.1. In Table 1 the phonetic charts of the principal languages
of the area are shown. The relative geographical arrangement of the
languages is approximately as shown below. See also the map.

	Tolowa		Klamath-Modoc	
[Yurok]	KAROK	SHASTA	ACHOMAWI	
[Wiyot]	Hupa	CHIMARIKO		ATSUGEWI
Mattole		Wintun	YANA	
Kato	(Yuki)			
	POMO	Lake Miwok	Maidu	WASHO
	(Wappo)		S.S. Miwok	

(Languages in plain type, without brackets or parentheses,
are Athapaskan; languages in square brackets are Algonkian-Wiyot-
Yurok; languages in parentheses are Yukian; languages in capital
letters are Hokan; and languages with underlining are Penutian.)

Areal vs. genetic characteristics are in many cases rather
difficult to distinguish. The Athapaskan languages (Tolowa, Hupa,
Kato) have three series of stops and affricates (plain, glottalized, and
aspirated) and some of the Hokan and Penutian languages of the area
share this trait. Those that do are Chimariko, Yana, and Pomo
(Hokan) and Klamath, Wintu-Patwin, and Lake Miwok (Penutian).
Since the Athapaskan languages are generally assumed to be late-
comers in the area (and this is well-supported by archaeological as
well as linguistic evidence), it is not suggested that this trait spread
from Athapaskan into Hokan and Penutian or vice versa. Rather it

appears to be a trait of a much larger geographical area including
some Penutian and Hokan languages to the south and even languages
in Mexico and Central America as well as the West Coast of South
America.

Table 1

Phonetic charts of Languages of Northern California

TOLOWA (Athapaskan)							HUPA (Athapaskan)						
ʔ		h					ʔ			h			
kw		ƙw	xw										
k		ƙ̓	x						q̓				
							k			x			ŋ
		ǯ̓	ṣ̌				ky	kyh	ƙy				
č	čh	č̓	š	y			č	čwh	č̓			y	
	ch		s				c	ch	ć	s			
			ł	l					x̣̓	ł	l		
t	th	t'			n	ń	t	th	t'				n
p				w	m	ḿ			W		w	m	

YUROK (Algonkian-W.-Y.)					WIYOT (Algonkian-W.-Y.)				
ʔ		h			(ʔ)		h		
kw	ƙw				kw	kwh			
k	ƙ̓		γ		k	kh		γ	
č	č̓		y		č	čh	š		y
		s			c	ch	s		
		ł	l				ł		l
t	t'		r	n	t	th		r̥ r	n
p	p̓		w	m	p	ph		β w	m

Table 1 (Continued)

KAROK (Hokan)

```
ʔ   h
k   x
č  (š)      y
    s

t   θ      r   n
p   f      v   m
```

SHASTA (Hokan)

```
ʔ        h
k   k̯    x
č   č̯         y
c   c    s

t   t         r   n
p   p         w   m
```

YANA (Hokan)

```
ʔ              h
k   kh  k̓     x
č   čh  č̓  š  y
                   l
t   th  t'     r   n
p   ph  p'     w   m
```

KLAMATH (Penutian)

```
ʔ              h
q   qh  q'
k   kh  k̓
č   čh  č̓       y   y̓
            s
            l   l
t   th  t'          n   ń
p   ph  p'     w   ẃ   m   ḿ
```

WINTU (Penutian [Wintun])

```
ʔ              h
q       q̓    x̣
k       k̓    x
č       č̓         y
            s
        ƛ̓   ł   l
t   th  t'     r   n   d
p   ph  p'     w   m   b
```

CHIMARIKO (Hokan)

```
ʔ              h
q   qh  q̣    x̣
k   kh  k̓    x
ṭ   ṭh  ṭ'
č   čh  č̓  š  y
        c̓   s
                l
t   th  t'          n
p   ph  p'     w   m
```

KASHAYA (Hokan [Pomo])

```
ʔ
q   qh  q̓
k   kh  k̓
ṭ   ṭh  ṭ'
č   čh  č̓  š  y
        c'   s
                l
t   th  t'          n   d
p   ph  p'     w   m   b
```

Table 1 (Continued)

WAPPO (Yukian)					LAKE MIWOK (Penutian [Miwokan])					
ʔ	h				ʔ		h			
k	k̓				k	kh	k̓			
ṭ	ṭ̓				ṭ	th	ṭ̓	s		
č	č̓	š	y	y̓	č		č̓		y	
c	c̓	s			c		c̓	s		
			l	l̓				ƛ̓	ł	l
t	t		n	ń	t	th	t̓	r	n	d
p	p̓	w	ẃ m	ḿ	p	ph	p̓	w	m	b

S.S. MIWOK (Pen.[Miw.])		H. PATWIN (Pen.[Win.])			MAIDU (Penutian)			
ʔ h		ʔ	h		ʔ	h		
k	ŋ	k kh k			k k			
ṭ								
č š y		č	č̓	y	č	č̓		
s			s			c̓ s		
l		ƛ̓ ł l				l		
t	n	t th t̓	r n d		t		n	d
p	w m	p ph p̓	w m b		p		w m	b

Back velar consonants (q, etc.) are highly characteristic of the Northwest Coast area (though rare in Athapaskan languages). Languages in northern California which have this trait are Klamath and Wintu (Penutian) and Chimariko and Pomo (Hokan). It appears to be an old trait of spotty but wide distribution including distribution along the Pacific Coast of North and South America.

Another oft-noted peculiarity of the Northwest Coast is the presence of voiceless spirantal and affricated l- sounds (ł and ƛ, etc.). These are common in all Athapaskan languages. They also appear to have spread into non-Athapaskan languages of northern California from languages further north. Thus we have ł in Yurok and Wiyot (Algonkian-Wiyot-Yurok) and both ƛ and ł in Wintu-Patwin and Lake

Miwok (Penutian), though in Wintu ɬ has an allophone ƛ. These sounds
do not occur in any Hokan languages of the northern California area.
The presence of ɬ far to the south in the Yuman languages (Hokan) is
a characteristic of a quite different linguistic area.

The fact that ƛ' occurs in several of these languages un-
matched by a plain ƛ appears to be a special subareal feature shared
by Hupa (Athapaskan), Wintu-Patwin (though Wintu has it allophoni-
cally) and Lake Miwok (Penutian). This is especially interesting since
Hupa deviates from many other Athapaskan languages in lacking ƛ
while Wintu-Patwin and Lake Miwok deviate from many other Penutian
languages in having any kind of lateral affricate.

So far we have examined phonetic traits which appear to be
especially characteristic of the Northwest Coast area and may very
well have spread into northern California from the north. Equally interesting are phonetic traits lacking to the north but found in northern
and central California.

Retroflex apical stops are found in several languages of the
area, but the northernmost one appears to be Chimariko (Hokan). The
type also appears in a belt extending eastward from Kashaya Pomo
(Hokan) and Wappo (Yukian) through Lake Miwok to Sierra Miwok
(Penutian). In every case whether there are three varieties (plain,
aspirated, and glottalized), as in Chimariko, Kashaya Pomo, and
Lake Miwok, or two varieties (plain and glottalized), as in Wappo, or
only one (plain), as in Southern Sierra Miwok, depends on the treatment of the stop series as a whole in the particular language. The
retroflexion trait appears to be one that is shared with languages to
the south, particularly Yokuts (Golla, 1964).

Other special traits have a more limited distribution. Few
languages of the area have both ḻ and ṟ. Those that do are Yurok and
Wiyot (Algonkian-Wiyot-Yurok), Wintu-Patwin and Lake Miwok (Penutian) and perhaps Yana (Hokan). The presence of both ḻ and ṟ in Yurok
and Wiyot is associated with consonant symbolism (see §3) and every
word that appears with ḻ could also theoretically appear with ṟ. In
Yana the distinction may be subordinate to another feature; in other
words, ṟ is probably an allophone of ṯ. The remaining languages
which have both ḻ and ṟ are Wintu-Patwin and Lake Miwok. In

Wintu-Patwin r̲ has a more limited distribution than l̲ but the distinction seems to go back to the Proto-Wintun system (Broadbent and
Pitkin, 1964). Lake Miwok, on the other hand, has clearly been influenced here, as in a great many other phonetic traits (Callaghan,
1964), by the neighboring Wintun languages.

        Voiced stops (separate from voiceless unaspirated stops)
are rare in northern California but they are found in a narrow east-
west strip of languages including Kashaya Pomo, Wintu-Patwin, Lake
Miwok, and Maidu (but here with the added feature of implosion). It
should be noted that in the Northwest Coast area the voiced stops b̲
and d̲ occur in a few languages as a development from *m̲ and *n̲. In
this narrow strip of California, however, they always occur in addition to m̲ and n̲. The presence of b̲ and d̲ here is clearly a subareal feature which crosses genetic boundaries.

        2.2. In recapitulation of what has been said in this section,
a few special points can be made. There are several striking traits
which cross genetic boundaries. Some of these are shared with languages to the north, some with languages to the south, and some encompass much wider areas. For example, glottalized stops and affricates characterize (with only minor breaks) the whole of the Pacific coastal area of both North and South America. The presence of
back velars is spottier but it too encompasses roughly the same great
area. But affricates with spirantized lateral release, which are also
prominent along the Northwest Coast of North America, peter out,
as one moves south, approximately at the southern Patwin boundary.
This remains true even though sporadic occurrences crop up in other
widely separated places (e.g., some dialects of Cherokee formerly
along the Atlantic Coast and some dialects of Nahuat or Nahuatl in
Mexico).

        As a final point in this section, I wish to make a different
kind of observation. Most languages of the area bear more resemblance to their adjacent unrelated neighbors than they do to their
congeners. Thus Yurok has glottalized obstruents and Wiyot has aspirated obstruents even though neither of these traits is found in the
Algonkian languages, their closest relatives. And Lake Miwok, as a
matter of fact, is a classic example of a chameleon-like language
which reflects all the special traits of its neighbors, but looks

superficially very unlike its sister Miwokan languages (Callaghan, 1964). Contrast the Lake Miwok system with the Southern Sierra Miwok system in Table 1. In contrast to cases like these, Karok stands out as a language that seems to have been little influenced by surrounding languages. It has very few consonants (only 15 in fact, since š is merely a morphophonemic alternant of s̲) and these are of a very general nature of the sort that appear to be very close to the bare minimum for the languages of North America. In an unpublished paper entitled "Phonological Convergences in Western North America" (read in Berkeley in 1969), I postulated as a basic core of consonant sounds for North America, the following:

$$
\begin{array}{lll}
\text{?} & \text{h} & \\
\text{k}^{\text{w}} & & \\
\text{k} & & \\
\text{č} & & \text{y} \\
& \text{s} & \\
\text{t} & \text{l} & \text{n} \\
\text{p} & \text{w} & \text{m} \\
\end{array}
$$

Karok is thus seen to have little more than this bare minimum. It would be premature to speculate on what this means either areally or genetically, though two questions are unavoidable. (1) Is Karok, in the simplicity of its phonetic system, a relic, so to speak, of the early Hokan system? After all, if we were to add q̲ (which is found both in Pomoan and in Yuman) and if we were to assume that glottalization and aspiration, as in Pomo, arose from the operation of early morphophonemic rules, we could argue that Karok has a consonant system which is very close to that which needs to be assumed for Proto-Hokan. (2) Since Karok appears to be very different from most of its neighbors in its phonetic system, does this mean that it has been in its present location longer than the surrounding tribes, especially those to the west, even though in recent times its closest associations have always been with these tribes to the west? And has Shasta, whose phonetic system is close to that of Karok except for its glottalized series (see Table 1), been influenced in this trait by languages lying to the east and north? Definitive answers to these questions are not yet possible, but they serve to highlight the value of areal studies for new insights into genetic as well as areal problems.

3. Another extremely interesting areal trait of northern
California is the presence of some kind of consonant symbolism in
Yurok and Wiyot (Algonkian-Wiyot-Yurok), Hupa (Athapaskan), and
Karok and Yana (Hokan). Consonant symbolism is the substitution of
one class of consonant by another related class for the purpose of
expressing the diminutive (or sometimes the augmentative) or for the
purpose of characterizing the speech of handicapped persons (the
blind, the lame, etc.) or the speech of myth-characters (Deer, Bear,
etc.). The diminutive-augmentative type of symbolism was perhaps
most highly developed among the Wishram (Chinook) Indians of Oregon. On the other hand, the Nootka of Vancouver Island appear to
have had the highest development of consonant symbolism for the purpose of characterizing the speech of the handicapped and of myth-
characters (Sapir, 1915).

The northwestern corner of California, which was inhabited
by the Tolowa, Yurok, Wiyot, Karok, and Hupa tribes, has long been
cited as a classic case of cultural homogeneity existing across sharply
distinct linguistic boundaries. Although the genetic cleavages are as
clear as ever, in recent years instances of linguistic as well as cultural diffusion have also been described for the area (Bright and
Bright, 1965; Haas, 1967, 1970). In describing the phonetic traits
of the languages of this area, we noted that Karok has remained un-
modified. But when we turn to the problem of consonant symbolism,
we see that Karok shares several traits with its geographical neighbors. See Table 2. Although these traits give every evidence of
having been diffused (since they cross three genetic boundaries), it
is not possible to determine their origin. In all probability the traits
came into northern California from the north and one could hazard
a guess that Hupa, which has the most kinds of symbolism and is also
a relative latecomer to the area, was the instrument of diffusion.
Still the direction of change differs between Hupa and, say, Yurok,
and this fact poses problems about the matter. Tolowa and perhaps
other nearby Athapaskan languages also show traces of the symbolism
but our records of most of them are very scanty.

Diminutivization processes in the area are of three types:
(1) change of apical stop (in Karok, spirant) or c̲-affricate to č̲-af-
fricate or vice versa, (2) change of s̲ to š̲ or vice versa (Hupa W is
from *š̲), and (3) change of l̲ to r̲ or change of r̲/l̲ to n̲. In Wiyot

Table 2

Consonant symbolism in northern California

Yurok	Wiyot	Karok	Hupa	Yana
t č	t, th c, ch č, čh	θ č	č c	
			čwh ch	
			č̣ c̣	
	s ś		W s	
l r	l r	r n		l n

there is an added dimension of augmentative in the first type so that
t → c (dim.) → c̣ (aug.). There is also a curious similarity in the phonetic shape of the diminutive suffix in three genetically distinct languages, viz. Wiyot -oc, -ic; Karok -ič, -ač; and Hupa -c, altered
from -č. Yurok diminutive forms do not require a diminutive suffix
and in Hupa some forms are also diminutivized without the use of the
suffix. Yana required the use of a suffix, -p̓a in the singular and
-cheeki in the plural.

Whatever the origin of the consonant symbolism found in
northern California it is clearly a diffused trait which has crossed
several genetic boundaries. Consonant symbolism appears again in
southern California (e.g., Diegueño, Langdon, 1971), but at the
present time it is not suggested that its appearance in these two widely
separated areas is the result of diffusion between the two areas.

4. The numeral systems found in northern California are
basically decimal, quinary, senary, or quaternary. Succeeding sets
in each system are built up of combinations derived by addition, sub-
traction, and multiplication. To make cross-language comparison
easier, these may be symbolized in the following way in the second
quine of a quinary system:

6.	+1	+1	+1	+1	−4	2x3
7.	+2	+2	+2	−3	−3	2x3+1
8.	+3	+3	−2	−2	−2	2x4
9.	+4	−1	−1	−1	−1	2x4+1
10.	(10)	(10)	(10)	(10)	(10)	2x5

When we have analyzed the various systems found in northern California in this fashion, we are sometimes able to make certain deductions about the typical system for each family and to cite some instances of probable diffusion of a system across genetic boundaries.

A formal analysis of several northern California languages (arranged by family) is given below. The Yukian situation is perhaps the most uncertain since all of the languages except Wappo are now extinct. But the Maidu information is incomplete and shows two competing systems as far as it goes.

Numeral Systems of Northern California

Algonkian-Wiyot-Yurok

Yurok. 10.
Wiyot. 10.
(Algonkian languages are mostly quinary, e.g. 1+, 2+, 3+, 1−, 10, and other varieties.)

Athapaskan

Hupa. 10.
Mattole. 10.
Kato. 5. +1, +2, +3, +4, 10.
(Athapaskan languages everywhere are mostly decimal.)

Hokan

Karok. 5. (1)+, 2+, 3+, (?), 10.
Shasta. 5. 1+, 2+, 3+, 4+, 5(x2 ?).
Atsugewi. 5. 1+, 2+, 3+, 4+, 10.
Yana. 5. 1+, 2+, 3+, 4+, 10.
Chimariko. 5. 1+, 2+, 3+, 1−, 10.

Achomawi. 5. 6, 2+, 4(x2 ?), 1(-), 10.
                 6+2
Washo. 5. +1, +2, 4 rdpl., (?), 10.
Pomo (Eastern). 5. 6, +2, 2x4, -1, 10.

Penutian

Klamath. 5. 1+, 2+, 3+, 1-, 10.
Wintun.
  Wintu. 5. ()x3, 7, (2 ?)x4, -1, 10.
  Hill Patwin. 5. ()x3, ()x3+1, 2x4, 2x4+1, 10.
Maidu. 5. 3x2, 3x2+1, —, —, 5x2.
          5. +1, +2, —, —, 5x2.
Miwokan.
  Lake Miwok. 1, 2, 3, 4, 5, 6, 7, 2x(4), 1-, 10.
  S.S. Miwok. 1, 2, 3, 4, 5, 6, 7, 8, 9, 10.
  C.S. Miwok. 1, 2, 3, 4, 5, 6, 1-, 8, 9, 10.
  Saclan. 1, 2, 3, 4, 5, 6, 1+, 2+, 3+, 10.

Yukian

Yuki. 1, 2, 3, 4, 5, 6, 7, (2x4 ?), +1, +2, +3, +4.
                            (9) (10) (11) (12)
Wappo. 1, 2, 3, 4, 5. 1+, 2+, 2x(?), 1-, 10.

Evidence of diffusion of ways of building numerals above five (or
some other base) is seen in several cases. The most interesting are
the following:

(1) If Yurok and Wiyot had a numeral system like that of
most Algonkian languages it would be a quinary one. Since it is a
decimal system, it bears, as a system, more resemblance to the
system of some of its neighboring Athapaskan languages.

(2) Kato is clearly out of step with all the Athapaskan languages, but appears to have been influenced by the formal system of
some of the Hokan languages, particularly Karok, Shasta, Atsugewi,
and Yana, even though at the time of discovery Kato was geographically closest to Yukian and Wintun languages. This might mean that
Kato has rather recently come to be in its present position as the
most southerly of the California Athapaskan languages. It may have

moved or other tribes may have intruded between Kato and its possible earlier Hokan neighbors.

(3) The various Hokan subfamilies are not at all closely related to each other. Therefore the fact that Shasta, Atsugewi, and
Yana all share the feature of +1, +2, +3, +4 in the formation of the
second quine can be as easily attributed to contiguity as to genetic
relationship. The same thing applies to Karok, Achomawi, and
Washo, which differ from Shasta, Atsugewi, and Yana in the ambiguity in the formation of 9. Achomawi has other special features
which are mentioned below.

(4) Klamath and the Wintun languages are also basically
quinary, but Klamath resembles the northern Hokan languages more
than it does the Wintun languages in the formation of the second quine;
and in the formation of 9, it most closely resembles Achomawi, a
Hokan language not far removed geographically.

(5) The Wintun languages stand out as making considerable
use of multiplication in forming numerals of the second quine. Some
neighboring languages appear to have been influenced by this feature.
Eastern Pomo, in its formation of 8 and 9, appears to have been influenced by Wintu. Maidu, in one of its systems, may have been influenced by Patwin.

(6) The two Maidu systems are fragmentary and cannot be
clearly characterized. The first system resembles Patwin, as has
just been mentioned, and may be quinary as Patwin seems to be. However, lacking the words for 8 and 9, it is not possible to be sure,
since if Maidu 8 and 9 were 3x2+2 and 3x2+3, respectively, the system might have been senary. Note that Achomawi, a nearby Hokan
language, has an alternate form for 8 which is 6+2.

The second Maidu system is clearly quinary since 6 and 7
are +1 and +2, respectively. In this feature it appears to be like
Washo, its Hokan neighbor to the east.

(7) The Miwokan languages show several interesting features. Saclan is a senary system (or perhaps better a trinary system after 6) and in this it resembles some of the Costanoan languages

(Beeler, 1961), not shown here. Central Sierra Miwok appears to retain a trace of this in its word for 7, but this could also be the influence of one of the Maidu systems.

Lake Miwok, in its word for 8 as 2x(4), may show the influence of its near neighbor Patwin, especially since it shows such influence in other ways as well (Callaghan, 1964).

(8) An early recording of Yuki (Barrett, 1908) seems to indicate that the system was basically quaternary, though the build-up is clear only after 8 is reached. But Wappo, a Yukian language separated from its congeners by Pomo intrusion, is quinary, perhaps from Pomo influence.

5. There are clear evidences of diffusion in pronominal forms in northern California. See Table 3. Although Wiyot and Yurok retain the Proto-Algonkian system and the Athapaskan languages (e.g. Kato) the Athapaskan system, the systems of the Hokan, Penutian, and Yukian languages give the impression of belonging to a single diffusion area.

Table 3

Some pronoun sets of northern California

	Yurok	Wiyot	Algonkian	Kato	Karok	Shasta	Pomo	Achomawi
S 1	ne-	d-	*ne-	ši·	nani-	ya·ʔa	ʔa·	it
2	ke-	kh-	*ke-	niŋ	mi-	ma·ʔi	ma	miʔ
3	we-	w-	*we-	(pi·)	mu-	kwač	mukid	peka·

	Klamath	Wintu	Maidu	S.S. Miwok	L. Miwok	Yokuts	Wappo
S 1	ni	ni	ni	kan·i-	kanni	na·/	ʔah
2	ʔi, mi	mi	mi	mi·ni-	mƚi	ma·/	mi·
3	pi	pi	mỹ	ʔis·ak-	ʔƚi, ʔƚti	ʔama·/	cɛ́ʔ

The most prominent feature is n- in the first person paired
with m- in the second person. This is found in Karok (Hokan) and in
Klamath, Maidu, Wintu, and Yokuts (Penutian). The use of m- in the
second person (though paired with something else in the first person)
is even more pervasive and includes Shasta and Pomo (Hokan), Miwok
(Penutian), and Wappo (Yukian).

But the total picture of diffusion of n- and m- in the first and
second persons goes beyond the area being studied in this paper and
so the problem really needs to be attacked on a larger scale. The use
of n- in the first person (paired with other things in the second person as well as with m-) is also very widespread and in this wider context the first person n- in Algonkian-Wiyot-Yurok is also part of the
picture.

6. The unravelling of the prehistory of languages is a slow
and painstaking process. Even where genetic relationship is clearly
indicated, as in the case of the Athapaskan and the Algonkian-Wiyot-
Yurok families, the evidence of diffusion of traits from neighboring
tribes, related or not, is seen on every hand. This makes the task
of determining the validity of the various alleged Hokan languages
and the various alleged Penutian languages all the more difficult. It
does not, however, invalidate the many important studies attempting
to trace genetic traits throughout Hokan and throughout Penutian. It
does, however, point up once again that diffusional studies are just
as important for prehistory as genetic studies (Haas, 1969) and what
is even more in need of emphasis, it points up the desirability of
pursuing diffusional studies along with genetic studies. This is nowhere more necessary than in the case of the Hokan and Penutian languages wherever they may be found, but particularly in California
where they may very well have existed side by side for many millennia.

REFERENCES

Barrett, S. A. 1908. The ethno-geography of Pomo and neighboring
        Indians. University of California Publications in American
        Archaelogy and Ethnology 6.1-332.
Beeler, Madison. 1961. Senary counting in California Penutian.
        Anthropological Linguistics 3(6).1-8.

Bright, Jane O. and William Bright. 1965. Semantic structures in
    northwestern California and the Sapir-Whorf hypothesis.
    Formal Semantic Analysis, ed. by Eugene Hammel. Ameri-
    can Anthropologist (Special Publication) 67.5 (Part 2).
    249-58.
Broadbent, Sylvia M. and Harvey Pitkin. 1964. A comparison of
    Miwok and Wintun. Studies in Californian Linguistics, ed.
    by William Bright. University of California Publications in
    Linguistics 34.19-45.
Callaghan, Catherine A. Phonemic borrowing in Lake Miwok. Studies
    in Californian Linguistics, ed. by William Bright. Univer-
    sity of California Publications in Linguistics 34.46-53.
Golla, Victor K. 1964. Comparative Yokuts phonology. Studies in
    Californian Linguistics, ed. by William Bright. University
    of California Publications in Linguistics 34.54-67.
Haas, Mary R. 1967. Language and taxonomy in northwestern Cali-
    fornia. American Anthropologist 69.358-362. [In this
    volume, pp. 328-38.]
_____. 1969. The prehistory of languages. The Hague:
    Mouton.
_____. 1970. Consonant symbolism in Northern California:
    A problem in diffusion. Languages and Cultures of Western
    North America, ed. by Earl H. Swanson, Jr., pp. 86-96.
    Pocatello: Idaho State University Press. [In this volume,
    pp. 339-52.]
Langdon, Margaret. 1971. Sound symbolism in Yuman languages.
    Studies in American Indian Languages, ed. by Jesse Sawyer.
    University of California Publications in Linguistics 65.149-
    73.
Sapir, Edward. 1915. Abnormal types of speech in Nootka. National
    Museum of Canada, Geological Survey Memoir 62. Anthro-
    pological series no. 5. Ottawa. (Reprinted in Selected
    Writings of Edward Sapir, ed. by David G. Mandelbaum,
    pp. 179-96. Berkeley: University of California Press,
    1949.)

Author's Postscript

My earliest interest in linguistics was sparked by a small volume on comparative philology and this led me, in the summer of 1930, to enter the University of Chicago in order to pursue studies in that field. But I was soon attracted to the study of unwritten languages and the broader aspects of linguistics in a series of seminars given by Edward Sapir of the Department of Anthropology. At the same time I continued my study of the more traditional topics in comparative philology, including Sanskrit, Gothic, and Old and Middle High German. It was in this connection that I met another famous linguist, Leonard Bloomfield, who was my teacher in the Middle High German course.

In 1931 Sapir accepted an appointment at Yale and I was among those of his Chicago students who followed him there. At Yale I had the opportunity to study under three other leading linguists of the time: Edgar Sturtevant, the Indo-European and Hittite scholar; Franklin Edgerton, the Sanskrit scholar; and Edward Prokosch, the Germanic scholar. But Sapir's seminars remained the high point of those years. The breadth of his knowledge of languages, both written and unwritten, was phenomenal and his ideas were both fresh and provocative. He taught that so-called "primitive" languages were not really primitive at all but were as full of intricacies and subtleties as any literary language. To the consternation of his colleagues he could and did speak of Navajo and Greek, or of Zulu and French, in the same breath. His own teacher had been Franz Boas and from him Sapir had gained the broad anthropological perspective that so many traditional linguists lacked. Of course the greatest advantage that men like Sapir and Boas possessed was the knowledge they had gained in their direct experience with a variety of unwritten languages through field work. Sapir was interested in child language, in men's and women's speech, in consonant and vowel symbolism, and in typology and universals. He was also interested in the genetic comparison of unwritten as well as written languages — he had been trained in Indo-European and Germanic as well as anthropology — and in particular he was interested in broad genetic classifications. Boas's work too reflects many of these same interests except that he refused to take broad genetic classifications seriously and emphasized instead the necessity of investigating examples of the diffusion of linguistic traits; he was thus an early advocate of the concept of the linguistic area.

It is fortunate that I began my linguistic studies at the time I did. It was an era of greater freedom than those which followed and all kinds of innovative ideas were in the air. But not long after this linguistics became dominated by structuralism through the influence of Bloomfield's book Language which appeared in 1933. While structuralism was important in fostering a rigorous method of analyzing and describing languages, its basic tenets were set forth in such a way as to preclude the consideration of those broader facets of linguistics which loomed so large in Sapir's work. The fresh perspectives so characteristic of Sapir's linguistics were labelled "mentalistic" and were considered unsuitable topics for linguists to study. But as a consequence of my early training under Sapir I was able to retain a deep interest in these broader topics and it is clear that, without this interest, many of the articles of the present volume would never have been written.

Field work has always loomed large in my linguistic experience. American Indian languages that I have worked on in the field include Nitinat (in collaboration with Morris Swadesh), Tunica, Natchez, Creek (Muskogee), Koasati, and Yurok. But I was also one of those who, during World War II, applied field techniques to literary languages in order to devise methods of teaching them in their spoken form. And so I worked for a number of years with native speakers of Thai in order to produce teaching materials of various kinds, including teaching materials for the written as well as the spoken form of the language.

Although I have always enjoyed working on linguistic problems and writing about them, I must confess that the most rewarding part

of my career has been the opportunity to participate in the training of
several generations of linguists at the University of California,
Berkeley. Many of our former students are now teaching at some of
the finest universities in the United States and Canada and some as
far away as Southeast Asia, India, and Australia. And now that many
of Sapir's ideas are receiving a new appreciation in the present era,
it is a great satisfaction to me that all of these former students show
in their work the influence of Sapir's thinking.

In conclusion I wish to express my sincere thanks to Dr.
Anwar S. Dil for the thought and care he has taken in the selection of
the articles which appear in this volume.

Berkeley, California
March 1, 1978

Bibliography of Mary R. Haas' Works

Compiled by Anwar S. Dil

List of Abbreviations:

AA	American Anthropologist
IJAL	International Journal of American Linguistics
JAF	Journal of American Folklore
JAOS	Journal of the American Oriental Society
Lg	Language
UCPL	University of California Publications in Linguistics

1932   (With Morris Swadesh). A visit to the Other World, A Niti-nat text (with translation and grammatical analysis). IJAL 7.195-208.

1934   (With George Herzog, Stanley S. Newman, Edward Sapir, Morris Swadesh, and Charles F. Voegelin). Some orthographic recommendations. AA 36.629-31.

1935   A grammar of the Tunica language. Ph.D. dissertation, Yale University. Published in revised form under the title Tunica, 1941a.

1936   Review of Tonkawa, An Indian Language of Texas, by Harry Hoijer. AA 38.115-16.

1938 a. Geminate consonant clusters in Muskogee. Lg 14.61-65.
      b. Review of Tonkawa, An Indian Language of Texas, by Harry Hoijer. IJAL 9.122-24.

1938 c. Review of A study of the Kanuri Language: Grammar and
         Vocabulary, by Johannes Lukas and A grammar of Chichewa:
         A Bantu Language of British Central Africa, by Mark Hanna
         Watkins. AA 40.507-09.

1939   Natchez and Chitimacha clans and kinship terminology. AA
         41.597-610.

1940 a. Ablaut and its function in Muskogee. Lg 16.141-50.
     b. Creek inter-town relations. AA 42.479-89.

1941 a. Tunica. Handbook of American Indian Languages, ed. by
         Franz Boas, 4.1-143. New York: J. J. Augustin.
     b. The Choctaw word for 'Rattlesnake'. AA 43.129-32.
     c. The classification of the Muskogean languages. Language,
         Culture, and Personality: Essays in Honor of Edward
         Sapir, ed. by L. Spier, A. I. Hallowell, and S. S. Newman,
         pp. 41-56. Menasha, Wisconsin: Banta Publishing Com-
         pany. [Book reprinted, Salt Lake City: University of Utah
         Press, 1960.]
     d. Noun incorporation in the Muskogean languages. Lg 17.311-
         15. [In this volume, pp. 294-301.]
     e. A popular etymology in Muskogee. Lg 17.340-41.
     f. [Notes on the economic uses of gourds among the Creeks.]
         Gourds of the Southeastern Indians, by Frank Speck, pp. 89-
         91. Boston: The New England Gourd Society.

1942 a. Comments on the name 'Wichita'. AA 44.164-65.
     b. Types of reduplication in Thai. Studies in Linguistics 1(4).
         1-6.
     c. The use of numeral classifiers in Thai. Lg 18.201-05. [In
         this volume, pp. 58-64.]
     d. The solar deity of the Tunica. Papers of the Michigan Aca-
         demy of Science, Arts, and Letters 28.531-35.
     e. Beginning Thai. Dittoed materials, Department of Oriental
         Languages, University of Michigan, Ann Arbor.

1943   The linguist as a teacher of languages. Lg 19.203-08. [Re-
         printed in Readings in Modern Linguistics, ed. by Anwar S.
         Dil, pp. 75-85. Lahore, Pakistan: Linguistic Research Group
         of Pakistan, 1964.] [In this volume, pp. 95-103.]

1944   Men's and women's speech in Koasati. Lg 20.142-49. [Re-
          printed in Language in Culture and Society, ed. by Dell
          Hymes, pp. 228-33. New York: Harper and Row, 1964.]
          [In this volume, pp. 1-11.]

1945 a.   Dialects of the Muskogee language. IJAL 11.69-74.
     b.   Review of Thai-English Dictionary, by George Bradley
          McFarland. JAOS 65.270-73.
     c.   Thai phrases. Dittoed materials, Army Specialized Training
          Program, University of California, Berkeley.
     d.   Manual of Thai conversations. Dittoed materials, Army
          Specialized Training Program, University of California,
          Berkeley.
     e.   Thai reader (in phonetic writing). Dittoed materials, Army
          Specialized Training Program, University of California,
          Berkeley.
     f.   (With Heng R. Subhanka). First Thai reader (in Thai alpha-
          betic writing). Dittoed materials, Army Specialized Train-
          ing Program, University of California, Berkeley. [Re-
          vised and expanded as Thai Reader, 1954c.]

1946 a.   A grammatical sketch of Tunica. Linguistic Structures of
          Native America, by Harry Hoijer et al. Viking Fund Publi-
          cations in Anthropology 6.337-66.
     b.   (With Heng R. Subhanka). Spoken Thai. Book I (1946), Book
          II (1948). New York: Henry Holt and Co.
     c.   A Proto-Muskogean paradigm. Lg 22.326-32.
     d.   Techniques of intensifying in Thai. Word 2.127-30. [In this
          volume, pp. 53-57.]
     e.   Review of International Journal of American Linguistics,
          vol. 10, no. 1, and vol. 11, nos. 1-4. JAF 59.335-36.

1947 a.   The development of Proto-Muskogean *k^W. IJAL 13.135-37.
     b.   Some French loan-words in Tunica. Romance Philology
          1.145-48. [= Some French Loanwords in Tunica. In this
          volume, pp. 89-92.]
     c.   Southeastern Indian folklore. (A section of "Folklore Re-
          search in North America.") JAF 60.403-06.
     d.   Phonetic dictionary of the Thai language. Vol. I, Thai-Eng-
          lish; Vol. II, English-Thai. Berkeley: University of Cali-
          fornia Press.

1947 e.   Review of <u>Grammaire Laotienne</u>,by J. -J. Hospitalier. <u>Lg</u>
          23.303-05.

1948 a.   Classificatory verbs in Muskogee. <u>IJAL</u> 14.244-46. [In this
          volume, pp. 302-307.]
     b.   Review of <u>The Indians of the Southeastern United States</u>, by
          John R. Swanton. <u>JAF</u> 61.89-91.

1949   The position of Apalachee in the Muskogean family. <u>IJAL</u>
          15.121-27. [In this volume, pp. 282-293.]

1950 a.   On the historical development of certain long vowels in
          Creek. <u>IJAL</u> 16.122-25.
     b.   <u>Tunica texts</u>. <u>UCPL</u> 6.1-174. Berkeley: University of
          California Press.

1951 a.   The use of numeral classifiers in Burmese. <u>Semitic and
          Oriental Studies</u>, <u>University of California Publications in
          Semitic Philology</u> 11.191-200. [In this volume, pp. 65-81.]
     b.   The Proto-Gulf word for <u>Water</u> (with notes on Siouan-Yuchi).
          <u>IJAL</u> 17.71-79.
     c.   Interlingual word taboos. <u>AA</u> 53.338-44. [Reprinted in <u>Lan-
          guage in Culture and Society</u>, ed. by Dell Hymes, pp. 489-
          94. New York: Harper and Row, 1964] [In this volume,
          pp. 12-21.]
     d.   The declining descent rule for rank in Thailand: A correc-
          tion. <u>AA</u> 53.585-87. [= The declining descent rule for
          rank in Thailand. In this volume, pp. 48-52.]

1952   The Proto-Gulf word for <u>Land</u> (with a note on Proto-Siouan).
          <u>IJAL</u> 18.238-40.

1953 a.   <u>Tunica dictionary</u>. <u>UCPL</u> 6.175-332. Berkeley: University
          of California Press.
     b.   The application of linguistics to language teaching. <u>Anthro-
          pology Today</u>, ed. by A. L. Kroeber et al., pp. 807-18.
          Chicago: University of Chicago Press.
     c.   Sapir and the training of anthropological linguists. <u>AA</u> 55.
          447-49.

1954 a. The Proto-Hokan-Coahuiltecan word for 'Water'. <u>Papers</u>
         <u>from the Symposium on American Indian Linguistics</u>, <u>UCPL</u>
         10.57-62. Berkeley: University of California Press.
     b. Foreword to the Second Printing and Addenda to the Biblio-
         graphy. <u>Thai-English Dictionary</u>, by George Bradley
         McFarland, pp. i and xxii. Stanford: Stanford University
         Press.
     c. Thai reader. Pp. 1-216. Washington, D.C.: American
         Council of Learned Societies.

1955   Thai vocabulary. Pp. 217-589. Washington, D.C.: Ameri-
         can Council of Learned Societies.

1956 a. Natchez and the Muskogean languages. <u>Lg</u> 32.61-72.
     b. <u>The Thai system of writing</u>. Pp. 1-116. Washington, D.C.:
         American Council of Learned Societies.

1957   Thai word games. <u>JAF</u> 70.173-75. [Reprinted in <u>Language</u>
         <u>in Culture and Society</u>, ed. by Dell Hymes, pp. 301-04.
         New York: Harper and Row, 1964.] [In this volume, pp. 22-
         26.]

1958 a. Algonkian-Ritwan: The end of a controversy. <u>IJAL</u> 24. 159-
         73.
     b. Notes on some PCA stems in /k-/. <u>IJAL</u> 24.241-45.
     c. A new linguistic relationship in North America: Algonkian
         and the Gulf languages. <u>Southwestern Journal of Anthro-</u>
         <u>pology</u> 14.231-64.
     d. The tones of four Tai dialects. <u>Bulletin of the Institute of</u>
         <u>History and Philology</u>, Academia Sinica (Taipei) 29.817-26.
     e. Thai language. <u>Encyclopaedia Britannica</u>. 21.935. (Volume
         and page numbers as in the 1973 printing.)

1959   Tonkawa and Algonkian. <u>Anthropological Linguistics</u> 1(2).
         1-6.

1960 a. Differences among languages and problems of language
         learning. <u>California Schools</u> 31.35-37.
     b. Some genetic affiliations of Algonkian. <u>Culture in History</u>:
         <u>Essays in Honor of Paul Radin</u>, ed. by S. Diamond, pp.
         977-92. New York: Columbia University Press.

1961 a. Comment on Floyd G. Lounsbury's 'Iroquois-Cherokee linguistic relations'. Bureau of American Ethnology Bulletin
180. 21–23.

1962   What belongs in a bilingual dictionary? Problems in Lexicography, ed. by F. W. Householder and S. Saporta, pp.
45–50. Bloomington: Indiana University Press. [= Publications of the Research Center in Anthropology, Folklore,
and Linguistics 21. 45–50.] [In this volume, pp. 104–109.]

1963 a. The Muskogean and Algonkian words for Skunk. IJAL 29.
65–66.
     b. Shasta and Proto-Hokan. Lg 39. 40–59.

1964 a. (With the assistance of George V. Grekoff, Ruchira C.
Mendiones, Waiwit Buddhari, Joseph R. Cooke, and Soren
C. Egerod.) Thai-English student's dictionary. Stanford:
Stanford University Press. Pp. xxix, 638.
     b. Athapaskan, Tlingit, Yuchi, and Siouan. XXV Congreso
Internacional de Americanistas, México, 1962. Part 2,
pp. 495–500.
     c. California Hokan. Studies in Californian Linguistics, ed. by
William Bright, UCPL 34. 73–87.
     d. Foreword. The Wiyot Language, by Karl V. Teeter. UCPL
37. v–viii.

1965 a. Is Kutenai related to Algonkian? The Canadian Journal of
Linguistics 10. 77–92.
     b. 'Other-Culture' vs. 'Own-Culture': Some thoughts on L.
White's query. AA 67. 1556–59.
     c. Foreword. A Vietnamese Grammar, by L. C. Thompson,
pp. vii–ix. Seattle: University of Washington Press.

1966 a. Wiyot-Yurok-Algonkian and problems of comparative Algonkian. IJAL 32. 101–107.
     b. Historical linguistics and the genetic relationship of lan-
guages. Current Trends in Linguistics: 3: Theoretical
Foundations, ed. by T. A. Sebeok, pp. 113–54. The Hague:
Mouton and Co. [In this volume, pp. 220–281.]

    c. Addenda to review of Bloomfield's 'The Menomini Language'. AA 68.521-24.

    d. Vowels and semivowels in Algonkian. Lg 42.479-88.

1967 a. The Proto-Algonkian word for 'sun'. Contributions to Anthropology: Linguistics I (Algonquian), National Museum of Canada, Bulletin No. 214, Anthropological Series No. 78, pp. 60-65. Ottawa: Department of the Secretary of State.

    b. Roger Williams's sound shift: A study in Algonkian. To Honor Roman Jakobson 1.816-32. The Hague: Mouton and Co.

    c. The development of Proto-Algonkian *-awe-. Studies in Historical Linguistics in Honor of George Sherman Lane. University of North Carolina Studies in the Germanic Languages and Literatures 58.137-45. Chapel Hill: University of North Carolina Press.

    d. Language and taxonomy in Northwestern California. AA 69. 358-62. [In this volume, pp. 328-338.]

    e. On the relations of Tonkawa. Studies in Southwestern Linguistics, ed. by Dell Hymes, pp. 310-20. The Hague: Mouton and Co.

    f. Southeast Asian languages. Encyclopaedia Britannica 20. 1017. (Volume and page numbers as in the 1973 printing.)

1968 a. The last words of Biloxi. IJAL 34.77-84.

    b. Notes on a Chipewyan dialect. IJAL 34.165-75.

    c. The Menomini terms for playing cards. IJAL 34.217. [In this volume, pp. 93-94.]

    d. Haas's reply to Hockett. [Hockett's reply to Haas's comments on Bloomfield's 'The Menomini Language'.] AA 70.570.

    e. Author's precis [of 'Historical linguistics and the genetic relationship of languages'] and Reply [to reviewers]. Current Anthropology 9.127-28, 171.

1969 a. 'Exclusive' and 'Inclusive': A look at early usage. IJAL 35.1-6. [In this volume, pp. 164-175.]

    b. Internal reconstruction of the Nootka-Nitinat pronominal suffixes. IJAL 35.108-24.

   c. Grammar or lexicon? The American Indian side of the
question from Duponceau to Powell. IJAL 35.239-55.
[= The problem of classifying American Indian languages:
From Duponceau to Powell. In this volume, pp. 130-163.]

   d. Burmese disguised speech. Bulletin of the Institute of History and Philology, Academia Sinica 39(2).277-85. [In this
volume, pp. 27-38.]

   e. Swanton and the Biloxi and Ofo dictionaries. IJAL 35.
286-90.

   f. Sibling terms as used by marriage partners. Southwestern
Journal of Anthropology 25.228-35. [In this volume, pp.
39-47.]

   g. Review of Yao-English Dictionary, by Sylvia J. Lombard,
compiler, Herbert C. Purnell, Jr., editor, Southeast Asia
Data Paper 69, Ithaca, Department of Asian Studies, Cor-
nell University). AA 71.367-68.

   h. The prehistory of languages. The Hague-Paris: Mouton.
120 p. [Reprinted in 1978]. [Chapter 5, "Prehistory and Diffusion", pp. 78-97. In this volume, pp. 308-327.]

1970 a. Consonant symbolism in Northwestern California: A problem in diffusion. Languages and Cultures of Western North
America, ed. by Earl H. Swanson, Jr., pp. 86-96. Pocatello: The Idaho State University Press. [In this volume,
pp. 339-352.]

   b. Review of New Views of the Origin of the Tribes and Nations
of North America, by Benjamin Smith Barton, [1797] (1968).
IJAL 36.68-70.

   c. Review of Current Trends in Linguistics: 2: Linguistics
in East Asia and South East Asia (1967), ed. by T. A.
Sebeok. AA 72.188-90.

1971 Southeastern Indian linguistics. Red, White, and Black:
Symposium on Indians in the Old South (Southern Anthropo-
logical Society Proceedings, No. 5), ed. by Charles M.
Hudson, pp. 44-54. Athens: The University of Georgia
Press.

1972 The structure of stems and roots in Nootka-Nitinat. IJAL
38.83-92.

1973 a.   The expression of the diminutive. <u>Studies in Linguistics in</u>
          <u>Honor of George L. Trager</u>, ed. by M. Estellie Smith, pp.
          148-52. The Hague-Paris: Mouton. [In this volume, pp.
          82-88.]
     b.   American Indian linguistic prehistory. <u>Current Trends in</u>
          <u>Linguistics: 10: Linguistics in North America</u>, ed. by
          Thomas A. Sebeok, pp. 677-712. The Hague-Paris: Mouton.
     c.   The Southeast. <u>Current Trends in Linguistics: 10: Lin-</u>
          <u>guistics in North America</u>, ed. by Thomas A. Sebeok, pp.
          1210-52. The Hague-Paris: Mouton.

1975 a.   What is Mobilian? <u>Studies in Southeastern Linguistics</u>, ed.
          by James M. Crawford, pp. 257-63. Athens: University of
          Georgia Press.
     b.   Problems of American Indian philology. <u>Language and</u>
          <u>Texts: The Nature of Linguistic Evidence</u>, ed. by Herbert
          H. Paper, pp. 89-106. Ann Arbor: Center for Coordination
          of Ancient and Modern Studies, University of Michigan. [In
          this volume, pp. 176-193.]

1976 a.   Boas, Sapir, and Bloomfield. <u>American Indian Languages</u>
          <u>and American Linguistics</u>, ed. by Wallace L. Chafe, pp.
          59-69. Lisse: The de Ridder Press. [= Boas, Sapir and
          Bloomfield: Their Contribution to American Indian Linguis-
          tics. In this volume, pp. 194-206.]
     b.   The Northern California linguistic area. <u>Hokan Studies</u>, ed.
          by Margaret Langdon and Shirley Silver, pp. 347-59. The
          Hague-Paris: Mouton. [In this volume pp. 353-369.]

1977 a.   Tonal accent in Creek. <u>Studies in Stress and Accent</u>, ed. by
          Larry M. Hyman. <u>SCOPIL</u> 4.195-208. Los Angeles: Uni-
          versity of Southern California.
     b.   Nasals and nasalization in Creek. <u>Proceedings of the Third</u>
          <u>Annual Meeting of the Berkeley Linguistics Society</u>, pp. 194-
          203. Berkeley, California: Berkeley Linguistics Society.
     c.   From auxiliary verb to inflectional suffix. <u>Mechanisms of</u>
          <u>Syntactic Change</u>, ed. by Charles N. Li, pp. 525-37. Austin:
          University of Texas Press.

d. Anthropological linguistics: History. <u>Perspectives in An-</u>
<u>thropology 1976</u>, ed. by Anthony F. C. Wallace et al. A
special publication of the American Anthropological Association, no. 10, pp. 33-47. [For revised version see 1978a.]

1978 a. The study of American Indian languages: A brief historical
sketch. In this volume, pp. 110-129. [Revised version of
1977d.]

b. Linguistics and history. <u>The Scientific Study of Language</u>;
<u>The Role of the Linguistic Society of America</u>, ed. by Anwar
S. Dil, pp. 136-47. Abbottabad, Pakistan: Linguistic Research Group of Pakistan, forthcoming. [In this volume,
pp. 207-219.] (Presidential address to the Linguistic Society of America, December 1963, Chicago, Illinois.)

c. Author's postscript. In this volume, pp. 370-72.